DUBLIN VOICES

AN ORAL FOLK HISTORY

DUBLIN VOICES

AN ORAL FOLK HISTORY

Kevin C. Kearns

GILL & MACMILLAN

Gill & Macmillan Ltd
Goldenbridge
Dublin 8
with associated companies throughout the world
© Kevin C. Kearns 1998
0 7171 2650 1

Print origination by
O'K Graphic Design, Dublin

Printed by
MPG Books Ltd, Cornwall

This book is typeset in 10/13 pt Plantin

A catalogue record for this book is available from the British Library.

1 3 5 4 2

Dedication

To Cathe, blithe spirited companion

"The true makers of history are the people."
(Theodore C. Blegen, *Grass Roots History*, 1947)

"Nothing less than the whole of the past is needed to explain the present, and in this difficult task we cannot afford to neglect the unrecorded past."
(E. Estyn Evans, *Irish Folk Ways*, 1957)

"Oral History and folklore can no longer be viewed as curious anachronistic beliefs but as the very roots of Dublin's historical, geographical and social identity."
(North Dublin Inner City Folklore Group, *Living in the City*, 1992)

Contents

1

Introduction

"The folk, the masses of people, possess a culture and a history well worthy of study."
(Richard M. Dorson in Oral History: An Interdisciplinary Anthology, *1984)*

*"Narrative is ageless. The impulse to tell a story and the need to listen to it have made
narrative the natural companion of man throughout the history of civilisation."*
(Linda Degh in Folklore and Folklife, *1972)*

Dubliners are renowned connoisseurs of savoury narrative. They are
addicted to talk, gifted at storytelling, always appreciative of a lively or
fascinating tale. Indeed, there is a long tradition of rich verbal expression and
oral history in Dublin with one generation—around the dinner table, in front of
the hearth, ensconced in the local pub—instinctively passing down to the next
its treasury of life experiences, family heritage, customs and folkways. Listeners
were attentive and often enraptured by vivid accounts, more captivating than
clinical written records, of earlier life and historical events. Thus, in the age
before radio and television, narrators and storytellers provided profoundly
satisfying entertainment as well as imparting historical knowledge. This form of
intimate oral transmission flowed naturally within most families and enriched
each individual who, in turn, carried it down to his or her descendants. In his
Autobiography, W. B. Yeats cites the "poignant memory" of his mother passing
down stories and oral family history to him and his sisters—"She would spend
hours telling stories . . . she had a great depth of feeling."[1]

This valuable oral tradition survived well into the first half of this century.
Historically and emotionally it linked one generation to another and created a
strong sense of family origins, pride and continuity. This is exemplified by Tom
Byrne, 80, one of nine children who grew up along the docks in a seafaring
family. His father was an adventurous seaman and his grandfather the skipper
of a sailing schooner. When they returned from long voyages to exotic places
they would regale young Tom and his siblings with colourful tales:

"When they went away it'd be eighteen months or two years. A long trip, maybe off to Calcutta, Bombay, Oregon, Australia. When they'd come back they'd be sitting around and as kids me father'd start telling us stories. And they were really *very* good storytellers. They seemed to have good retention and they could paint sort of a mental picture for you. So I suppose in that way I might have inherited a little of that."

Today Tom Byrne is well known as one of Dublin's natural storytellers and an archetypal oral traditionalist. He is also one of a vanishing breed of "old-timers" who constitute an invaluable repository of original oral folk history and urban lore. The personal histories of such "common folk", often as historically significant as they are individually interesting, lamentably tend to go unrecorded for future generations. As the twentieth century wearily sets over Dublin's venerable cityscape many a unique species of Dubliner will soon be extinct—the likes of shipwrights, tram drivers, stevedores, hatters, lamplighters, factory workers, coopers, railway steam engine drivers, "pirate" busmen, World War II soldiers, daring fire brigade men, heroic rescue workers in the wake of the 1941 German bombing and countless others. Common folk all—but often with *uncommon* life experiences well worthy of being recorded and preserved for posterity.

Both the oral tradition and social environment in which it flourished are fast fading and the reality looms that these stories will one day be lost for ever. Most of the storytellers are now aged between 70 and 95 years and their days are numbered. Yet, many possess a remarkable memory bank, a keen clarity of mind and great descriptive powers. In the early 1990s Bertie Ahern, TD and Minister for Finance, publicly recognised the value of this oral heritage when he proclaimed that Dublin is a "store-house of history and lore" in which "ordinary, decent people in the inner-city heartland" still retain a strong "folk memory" that should be tapped before it vanishes.[2] Regrettably, most do not have the inclination or literary skills to chronicle their own memoirs. Thus, as E. Estyn Evans contends in *Irish Folk Ways* to capture this "living past" one cannot rely on traditional historical archival methodology.[3] It can only be gathered and preserved through the oral historical approach before it perishes with the informants. This task is challenging and immensely rewarding, for as seasoned oral folk historians continually discover:

"The old survivors are walking books."[4]

THE NATURE OF ORAL FOLK HISTORY

"Memory is the treasury and guardian of all things."
(Cicero)

Oral history may be defined as "primary source material obtained by recording spoken words—generally by means of planned, tape-recorded interviews—of persons deemed to harbour hitherto unavailable information worth preserving".[5] This includes "reminiscences, accounts and interpretations of events from the past which are of historical significance".[6] It is a relatively new branch of historical research, born of Colombia University's pioneering oral history programme in the late 1940s which coincided with the invention of the tape recorder. Initially, large cumbersome reel-type machines were used, followed by the advent of small portable cassette recorders which greatly facilitated the taping process. The original purpose of oral history was to record the memories of famous people such as political figures and business barons. From the outset, oral history proved to have "certain advantages over the written record".[7] It provided freshness, candour, clear verification of the source and the opportunity to clarify subject matter through verbal re-examination and direct questioning. Thus, recorded reminiscences of presidents, prime ministers and military leaders were a valuable supplement to the often staid archival records. Hoffman even contends that "when undertaken in the most professional way, oral histories may be superior to many written records", noting that "archives are replete with self-serving documents, with edited and doctored diaries and memoranda written 'for the record'".[8]

The evolution of oral history from the focus on elitist types to ordinary people occurred largely in the 1960s as oral historians began to explore the realm of folklorists working with country and small-town folk in such settings as Appalachia. They found that farmers, ranchers and miners retained a strong oral tradition with their own unique body of history, customs and lore. Initially, some folklorists were wary of the interlopers. However, as Harvard-educated folklorist and historian Richard Dorson explains, the "inherent kinship and harmony between oral history and folklore" soon became recognised as "the old rigid polarisation between history, as scrupulously documented fact, and folklore, as unverified rumour—often equated with myth and legend—was beginning to break down".[9] Gradually, a new academic discipline known as "oral folk history" emerged from the synthesis, or as Danielson more poetically puts it, the happy "courtship of folklore and oral history".[10] Oral folk history became an "accepted literary genre" based upon the realisation that *ordinary* people, or "common folk", possess their own culture, lifeways and experiences worth recording and preserving.[11] This created a "new kind of history—a history not of captains, kings and presidents but of farmers, workers, immigrants and the like".[12] Evans, having studied the folkways of the rural Irish for decades, concluded that ordinary people in home, field and workplace "have done more to shape our instincts and thoughts than the trampling of armies or the wrangling of kings which fill the documents from which history is written".[13]

Oral folk historians at first concentrated on the rural realm, restricting the term "folk" to inhabitants of farms, villages and small towns. But as some innovative oral historians began casting a wider net, they turned their attention to urban populations which they called "city folk". Here they discovered that such types as factory workers, dockers, trade unionists, tradesmen and shopkeepers—like their "country cousins"—embodied their own oral history and urban folkways. But as Dundes explained back in the 1960s some traditional folklorists initially eschewed the notion of "*city* folk", regarding it as a contradiction of terms: [14]

"Some folklorists mistakenly identify the 'folk' with peasant or rural groups. If one were to accept this narrow conception of folk, then by definition one would have to conclude that city dwellers were not folk and hence could have no folklore."

Once urban oral history began to appear in print most academic sceptics conceded the legitimacy and value of the research findings. As Messenger confirms, by the 1980s folklorists and oral historians were "no longer bound by narrow concepts of who and what constituted 'folk'", contending that the "traditions of city folk" were just as complex and rich as those of their rural counterparts.[15] This expansion of both terrain and social types allowed oral historians to record the "rich ability of people in *all* walks of life to express themselves";[16] whereas, previously, most traditional archival historians had "no interest in the point of view of the labourer" and summarily dismissed the "life experiences of women" as irrelevant.[17] But when oral historians broaden their scope the "life experiences of people of all kinds can be used as raw material and a new dimension is given to history".[18] This nascent documentation of the "unofficial, unnoticed lives of ordinary people" is what some practitioners like to call "grass roots" or "real world" history.[19] Most importantly, proclaims Thompson, this form of original oral narrative research serves to truly *democratise* history by finally giving expression to common and generally forgotten folk.[20]

Oral folk history can significantly supplement and clarify (even correct) the standard written record by documenting the participatory experiences of ordinary people in historical circumstances or events. This book is replete with powerful case studies. For example, in Bernard Share's excellent *The Emergency: Neutral Ireland 1939–45*, a definitive work on the wartime period, there is only scant mention of two dramatic historic events—the 31 May 1941 German bombing in the heart of the city, and the bold dispatching of Dublin fire brigades to blazing Belfast a month earlier. Share expresses that "Dublin was to suffer" from the four bombs dropped that clear night, citing the official record of twenty-seven people killed, forty-five wounded, twenty-five houses completely destroyed and another three hundred rendered unfit for human habitation.[21] Surely few historic events in this century had a more personally traumatic impact on common Dubliners than this disaster. Yet, official documents and historians' references to this tragedy fail to provide a genuine *feeling* and *understanding* of the suffering and anguish experienced by city folk on that fateful night. Here is precisely where oral testimony can offer poignant insight to a historic event. Alec King, 85, was one of the first Rescue and Demolition Officers on the grisly North Strand scene, literally minutes after the bomb exploded. His vividly detailed description of destruction, human reaction and rescue efforts over the next sixty frantic hours provides a unique and most authentic account:

"We were the first squad to arrive. And to *see it* . . . *devastation*! The whole scene is still embedded in my brain . . . gaping floors, empty beds. There was *nothing* left. We had all sorts of equipment but we discovered we could only use what God gave us, our *hands*. We found people cut, bruised, their limbs missing. Our own squad that night collected eleven or twelve people, dead or alive or maimed. I got the head out of a woman with long black hair. The neck was severed from the body. Completely! Her eyes were *wide open*, *staring* at me . . . as if to say, 'What have you done with me?' We discovered the body and I took the shoulders and open neck and we started to the stretcher and all the blood in the carcass—it was hot and sticky—it flowed out on me. *All* over me. I worked for sixty plus hours, never had a break. My fingernails were gone, nothing but red pussy sores and I was cut and bruised all over the place. It's all photographed on the brain—31 May 1941. A week later the men, we met for the first time and had tea . . . and some of us cried."

Only through oral testimony could such human emotion and detail emerge. Furthermore, his body count conducted on the scene contradicts the official total. He contends: "I reckoned that thirty-nine people that night were killed. Some said it was only twenty-eight, but I have it on good authority that it was thirty-nine. I have proof of it."

Referring to a similar wartime episode, Share writes about "de Valera's dispatch of the Dublin fire brigades northwards at the time of the 1941 Belfast bombings at some considerable risk to his neutrality policy".[22] But, again, these few lines tell us nothing about the dramatic event itself. The few surviving participants remain our most reliable source of historical information. Jack Conroy, 78, was one of the heroic band of fire-fighters who volunteered to race to the aid of their Belfast brethren during the German blitz of April 1941:

"Now Belfast, they were bombed, *blitzed* completely. They weren't able to control it. We were pulled out of bed at half six in the morning from Buckingham [Street] station. They called for volunteers and single men. So we made up a crew of five of us and we went to Belfast. And our station officer said to us: 'Well, you're going out and God knows when you'll be back!' And we accepted that. I was young, 22, there was a spirit of adventure . . . didn't know what was facing us. We saw the refugees and cars coming along the roads, all *beating south* across the border. Fleeing. In the centre of the city we saw *all* the shop windows shattered. And streets of workers' cottages *flattened*, a pile of bricks. *Completely* flat. Who was underneath them I don't know . . . never found out either. Fires were widespread, especially in the flax mills. Our job was putting out what was left. So we went in the flax mills and *huge blazes*. Terrible heat. The Germans let these incendiary bombs down like hailstones, set fires *all over* the place and we were walking through them, kicking them out of our way."

Another illustration of the value of oral verification is that rendered by workers in Dublin's grim factories early in the century. Labour historians have written much about the city factories and workforce, commonly referring to the "deplorable conditions" under which men and women toiled. But their scholarly analysis is generally devoid of insights to the actual experiences and feelings of the workers themselves. For instance, Dermot Keogh's book, *The Rise of the Irish Working Class*, is really more a treatise on unionism, politics and labour leaders than a study of the real working class. Speaking of the appalling conditions in many factories he comments, "the lot of womenfolk was harsh", but basically only makes reference to their long hours and low wages which scarcely conveys their real hardship.[23] By graphic contrast, women in this book who worked in tailoring, soap and biscuit factories back in the 1920s and 1930s fill in the details of how they daily had to cope with unhealthy conditions, dangerous machines, serious accidents, twelve hour work shifts, standing and bending over the entire day, and religious discrimination.

Similarly, in his highly regarded work, *Dear, Dirty Dublin*, O'Brien asserts that factory workers were "extremely vulnerable to victimisation by employers" and cites the "total neglect of safety and inspection in unsanitary workshops".[24] But there is little documentation of such stressful conditions. Arthur Murphy, 80, worked in Winstanley's shoe and boot factory from 1933 to 1984, over a half-century. His memories *humanise* detached accounts of historians:

"Oh, conditions were primitive. The factory was stone walls, whitewashed, and very rough, but no windows. Very dusty, a three or four inch layer of dust on the wooden beams and an inadequate extraction of the dust. Leather dust clogging up your lungs. Oh, I finished up with acute bronchitis and many men came out of it with the same complaint. And the noise from the presses cutting out the leather was *unbearable*. And it was one of the more risky jobs. Most of them had fingers missing, or bits of fingers. It was accepted. Fear of being sacked. People were *afraid* to express it. And the management and office staff was all Protestant, wouldn't *oblige* a Catholic in the office. We sort of accepted our lot."

Such "real world" personal testimony illustrates how oral folk history both supplements and enlivens the conventional written record.

DECLINE OF THE ORAL TRADITION

"Party pieces were part of the oral tradition."
(Pete St John, Jaysus Wept!, *1984)*

"A human voice, fresh, personal, particular, always brings the past into the present with extraordinary immediacy. The words breathe life into history."
(Paul Thompson in Oral History: An Interdisciplinary Anthology, *1984)*

In times past, people customarily kept detailed journals or diaries and wrote lengthy correspondence. Such personal written records comprised a wealth of primary source material for historians. But with the invention of the telephone, improved transportation links and the accelerated pace of modern life, the leisurely practice of putting pen to paper to express thoughts and register experiences declined sharply. As a consequence, the simple art of conversation became more important as a means of transmitting and retaining history within families. There was a strong tradition in most Dublin families of elders passing down information by spoken word. O'Keefe, in her book, *Down Cobbled Streets: A Liberties Childhood*, tells how "my mother liked to talk about her schooldays" and "old-fashioned cures were handed down from grandparents".[25] Back then narration was a natural and pleasant way of passing the time. Similarly, in *Cowslips and Chainies: A Memoir of Dublin in the 1930s*, Crowley fondly recalls sitting mesmerised on her mother's or aunt's lap "taking in every word" as they told her lengthy stories about things that had happened in the family long ago.[26] This is how she learned about her roots and came to be a gifted storyteller herself. This oral tradition flourished well into mid-century in most homes.

It was also an old Dublin custom at family gatherings for adults, and particularly elders, to "tell tales" about past family figures and events. At family parties—or outright hooleys—everyone was *expected* to make some contribution in the form of music, song or narration. Narratives could be stories, poems, recitations, observations, witticisms or accounts of interesting personal experiences. All formed part of the family's unwritten heritage. Somewhat wistfully, Pete St John recalls how this "art of expression" thrived within families during his childhood and "party pieces" were a vital part of the oral tradition:[27]

> "Every adult in the family was fully expected to have one . . . in short, once you were over 18 you better have some feckin' act that you were ready to do, drunk or sober, on call, anytime in all places. A family party called for everyone to do their bit. The party piece was a special kind of recognition . . . these party pieces were personal . . . worthy of their personal history."

But with the appearance of radio, television, videos and computers the oral tradition in home and pub has declined precipitously. Furthermore, it is no longer so common in Dublin for three generations to live under the same roof communicating intimately on a daily basis. Increasingly, each generation tends to exist within its own social milieu, with ever diminishing verbal interaction within the family unit. Today family members are often so scattered across Dublin that they no longer see each other with the same degree of frequency. Thus, the familiar social environment which was so conducive to oral historical expression has deteriorated. Simply put, *meaningful* and *substantive* personal communication both within families and among friends is no longer the common form of intimate social interaction it was in a more leisurely and reflective age.

Many older Dubliners cite television as the major culprit in this decline. Mary Bolton, 78, of Stoneybatter, one of the city's oldest neighbourhoods, laments on how her home was always jammed with family and friends talking and sharing life and feelings: "People got more out of life then. But when television came in the whole body seemed to go out of it. It changed the *whole* atmosphere. Television was the *ruination* of the world." Television even invaded the local pub, long a bastion of the conversational art. Old-timers now grouse that they can no longer chat with cronies over the noise of the "infernal picture box" blaring above their heads. As Joe Cox, 75, opines: "TV has ruined conversation. Today it's 'Come in, sit down, and shut up.' Conversation is gone . . . and they shouldn't have it in the pub at all." To many, television is the curse which dealt the death blow to traditional conversation and oral history in Dublin family life.

Today the heartfelt lament of many elderly people is that "Nobody cares, nobody listens." This accentuates their sense of loneliness and isolation. Virtually all the individuals featured in this book expressed sadness and sometimes bewilderment that their children and grandchildren now exhibit little or no interest in hearing about their life experiences and family roots. Thus, they see themselves as the last link in the long family chain of oral transmission, painfully aware that with their passing much of the family's verbal heritage will die. The *positive* aspect of this social situation is that they are now especially eager to share it with an attentive oral historian. It is comforting to them to know that their life stories will be recorded and preserved in written form for future generations. Ironically, quite often when their words finally appear in an oral history book their relatives absolutely marvel at the revelations, commonly blurting, "Why, I had no *idea* my grandfather had such experiences!"

THE SEARCH FOR SOURCES

"It is surprising how much oral tradition can be picked up anywhere . . . one may have the luck to bump into a good informant in a shop, in the pub, on the road . . . almost anywhere."
(*Donald A. MacDonald in* Folklore and Folklife, *1972*)

In Ireland the terms "folk", "lore" and "oral history" are still strongly associated with country life and rural villages. It has only been in the past decade or so that *urban* oral history and folkways have been recognised as worthy of study and chronicling. Irish "urban folk" are increasingly seen as possessing their own unique oral history and lore similar to that of Appalachian inhabitants or Gaeltacht dwellers. This was acknowledged by Comhairle Bhealoideas Éireann

(Folklore of Ireland Council) when they affirmed the "similarity between traditional customs and social attitudes of Gaeltacht people and those of native Dubliners", hence noting the "importance and urgency of recording the lore and idiom of Dubliners".[28] Dublin is especially fertile ground for the extraction of rich oral folk history because in such old neighbourhoods as the Liberties, Stoneybatter, Ringsend and the Northside the oral tradition, customs and lore have been preserved by the large elderly population. These surviving Dubliners, born and reared early in the century, now constitute an invaluable repository of oral folk history. Old tradesmen, factory workers, cinema ushers, hotel concierges, all have their own fascinating tales to tell.

The challenge is to "track down" members of the "old crowd", as they are affectionately known. As Brewer explains in *The Royal Constabulary: An Oral History*, it is both important and urgent to seek out this "small number of survivors whose life experiences will be lost to future generations once they pass from the scene".[29] In this search the oral historian is akin to an explorer. MacDonald likens him to a hunter or prospector;[30] or as Starr adventurously puts it, oral historians are "modern muses armed with tape recorders in quest of first-hand knowledge that would otherwise decay".[31] Indeed, one must be curious, imaginative, persistent and possess good exploratory instincts. Over my twenty-five summers of field research in old inner-Dublin neighbourhoods I have made countless friends and established a sort of "bush telegraph" in terms of gaining information and leads to good potential oral history sources. However, this task has been made considerably more difficult in recent years by urban renewal schemes which have demolished old neighbourhoods and transplanted their occupants to scattered suburban housing estates. As a consequence, many native inner-city folk have severed their ties with their home turf and faded into the larger urban fabric. Fortunately, many men are accustomed to returning on weekends to their old local pub where they can be contacted. Women, too, often make excursions back into the old areas for purposes of shopping or social visitation. And, of course, there is always the element of happy serendipity in the search, when one finds by pure good luck an excellent informant along the path or in a pub.

Once contact is made the oral historian must assess the potential of the informant and immediately endeavour to create a bond of trust. The inquisitive academic is often initially viewed with a healthy degree of suspicion as to motives. The most common hesitation—or overt resistance—on the part of prospective informants is the query, "Now *why* would you have any interest in talking with me? I've nothing special to tell you." It is precisely at this tentative moment that the oral historian must try and establish an identity link with the interviewee. This "cultural likeness" association, as Gluck calls it, becomes crucial to future success.[32] As she explains, "cultural likeness can greatly promote trust and openness, whereas dissimilarity reinforces cultural and social distance."[33] A bond of trust and easy rapport allows the oral historian to explain his honourable objectives and is vital to the flow of honest conversation. Conrad M. Arensberg in his classic, *The Irish Countryman*, tells what a daunting challenge it was for him to plumb the heart of Irish folk society as an "inquisitive, even importunate, stranger in a foreign land, seeking out intimacies and sanctities scarcely acknowledged among friends and fellow countrymen".[34] He found himself "utterly dependent upon the hospitable good nature and the intelligent understanding of the people among whom I worked".[35]

Dublin city folk are no less wary than their country counterparts. But in researching this book over a period of three summers I had many advantages over Arensberg's plight. That I am Irish-American possessing a pure Irish name, Roman Catholic, educated by the clergy, have spent twenty-five summers in inner Dublin working among the plain people and have written six books on the city, served to facilitate the creation of mutual identity and trust. But, like Arensberg, I was ultimately dependent upon the good nature, kindness and remarkable verbal gifts of Dublin's "natives".

Because many informants are well advanced in years there is always a sense of urgency to conduct taped interviews as soon as possible. It commonly happens that an individual passes away shortly before or after the scheduled interview. A typical example was that of Bobby Walsh, 85, Dublin's oldest surviving cattle drover, whose oral history in *Stoneybatter: Dublin's Inner Urban Village* provided an original account of a "lowly" drover's life early in this century. Confessed Walsh:[36]

"It was a rough life. You'd no money. It was all pennies and coppers . . . you were half starved. The old drovers now, they're all dead and gone. I'm the oldest drover still alive. Oh, God, I don't think I'll live much longer."

He died three weeks after speaking the prophetic words—and thus never saw his story in print.

THE "ART" OF TAPING ORAL HISTORY

"Empathy is extremely important in oral history."
(Ramon Harris, The Practice of Oral History, *1975)*

When conducted in its highest form by a skilled practitioner, Hoffman regards the recording of oral history as an "art".[37] Surely, there is no form of historical research more challenging and rewarding—or emotional. I usually met with respondents in their home or local pub, the settings in which they were most comfortable. This was most conducive to the natural flow of conversation and reflection. Taping sessions typically lasted from two to four hours. Some individuals were revisited to expand on salient points or clarify a dangling theme. Their lengthy narratives, some running to fifty typed pages, were condensed and arranged topically and sequentially for literary cohesion. But their original vernacular and intonations were not tampered with in any manner, for an informant's words "may be idiosyncratically phrased but all the more expressive for that".[38] Indeed, no novelist could duplicate the purity of their speech and expressions.

The oral historian cautiously probes the mind and memory of respondents with all the sense of wonder and expectation with which an archaeologist meticulously unearths a precious dig site. Promising prospects can prove to be fascinating discoveries or disappointing vacuums. The process is highly exploratory, replete with grand revelations, drama and often intensely emotional moments. As Gluck affirms, the "oral history interview is a human interaction and the same kind of warm human responses expected in other interactions should govern our behaviour".[39] Thus, empathy, patience and sensitivity are vital requisites. The oral historian must always retain a delicate balance of objectivity and sensitivity in response to every human emotion from sadness to joy to anger. Oral testimonies are filled with poignant accounts of hardship, suffering, heartbreak, tragedy and despair as well as unbounded joy, earthy wit and humour. Commonly, a person will be reduced to tears when recounting painful episodes such as a serious illness, loss of loved ones, abusive treatment or loneliness. For many elderly persons, sharing their innermost feelings is visibly therapeutic as they realise a sense of "release" in having revealed to another person long-held experiences and emotions. After a long and emotionally wrenching taping session both interviewer and respondent can feel quite fatigued.

Several examples serve to illustrate the range of human emotions expressed in oral testimonies. Willie Murphy, 87, of Ringsend tells of his fear and hatred of the dreaded Black and Tans early in the century:

"I had dealings with the Black and Tans. *Bastards* they were! One of them chased me down Pearse Street but I run and he couldn't fire into the crowd. When they'd get whiskey it was terrible. Oh, they went mad altogether. Oh, they were the *scum* of England. They were *murderers, rapists.*"

Docker Martin Mitten, 82, who knew James Larkin, remembers the deep feelings and actions of the hungry dock workers toward the detested scabs who took their jobs during the strike of 1925:

"Now that was a *bitter* strike. Ah, brothers split over that. They brought men up from Wicklow and employed them on the docks. They was known as 'scabs'. I seen me mother and all the women in the big [tenement] houses throwing scalding water down on top of the scabs. And some of the older fellas was running alongside the scabs' carts in Townsend Street with whips lashing the horses to make them jump up. Then detectives came down and firing shots in the air to stop the people from attacking the scabs, to stop the scabs from getting bashed . . . murdered. Oh, that went on for years afterwards, that bitterness."

Oral history sometimes penetrates the very heart and mind. At age 95, Frank

Wearen's life has nearly spanned the entire century as he personally knew Maud Gonne and Countess Markievicz. As a teenager he joined the IRA, carried a revolver, engaged in raids against the British, was imprisoned and endured an excruciatingly painful twenty-seven day hunger strike in Mountjoy Prison. He recalls the physical and psychological horrors of the experience:

"I had headaches, *dreadful* headaches. And if you had bad teeth that was the first thing that deteriorated. You got no end of pain. Get up in the middle of the night roaring and bawling, 'Oh, doctor, get a pair of pliers and pull it out!' You'd be that frantic. But I'll tell you what was terrible *worse*. You were dreaming every night only of fancy food . . . cake shops, ice cream, fish and chips. And you'd wake up roaring and bawling. A *hell* it was, a hell on earth. It was pandemonium . . . Jesus, it was dreadful. And there was big strong men there and they lost their mind. They went delirious. I was *determined* to either come out on me feet or come out *dead*."

Some narratives express great love and compassion, such as that of John McCormack, a powerful former light-heavyweight Irish boxing champion. His father, "Spike", a notorious street fighter and boxing champion himself, was one of the most legendary Dublin figures in this century. He was famed and loved not only for his fighting feats but also for his role as hero of the downtrodden, idol for hordes of street urchins and acts of generosity to the poor. Upon Spike's death, *Evening Press* journalist Adrian McLoughlin hailed him as a genuine Dublin "folk hero" of the common people.[40] Yet, outside of newspaper articles about his boxing matches, virtually nothing has been recorded about his extraordinary life and role. But through his son's poignant narrative—the longest in this book—Spike comes to life again in the old cobblestoned streets. Sitting before the tape recorder like a gentle giant, John recounts his father's bloody brawls along Gardiner Street and speaks in tender tones about the love and compassion he felt for his "Da":

"He was *bred* to fight. He had this fighting spirit. The man was a pit bull! Oh, *could* he fight! But a gentleman. Oh, he was a lovely person, in *every* way . . . his nature. I loved my father . . . I idolised my father. He died at home. We got him some brandy cause his mouth was dry and his tongue felt three or four times its normal size, cause of the radiation and morphine he was taking. It eased the burning sensation in him. He wasn't short of brandy that night he died. And you know the way they hallucinate? I'll never forget this. He dozed off and woke up again and says to me, 'Am I still Spike?' And I says, 'Yeah, dad, of course you are.' It was a shock. Like, for me, to think that he didn't know who he was. That morning he died . . . and then when he's gone it hits you. I loved my father. Older people still say today, 'Oh, you're Spike's son.' . . . I'm young Spike."

Contrasting with oral testimonies which express sadness or anger are those which are delightfully light hearted, joyful, even hilarious, as when Charles Webb, head porter at Trinity College, shares his recollections of the high jinks of mischievous students some four decades ago; or Shelbourne Hotel concierge Jimmy Dixon's humorous description of guests Laurel and Hardy. No less amusing are Savoy Cinema usher Herbie Donnelly's stories of personally meeting the great film stars of the day, such as Gene Autry, Judy Garland, Bob Hope, Gracie Fields, Danny Kaye and his favourite, James Cagney, who spoke and strutted "exactly like he did on the screen". Oral history, indeed, includes the full range of human emotions.

CHRONICLES OF A VANISHING BREED

"Oral historians are haunted by the obituary page. Every death represents the loss of a potential narrator and thus an absolute diminution of society's collective historical memory."
(Cullom Davis, Oral History: From Tape to Type, *1977)*

The individuals chronicled in this book are true survivors, a vanishing breed of *real* Dubliners from bygone days. As preservers of the oral tradition their generation is the last link with family heritage and Dublin oral history and lore. Collectively, they represent a colourful collage of Dublin life earlier in the century. Their diversity runs the gamut from butcher, barber, undertaker, cutler and grave digger to railway man, tobacconist, seaman, soldier, legendary fortune teller and wartime hero. Yet all are common folk embodying values, lifeways and customs which have largely disappeared from the Dublin scene. All were selected for their significant personal or historical life experiences and narrative abilities.

Even such perceived "lowly" types as chimney sweep or grave digger reveal a proud heritage in their trade as they describe its origins, techniques, tools and lore. They also explain old customs and practices now extinct, which need to be set down for the historical record. At first glance, some types might appear decidedly uninteresting and insignificant. For example, a barber's life and trade might seem unworthy of historical documentation. But back in the 1920s barbering in Dublin demanded a rigorous five year apprenticeship and involved using instruments and treatments long obsolete which would likely fascinate people today. Only by recording the few surviving barbers who three-quarters of a century ago used mud packs, hair singeing devices and hair restoration treatments can we preserve such practices. Similarly, David O'Donnell, 76, one of Dublin's last coopers, tells of an old custom he learned from his father after a long day working with rough wooden casks:

"Your hands would crack like a horse's foot. At the end of the day they'd be just solid welts. I'd get a crack down along here and it would be quite deep and I often stitched it up with a piece of thread when it would become really open. It was like leather. Then when I came home I'd put tallow on my hands. I'd do it in front of the fire because that's what my father used to do."

Chimney sweep James Rooney can trace the ancient trade in his family back to 1834. Through the strong oral tradition in his family he learned from those before him about the "old days" when sweeps would literally buy small children from orphanages and force them to climb up dangerous chimneys, sometimes getting stuck or burned to death:

> "They used to sell children out of the orphanages and they'd beat them up the chimneys to clean them. Oh, made to go up *into* the chimney. Get the children small and made to climb up, with their feet. It must have been awful altogether."

Some individuals link us to an even more distant past. John Read Cowle, 90, is the last genuine cutler in the city and proprietor of Dublin's oldest surviving shop dating back to 1670 when his family began by making swords. Leslie Taylor is the master bell ringer at Christ Church Cathedral which was built nearly a thousand years ago. He proudly relates the heritage within the stone belfry:

> "This place *exudes* history! This is the *tradition*. Some people go on ringing till they're 80 or more. The ancient tradition is a serious business. We ringers of Christ Church are the upholders in our time of a beautiful tradition of ringing great and noble bells, bells whose sound can send ripples up the spine. I'm one of the people who have serviced the cathedral in some way since its foundation in 1038. I'm *part* of the bells. We're the successors. I'd like to die in the belfry . . . when I'm ringing."

Sometimes the spoken word can almost put us in personal contact with past famous figures. Herbert Pembrey, 87, is the proprietor of Greene's bookshop, a literary institution to Dublin bibliophiles. He began working in the shop for his father as a young man and exchanged pleasantries with the literary luminaries of the day:

> "I came here on 12 March 1928 and I've been coming in ever since. In those days we were mostly a lending library. We had six [outdoor] stands then with books ranging from a penny to a shilling. Oh, books were treasured in those days. It was a browser's paradise! We had W. B. Yeats and George Russell, A. E., and Jack B. Yeats. Very often they'd come in. You'd make chat with them. Oh, I knew them well. W. B. was a great man. He'd drop in for a chat. And Samuel Beckett often came over but he was never a very friendly fellow. He was very quiet, a bit eccentric."

His nonchalant tone in recounting conversation with Yeats, Oliver St John

Gogarty or Brendan Behan almost puts the listener beside the little bookshop counter seventy years ago.

A number of oral testimonies are historically valuable for revealing unrecorded folklore or for providing behind-the-scenes accounts of important events. For nearly a century it has been part of the folklore of old railway men how some of the steam engine drivers used to smuggle arms for the IRA to different parts of the country at great risk. But the details of such smuggling exploits have never been recorded. Since they are today held only in the memory of very few men they are in danger of being lost. Paddy Whelan, 85, a railway steam engine driver like his father before him, provides a unique detailed description:

> "My father used to carry guns down to different places from Dublin for the IRA. They'd be brought to the [locomotive] shed in Inchicore at night by some of the IRA fellas. Or maybe they'd have girls bring them in. They'd be in, like, plastic bags and a big long lump of string tied out and a cork on top. And it'd be dropped down into the water tank of the engine. Now on several occasions the Black and Tans searched my father's engine. They shovelled the coal off it, done *everything* looking for guns. And when they got to Cork or wherever, they filled up the tank and put their hand in till they got a bit of cork—cause the cork would float on the top of the water. Pulled up the cork and they had their guns!"

A last example is that of the "behind-the-barricades" oral historical exposé of the famous media-dubbed "Battle of Hume Street" in 1969. Over the past third of a century much folklore had built up around this impassioned spectacle in the streets of Dublin. But apart from the external articles written by journalists covering the event, no detailed "inside" account has ever been recorded. Urban activist and preservationist Deirdre Kelly played a major role in the dramatic struggle. She was one of a group of idealistic college students who occupied threatened old Georgian buildings for nearly six months during which (at considerable physical risk and some harm) they battled greedy developers and hired thugs. Her explicit narrative of the strategies and emotions of the participants provides a valuable historical chronicle of the event.

From the aforementioned oral history examples it should be apparent that such meticulously documented factual information is not likely to be found in library archives. These vivid personal testimonies not only significantly supplement and clarify existing records but profoundly *authenticate* and *humanise* historical circumstances and events. Only through the oral historical process of tape recording survivors can such original information be preserved for posterity.

"Alas, we cannot interview tombstones."[41]

2

Calls to Duty and Destiny

ALEC KING—WORLD WAR II RESCUE AND DEMOLITION OFFICER,
AGE 85

Having endured terrible physical pain early in his life, as well as witnessing his father's long agony from a war wound, he was imbued with a great sense of empathy for the suffering of others. Thus, he volunteered to become a Rescue and Demolition Officer and was one of the first men on the horrifying North Strand scene when the German bomb exploded on 31 May 1941. His heroism saved lives and inspired those around him. He recounts the tragic event in gripping detail.

"I was born in 1912 and my father came out of the [British] army in 1917 and he was dying from mustard gas. But now in 1933 I had a brain operation and my father looked after me. My mother wouldn't come near either of us. I don't know why. My sister came along when I was 6 and I was just pushed out in the cold. There was no love, no nurturing, no nothing at all. She was cold. But I was very close to my father. He thought the world of me. But I was dying. I had a night to live. And I used to go unconscious and my face was all crooked and I was in terrible pain. I knew nobody and I ate nothing and I dropped down to about five stone and there was nothing left of me. And the doctor said to my father standing at the end of the bed, 'I can do nothing for him. He'll have a night to live and he'll be dead in the morning.' And I don't know whether the Lord helped me or what but I just *sat up!* And the two of them looked at each other.

"So the doctor started the operation on me at ten minutes to six at night and finished at twenty minutes to two in the morning. It was hammer and chisel on part of my skull. It was that serious. Two nurses collapsed in the operating theatre at the operation . . . it was so horrible. The doctor was stripped to the waist with just a mask on his face and a hammer and chisel and saw. It was only touch and go. But I came to and survived . . . don't know how. I could have been brain damaged for life. Oh, it was a miracle. And in those days they had ether and it used to burn the face off you, and when I was coming to I saw what I thought was heaven . . . I was dead. If you can imagine an avenue of green grass with lovely beech trees in early morning, soft beech leaves, and right at the very end the sun was shining and there was a shimmer on the lake and the dew in the morning was rising. And I thought I was in heaven. To me, it *was* heaven. And there was a nurse beside me swabbing my face where the ether had been with ice cold water on my forehead and this was the lovely spring feeling . . . I can still feel it.

"And then my father died in 1934. He had seventeen years of agony, struggling to keep alive. His lungs were burned away by the mustard gas and I've never seen a person screaming his heart out like that. Oh, it was *unbelievable*. He dropped down from eleven and a half stone to five stone. There was literally nothing left of him. He was home all the time and I did everything for my father. When he was in bed dying I did the cooking for him. I'd get him his cigarettes and when he was in really bad pain I'd pop down and get him a drop of the hard stuff, a drop of whiskey, to help him. I'd do anything under the sun for him. And when my father died she never saw him. Didn't even see him in the coffin. She showed no emotion. It was like an iceman. Oh, my mother was callous . . . callous to the last.

"In 1939 I was living in Milltown and I was asked by the firm I was working for, Crampton's the builders, to join the ARP—that was the Air Raid Precautions—and to go to the anti-gas school and learn about these gases if an air raid came. It took five months and you had a great big heavy gas mask on you and you were climbing over bushes and ditches and doing daft things really. But I was made a Chief Air Raid Warden and I had the Ranelagh district. Had to notify everybody to keep indoors and the windows had to be sealed in case we got gassed by the Germans or the British—or the Americans. Anyway, one day I got word that 'you've been taken from the ARP and you're to start with the Rescue and Demolition in Number 6 Area', which was down in Ballsbridge. So I had to go down to the Rescue and Demolition and teach *them* all the gas routine that I'd learned. And then I became Chief Rescue and Demolition Officer. I had eighty men underneath me. We were all volunteers. We had a blue helmet with 'R & D' on the front of it, a type of boiler suit, and wellington boots and an axe—I *still* have it. I'd meet with my men in Crampton's stockyard beside the Dodder river and we had permission to use *anything* we wanted for rescue and demolition work. We could use planks and ladders and crowbars, welding equipment, all this sort of stuff. And lorries.

"Now before the bomb fell I had a sixth sense. I've had it all my life. It just gives you the shivers. And I had this on 31 May 1941. I came home from Crampton's and had my dinner and went out in the garden and started to dig around for the spring, sew seeds and plant things. And about half eleven my wife went up to bed but I just couldn't settle down . . . there was *something* wrong. There was a couple of planes buzzing around and I didn't know what it was. So I put on my boiler suit and got into my wellington boots and headed off down to the depot. And when I was about 300 yards or so at a crossroads there was a car coming and I stopped to let it go by cause I was on a bike. And at that time there was a terrific '*Whoof*' in the distance. And I thought, 'That's not an ordinary bang. There's something wrong here.' And about ten or fifteen seconds later I got a feeling of hot air on the left side of my face. And there was a telephone box across the road and I rung the depot and Tim Conlon was the night watchman and he was all shivering and shaky and he said, 'I've just got a call from headquarters that there's been a bomb dropped at the North Strand', and I was to gather all my force together and get there as *quick* as we could. So I went down and put on my gas mask and my belt with the axe and started to load the lorry and the first eight men that came in I took them. Our lorry driver was supposed to be Ned O'Loughlin that day but he was out on the North Strand when the bomb fell and Ned was fired fifty or sixty yards down the road and he was *peppered* with glass. And he went 'queer'. He was a cabbage. He never knew.

"We were the first squad to arrive and there was *no* organisation at the North Strand and the first thing we met was the LDF, the Local Defence Force. And they wouldn't let us through! We said we were the Rescue and Demolition. We were *on orders* to get through and *rescue* people. 'Nope. Our orders is that nobody comes through.' So I went back to the lorry and said, '*Right*, I've got four hefty fellas'—and I wasn't small myself—and we took the heads off the picks and took the pick handles and *you talk about hurling*! We saw the LDF going half the length of the field! And then Johnny Lawless put his boot to the accelerator of the lorry and we went through like *lightning*! And we were the first there. And to *see it* . . . *devastation*! I can still see it. It was *unbelievable*. The whole scene is still embedded in my brain, in my eyesight. I can see the whole scene . . . gaping floors, beds empty. There was one person who was fired out of the house when the bomb fell, *on a mattress*, and landed in the convent garden and wasn't hurt. And her sister in the room was killed. It was unpredictable. But there was *nothing* left. There were people hanging around that didn't know what to do with themselves. They were in a daze.

"So we unloaded everything off the lorry and we started working. Where to start we didn't know. We saw a huge flame away in the distance. It was the whole gas main lit up. And then the gas main went out and we had to use our own acetylene lamps which we had in those days. Now we had all sorts of equipment with us there when we arrived but we discovered that the only thing we could use was what God gave us, our *hands*. And if you took one brick out you had to *watch it* that half a ton didn't fall down on you. It was a *feat* of unknown engineering. And I was three times stronger than the normal man cause you get a person who has gone 'bats', that's gone mad, they have the strength of three men. You're not yourself. You felt the strength . . . adrenaline was *up high*! A hundred per cent, *over* a hundred per cent. And you lifted things that you couldn't have lifted before. I lifted a board of timber eight inches square and fourteen or sixteen feet long. I *shifted* it about a foot to get into a call or whisper we heard. And I went back there about three days later and *no way* could I move that block of timber. Impossible!

"We found people who were in pretty bad shape, cut, bruised or part of their limbs missing. Our own squad that night collected, I think, eleven or twelve people, dead or alive or maimed. And this is where the sixth sense came in too. You'd suddenly stop and say, '*Hush*, lads', and you'd listen. Everybody with their ear to the bricks. And you'd listen for a faint call or a faint cry or a faint whisper, or something. Where it came from you couldn't tell because one echo would bounce off a wall, off a fireplace, off an upturned bed, and you wouldn't know *where* it was and you had to go very gently. I was up on a landing, the first storey, on one of the rickety floors, and I saw in the corner a wicker chair and a big sheet of galvanised iron on the chair. It must have been blown there by the grace of God, because I *lifted* away the sheet of corrugated iron and in the wicker chair was a *lovely* little golden-haired child. Now I didn't know if it was a boy or a girl. And when I lifted the corrugated iron away it sat up and rubbed its eyes and started to cry for somebody. And I picked him up in my arms and I'd say he was around fifteen months old, roughly. And I took him up in my arms with the blankets, cause he was wrapped up for the night in the chair, and I brought him down and some of the people took him from me and said, 'We'll look after him, sir.' He was intact. I can *still* see him, lovely curly fair hair. And then one man just appeared out of the rubble and dirt and dust and he had *no idea* who he was, *where* he was. *Nothing!* It was *unbelievable*. He appeared out of *nowhere*. It was like the Phoenix, like a *zombie!* It was like one of those things appearing on the horror films you see, that this person just appeared out of the dust like a zombie. And some people recognised him and they brought him away and I didn't ever know what happened to him. He may have died or he may have been like that for the rest of his life.

"You were always afraid because you never knew when there'd be five or six tons of rubble that could suddenly collapse down on you. But we were working away and I put my hand in and I said to the lads, '*Quiet!* I've found *hair.*' So we had to do everything then very, very gently, lifting each brick. So eventually I got the head out of a woman with long black hair. The neck was severed from the body, completely, her eyes *wide open*, *staring* at me. I can still see her and her eyes staring at me as if to say, 'What have you done to me?' And when I eventually got her out there were white tubes hanging out from her neck that must have been her breathing and guts and that sort of thing. Eyes *wide open*. See, the eyes won't close unless you put a penny on them when you're dead. It's a muscle reaction. So I took this head down to the first-aid people and they put it on a stretcher and I said, 'Stay where you are, I've got to find the rest of her.' So we started to work away and we discovered the body and we started to lift it out slowly and I took the shoulders and open neck where you could see into the cavity. And the whole body came out then in one piece. A couple of the lads took the legs and we started to go down to the stretcher. And on the way down all the blood that was in the body, in the carcass—it was hot and sticky—it flowed out on top of me. *All* over me. I can still feel it. I was clammy . . . oh! But we never thought of washing ourself. That didn't matter. There was *more* people in there that we had to get out! And as the night wore on I discovered that the front of my suit was getting terribly heavy and it was all the dirt and filth and dust just hanging on to the blood, and your hands were caking. When you would move your hand the lumps would fall off, with red underneath and black on top. And when we brought that woman out a priest came along, a little man, his name was Father O'Reilly, and he was there on his hands and knees giving her the last rites and he was crying his heart out.

"And you'd see a person [on their knees] praying and you'd take no notice. You'd just think, 'She's doing her own little bit.' And you might even get five or six collected together praying and they'd have the rosary beads out. They were shocked. I don't think they really realised until a few days later. There were one or two women who went berserk, weeping and wailing, and they were carted away. But other women were really very, very strong. They were *super* people in North Strand. They were *brilliant*. They wanted to come and help us rescue people and we just explained to them very quietly, 'You may not know the art of taking bricks apart. You have not had the training that we have had, and you *may* kill somebody by accident.' But the people who were around, we'd hand them out these big baskets about three feet high and two foot across which we put rubble into, slates and bricks. And they'd carry it away and dump it in the middle of the road. In that way they were a great help. I could never thank them enough for all their help. And we were handed tea in a mug or a jam jar and handed sandwiches. We ate them and didn't know what was in them. Could have been rats, bits of dead dog or horses or humans . . . you wouldn't know, you just ate them. To wash down the dirt and filth in your throat. And the tea, it was like a godsend. It was like a Mecca. And as the tea got down to the bottom it got stronger and stronger and you needed a knife and fork to cut it! You could chew it! But *anything* to get rid of that *awful* dirt and filth.

"People around there were very sensible, very solid. They stuck together, they were as close-knit families as you ever could find. But I think they were dazed . . . that a German would drop a bomb on them. Why? We never did anything to the Germans. The German planes had a kind of 'whoo, whoo, whoo', a kind of throbbing sound. It would get on your nerves after a while. This particular plane had been flying around Dublin for about an hour and after a while the army anti-aircraft pinpointed him. My own reading of the matter was that he just jettisoned his bomb. He said [to himself], 'Look, I've got to get back, the fuel is going down, good luck', and he pulled his lever and that was it. He headed out to the sea and got his route going back and he was shot down in the Irish Sea. I got that from some of the British pilots, pilots that I had known in grammar school.

"I worked for sixty-plus hours. I never had a break. *Sixty* hours. I reckoned that thirty-nine people that night were killed. Some said that it was only twenty-eight but I have it on good authority that it was thirty-nine. I have *proof* of it. The bomb fell early Saturday morning around about 2.00 and I didn't get back home till Monday. Mentally, everything was drained out of me. When the Rescue and Demolition squads were done the Corporation workers took over. And when I got home finally the first thing I wanted was a bath, and then to bed. And when I stripped in the bathroom, took off my boiler suit and my underpants, I discovered I had a ring about an inch and a half around my stomach, all raw, and this was from the *bugs* who couldn't pass the elastic of my underpants so they decided to eat underneath it. See, the bugs worked up from the legs up and they couldn't get up under the elastic of my underpants. This all occurred because in the old days they built houses with plaster and horse hair and cow hair and the bugs got in there. And I was *covered* in blood. My wellington boots were thrown out the window. And when I got into the bath there was a scum thick on the top with bugs, *every* sort of bug. And I got a big bottle of Jeyes fluid and I lashed the whole lot into the bath and I got in. And the *pain* around my stomach was something, from the raw flesh and the Jeyes fluid. And I started to push the scum down toward the end of the bath with my hands and when I pulled the stopper out it took a long time to drain away. I had to get a bucket to clear out the bugs. Anyway, then I got the best disinfectant you could get and that was a bottle of whiskey and I poured whiskey over my stomach and by that time I was up around where the electric light was with the pain of it. Then I had a right good feed and I went to bed.

"But then I went back on the Monday afternoon and I saw just that much of a woman's shoe, just the little pointed toe. And I went to lift this up and I couldn't get any movement out of it at all. So I started to excavate a bit and I discovered there was a foot in it! And from the foot I discovered there was legs on it. And from the legs I discovered there was a body on it. And three other workers came over and we started excavating and we found a young lady of about 19 called Fitzpatrick and her nose and breasts were sheared off like you would see with an electric carving knife. It must have been a girder or a block of timber that had just come down and severed her. Whether she had been killed by it or just laid there wounded and died eventually I don't know. One will never know.

"Days later people came from far and near to look at it. Of course, there were reports in the papers all over the place. And when it was all over then I felt sort of sorry that it [the rescue] had to stop . . . I was so *hyped up* at the time. I lost my glasses. They were smashed. I lost my watch. It was smashed. And my fingernails were gone, there was nothing but red, pussy sore things. And I was cut and bruised all over the place. But at the time you were numbed to it. That was a minor thing, because you had people in there who were far worse with no arms and no legs, maybe no head, like that woman. You didn't think about it, you just kept going. It's all photographed on the brain—31 May 1941. And about a week later after it was all over all the men we met for the first time and had tea . . . and some of us cried . . . over what happened. They were great. The only thing I have to show for it is a bit of an old medal they sent out to me, the Department of Defence. Got that three or four years later. No ceremony at all, just sent out to me."

JACK CONROY—WORLD WAR II FIRE BRIGADE, AGE 78

In April of 1941 he was rudely roused from his fire station bunk and informed about the German blitz which left Belfast blazing. De Valera wanted to dispatch volunteer Dublin fire brigade men to assist their beleaguered brethren in the North, at considerable risk to his policy of neutrality in the war. At age 22 he responded to the call to duty as he raced north to extinguish fires, clear rubble and save lives. The valorous actions of his band of men went largely unheralded and unrecorded. His precise narrative chronicles this historic event.

"We lived in a little square off Oxmantown Road and there were seven children. My father was in Dublin Corporation and at that time all the streets were paved with these paving stones, setts. It was a trade they served seven years to, as apprentices. Oh, there was an art to it. He worked at that and he was a foreman at 21 years of age. And my father never drank in his life. He lived for two things, his family and his job—nothing else. And he used to laugh and say 'Arthur Guinness is my best friend', because the other guys would spend half their day in the *pub*, so they wouldn't get a promotion. But he never drank and he was very steady, very industrious and very conscientious. When he retired after fifty-odd years in it he was chief inspector of the paving department, the streets department now.

"I went to a national school in Marlborough Street and from there I progressed to what is now called the vocational education colleges. At that time they were called technical schools. It was a school of retail distribution and when I was 18 I got a position in a drapery shop, men's outfits. And I stayed there for about three years. I was 21 and at that time my brother, Michael, had been in the fire brigade for three years. It was a *permanent* job, a permanent *pensionable* job. It *appealed* to me. There was a certain amount of glamour attached to it I suppose. And there was always the feeling that you were doing something worthwhile. They needed extra men and there were *hundreds* of applicants. There were thirty-two new men taken on. We had to do a bit of an examination. 'Twasn't very much. To me it was nothing, child's play. And, of course, a physical test, and I was in!

"There were just four fire stations in Dublin then. One still exists in Tara Street. There was one station on Amiens Street. It was on Buckingham Street. And now I never saw Buckingham Street until the *day* I was told to report, didn't know where it was. There was only a crew of six men on each day and we had the one appliance, five men on the appliance and one man on the telephone. We were on duty then for one day—on from 10 a.m. to 10 a.m. In turn, we cooked our own dinner, the midday meal. And some of them were bad cooks, I'll tell you. I was a good cook, bacon and cabbage or steak and onion, nothing fancy. But when the bells would go we all had to get out and the dinner could be half cooked and it was just *left* there.

"And the station could be damned cold in the winter, especially when the war started and fuel went scarce. Terribly cold and there was no coal to be had. There was an old boiler that used turf and it was only lit on odd days during the week. Freezing cold. I'll tell you what we used to do. A lot of the lads there were fond of their beer, the pint, and they used to get these pint bottles sent up from the local pub. A fella [porter] would come with a big basket, *into the station*, in the evening time. Oh, that was allowed. Now if anybody went over the limit they'd be pulled up and reprimanded before the chief. So we used to fill the pint bottles with hot water and put them into the bed, two or three bottles of hot water. But some of the lads would come and get into their bed and find three bottles of *cold* water that the fellas had put in on them—a bit of a joke. Oh, we were very close. And I'll tell you this much now. If you didn't like a guy and he didn't like you, or if you had a falling out for some reason or another . . . but when you went to a fire that was all forgotten, that fella'd go in and pull you out by the legs if he had to. Once you went to a fire all animosity or differences were forgotten. You worked as a team.

"We had a uniform with what they call a military collar. It was dark blue with a red band on the tunic and down the side of the leg and the pockets had red piping. And, oh, brass buttons, polished. You scrubbed the buttons with Brasso. Then they gave us these Dunlop boots, wellingtons if you like, big heavy ones. We were very badly equipped. Now we had a month's training in Tara Street—the bare essentials—like how to run the hose out and connect up to the engine, and using ladders. Oh, God, they had a drill tower that was five storeys high, a wooden structure with blank windows in it, and we had to go up that with a hook ladder. I was a bit nervous. You hooked the ladder [in a window sill] and you climbed up it and then you put one leg in through the window, straddling the window sill, and then put the ladder up again. It was fairly light, made from some sort of ash wood with a big long hook. And you had to sort of lean out and get it up into the next window. Anyway, we'd go up the whole way and then come down again.

"Then they had a smoke hole. It was like a big manhole cover, and down below was a square cavity about six feet square and maybe four or five feet high [deep]. And they'd put oily rags and all sorts of stuff down there and set it on fire and put the lid on it, and the smoke would be so thick that you couldn't see your finger in front of your nose. And we'd be sent down there one at a time for three or four minutes maybe. Almost suffocated! And I said to the officer in charge one day, 'You wouldn't get smoke like that' and he said, 'Oh, indeed you *do*. Wait until you go out yourself.' Which I *did* find. Then I took up driving and we'd go on one of the appliances all around the city for a couple of hours, just to get the feel of it. They were heavy enough. They were Leland and Merriweather appliances. It was a good fire engine. Merriweather built the body and Leland was the engine. In those days the traffic was in *no* way what it is today, and we had a clanging bell.

"We had very poor facilities. But we had a dartboard or a ring board and we played cards, played bingo. We even ourselves had to *hire* a radio. There was a firm in town that specialised in hiring out radios. We paid so much per week and the mess man would collect the money. During the war years we were very fond of listening to Lord Haw-Haw and the war news. And many a time we played cards *all night*, wouldn't go to bed. We'd still be playing cards in the morning when the other fellas would be getting up, pontoon, poker. Now I started at £3.12.6 a week wages and I remember this particular night we were playing pontoon and you could lose a lot of money. I was losing thirty shillings, which was nearly half a week's wage, and about 12.00 there was a turnout [alarm] and *down we went* and left the money on the table. But when we got back we started playing again and I got my money back in about a half an hour's time.

"Now in 1936 there was a big tragedy here in Pearse Street and three men lost their lives. Strange thing about it, I was courting a girl at the time and was on my way home about half eleven at night and I came up into the middle of it and it was *blazing*. And I spoke to one of the firemen and he said, 'Three of the lads are missing.' Anyhow, this fireman was at a hydrant there and he says, 'There's no pressure, there's no water.' And the station officer came to him and said, '*Open up* the pressure.' And he says, '*I can't*, the water's *not there*.' There was no water left. And there was a big inquiry went on for weeks and weeks about that. There was four guys went into that building and only one came out and I soldiered with him years later and the poor fella, he was a nervous wreck, a nervous man completely. There were three older guys than he was, he was *so new*, a recruit, he hadn't even got a helmet. They went off one way and he didn't go with them and there was an explosion and they went down. And he was always nervous, almost destroyed. At the tribunal he was asked, '*Why didn't* you go with the other men?' And he answered, 'It was an act of God.'

"After the inquiry then this army man took over as chief, a Major Comerford. Oh, he was a spit and polish merchant. He had us marching up and down in the barracks square. Oh, God, yes. He had an ex-sergeant in the army come in twice a week to drill us and teach us how to salute. I enjoyed it but some of the older men didn't like it. But it made us fit. Comerford turned the place inside out. His word was law. A good man. And he used to *time* us with a stopwatch and we had *one minute* [to be out when the alarm bell sounded]. *One minute*! Oh, we didn't waste any time. We *wanted* to get out and do our stuff. At night we did what was called 'make down'. You could take off your boots and trousers together and lay them beside your bed with the trousers *outside* the boots. And then you'd *jump* up and pull up your boots and trousers in one go. And I needn't tell you, we didn't sleep in pyjamas! But he'd come along and have the man pull the alarm switch and he'd have the stopwatch in his hand and we had *one* minute.

"Now the bomb in 1941, I *saw it all*. We *always* knew the sound of the German bombers, they had a most peculiar beat that went 'drum, drum, drum', a throbbing sound. They used to use the east coast of Ireland to come up and maybe attack Liverpool. *Many* a night we'd hear the bombers overhead. But this night I was home and the sound of the bomb coming down was a whistle and then '*plump*'. My father and me put my mother and sister under the stairs for protection. And I had a lovely new bike and I took off on it down to

Buckingham station and it was filled with civilians who got scared and came in for help. Now two small bombs had come down on Summerhill and North Richmond Street. So we were trying to quiet the people down but one fella says, 'No, they're still up there. I can hear them.' And *with that* the North Strand bomb came down. I can honestly say I never heard it and I was only a few hundred yards away from it. *Never* heard it. All I know is that whatever percussion there was we were thrown in a *heap* on the floor. *Thrown* down. Every bell in the place went off and *clouds* of dust came down from the ceiling. It was so near that we all thought the bomb fell in the back yard.

"So there was just two of us [firemen] there cause the engine was out in Summerhill and we were sent down on foot to the North Strand. The two of us had our steel helmets on us and we were running and the other fella was seventeen stone. As we were going past the Five Lamps there was *mobs* of people coming up, *running away* from it in their night attire and all shouting, 'It's *down there*, firemen, it's *down there!*' Oh, they were in a shocking state . . . shocking state all the people and children. I'll never forget all these people running down pulling kids by the hand, putting overcoats over their night attire, *hysterical* shouting and screaming, 'It's *down there*.' And the ambulances were going back and forth. We run down as best we could and you could see a huge cloud of dust as you were coming near the crater and we saw a figure lying along the kerb stone. And we looked to see could we help him and his *head* was gone! The blast blew his head off. Bleeding . . . just lying there.

"So we made our way down and there was a *big thick* haze of dust cause the house'd collapsed like a pack of cards. They were *old* Georgian type houses, tenement houses, with shops underneath them. I'll never forget it. We were one of the first on the scene. And just as we got near to it there was a big 'puff' and the gas [main] went up in flames and the whole thing then, of course, was ablaze. And we couldn't do an awful lot. But we were there all the night pulling people out of it, all night through the dawn, through daylight. There was about thirty people killed. It was *pitiful* looking at little babies . . . like little waxen dolls that they were pulling out. Some of them fell, came down from the top floors on top of the rubble. Quite a few babies, maybe a half a dozen or so. Killed. Dead. Innocent. Now I hadn't seen much before of death. That was really my first contact with *violent* death. But *somehow* it slid off you, sort of. You were there to do something and you *did it*. The night went by very, very quickly. And we saw the size of the crater when daylight came and it was about twenty feet deep, a *massive* thing. You could put a house into it. It must have been an unusually big bomb. About thirty-odd people killed. Don't know how many injured. Must have been scores. I'll never forget it.

"Now Belfast, that was in April of 1941, before the North Strand bombing. They were bombed badly, *blitzed*. Blitzed completely. The story was that they lost complete control of the whole thing. They weren't able to control it. We were pulled out of bed at half six in the morning from Buckingham station. And we were standing around saying, 'What's going on?' We didn't know, just left there standing, five or six of us. So eventually we found out that Belfast had been bombed. Now we never thought we'd be going to Belfast. And the power that be didn't think that either because there was no *provision* made for it. It was a request from Belfast for help. But we didn't know what the hell was going on, standing there. Now they called for volunteers and single men. My brother was down in Dorset Street [station] and I told our station officer that he's married and I'm not. And he wouldn't send two men from the one family.

"It was 9.00 before we moved out. We didn't go on our appliance. That was kept back. We went on one of these ARP [Air Raid Precaution] vehicles they called a tangye. It was for the auxiliary fire service personnel. It was like our appliances but the bodywork was rather basic and done cheaply. It was a dark grey. So we made up a crew of five of us and we went off to Belfast and we were told that we could be days there, could be weeks there. We were told to bring spare uniforms with us, spare this and that. And when we were going out the gate our station officer said to us, 'Well, you're going out and God knows when you'll be back!' And we accepted that. I was young, 22 years of age. You know, there was a spirit of adventure. I was *pleased* to go . . . didn't know what was facing us . . . just 'things are bad up there'. And we were told going up to Belfast to fill up with petrol at *any* station this side or the far side of the border, cause we were short of petrol. We crossed the border and stopped in Newry and filled up and got off to stretch our legs and this woman came up and said, 'Where are you from?' And we said Dublin and she said, '*Dublin?*' She couldn't believe it, that we had come up from Dublin, the Free State as they called it then, to help them out. And we went into a couple of pubs—and they shouldn't have been open but they were—and we hadn't got to spend a penny. It was Thursday and our payday was Friday and we had no money in our pockets. We'd go into the pubs and the barman'd say, 'What are you having?' *Whatever* you wanted, they gave. And there was this one old Belfast chap sitting by himself in the corner drinking his whiskey and he said, '*Up de Valera!*'

"The first thing then we saw was the refugees and cars coming along with perambulators tied on top of them and bedding on top and they were all *beating* south across the border. Fleeing. And they went fleeing by foot out to the nearby mountains near Belfast and they stayed out there for weeks. Now to give the Germans their due, on that particular night they bombed the northern part of Belfast which was an industrial site. It was where the flax mills were. Belfast was known for its linen and they had these *huge* flax mills. And we passed through the centre of the city and all we saw was *all* the shop windows shattered, glass lying all over the place but no structural damage. And the British Army had been at it all night long and they were sitting along the footpath, all these officers, and the firemen the same, all exhausted.

"Now the fires were *widespread*, fires everywhere, especially in the flax mills. The Germans let these incendiary bombs down like hailstones. This is what did the damage, set fires *all over* the place. And we were walking through them, kicking them out of our way, what was left of them, bits and pieces. And there were streets of workers' cottages *flattened*, a pile of brick. *Completely* flat. Who was underneath them I don't know. I never found out either. So we were sent in and kept busy in the flax mills. Our job was putting out what was left. And *huge* blazes, *vast* huge blazes. Terrible heat. And as I came to this particular spot to pull the hose an oil pipe burst and hit me with hot oil and luckily enough it hit the back side of my helmet. And at that time our protective clothing was very basic. It was called a slicker, a big long black rubberised coat. So it hit my helmet and ran down the back of my slicker and the heat of the oil lifted all the coating off the slicker. So we did our stuff and the soldiers there came along with their mobile kitchens and they sent out to us big cans of tea and sandwiches and hard-boiled eggs and the soldiers were all sitting down along by us telling us of their experiences and they claimed that the Germans came down and machine-gunned the streets. Later we went back to the station in Belfast in Chichester Street and got a meal and they had all mattresses laid out on the floor for us. And in the station we were grimy and dirty and washing ourselves. But about ten o'clock word came to pack up, that we were going home . . . they were the best times of my life, great camaraderie."

Paddy Launders—World War II Seaman, Age 75

In 1942 he joined the British Merchant Navy, carrying high explosives to the most dangerous war zones. His ship narrowly escaped being sunk by a torpedo from a German submarine. Shortly thereafter, he witnessed at a distance of only a few hundred yards the horror of a companion vessel blown "into oblivion" with a full crew of English and Irish mates aboard. But he survived the war intact and even brought home a few pounds of precious tea from India for his father.

"I'm a three generation Dublin man, born in the centre of Dublin in North King Street. My father was a carter in the Dublin Corporation. He was a great horse man, had a great understanding of horses. There was nine children in our family. Conditions were atrocious in the tenements. There was seven families in our open-door tenement. We had only one room. Shared one toilet in the yard. One water tap. We had an open fire, turf and coal for fuel. And paraffin lamps. There was no way my father's money covered feeding eleven mouths so we went to the pawnbroker. Everybody around you was in the same, or worse, position. And everybody *helped* one another. But we didn't starve, us kids. Do you know why? Because we had the fruit markets next to us. And it didn't require stealing. See, there was always some pickings left there, lovely bunches of grapes, apples, a pear. Potatoes as well. And we'd go to the back where the waste ground was and we'd cook the potatoes, just over a fire, and we'd have a baked potato. So I never knew the pangs of hunger, because of our wits. We found a way to supplement. And we weren't thieving.

"In those days we didn't go for trips. But my father would say, 'We're going for a ramble' around Dublin. By foot. We'd go for a ramble down along the quays. And I remember in 1932 when I was 10 years of age and I'm walking down there with my father and there was a sea of ships and there was a carrier ship and the cook was on the stern by the galley and he was a coloured man, probably from Liverpool. And he speaks to my father and he goes in and brings me out a piece of plum pudding. And it was the sweetest thing I'd ever tasted. And now that set me off thinking, 'That's the kind of life I want, if you can get things like that.' So that was my first impression of ship life. And my father says, 'That man, he's from Senegal'—now he might as well have said he's from Donegal—'That's in Africa and that's where the blackest people come from.' Now my father was just an ordinary working man but he was pretty well versed and he done a lot of reading and he tried to pass it along to me.

"I was sent to this school in Great Strand Street which was right down on the quays. I was anything but a star pupil. But I always wanted to get out of where I was [in the tenements]. That was my goal in life. Cause I saw my mother crying because she didn't have *one* shilling and sixpence for the rent. And to this day it even breaks my heart. And so I *swore* I would *never, never* be idle . . . if I had to go to the Klondike to dig for gold, but I would never be idle if I could go anywhere to find work. So I came out of school at age 14 and the local laundry employed me as a van boy for twelve shillings a week working about sixty hours. I went out on the horse and dray with the man delivering the laundry. And I helped to clean out the stable and I'd take the horse to the farrier to be shod. And I'd ride him down and back and that was a thrill, a city kid getting a touch of country life.

"Now at the outbreak of the war I was in my last week or two on the laundry job. Incidentally, they let me go because I was due for a raise, no other reason. I was on twelve shillings and I was to go on to eighteen shillings. So they found it more economic to employ another boy. But I didn't mind cause I wanted to do something else. I wanted to go somewhere. And there was a war on. And I was with the van man and there was a lady in Clanbrassil Street—I'll never forget it—and she gave the van man a Birmingham newspaper. And it was like my opening up the Bible for the first time when I found four or five full pages of situations vacant. So, needless to say, I thought, 'There's no problem', and I told my mother. Between her and me we made up thirty shillings and I went on the B & I boat and arrived in Liverpool at 3.00 in the morning. And I fell asleep in the park out of fatigue. And I remember my first day in Liverpool in England. The first thing I found peculiar were the large balloons. They were a dirigible and they were anchored with a strong cable to a mobile winch machine and they were driven around vulnerable areas to stop German dive-bombers. That was my first vision of wartime England.

"Anyway, I woke up in Liverpool to meet a crowd of pessimistic Dubliners who were saying there was no work in this place. So I headed up in the train to Birmingham and got a job in the factory reaming metal rods. Then I got a job as a general labourer wheeling concrete from a mixer. Then I realised that if I stayed in England I was due for recruitment—and I knew I wasn't going home because there was no work. Then I was bombed out in Birmingham. There was an air raid. It blew out the window where we were sleeping and blew down the hall door. So I went back to Liverpool and applied to join the Merchant Navy. This would be 1942. And I went away on a deep-water tramp steamer carrying general cargo. Like, when we done the run to Malta, during the siege of Malta, among our items was Christmas pudding for the officers. But 99 per cent of my cargo after that was *high* explosives, *high* octane petroleum. We carried *thousands* upon *thousands* of jerrycans with high octane petroleum for the aircraft. The jerries invented a tin can with a handle on it for carrying petrol and that's known as a jerrycan to my generation. Tin cans of about five gallons. And now when you consider that this ship that I was on was a *coal-burning* vessel! And it had a coal-burning galley for cooking the food! And on this ship every second man smoked! And I done seven convoys carrying 100 per cent inflammable bombs in the hold.

"I was a fireman and you put in four hours down in the stoke hole in that degree of heat. I was shovelling coal to raise the steam, pure and simple. Shovelling coal. I done that over an eight year period. We had a No. 7 shovel. An ordinary concrete worker used a pear-shaped shovel but we used a flat, square shovel, a big size called a Number 7. It was killing! You had to do it for four straight hours. You'd have a sweat rag around your neck and into the corner of your mouth and you *sucked* that as a lubricant. It would wind up grimy. And your face was black. We used to put Vaseline around the rims of our eyes so that when you washed yourself the black coal would not have been next to your skin. It would be on the Vaseline, which is a grease. And my hands were all welts. And the food we got on the ship depended on your cook and they'd say that some of the cooks came out of the munitions factories and they'd bake bread that you could put in and use as shells! We lived by broaching the cargo. In the cargo we had tins of fruit, like pears. That's what we survived on. But the officers knew.

"My first trip was going around the Cape in Africa. That was general cargo. Then I went to Bombay. And I done four trips to the relief of Tripoli. But on the *next* ship I went up to the war zone to the Suez Canal. I done seven or eight trips *completely surrounded* by belligerent Germans and U-boats. There could be about twelve ships in our convoy. Now when we went with the convoy to the Siege of Malta we had four ships and eleven destroyers and a battle cruiser as an escort. See, Malta was the most besieged and bombed island and the most strategic in the North African campaign in the Mediterranean. And it held out for two years. We were carrying explosives and everything and we *had* to get through. But, see, I was young and my mother's prayers were with me. So I never had any fear. But I seen men wanting to jump over the side, older men than me, more experienced men than me. I seen men panicking. I didn't understand the psychology of it. I only knew the way I felt.

"We had with us the *fastest* destroyers in the British Navy. They were light anti-aircraft destroyers. They were able to do fourteen knots and were [supposedly] unsinkable. But I saw one of them going up in smoke. The torpedo anticipated his course, or the submarine anticipated his course, and hit him. All I seen was a blob of smoke. And that was one of our escorts. And the ships that

I saw getting blown up, there was nothing dramatic about them as you would see in a war film. They just went up completely in smoke—end of story. One time this U-boat came up and shot a torpedo. It had us for the target, but it missed us, missed the second ship likewise, and slammed into the third and she went down in *minutes*. And we were told to '*Keep going, keep going*, or they'll get you!' You wouldn't give any mind to breaking rank or going to pick up survivors. Do you understand? You weren't allowed to do that. That was the escort's job. She went down in a matter of minutes. She had a crew of about forty and I heard that there was seventeen picked up. And you can just imagine, even if they *were* picked up in a sea of oil, how many of them survived. For me it was a shock to see.

"But one time we were around Gibraltar and were heading home and we thought, 'Thank God, now we're heading home.' And this was in the month of July. It was a day like you were sailing on your millionaire's yacht, lying back, not remotely concerned with war, a *beautiful* Mediterranean day. And we were sailing along beautifully and the next thing we seen a vessel coming toward us from the west and they came as close as they could be and now this was a British assault craft and *packed* with men and they would have been carrying oil as well. So they came as close as could be and we done the usual sailor's thing which was calling out to them, 'Anyone from Dublin?' 'How's Liverpool playing?' You know, the usual thing. And I'm standing over the railing as the ship goes by and we're just looking at it and it just goes a thousand yards or so by—no great distance—and I had a great feeling of peace . . . and the *shock*! That ship went into *oblivion*! And I'm looking at it. A torpedo, a U-boat. Even now I can remember the shock. There was a *tremendous* explosion. Our captain had radioed them that this submarine had gone *under us*. Now I didn't see anything, *hear* anything . . . but what I saw was our friends lost. They were not any more than a half a mile away from us, could have been less. *Clearly*!

"Now my father asked me, 'There's two things I want you to bring back, Paddy. Number one is *you* and number two is some tea.' And I bought a beautiful 5 lb packet of tea in India, this lovely box of tea. But it was stolen. Well, you talk about being disappointed! That *broke* my heart. But my shipmates, the Lord rest them, dipped into theirs and made up about 2 lb of tea for me. Now I'm an Irish national through and through, to the core. I believe in the unity of this country. I *love* this country. But I have sailed with Englishmen and they're as good as any in the world, the same as us Irish is good. And they were *men*, men in *every sense* of the word."

Henry "Ginger" Kelly—World War II Soldier, Age 82

He gave up parking bicycles and cars on Abbey Street to join the British Army in July of 1940. He was promptly dispatched to the French Front with virtually no training or arms. With the fearsome German Panzer tank troops in hot pursuit, his company was driven south to Dunkirk which became one of the great killing fields of the war. Here he witnessed a horrifying massacre by German pilots flying so low he could see their laughing expressions. He helped to bury the dead, including heaps of children, in mass graves. Only fifteen of the eighty-seven men in his company came back alive . . . "War is a cruel thing", he reflects.

"'Ginger', that's a nickname. I was born on Cook Street, in 1910. Me father was in the First World War. I was in the last one . . . Hitler . . . oh, I was chased out of Dunkirk. I'll tell you the whole story. But me father was in the war and me mother died when I was 8 years old and I'd a brother 4 years old and a sister 12. And me aunt couldn't keep us cause she was married with a house full of kids and she put us into a convent. When I come out of the convent I was put in another school for five years. And then I went into a place called Artane run by the Christian Brothers. And then when I was 16 I was sold to a farmer down in Roscommon for two bob a week. Rough, *rough*. He used to kick me and belt me and I run away from him, come up to Dublin and I hadn't a crust of bread and I had to mind cars.

"I started at Wynn's Hotel on Abbey Street minding cars for tuppence or thruppence. They'd give me anything, apples, oranges, maybe a packet of fags [cigarettes]. I got married in 1930 and I was minding cars and bicycles. Bicycles used to be all parked in the middle of O'Connell Street and Abbey Street and any ordinary bloke could mind bicycles. You could watch forty or fifty bikes. Just looking for a living. I used to go home with about four or five shillings in copper, old pennies. It got stew for the kids. Now I was getting a bit fed up with this minding cars and bicycles for tuppence and thruppence in hail, rain and snow, standing five, six, seven hours out in the rain. And I said to the wife, 'Well, Hitler is started', and that was in September. I remember it very well, a Sunday morning. And the wife says to me, 'You're going to join the [British] army.' See, there was seven kids by this time.

"So I went to Belfast and joined up at the depot, was dressed out, sworn in, put up for a fortnight and then moved over to England outside Liverpool. And after about a month we were shipped over to France. We arrived in Le Havre and went up to Belgium, riding in cattle trucks. Hitler had nearly got the Channel Islands at the time. He was on the verge of coming, so we had to be fast. Now I'll tell you another thing. When I joined up and went over to France they'd no rifles to give us, so they gave us old rifles from the First World War— that's how *desperate* they were. We went through France and Belgium like that with the old big long rifles like Davy Crockett used. And half my company had *no* rifles when they sent us over. They were trying to make a crowd to frighten them [Germans]. *Churchill!* To give you an idea, there was one of my officers with one eye and another with one arm. They were in the First World War. True as God!

"So we were in cattle trucks and you know the water that comes out of the side of the train? The pipe? We started making tea with that! Full marching orders and nothing, only a tin of salty sausages each and a tin of dog biscuits. True, true! And we're having a drink of this tea and a dispatcher pulls in on a motor bike and sees the commanding officer and says Hitler is about three miles away with about 500 tanks. 'Get back on the cattle trucks. *All the way back*, to Dunkirk this time. This was about August 1940. Now there's a road about two miles outside Dunkirk and a canal on one side and a field on another and there were refugees with beds and horses and bicycles and women and children and the jerries [German pilots] are coming over and the planes are so low they're looking at me with their goggles on and they *mow down* the people. *Mow* them all down. And we had to bury the lot of them. Eighty, ninety or 150 in a grave and an old blanket around them and slop them in . . . a few prayers and the bulldozer covers them over. This is true. Now are you taking all this *in*? Anyway, we buried a lot of dead . . . kids, girls and boys, 12 and 14. Ah, but what could you do? War is a cruel thing . . . a very cruel thing.

"Then we went into this big mansion—some big French fella must have owned it—and we were taking all the wounded in there and burying all the dead off this road which was quite near it. And now I'll tell you this. I don't like saying it. Maybe I'll be wrong in saying it to you, but there was a lot of fellas filling their kit bag with blah, blah, blah. Do you understand me? One fella I seen, a fella called Stewart. I'll never forget it. He went over to a dead French officer and took a solid gold watch that size off him. They came back with kit bags full! But we were in this big mansion with the wounded laying on the stretchers waiting for the Red Cross ambulances to come. And we had a big red cross laid out on the ground to let them [Germans] know—but they very seldom respected that, you know. So I goes down to the cellar anyway, me and about five or six of me mates, and, *oh*, there's wine! You know, the wine cellars. Ah, there's vin blanc and sour wine and I come across this bottle and I'll never forget it—*Benedictine*! Like red blood. And I drank two bottles of it. I was drunk. I was *stupid* on this Benedictine. I never had it before. Red blood it is. Jesus, me ears were numb! And I go out after this Benedictine and the jerries looking down at me from their planes and they're having to drag me back in.

"Anyway, then I went down to the beach and Dunkirk was as flat as that floor, on the harbour. Honest to God, they levelled out Dunkirk. I got to the beach and there was about a quarter of a million people on it. And no uniforms, no shorts, some in their bare feet, beards, not shaved . . . all sorts, Poles, British, French and they're all pushing on this pier. Ah, for God's sake, there was chaos. About a quarter of a million on the beach, no tunic, no rifles. They were waiting [for ships] to take them over [to Britain] but these bombers were coming over every half-hour and they done the ships as well as Dunkirk town. And I couldn't run quick enough. I took off me army boots and put on my runners. I was scared. I'm no hero. Jerries were coming over every half-hour, twenty or forty of 'em, *looking out* at you, they were *that* low. Oh, God, they were looking out at you—*laughing*! And there were two hospital ships in the harbour with wounded on them and they were in half with the decks on fire with barrels of oil. And I was out in the water up to there [chin]. So there was two or three days waiting, for rowing boats, motor boats, yachts, muck boats, dredgers, and they were afraid to come over because they were blasting Dunkirk. It was *chaos*.

"But I didn't get a scratch. I was lucky. I took me turn in the queue and I got on a bloody big old boat like a dredger for muck and mud and nothing in it, nothing at all. You had to go down a rope to get into it. It was like a bowl. We should have got over to Dover but we got to Ramsgate and it was that bad that I hadn't a smoke. And the English people were naturally all waiting there and do you know that about sixty cigarettes were put into me hand and about a tenner. Ah, fair play to them, they were doing that for us. And tea waiting, and sandwiches, a train waiting, all the lot. Everything was laid out. Anyway, fifteen of my company was all I could see come back, out of eighty-seven. Fifteen of us come back. Now where the others were I don't know. Anyway, I got a pension out of it—£14 a week."

PADDY FINLAY—WORLD WAR II FIRE BRIGADE, AGE 81

He joined the Dublin Fire Brigade at age 22. Combating fires in the old tenements could be a terrifying experience. Once, when carrying a woman down a ladder from a blazing tenement room, her clothing ignited, burning his face and hands—but he saved her life. In April of 1942 he volunteered to assist Belfast fire-fighters during the German blitz. He could have lost his life when a towering brick wall against which his ladder was placed collapsed just seconds after he descended. Saving countless lives over his forty-one years in the brigade gave him a "great sense of achievement".

"My father was with the Dublin Metropolitan Police and after that he worked at Kennedy's Bakery and I used to give him a hand out. Now on one occasion, and I was only 12 at this time, my father wasn't able to work this day and the manager says to me, 'Well, you give him a hand sometimes, so go down to the stables and take out the van', the horse van. So the yard man assisted me with getting the van out and we yoked up the horse and I proceeded up Parnell Street, took the load of bread for the day. I just took off. *On my own.* And I met very prominent people on this route, the widow of the late Arthur Griffith, and I also knew Dan Breen. The horse knew every foot of the way and I'd give him the oats and a drink. Later on when I was 15 I conducted buses. To qualify for a licence then it was necessary to be 18 but I looked old for my age.

"Now how I got into the fire brigade is this. I was 22. There were thirty-two positions [open]. I went to a politician friend of mine and he wrote a few lines indicating that I was a successful candidate. And it was normal procedure to get a letter from your parish priest and I had that cause I had been an altar boy. There was no test as such but you produced the appropriate credentials, your education and anything you were involved with. Now there was something like 600 applicants for this position and I'm happy to say that I was one of the thirty-two. So I was taken into the fire brigade and we got five or six weeks' training. You were provided with a uniform but you were *not* provided with any waterproof protective clothing. It was a dark blue cloth uniform with red beading down the front and on the side of the legs and like a Prussian collar. Just cloth. And a pair of rubber boots and a cork material helmet. No gloves! You had *bare* hands. And *no* breathing apparatus—you had to *eat* the smoke!

"I spent 90 per cent of my service in Tara Street. Forty-one years. We were provided with accommodation in dwellings similar to English barracks, a three-floor structure of red brick. The procedure was that you'd rise at half six, get out of bed and you'd wash and shave, have breakfast then and do cleaning. Wash and scrub the floors, clean the brasses, mop and clean the offices. In the station you were obliged to wash and scrub the floors like sailors at sea. And, I might add, sailors were the *most acceptable* person—in their opinion—to become a suitable fireman. It was because they were used to being in a confined area living together and they were good mixers. Training consisted of running out the hose, connecting branch pipes, connecting the hose to the pump and holding the jet and directing it on to an imitation fire. They had a structure of timber erected and it had four floors and imitation windows and they had a hook ladder and you were obliged to climb it and rescue people, place them on the ladder and lower them on a rope. Now that was a very dicey drill. There was a number of men that couldn't cope with it.

"Now there was no mess as such for the men. We'd have to go and get a head of cabbage or piece of bacon or corned beef and cook it *ourselves*. No cook for us, no nothing! You wouldn't *believe* it. And a lot of men then drank a lot. Oh, yes, they used to *smuggle* it in, mostly stout. Now this is one for the book: what some of them used to do was they got their rubber boot and got a rope tied on the boot and they used to *lower* the boot down on the side street. And they had a guy used to come over from the pub and put the bottles *in* the boot and they used to pull it up, cause they couldn't come in the front gate! And no one was the wiser. Oh, they were up to every trick. Now they were *forbidden* to drink. Oh, they would have been sacked.

"As soon as a fire call was received the bells would *ring* throughout the station. And the men would proceed to their appliances and hop on. And you'd have to be out in fifty-nine seconds. Even at night! It was amazing. When you'd go to bed at night you'd have your boots in front of you and your pants down low and you'd just *jump out* and jump in and pull it up. Now on going to the fire your emotions would be 'What's in store for us? Is life at risk?' On arrival the officer would make the command and each man'd do his job. And the officer would ascertain if there were any persons within the premises. But even if we were assured that there was no one in there—and I learned this from experience—*never* take their word. I always ensured that I checked out the premises from A to Z. And we had a hand torch, that's all. Now we also had an ambulance service. We had two ambulances in Tara Street and they were left over from the Spanish Civil War. It was like a field ambulance. You could put six stretchers into them. They were like bread racks. And now when you brought in a B.I.D.—that's brought in dead—to a hospital, you received £1 from the doctor. He gave you a £1 note, to the fireman. Because he used to get £6 for the P.M., post mortem. And they'd often say, 'Don't forget now, get as many as you can and bring them in.' They made a bid!

"Those old tenement houses, they were something! When we'd go into an old building on fire we'd go into the hall and we'd keep our head as close to that jet of water cause that's pure air. See, the air coming in with the water was fresh . . . and *cool*. And in tenement dwellings in Dublin years ago a lot of down-and-outs were in the hallways, for shelter at night. And with a tenement fire you'd get the water in but your prime concern was to *rescue* those within. And they were all timber staircases. And as soon as the fire developed inside and the door was smashed the *rats* were leaving. And *at* a fire there'd be hundreds of people. Fire always seems to attract large numbers of people. And they can be an obstacle because they're in your *way*, like, if you're looking for a hydrant or have to lay down hose. Now when I was a young fireman there was these two eccentric ladies and there was smoke there but no great fire. So we jumped off the appliances and ran up the pathway to the door and the lady was standing on the window ledge and we *appealed* to her to *stay* where she is and we'd take her down. And they must have had about *fifty* cats . . . they were eccentric. And, oh, Jesus, didn't she jump! Oh, jumped about eighteen feet and she broke both legs.

"Now once there was a fire in Cuffe Street. And on arrival at this fire I saw a lady hanging out the window, hanging out through the window. And there was a good fire inside. Now there was an iron bar across the bottom section of the window to prevent children from falling out. Now she was a *large* woman and her big breasts were out over it. Now you couldn't get her out! So I took an axe and hacked the bolt that was securing the bar and removed it. Then I put my feet through the rungs of the ladder and I *dragged* her out of the room and placed her on the ladder. But as *soon* as I got her out her clothing ignited and *burned* like a torch because the flames shot up and caught us against the wall. My forehead was burned, and my hands. But I *still* held on to her. She had become unconscious. And by the time I got her down to the ground her clothes were only in tatters. Then we brought the ladder up to investigate the room. But when the [extension] ladder went up it moved and caught my foot. I could have severed my foot. They took me to the hospital and I was laid out and when I come to *those who died* were laid out on the floor *beside* me. But can you *imagine* waking up and seeing the dead? To this day it upsets me.

"I had the experience of seeing human spontaneous combustion. I had two of them. This is where the body ignites, burns, without even damaging the clothing they're wearing. I had one in Harcourt Street and one in Ringsend. The body burns . . . oh, it burns to a *cinder*. And very often the clothes are left there untouched. But the body's consumed in fire, human spontaneous combustion. The lady in Harcourt Street was seated on a couch and the body was burned and we had to be terrible careful lifting the body. We had to use shovels because it'd burn the hands off you. Oh, yes. And we had to shovel her on to a wet sheet to hold it together. The skull and the bones were still there, but the flesh was gone. And I found there was a considerable number of baby Power's bottles in the room. She was obviously living alone.

"When the war years came they changed the colours [of vehicles] to grey, for security. And they muffled the headlamps. And in addition to the regular personnel they recruited an auxiliary group and they were great lads. Now at this time I was located at Rathmines station and we got a phone call, which all stations got, requesting all personnel to proceed immediately to Tara Street station. And on arrival we assembled in the appliance room and we were addressed by Major Comerford. He informed us that Belfast had been severely bomb damaged and they sought assistance. I remember it was 16 April 1941. See, what occurred in the North was this—and England was at fault. She stripped them of their fire appliances. They were gone to protect Brixton and London. And that's how Belfast was caught napping. Belfast had no proper defence. The Northern authorities got in touch with Dev [de Valera] and he in turn got in touch with Major Comerford. And we were assured that if anything happened to us our families would be taken care of. Oh, it was a volunteer basis. And *umpteen* didn't go! And for some reason I was of the opinion that the Northern firemen would not protect Catholics. For some *extraordinary* reason. You see, it was *bred into* us here. But did I learn a lesson!

"So I volunteered. Oh, I think there was over 140 or 150 of us, from Dublin, Dun Laoghaire, Dundalk. We went up on an open vehicle. We had an idea of what we were going to encounter when we met the refugees leaving. It reminded me of the pictures I saw of refugees in Belgium and France, coming along the road with handcarts with anything and everything, and walking. When we passed Newry we were met by the RUC and they guided us along. And I could see even at that distance the flames in the sky and the flashing. And, funny thing, fear never occurred to me. The last of the [German] planes were still there and you could see them firing at them. So we got off the appliance and went into Chichester Street to ascertain where we would work. In Chichester Street was where the station was. And the chief officer's name was Smith. And I enquired from a junior officer, 'Where's your chief officer?' And he was *in under* the table—and he wouldn't come out! In front of his own men! Oh, the blitz was on. He *wouldn't* come out. So I dealt with another man.

"There was a thousand killed that night. My God! And all afire. And the *amount* of bodies. I saw one underground shelter where the water main burst and the bodies were floating like corks. So we went around and there wasn't much sense worrying about the factories because they were all done. But the *smaller* dwellings—they were red brick—they were all evacuated, people all gone. We worked on any fire where there was a chance of saving anything. But it got to the stage where you could save *nothing*. The whole thing was gone. So you'd be going around to see if there was any people injured and I found several. Oh, yes. The only meal I had was from the Salvation Army, corned beef and cabbage, and I was sitting on the sidewalk. And then I nearly met my Waterloo. I put this ladder up against a red brick structure, went aloft on the ladder and got on to the parapet. And I put my foot against it and it moved out and moved in again. 'By Jesus, what am I in for here?' So I *sneaked* down the ladder, careful not to disturb it, and I *don't think* I'd gone a hundred yards when that *whole* wall came down! Wasn't that luck? And I was standing looking at it coming down. Was I praying?

"I found the RUC men *terrific*. And the *praise* we got that night from them! None of our men were lost that night, not even injured. But we had the courage to face up to it. Umpteen people to this very day shake my hand. To this very day we're [Dublin and Belfast fire-fighters] great pals. I write to them and they write to me. I was in for forty-one years. I retired in 1979. *That* was my life. I'm happy to say that I was a guy in a position that he liked. It gave me a great sense of achievement to save a life. I *loved* it."

3

Historic Helmsmen
of Road and Rail

TONY GALLAGHER—"PIRATE" BUS DRIVER, AGE 94

He was one of the flamboyant "pirate" bus drivers who raced through the streets of Dublin in the 1920s boldly stealing passengers from CIE. The frenzied competition with rival drivers and conductors led to an unmitigated free-for-all and sometimes wild fisticuffs in full view of passengers. He confesses that his band of pirates were "devils driving mad" which endangered passengers since vehicles were poorly maintained. Now in his mid-90s he still visibly gets a thrill recounting those exciting renegade days.

"I was born in 1903 . . . I think. I can remember the 1916 Rebellion well. I remember me father going out with an old horse to bring me grandmother and all the aunts to a place far away from where the trouble was on. The rebellion was in the city. Oh, I saw it a couple of days after the surrender. Ah, I saw houses flattened and burning and all like that. I saw Dublin flattened during the 1916 Rebellion and again in the Civil War.

"I remember the Black and Tans well. We wanted our freedom. They opened the prison gates wide to get these guys out and send them over here to put us down. Oh, the Tans were *buggers*! They were all criminals in for murder and everything. There was a curfew at 10.00 and they had armoured cars that used to go around. They had a Rolls Royce engine and you wouldn't hear it going around. And if you weren't shot dead you were lucky, if you were caught out after the 10.00 curfew. They didn't care *what* they did with you. They'd tie a rope around you and drag you behind a lorry on the street. Yeah, I knew some fellas they did that with. And they'd turn their guns on you and you could be shot. I knew a fella that was shot. Dead. There was a place out here, on a lonely road, out in Drumcondra, and they used to leave a *heap* of the dead there at night, a whole *heap* of them.

"The best time of me life I spent driving a bus. This was in 1927. I was driving for seven years. You see, we were private buses. We were called 'pirates'. See, we'd put 'private' [sign] up and we could go where we liked. We could go to a CIE bus stop and *take them* [passengers]. Oh, we used to do terrible things! We were pirates . . . we were pirating. My company was the Whiteline Bus Company. My boss was named White . . . the Whiteline. We had seven buses and seven drivers. On the morning shift we'd work from half seven to 4.00 in the evening and in the evening shift you'd work from 4.00 to 12.00. You had a day and a half off. I got thirty shillings a week. Our fare was the same as CIE. You'd get on for thruppence. We'd no uniform. Nothing. We went *everywhere*. O'Connell Street was the busiest. Oh, we'd drive *fast*. And I was experienced in driving in frost and snow. I didn't give a *damn* about it. Right on through, in and out, in and out.

"I was fit to take care of my own bus as a mechanic. Badly maintained they were. The CIE buses were better buses and better kept. They were a big bus and we were small compared to them. But CIE buses, they were always maintained, they were well kept. But our own buses, you'd get a load and the brakes would tighten up and burn out and when you'd get back into town you'd have *no* brakes. Dangerous! My bus had an electric horn and we had a spare tyre underneath. I was coming in one night and I picked up a *huge* load and I got a puncture. Oh, had to get them all out of the bus and I jacked up the bus and did the whole lot. And you wouldn't believe what the puncture was—it was the bone out of a chop, stuck in the tyre.

"So we were private buses and CIE wanted it [business] all, but we used to get in between them and steal the time off them. We'd *take* the CIE passengers. See, they'd keep a rigid time and *we wouldn't* . . . we'd *rob* them. We'd be the first to the people and that way we'd get more passengers. It was a free-for-all. See, we were *supposed* to keep a timetable too but we'd steal time off them. Oh, we did whatever we liked. We were *ahead* of CIE everywhere. We were always before CIE. And we were *faster*. We were like devils driving mad. We'd no thought for anything driving . . . oh, *in* and *out* and *anywhere*. *Wild!* There was one fella, 'Stewy' Browne, and Stewy, he'd go anywhere. I saw him one day and he hadn't a *pane* of glass in his bus. He was after getting caught between two trams. One tram going one way and the other tram going the other way. And he got jammed.

"And there was no set spot for stopping. Ah, you'd stop anywhere. And it'd start a row. Well, the lads on CIE kicked up and come to beat us up—and we *wouldn't have it*. We'd retaliate . . . *fighting!* Oh, you had to be tough. You had to use these [fists]. See, CIE had a conductor and a driver and the conductor wore a [metal ticket] punch with a long string down around their neck and he'd *whip* that off and give it to you on the top of the noodle if you didn't jump away beforehand. We didn't have a conductor, only the driver. So it was two men against one. They'd board your bus and say, 'You should be ten minutes gone.' Well, he'd be right—but we weren't *going*. We didn't have to keep to a time. No, we could go as we liked. We were always rough and fighting. They were *tough* times.

"Now I was driving a twenty-seater—but we often had *seventy* on it. The law permitted only twenty. But we'd always carry three times more than we *should* carry. Then the police, they'd board us and stop us. The police would come along and write it down cause overloading the bus *was* a danger to the public. And you'd say to him when he was getting out, 'I'll bring you out a large whiskey', and he'd be waiting then [later] at Rathmines or O'Connell Bridge. And you'd give him a bottle of whiskey—a bottle of whiskey was cheap then— and then he wouldn't register it. He'd scratch it out of his book.

"At O'Connell Bridge in the middle of the city I was the last bus and all the locals around were half-drunk and they were hard tickets . . . *rough* characters. But they *all* knew me well. One time I came to Rathmines and these two fellas got on that had revolvers. They had two revolvers. And I jammed on the brakes and I told the people to get out. They must have been two IRA men. And I hit one fella a *belt* and then I was in between them and got into a scrap. And I got the grandest black eye you'd see out of it. But we loaded up again and got home safe and sound. Another time I had a fella and he used to train the IRA and the police was looking for him and he was sitting at the emergency [exit] and he says to me getting in, 'If anything happens, go slow through the village of Rathfarnham and I'll jump out the back.' So just as I come to the village of Rathfarnham the police stopped me. I let them in and *out he goes* through the back door and *away* with him. He was scot-free.

"All us drivers was well-off men. Our fathers and all was well off and we weren't depending on it for our wages. We were doing it for the 'gas' and meeting people and *excitement*. Yes. It was excitement . . . and meeting birds [girls]. We were all well-dressed young fellas. Sure, I used to bring my friends around free. They knew I'd be driving and bring them in. I'd bring *loads* of them in free and then bring them home. The till was in front of us and passengers just dropped it [coin] in, but if it was anyone you knew you just shoved your hand and rattled it and hit the money in the till to make it sound right. So you could take anyone you liked aboard. They were all my friends. And we used to have plenty of girls after us. I remember this one driver, David Stanley, and one night he had the *full bus* of girls on after him. There wasn't a *paying* one on it. Oh, we'd have a string of girls following us. We could have a whole load of girls and we'd do a run for nothing with the women. One time I was going across this one place with the bus and there was only a girl that I used to go with on the bus. And I got out of the driver's seat and went back and had the bus going by itself and I *sat beside* her. And the bus was going by *itself*! And here she was [screaming]! It was just the two of us. She was coming out on the run to keep me company. I just put it in top gear and got up and went back and sat beside her. Oh, I was halfway down the bus . . . but it was a wide straight road and there was no traffic. Oh, I had a good time.

"And you never thought you were a bus driver, people were so kind to you. They'd bring you chocolates and cigarettes and they treated you decent. And people used to give me tickets for shows in places like the Theatre Royal and for different dances and all. They were all friends. Everyone knew all the drivers and liked us. But now the snobbish Protestant people, they'd take the CIE buses. They felt they were safer—and they were *right*. But others wouldn't care, they just wanted to get there and back as *quick* as they could. And if I was on in the morning I'd have a certain crowd and I'd stop at their house and get them up out of bed and wait for them to get ready. And we'd blow our horns for them to come out. Now there was one woman, an old moss gatherer, she was a down-and-out and she used to sell moss from an old basket she carried on her side. Moss, kind of green stuff they used for putting in flower baskets. And she used to pick flowers and bring them into Dublin and sell them to the gentry. And I'd stop and let her out and sometimes she'd pay me and more times she didn't. I never bothered. She lived in a little shack on the side of the road and she'd ring the bell for stopping and she'd say to me, 'Mr Gallagher, let me down by the roses beside the door.'

"Finally we were taken over by CIE and Whiteline disappeared . . . into oblivion. Ah, sure, there was no future in it for us. We were only foolhardy and 'hard roots' so to speak. I was driving for seven years and then I went to cattle dealing. But I had good sport driving . . . we had a *good* time."

PADDY WHELAN—RAILWAY STEAM ENGINE DRIVER, AGE 85

From age 14 to 65 he was a dedicated railway man. Now, at 85, he has no compunctions about revealing some of the clandestine exploits and sheer shenanigans of his mates fifty years ago which are now part of railway lore among old steam engine men. He is esteemed as a great reservoir of railway history and a gifted storyteller about the grand old days on the rails.

"My father was an engine driver on the railway, fifty-one years, the same as I was. Now the railway at that time was a *family* job. Nobody could get into the railway except if you were a railway man's son or if some official in the railway recommended you. And the railway at that time was run by the Freemasons. I saw a time when they made the engines here in Inchicore and where *every* foreman was a Protestant or a Masonic man. And you wouldn't get anything except if you were one of them. You would get to a certain degree, but no higher. Locomotives for *all* Ireland were made here. It was one of the biggest workshops in Europe at one time.

"Now me grandfather was a farmer in County Meath and when me father came to Dublin a railway man that he knew, a foreman, got my father a job as a cleaner that cleaned the engines. To be an engine driver at that time you started as a cleaner. You worked at cleaning the engines for maybe five or six years. I remember me father and those cleaners and when they'd be getting a pair of shoes soled they'd only get one shoe soled at a time. They wouldn't have the money till next week to get the *other* shoe soled. Fourteen shillings and seven pence a week he had! And it was a hard job cause you had to oil the engines and where the firebox was, that had to be tallowed. When that was hot they rubbed that over with tallow and when that dried it put a lovely kind of clean shine on it, the firebox of the engine. And the outside of the engine had to be cleaned and buffed off. And the number on them engines was in brass and it had to be shined up, and all the injector handles and regulator and all the brass had to be cleaned up. Now they had Brasso at that time but who was going to *buy* the Brasso? So they used a kind of soft stone and they'd pumice that down, break it down with a hammer and make a pumice sand out of it and put some oil in that, a little paraffin oil, or a little spirits, and they'd clean and shine the brass with that. Oh, on any of those footplates you could shave yourself in any of them!

"My mother was a dressmaker and she used to make dresses for some of the lady people. She made dresses for a Lady Malone who lived in Fitzwilliam Square. And my mother made all our clothes. She made everything for us. You lived from day to day. My mother made all our shirts out of flour bags. She *had* to do that. She used to wash the flour bags and make the shirts out of them. The first long suit I wore she made. And me father soled our shoes and cut our hair. But they were great times and there was *colossal* contentment. Now there was a hundred railway houses in Inchicore. They were big three-bedroom houses. And they were maintained by the company, painted and papered and everything, done up top to bottom every four years for you. Oh, it was a great thing. The only people who got them, really, was drivers and foremen but my father got one as a fireman, cause my mother spoke to Mrs Malone who knew one of the head men on the railway and he got my father a railway house. But there was one snag in that. When you got pensioned off or sacked you had to go out of the house. You see, that was the *big snag* at that time.

"My father used to carry guns down to different places [in the country] from Dublin for the IRA. And the way they used to carry them was they'd be brought up to the shed in Inchicore at night by some of the IRA fellas. Or maybe they'd have girls bring them in. But they'd be brought in and they'd be in like plastic bags and a big long lump of string tied out and a cork on top. And it'd be dropped down into the water tank on the engine. Now on several occasions the Black and Tans stopped and searched my father's engine. They took every bit of coal off it, shovelled the coal off it, done *everything* looking for guns. And they couldn't find them. They could never think of looking in the tank. And then when they got to Cork or wherever, they filled up the tank and put their hands in till they got the bit of cork, pulled up the cork and they had their guns, cause the cork would float on the top of the water. My father went out on six shillings a week pension. *Six shillings* a week pension till the day he died. That was a terrible thing to give a man, wasn't it? After doing *fifty-one* years.

"So a cleaner would put the tallow on the front of the engine and the firebox, just rub it in when it'd be hot and the tallow would melt and put a kind of oilish appearance on it and it'd make it shine. And women, if a child got whooping cough or anything, they'd get a bit of the tallow off the engines and get a bit of brown paper and rub the tallow on it and put it over the child's chest and it'd break up the whooping cough [or congestion]. And then there was another way they used to cure whooping cough up there too. In Inchicore they had a big creosote plant for creosoting the raw timber planks that the tracks run over. The creosote, it's a kind of black liquid and it preserves wood. Well, now at that time any children that had whooping cough, there was a doctor and he'd give them a note and the mother would go up with the child to walk through the fumes of the creosote and that would cure the child's whooping cough.

"The drivers at that time were the *elite* of railway men. They were the men that were looked up to. At that time each driver had his own engine and you wouldn't be allowed to *walk across* his engine! Drivers got a big heavy coat, a pilot overcoat, every three years. A big heavy black coat. The driver, he was a notch above the others. And years ago I saw some of them that'd go in with spats and gloves on them. And you'd often see his mate, the fireman, when he'd [driver] be getting on, you'd see him [fireman] with one of the white towels and he'd clean the handrail so me man wouldn't dirty his hands getting up. See, they had that respect for him. Oh, I remember one old driver now—he had a beard down to here [chest]—and he was a Scotchman and he used to say, 'Is the trimmings right? Well, then you'd better go and *piss* because there's no time for pissing on this job!' That was the kind they were, you know? *They* were the man!

"The engine would come in and the driver would bring his engine back into the shed and he'd get off the engine and then he was finished. He signed off then and he went home. Now that engine would be ready for him the next morning. At that time drivers *always* had the same engine and, oh, they were *very particular* and that was *their* property. The drivers would be going out again then at 2.00, 3.00, 4.00 in the morning and at the houses in Inchicore they had night callers, fellas that went around calling them. They'd go to their houses and knock on the door till they got an answer from the husband or wife. They were all fellas that were always elderly men that had failed eyesight tests, got an injury or something else like that. The night callers went only to the railway houses where there was drivers.

"After about seven or eight years of cleaning engines a man would go to fireman. Drivers always had one fireman with them. The fireman's job was nothing only to fire the engine. Shovel the coal. See, the engine before it went out was filled with coal. The steamraiser would have the coal down in the bunker and then the firemen would have to fire from that into the firebox. The fireman would be on the train but the steamraiser would be in the station. The steamraiser, he lit the fire in the engine to get up the steam. And when you'd come into a station like at Portlaois or Ballybrophy there'd be a steamraiser there and he'd run up and *jump* up and fill up the bunker with coal for to save the fireman that trouble. Because, actually, what happened was that coming into Ballybrophy one time a fireman got up to fill his bunker—and maybe he wanted to go over and get a pint while the train was getting water—so what happened was he was coming along filling it [on top] and in the excitement he forgot about the low bridge and his head hit it and he was made *mush* of. After that then they stopped firemen from getting up while the train was in motion. Then when the engine would come into the station the steamraiser would drop the old fire into the pit, what would be left, and the burning stuff would go down on to the ground and be taken away. That used to be taken away by men for to make bricks out of it. Mix it with stuff. There was houses around here built out of it. And it was great for making pathways. But they'd take the big clinkers out of it cause that was coal.

"A fireman then, after about eight years, could start out on the shunting engines, the engines making up carriages and making up trains in a yard. It was all on seniority. Shunting engines were small engines just for making up trains. Then from the shunting engines they'd go out on the goods trains. And then if men were any good on the goods trains they were picked and got on to the mail and passenger trains. So it would be about fourteen years before a man could get driving. And it was all *steam* engines then. Oh, I *worked* on them for years. Steam engines went out about twenty-five years ago. Now preserving your steam, that was the skill, and some drivers were great for that. Me father was very good at that. And there was no window wipers. You had to look out the side for a signal. Sometimes you couldn't see with the dirt and coal and dust, couldn't see through it. If you got a bit of coal up under your eyelid it would just be a terrible job to get it out. You'd have to lift the lid with a bit of a match and snip it out.

"Railway men always went to their own pubs. There was one in Kingsbridge, the Royal Oak. That was a railway man's pub. If you'd be in a pub with them drinking it was *nothing* only *railway talk*. Their whole life! It meant more to them than their family—because if they lost their job they've *no* family. Do you understand? Their job had to come first. Now my father, every Sunday morning, would bring us up by the hand to the shed in Inchicore to see that his own engine was cleaned and properly trimmed. And there'd be two or three men going out to see their engines the same morning. They'd go up on their *own time* to see their own engine, to make sure that everything was right. Oh, the old railway men, they were a special breed, a great breed. And the tram men were, like, more or less inferior to the railway men. Well, 'inferior' isn't the right word, but the railway men thought themselves above. Oh, the railway men were a tough crowd of men, but very good men and very honest and decent men. Oh, and the best family men in the world, the railway men were. *All* railway men at that time got on very well together. You could *kill* a fella at that time and nobody'd tell on you. There was a terrible bond between the railway men.

"Back then railways meant *everything* to people. There was no country buses or anything like that. You had no other way of getting anywhere except by railway. Every little town had a railway station and outside every station was cafés and all pubs and little shops and they all benefited by it. Oh, the railway brought cattle and all kinds of horses. Drovers would bring them down where there was big fairs at Ballinasloe. You'd have sixty-five wagons on a train and about twenty cattle in each wagon. And there were special newspaper trains at 3.00 in the morning and at 5.00 in the morning. They brought papers like the *Herald* and the *Independent* and the *Press* and went out and dropped them off at different stations. So people depended on the trains for *everything*.

"All different people rode the train then but the wealthy people travelled first class. See, there was first class and second and third. About 1930 they knocked off all second class and then it was all first and third. In first-class carriages you had a white thing behind for your head and a rug on the seat and in the wintertime you had a foot warmer. They had a piece of steel about three foot long and about nine inches wide by four inches and they had boiling water in those for the first-class passengers to keep their feet warm for hours. And the first-class passengers had cushions on their seats. And at that time they had tea baskets for a shilling. You got a pot of tea, a cup, a saucer, a nice bit of currant cake, a biscuit and a sandwich for a shilling. Dining cars were used only on the big mainline trains. Like, one dining car we had we used to have to light a fire in it with coal to cook. It was very elegant then. And there were a lot of special trains. Like, the big shops in Dublin would run a special train for shopping. Say the fare now from Cork or Limerick was about ten shillings to Dublin. And if you spent more than £3 or £4 in the shop they'd give you back your fare. Oh, hundreds of people'd come. There'd be twelve carriages with about a hundred in each carriage. Clery's used to do this all the time, and Arnott's. And then we had beer cars for the football matches.

"But I came out of school at 14. I was no good in school. And the minute I left school me father says to me, 'Now what do you want to do?' Says I, 'I want to go on to the railway and be an engine driver.' So he says, 'Righto!' So I started on the railway in Kingsbridge at age 14. I remember when I was starting out and was told, 'You know, my young lad, you're starting out and if you do anything wrong your father will be sacked.' Oh, that was the first thing you were told. And you were afraid of your living life! That was the way it was on the railway. So I started at Kingsbridge Station and I went into the office first as a kind of messenger boy. I was about six or eight months at that and I was let out oiling cattle wagons and railway cars. I was at that for a good while and there was an examination then for a train examiner. Well, I was *mad* for railway knowledge and I had a terrible lot of railway knowledge through my father as a young boy because I used to be up on the footplate with my father. See, if my father was going out on a night trip and it was a Friday night and I'd no school on Saturday, he'd bring me on the trip with him. And he'd bring me up to the shed and there'd be no one around and he'd let me fire the engine. Oh, I could fire an engine as good as *any* man. Oh, I did it for years. That was great excitement. Even when I was a supervisor [later] I'd get up with the fellas and give a hand to fire it with them. So I got appointed to examine the trains to see that the brakes were right and the vacuum was right and everything was right.

"Now the Monto area, the railway men were above that. No railway men were interested in women [prostitutes]. They were interested in *porter*, not women. Didn't bother about women but, by Christ, they drank porter. Very seldom would you get them drunk and if they were drunk somebody else covered up for them. Now if a fella [driver] had a few drinks the fireman took over the engine and he drove it. And the driver was put to sleep. I often saw a driver coming in with a few drinks and he'd be taken off and be put into the carriages and made to sleep and the fireman would take over and I'd maybe go over and fire the engine for him. I did that many times. Oh, some of the firemen would be better drivers than the drivers. Oh, I fired the engines for them and I *drove* the engines hundreds of times. There was nothing to driving. Sure, when I was 14 or 15 I could shunt a train.

"Now I had four brothers and four sisters and I'm the oldest of the family. And I had a *hell* of a big responsibility. Because when my father was away—and he was away nearly two or three nights every week—I was the boss. But my mother controlled the whole lot of us. Oh, she was a great woman, a Tipperary woman, a great woman. So there was five boys and a year between each of us and, my God, we were five whores! You have no idea how bad we were. We were *real* boys! No badness, but we were into *everything*, sports and everything that was going. We'd fight with ourselves and fight with everybody else. Oh, but she ruled us with an iron hand. My God, did she *wallop* us! But we *idolised the ground* she walked on. Now when I was 17 years of age I boxed for Dublin against Liverpool and I got the prize for the best fight of the night. I boxed a coloured fella. And I came back and I was as *proud*, as one of the fellas said, 'as a dog with two dickies'. And that was proud enough. And me photograph was in the paper and all. That was around 1929, and everybody was clapping me on the back and all. Oh, I thought it was the greatest thing in the world. But I came back home after 9.00 at night when we had to be indoors and she walloped the *bottom* off me. If you weren't in, you got walloped. So I went in and I remember—I can *see it now* . . . and she's in heaven looking down at me—and I opened the door and all the lads are sitting around with their mug of hot milk and a lump of bread and butter eating it before they went up to bed. And she says to me, 'This is a nice hour of the night for you to be coming in, *my boyo*! You're supposed to be responsible for those children when your father's away. A nice example you're giving them. Strip off and up to bed!' And she came up to me afterwards with a stick and she *walloped the backside off me*. She left me that I couldn't sit down, I was that sore. And I went into bed and cried me eyes out, covered meself up. I was crying because me feelings were hurt and because the other fellas, me younger brothers, knew I was after getting a hiding. But the next morning I got up and we were the best of pals.

"After I was working for a few years there was a job going on the brake gangs. We had three brake gangs on the railway. At that time every railway coach with an emergency brake on it had to be tested every three months. There was a smash down in the south of Ireland in 1911 or 1912 and there was a fella killed and they put it down to the brakes [failing]. So after that every coach had to be tested every three months. There'd be four men on each brake gang, four or six men. You travelled around the country. Oh, I liked that job. I was going all over Ireland. I did the Skull and Skibbereen, that was a little narrow-gauge railway, the Cork and Bandon railway, the Tralee and Dingle railway. They were all narrow-gauge railways and that was great excitement for a young fella from Dublin. I'd go out every Monday and come back every Friday. Now that meant I had to give up me boxing. And, thanks be to God, that was the luckiest thing that ever happened to me because I would have been punch-drunk and I wouldn't have been talking to you today, because I had eighty-one fights before

I was 21 years of age, and lost one of eighty-one. But I was just coming up in the international class when I would have been getting proper battling. And the fighting at that time was much harder than now. A fight was never stopped at that time till you were put on the ground, till you were knocked out.

"The people in the country, they were *waiting* for the engine to come along and you'd see farmers coming out to look, and they'd stop work in their field. Now the narrow-gauge rails down around Tralee and Dingle, they went through the bogs. And in the summer the fella [driver] going out with his railway, he'd leave maybe four or five wagons there and the fellas would load the wagons with turf. And he'd pick them up going back. And the same with cattle and sheep. They'd just leave the wagons there and the fellas would load them up themselves. Just stop out in the bogs where the cattle would be, and load them up. And sometimes when there'd be a high tide around Castlegregory you might have to wait three or four hours till the tide would go down before the train could go out. The water would come up and cover the tracks altogether.

"Now I remember years ago on the Tralee and Dingle railway. That was a *beautiful* railway, a narrow-gauge railway, from Tralee about thirty miles right up into the mountains into Dingle. It was lovely. Now I'd go out on that sometimes and I'd travel on the footplate with the fellas. Well, the driver, before he'd go out, he'd get maybe five or six different papers and he'd tie them up with a bit of old twine and he'd have them there on the footplate. And when the steam engine would be coming along you'd hear it and you'd see in the mountain maybe a half-mile away a sheep dog *running down the mountain* and he'd come alongside and they'd throw the paper and he'd grab the paper and *back* up the mountain with it. And then you'd go further on and you'd see another fella coming down . . . different farmers and their dogs. Dogs would take it in their mouth and bring it back. That was marvellous to see that. You know, coming from Dublin and seeing that.

"Wherever there'd be a railway there'd be railway plots, where the old railway fellas used to have potato and cabbage plots. It was where there'd be bits of waste land. You used to rent the plot for ten bob a year. See, you had to do that to supplement your income cause your wages was *small*. We had a railway plot too, outside of Inchicore. And now hundreds of boxes of fish, herrings and mackerel, and rabbits would be coming in from the country and the fellas on the train would fling it off one side of the rail out on to the road or in a corner of a plot and they'd [other railway men] get them. And there'd be a fry then for the night or for the next morning. And another thing we used to do, there'd be barrels of Guinness stout to go to the country and they'd just *fling off* one of the barrels, off the wagon, into the corner of the plot. There'd be maybe fifty wagons and they'd throw off one barrel out into the garden plot where it couldn't be seen and they'd have a place dug where they'd put it in. And then certain fellas would know where to go over and get their beer when they'd want it. And when it was empty just fling it back in and get another one. The railway men'd do that.

"Oh, the railway men were heavy drinkers, all good drinkers. But they could handle it. Now I'll give you a few instances. Now I'm not giving you *names* . . .

they're nearly all dead now anyway. Now all the Guinness beer went out to the country at that time by rail and there'd be fifty or sixty wagonloads. Well, we'd be doing the oiling and we'd be watching when they'd bring the beer down. And we used to have a little thing, a bit of iron like a corkscrew, and we'd put it in the barrel and then we'd have a hole and we'd put a bit of a tube in it and we'd give it a suck and the spirits would come out. Now we always had two or three oil cans, gallon cans, and one that we would never put a bit of oil in. And when we'd know it'd be full we'd take out the tube and put the little bit of wood back in the hold and get a bit of oil off the axle and we'd rub it over the outside and you'd never know anything was taken out of it. It fit perfectly back in. So we had our can of beer and then we'd get our oil can and pour some oil around it on the outside and there'd be oil running down it and anybody coming along, any inspectors, would think it was a can of oil for oiling the wagons. And when you'd be going home then you'd pick up your can of beer and go into the hut and the fellas would have the beer then.

"Now we had a railway watchman, a big fella, and he was a *great* character. He'd come in every morning, winter or summer, and he always wore a big mackintosh coat and he had a belt on and he had a quart can here and a quart can here, on each side hanging down, and he had the coat over them. Now he'd come by our hut and he'd lift the two cans off his belt and leave them down outside the hut. He wouldn't stop walking. He'd keep on walking. We'd take in the two cans, fill them with stout for him and he'd walk right around the yard, come back up around, pick up the two cans, put them on his belt and he'd go over to his hut. And he wouldn't come out till he was going home! And *not a word said*! And then when he'd be going home he'd come down by our hut and leave the two cans again, about an hour before he went home. And he'd walk around the yard again and we'd fill the two cans again and he'd put them on his belt and he'd walk home. And he was quite happy. *Everybody* was happy!

"Now I'll give you another good one. There was a publican down in the south of Ireland and he used to get whiskey sent down every month in barrels. And, of course, some of the [railway] old-timers used to go *mad* to get a sup of whiskey. And railway men knew all the tricks of the trade. But he used to buy the whiskey in the barrel by weight and when he'd weigh the whiskey there'd always be something short, because we always used to take about a quart of the whiskey out. It'd be taken out in a billycan. You only had to push in the corkscrew thing, put in the tube and plug it back up, similar to the way we did it with the Guinness. Anyway, this was going on for a long time and a special man was put on to watch the barrels, so they couldn't be tampered with. Now we knew what wagon the barrels would be going into. So the lads went over and bored a hole up through the bottom of the wagon. And the fellas loading the barrels into the wagon loaded the barrel of whiskey *right over the hole*, in the corner, where it couldn't be shifted. Now yer man is watching all the time, the detective. He got into the wagon and stood there till the wagon went out. So what did the lads do? They pretended that the door of the wagon wouldn't shut and they were *banging* on the door, 'repairing' the door. This other fella got underneath the wagon and through the hole he bored into the barrel and put up his tube and sucked and he got his quart of whiskey out of it. And he put the plug back in it, got a bit of stuff and dirtied it up, and it was never known. And the fella [detective] *never knew*. See, they were making the noise with the door and he couldn't hear anything. And when the whiskey barrel got down to the south of Ireland he could swear he was sitting on it. *Sitting on the barrel*—which he was! And they never knew *what* happened. It was a mystery to him . . . a mystery to *everybody*! Cause the weight was down on it. They were going on saying 'evaporation' and saying everything else. Ah, I saw those things myself . . . I was *part* of it.

"Another time we were going down to Kilkenny and there was this old fella, a terrible character altogether. He was the *ugliest* man in Ireland I'd say, but a born wit. Anyway, on this train there was a wagonload of boots. Now there was little lead seals on the wagon. So me man got out a long nail he had and he put it up through the seal and opened it. And he went into the wagon and lifted a box of new tan boots, *beautiful* boots. Came back out, pulled the seal back down, picked up a stone and hit the seal back on perfectly. You'd never know the seal was opened. So he comes in and there's five of us in the van sitting around the fire chatting. And he took off his old boots and went to the end of the van and he *flung* them away. There was holes in them and they were no good. So he then puts on the first one and it was a beautiful fit. And he put on the other and what was it? Two left boots! See, they always sent a consignment of left boots one week and right boots the next week—so they couldn't be pillaged. Of course, all the [other] fellas knew. So now he was in a terrible way. And so he had to get a knife and cut all this side out of the boot. So he had one new boot on him and the other one cut half in two and he was walking like this [hobbling] and here he was saying, 'Oh, it's me bloody old gout!'

"And now we had a general manager from the south of Ireland and he'd be doing good turns for people in the country, like getting their sons jobs and all. And every year around Christmas he'd be getting hampers of stuff coming up from all around the country, hampers and Christmas boxes with brandy, sugar, turkeys. Maybe there might be twenty or thirty of them. So we were there on the nightshift and this night there was about twenty hampers come in for this man. So we took one of the hampers and we were in one of the cloakrooms with it and we had the hamper open. I got a turkey out of it anyway, I know that. And there was a couple of bottles of whiskey and all the fellas started drinking. They were all fairly well jarred. And the next thing, who walks in among the whole lot of us, this detective fella. And the hamper there *open* and everything. Of course, we were all going to be sacked—about five of us. The first fella was a big fella. He was a shunter, and he walked over and when yer man started asking questions he hit him and knocked him unconscious, dragged him out on to the platform and gave him another few wallops. Next thing they ran over with the hamper and the stuff and *into* the firebox and burned it. The evidence was done away with then. And they took whatever they wanted. Got some of the whiskey and poured it all over me man, into his mouth and over his head and all over his coat and left him there. Next thing was they rung the police and says, 'There's a man here going berserk on the platform. We don't know what to do with him.' Two of the policemen come down from Kilmainham, went in and saw me man. After a while they got me man to, and when he come to he nearly went *stark mad altogether* . . . because they thought the man was elephants drunk! And they were trying to *hold him* and he was going to *beat them*. They didn't know what to do. So next thing was they had to get one of the cabbies that was there waiting for the train to come in and they got him in and he *broke up the cab*! So the *next* thing, they had to ring St Brendan's Hospital, the asylum, and they come down and put a strait-jacket on me man and had him tied and had to bring him off. And it was about two or three days before he got out. He knew *exactly* what had happened to him, but nobody else ever knew. There was never a word about it. But wasn't that a *quick thing* . . . quick thinking on the part of the railway men? Oh, nobody ever believed him at all. Oh, he was held up in the asylum but he finally got his job back. They thought he was off his bloody rocker!

"Then the war years were very bad for the railway. We had no fuel. Oh, we'd *no* coal. Then we were trying to mine some of our own coal here, the Arigna coal, hard coal and terrible. It burned the firebars out and everything. Oh, we ran on turf and logs and everything else. We got turf from the bogs. It wasn't in briquette form, just the way it came from the bogs. We were trying to work the engines on old turf and wet turf. And everybody'd give a hand shovelling it cause you had to put a hell of a lot of it in to fire it. But we weren't able to make [normal] steam. A trip from Cork that maybe'd take four hours, during the Emergency that took seven or eight hours running on turf. You got up a certain amount of steam and you ran it and she went down again and you had to wait for her to make up steam again. But, oh God, yes, turf kept the railways going.

"And during the war I used to go up to Belfast every week. I used to go up there to get a fight every Saturday night. I was a professional then [having returned to boxing for the money] and I used to get £30 and £40 pounds for a fight, which was terribly big money at that time. And my brother was working in Belfast and I used to bring him up a bit of sugar and then bring down a bit of tea. So I brought down a couple of pounds of tea one night and I says, 'I was afraid to bring down any more, Mammy, in case they'd stop me at the customs.' And me father looked at me and says, 'You're a *railway man* . . . and you're talking about *customs*? What's wrong with you? Are you light in the head? Get your bag of sugar, get a stone of sugar. Go down to Amiens Street a half an hour before the train goes out. Get in under the car and tie it up under the carriage on one of the bars. Put bags on it to keep it clean. And when you get to Belfast step out of the back of the train, cut your bit of twine and you have your sugar. And when you get your tea in Belfast you do the same.' And I says, 'I never thought of that.' So every time I went up then I used to bring back up about a stone of sugar and bring down about a stone of tea. I used to do that every week. I was supplying me *whole neighbourhood* with tea during the war.

"We were the last of the real crowd of railway men . . . the days of the steam. People in the country, they were *waiting* for the engine to come along. A diesel goes by now and nobody stops to look at it. No kids come out. Everywhere we went, everywhere there was a bridge, there was kids looking down waving to you. Just to be part of that . . . When diesel came in there was no life in it at all. Now even today if you show a kid a steam engine he'll go crazy over it, and adults as well. Oh, I used to have some of the leading doctors here and I used to get them passes to go on the train and stand on the footplates and they used to be *delighted*. Oh, you saw the end of that coming when you saw the first diesel come. And when the diesel came a different breed came in altogether. A lot of the old railway men got out of it. Very few of the older fellas stayed on to drive diesel. They were offered the opportunity but their *hearts weren't in it*. It just wouldn't suit them.

"Sure, a diesel fella goes on today and he's like a clerk or executive going on, the way he goes on dressed and with a briefcase. It's not like a working man at all. The old drivers, they were *working* men and they knew their engine inside and out. And if anything was wrong with their engine they could fix it themselves. It was *his* property. And when the diesels started coming in they were taking fellas out of college and putting them driving the diesels. And the new crowd . . . no respect for authority. We were very strict. If you went in in the morning and you were three minutes late you lost a day's pay. You were allowed three minutes. And if you had two lates you got a week's suspension. But when I went off the railway there was a different crowd coming in. I was in it from age 14 to 65, to 1976. It was in the blood. Oh, I had the *greatest time in the world* on the railway."

WILLIAM CONDON—TRAM DRIVER, AGE 95

Born in the last century, he began driving trams in the early 1920s amid a sea of bicycles and horse vehicles cluttering his tracks. He also had to contend with the aggressive pirate busmen who shamelessly stole his passengers. Navigating the old electric trams in frost and snow could be hazardous, while dense fog could be a real "death trap". But it was a civil age in which tram drivers were immaculately attired and highly respected and passengers were unfailingly courteous.

"I was born in 1898 and me father died when I was only 6 years old. My mother had no other means of living and an uncle took me down in the country. I was going around from one relation to another and then I joined the [British] army in 1917 during the First War. And after I came back from the army in 1919 you couldn't come into Ireland in a British uniform and they wouldn't allow you to bring your gun or rifle in. So I come back to a relative of mine in Roscrea and I started digging potatoes the day after arriving. I was very fit then, you know. I wore me uniform on the land working but never up in Dublin. I used to come up to Dublin to see me mother now and again and I met me wife there. She was my cousin cause her father and my mother were brother and sister. She was only 15 and we were going together for a long time. We dared not ask her father or me mother because being cousins they couldn't have it in those days. So we waited until she was 21 and I was 31 and we eloped. We went to the country and got married, and wrote them from down there to tell them about it.

"After coming out of the army it was hard at that time to get a job. So I come to Dublin then in 1922 and got on the trams for eight years and got married in 1930. The old tram men were nearly all countrymen. The old DUTC [Dublin United Tramway Company], they wouldn't give a city fella a job at all. City fellas were a different type from the countrymen altogether. And the countrymen were nearly all big men, particularly drivers, and you had to be five foot eight for the trams. And they were all respectable men. And you had to have a clear character. If your name was ever up in the law courts you couldn't get a job with the CIE. Oh, no, they wouldn't have anything to do with you. You had to have a priest from the parish you lived in verify that for you and the police from whatever station was in your parish. I was on the No. 14 tram, the Dartry tram. It used to run from the [Nelson's] Pillar to Dartry Road. I was conducting and then I went to driving. The old trams were electric with the trolley and all. Oh, the trams were grand. My wages was £2 17. 0. And there were check inspectors on the trams who'd check to see if you were doing your job and that you were properly dressed. We wouldn't be allowed to work if we didn't wear our tie and your shoes polished. And in the summertime you had a white top for your cap and that had to be washed and ironed. And they had what were called tram cottages for drivers and conductors. Up in Dartry there were about fifteen to twenty cottages in a circle and there was tram cottages over in Blackrock and Terenure. Lovely cottages and they're still there.

"I was about eight years at driving the old electric trams with the trolley. That line from O'Connell Street Bridge up to the Phoenix Park was a *sheet* of trams at that time, on both sides of the quays. You had inspectors—timekeepers—at different points and they always blamed the drivers for being late because he was the man that could make up the speed. But horses would hold the road in front of you and you couldn't pass 'em because you were on the rail. They'd drive on the track in front of you. *Oh, yes!* They were supposed to pull in but some wouldn't bother. We used to ring the bell, but they wouldn't bother. They'd look back and laugh at you! And we were tied to times . . . but they didn't care. And bicycles was the way of travelling then cause there wasn't many cars. And they'd swerve in and out in front of you. Oh, it was desperate. And you'd get the fella that'd ride up beside and put his hand on to get a drag along the tram. See, there was an iron bar on the edge of the tram. And children used to cling to that. Used to call it scutting. *Oh*, it was desperate.

"And frost and snow and fog. The fog was a death-trap. There was no window screen wipers in those days on the tram and you had to keep them clean with your hand. You used to have to stop here and there. Some fellas used a cut potato, cut it and rub it up and down on the window and that'd keep them from getting fogged and the rain would run down it. But the rain would beat down on the tram driver. You had a long topcoat, a big uniform down to your toes nearly. And when it was cold I'd wrap me hand up in a rag. Now tram driving was different than driving a bus. You couldn't stop a tram as quick as you could a bus. And you couldn't swerve because you were on a rail there and whatever you were going to hit, you hit it . . . if you couldn't stop. With a tram, if the rails were wet or greasy you couldn't stop it. From October on you'd get a damp, greasy wheel and it'd skid into something there very easy if a car come up or anybody was crossing you. Of course, you had a sand pedal there to press for the sandbox you had on the tram and when you pressed this pedal for emergency stops the sand would come down in front of the wheels. I often had to use that. And then I was on the Dalkey tram for a while. Oh, a beautiful tram, a luxury tram, that'd carry about ninety people. They were great big long trams, eight wheelers. You'd pass by motor cars and everything. They were easier driving than the smaller trams because you had more power and more power brakes. The thing standing in front of you was called the controller and the levers were on that and you had a power brake on it. And no matter how fast you were going, give that power brake a notch or two back and you'd find her coming back to you and the *roar* you could hear a mile away.

"The public in those days had more respect for the tram men than they had for the bus men. The tram men and the passengers in those days seemed to be nearer to one another, more familiar. See, nowadays you don't see the same bus driver more than twice a day. In those days you saw the same tram men going up and down on that route and he brought you in [to Dublin] in the morning, back home for your dinner [at noon], because they nearly all went back home for their dinner, and then you brought them back in again and back home again in the evening time. And then maybe back in to the pictures again at night. See, they *knew* one another by name. And back then you could get a parcel ticket on the tram for a bicycle or a basket [such as a street trader's wicker basket] and put it up behind the tram driver or stand it up on the stairs at the driver's end because there'd be no passengers going up and down there. Or a woman could put her pram up there. And you could get two bicycles on. People were different in those days. Oh, the politeness. And you were *respectful*. Children then wouldn't give you any impudence or anything like they do now. And if you'd get some old crotchety passenger who'd accuse you of doing something wrong you'd always get passengers to speak up for you. They'd stand up for you.

"At that time there were 'pirate' buses—independents. Tram men hated them. See, anyone could get a bus at that time and there were all types of buses. You could go and get a bus and drive away and pick up passengers anywhere along the road. They were ad lib. They went where they liked and gave the sort of service they liked. And they'd just cut in in front of you and pick up passengers in front of you. They were around the trams getting in front of you there to take your passengers, to pick them up. The pirate buses would only carry twenty, maybe thirty would be the most. See, the pirate buses would try to undercut the trams. They used to be able to *dash* in and out and take passengers if there was a queue. They'd pull up beside the queue and load up and *off* they went. The pirate drivers, a lot of them were gurriers we called them, a rough bunch. Oh, they were a desperate gang. They wore their own clothes, no uniforms. And they'd blow their horns at one another and hurling words and shaking their fists at one another. The attitude in the pirate business was, 'I'll do it my way', and rough language. Oh, people thought they were grand for a while. The young people went for the pirate buses but the average old tram passenger wouldn't understand them at all. A lot of tram passengers wouldn't get on it. They were inclined to be reckless drivers too. There was one bus that went on fire and there was a lot of people burned on it and they had no insurance. And that put a damper on the independent buses. People got afraid of them and eventually they went out altogether.

"Around 1930 the trams were going out and they'd eventually be gone. So a good few of the tram drivers went to bus driving. I had driven motor bikes and motor cars and lorries in the country but there were some of the tram drivers never drove a motor car in their lives. And they had to do the full training on the buses. Some tram drivers just couldn't go to bus driving, but those that did were very good. They had judgment. I was on a Leyland bus at first. It was a single-decker and carried forty. Then I drove a double-decker bus. Now the only thing with a double-decker bus was you had to be careful what route you go out, that the bridges were high enough to take it. There was a couple of low bridges down around Ringsend. Oh, there was two or three fellas that took the whole roof off their bus. That's true. One or two of them was coming back from the garage and they shouldn't have been coming that way at all. They were taking a shortcut back. They were in a hurry to get back to the garage. There was nobody up on top. Well, they were 'gone for the milk'—sacked!

"The bus driver had a bigger wage than the conductor. A driver always had the most responsibility. And he had to go before the doctor every so often and have his eyes tested. Buses were open at the back and people'd be running and get on and might trip and fall. And you'd have to stop the bus then and there'd be a big commotion. And children would scut the bus. As a rule, the same two men, driver and conductor, worked together. You could be there together for your lifetime. It was a good system providing you pulled together. But sometimes you'd get two different temperaments. The conductor would give you one bell to stop, two to go, and three if they wanted you to stop immediately. That was what we called an emergency bell. Sometimes if a passenger saw the conductor hop off to buy a pack of cigarettes or to change a pound, a smart fella'd stand up and ring the bell and you'd go—and leave the conductor behind. Ah, that was an old game they had on buses. Some conductors, they were very popular with the passengers. They'd have the little chat and the joke. At Christmas the conductor would get gifts. Oh, yes, a conductor was always tipped, always got a Christmas box. But never the driver. They had favourite conductors . . . but then there was conductors that wouldn't get a shilling. There was this one man and he always had a mean, cross face and they christened him 'Rhubarb' because he was like a big long stalk and nobody liked him.

"Traffic was easier in the war years because none of us could get petrol in those days. Only doctors and certain people got petrol. Lorry drivers, they got petrol. Cabbies got a certain amount, rationed, of course. And horses came back on the road. Oh, the cars were in the garages lined up. Now on the buses it was mostly diesel oil we used and there was plenty for the buses. As a matter of fact, they had to increase the buses because people who had cars had to go to the buses. And during the war years they relented on people standing up on the buses. They didn't mind us so much having people standing up. You *had* to do that to get all the people on, get them to work and get them home. Then when the war ended and petrol came back things started to get a bit congested and jam up again.

"But people were different in those days. In the morning people'd say, 'Hello, Mr Condon' or 'Hello, Billy.' Everyone getting on the bus in the morning said 'good morning' to you. Oh, the politeness! But nowadays nobody knows nobody. Today it's different. And the bus fellas today are a different type. We had a uniform with brass buttons and you had to have your boots cleaned and all. But nowadays they don't bother. They don't go in for dress today. In our day you had your shoes shined, trousers and coat clean, hands clean. Now they have open-necked shirts and everything. They've got dirty hands and they're half-shaved and don't give a damn."

4

Caretakers of Their Flock

JIMMY DIXON—CONCIERGE, SHELBOURNE HOTEL, AGE 65

As a child playing in St Stephen's Green he would peer across the street at the Shelbourne Hotel and watch with fascination as "lords and ladies" arrived in grand horse-drawn carriages. At age 14 he realised his dream when he became a pageboy at the historic hotel. Over the next fifty years he catered to the needs and eccentricities of the elite guests and met countless aristocrats, glamorous movie stars and powerful politicians. By the time he finally became the concierge he was an institution in his own right.

"My name is James but I'm known as Jimmy. I'm born in Fownes Street, that's really the old part of Dublin. I went to school there at St Michael and John's which is near the Halfpenny Bridge. Now how I got this position was I was an altar boy serving Mass after school every evening and the parish priest, a Father Byrne, asked me one day, 'What would you like to be when you leave school?' And I said, 'No idea!' But my mother used to take me up to St Stephen's Green here every afternoon after school to play and I used to watch looking over at the hotel here and seeing the horse-drawn carriages. Oh, when I was a boy looking across here I'd see lords and ladies and titled people of them days. The carriages and the big cars pulling up. Pomp and ceremony, you know. And I was just looking through the glass one day and I just wanted to be part of it. And I said to my mother one day, 'I'd love to work in the hotel, just to meet people.' And I was telling Father Byrne this, about the thing I'd love to be, and he said, 'Well, I have a lady who I know very well in the Hotel Shelbourne, the head housekeeper'—and her name was Mrs Duffy—and he said, 'I'll ring her up and see if we can get you an interview.' And I said, 'That'll be great.' So I came up one day when I was 14, because I left school when I was 14, and came up to Mrs Duffy and told her I just wanted the possibility for an opportunity. And she said, 'You would have to start as a pageboy, naturally.' So I was put on two weeks' trial.

"I started here in June 1946 as a pageboy. I learned with three others. At that time there was actually five pageboys, compared to today when there's only one. And we had this tradition where the first thing I learned was, of course, to be good mannered and nice to people. We had a head porter who used to inspect us every morning we'd come on duty, that our hands were clean, and our shoes, and our pillboxes. He was a powerful figure to us. We had a uniform with brass buttons and striped trousers and the pillbox was standard. Had to keep the brass buttons polished *every day*. And we used to have the white gloves and the collar and the silver tray when you were delivering messages to people. Each of us had a tray and we were responsible to keep that tray clean. I came up under a very tough man, head porter. He'd even time you when you were going out and say, 'You were fifteen minutes more than you should have been.' And always watching to see that you correctly called out the name or said 'Good morning' to them. In the first couple of weeks I was very nervous, I needn't tell you. Oh, *very nervous*. And I had two brothers and five sisters and I was the youngest. Oh, they were proud. They came up to see me about a week afterwards to see me in my uniform with the brass buttons and all. Really, what frightened me was the hotel was so big to me, so many rooms and so many people. And the story was that in room 526, which is on the fifth floor, this lady saw her husband who had died two months ago in the States. She saw his ghost in the room.

"We used to go on shift duty, like from 8.00 in the morning till 2.00 and 2.00 till about 10.00. Ten o'clock was the latest you worked as a pageboy. You had your breakfast and lunch and then in the evening had a meal at the staff canteen. The hotel provided that for you. My first weekly wage was ten shillings and sixpence in our old money. There were five pageboys here at that time and we used to have little seats we'd sit on and we had silver trays and most jobs was delivering letters and telegrams in them days to different bedrooms and people and collecting messages and paging people, *singing out* their names. We'd sing it out, like 'Mr Browne, please.' It was a tradition. We had a bell to get the attention of the people in the lounge, to get a bit of quiet. And we had to do a lot of errands and a lot of brasses to clean and ashtrays. And in those days we had a valet for every floor who would take care of laundry, pressing, cleaning or polishing shoes for all the guests. And the pages were like assistants to the valets and we'd give them a hand.

"It was all very wealthy people stayed here all throughout the forties and fifties and even up to the sixties—the racing people and also the hunting people. You had to have collar and tie to dine in those days. Those were very strict rules and they certainly enforced it. And it was mostly trunks back then they'd have, people staying for four or five days or a week or two weeks, a lot of heavy baggage. When you were a pageboy you wouldn't take much luggage but you'd help people with the small cases. The valet would help with the heavier stuff. In this hotel then it was mostly British people and they travelled by boat and train. In those days very few people used to fly. So you used to have to have a very good knowledge of rail and boat timetables, not only in Dublin and Ireland but in England for people going off to Holyhead. They'd say, 'Could we get a connection to Liverpool?' We used to have an English timetable and we'd be booking people on boats into deluxe cabins. People asked you for so many things. Your head would be spinning . . . and did you forget to give somebody an early morning call? Numerous questions you were asked. Some evenings you would go home and say, 'Did I forget something?' Cause if you gave them the wrong time for a boat you were in serious trouble. And tipping was not really important in them days. Not really. They used to give you gifts, like cuff-links or tie pins, from guests who stayed a long time and you'd be giving them a hundred per cent doing things for them.

"We got the hunting people. Hunting here in Ireland was very, very big in those days and this was one of the biggest things we had. People would come back in the evening after hunting and we had to clean those boots and jackets. The valet would spend hours to have those ready for the next morning and this is where the pageboy or junior porter would help out. Cause they could be here for a week and be hunting every day within a radius of maybe twenty or thirty miles around Dublin. That was a *big* job for us every evening, to give the valet a hand with the hunting gear. These British were all so very nice to people. But there was a tragedy about two weeks after I started as a pageboy. A pageboy in the hotel was shot down in one of the dressing rooms. He found a gun in some room and he was showing it to another pageboy and it went off accidentally. It was some of the hunting party people had these guns. It was terrible and I was only a couple of weeks here when it happened. He was only about 15 years of age.

"And we had a lot of racing fraternities staying in this hotel, mostly British. This was a great hotel for racing people. Like, Prince Ali Kahn in those days used to stay with us and all those big racing people. This was the *headquarters* for the racing people. Here and another hotel called the Dolphin in Essex Street. That was another great place to meet in the evening for the racing fraternity, like the Finns and the O'Briens. *Great* racing here in those days. And betting! If they weren't going racing themselves they'd ask you for the place to bet and you'd ring up the bookie shop near the hotel and we had an arrangement where you could send up the money later on. You know, just phone in the bet . . . on our word. And the head porter in them days was *really* a racing man. He used to go to most racing meetings himself and he knew *everything* about racing, absolutely everything. Some of the people would come over from England for an Irish race meeting and, well, maybe they'd want to have a bet on a horse in England. Now he [porter] would ring the bet through cause he had contacts through to Liverpool and London and he'd often ring his colleague in the Adelphi Hotel in Liverpool which, I believe, was a great racing hotel when the Grand National was on. Well, he'd ring his opposite there and have a bet on a horse there because a lot of the English trainers used to stay here and he'd get tips for horses, a lot of inside information. A lot of losers . . . but a few winners as well! Oh, I got a few good tips. They'd come on to you and say, 'I have a horse going tomorrow in England and he has a very good chance, have a £1 or £2 bet on it.' We wouldn't have a heavy bet because we were only junior porters, but the head porter, he used to bet heavy, like £20 in them days was big money.

"So you started as a pageboy and after about two years when you became 16 they either gave you a chance to go into being a waiter or a porter. You had a choice. I just liked the idea of the porter with the desk down there and so I became a junior porter and I was three years a junior porter. Then after that I became assistant head porter. And then the head porter who had been here for over thirty years, he retired and I was made head porter in 1968. The house assistants, or housemaids as we called them, they were under the supervision of the head housekeeper. She was over them and she would look after them and make sure the rooms were clean. A daily inspection of the rooms. They were completely separate from us altogether. Now social mixing between the housemaids and the staff porters, it was up to your discretion. Some would socialise together and go out in the evening. There was never any problem against that. And we used to have a staff party every New Year's Eve in our staff canteen down in the basement, a great party. And we used to get a lot of firms like Guinness's to bring in some beer for us and they would sponsor it like, sort of, a Christmas present for the staff. A great party.

"We had a few funny incidents. Like Stan Laurel and Oliver Hardy, they stayed with us in the fifties. And the stout chap of the two, we had cane chairs down in the lounge and he got into the chair one day and we couldn't get him *out* of it when the car was coming for him. So we had to just *pull* him out—and it ripped his trousers. It was highly laughable but we got them repaired. We had a lady who done all the repairs on the spot. They were great characters. And the Queen of Tonga, she stayed here and she was so big, about twenty-three stone, that we had to get a special bed. She stayed here on a state visit in the hotel but she was on her way to England, I think, for the coronation of Queen Elizabeth. And she had an entourage of about fifteen or twenty people.

"But one of the dearest persons we always had here was, of course, the late Princess Grace. And we have a suite here on the second floor named after her because she always would take the same suite. She used to come with the Royal Highness as well but they would never fly together. They would always come within an hour or two of each other. She would come here for different functions nearly twice a year. She was really the most charming person I've ever dealt with in my life. She was really something! She used to come down in the morning time and you would get a lot of people gathered in the hall here just to see her, just to have a look at her. And she would be told by her lady-in-waiting that there were a lot of people in the hall waiting to see her but she would *still* come down and say hello to them. I remember one morning the hall was *absolutely crammed* with people and she was going down to Grafton Street to shop. And she wouldn't use the chauffeur-driven car she had. The weather was fine and she walked down to go into Brown Thomas and Switzer's. Some people would want to go out the back way, away from the crowds, but she'd walk downstairs and meet the people. She was the most beautiful lady I've ever dealt with, one of the really great people.

"A very famous man stayed here and said to me one day, 'Jimmy, your desk here is like a stage and you are the performer and we're the audience.' It was very true. You've got to keep smiling here, you must be pleasant to people. You might come in some mornings and you might have a problem at home, you might have a headache, you might have a hangover, but you must always come in and smile at your desk. Also, what I think makes a good porter is to *remember* people's names, particularly people who have stayed here for a good while and come back, return guests. A good instinct of a porter is to have a good memory to remember names and to have a complete knowledge of what to see in Dublin. And you've got to be very diplomatic. You know, you might have a person who has too much drink on them in the evening time and gets obstreperous and you have to deal with him and be very diplomatic in the public areas. That's part of the job there behind the desk.

"People will say to me today, 'Why did you stay so long in the same hotel?' Because a lot of porters would have changed, but I just got to like the hotel. I did get some offers when I was assistant porter to go across to London to some hotels but my mother lived to a fair good age, so I decided to stay, and I liked Ireland. But the reason I liked the hotel and didn't want to leave here is that it was and, in my opinion still is, one of the traditional hotels in Dublin. The Shelbourne is an institution. We also have here on the first floor the Constitution Room where the constitution was drafted for the Irish Free State in 1922 and everyone asks to see that. I met *every kind* of person here, *every type*. I'll be sad when I retire. You have to retire at 65. It'll be a half-century!"

CHARLES WEBB—HEAD PORTER, TRINITY COLLEGE, AGE 64

He became a "raw recruit" porter at Trinity College at age 20, younger than many of the students he was to supervise. Upon entering the front gate, he found himself in "another world" enclosed by serenity and antiquity. Over forty-five years of strolling the old cobblestones in his familiar black uniform he grew into a father figure to generations of students. With visible nostalgia, he reminisces about the old formalities, customs, friendships and student pranks he so enjoyed.

"I'm Dublin. Born on Camden Street and living there all my life. My father was a salesman and he died when I was only 13. I wasn't very well educated, to be honest with you. I left school when I was 15. I was working at a wholesale chemist but the place closed down. So I was out of work. And I didn't want to leave home because my father had died and my brothers and sisters had emigrated and so I didn't want to leave home because my mother was there. Then I heard that there was a job going over here in the college and I applied. I would have been about a week or two off my twentieth birthday. They were very reluctant to employ me in the college as a porter because of my being so young. I would have been the same age as the students and they were afraid I'd get into hassles with them. They gave me a chance though. And my mother told me that she didn't think I would stick the job on account of the hours, nights and that kind of thing.

"Now I was never inside Trinity till that very day. Never! To me, Trinity College was a big place and kind of a hostile place to go into. I think people had ideas that it had been there since the time of the British and this is a Catholic country and they were banned there. Of course, there were Catholics in the college when I came here. And I'm Church of Ireland. That helped a lot, and I'll tell you why. You had to do services in the Church of Ireland, in the chapel in the college, and for Roman Catholic people it was against their religion to go into it at that time. So when you came in here as a porter you had to be a member of the Church of Ireland. And I had a reference from a clergyman. But they didn't bar Roman Catholics from working in other jobs in the college. And they wanted someone who wasn't going to fly off the handle and was sober.

"But Trinity was a kind of place of *mystery* to me. Like this lady who lived not far from me on Kevin Street said, 'Oh, Trinity College was taboo to us, we wouldn't go in.' The Catholic Church was a *big* influence in those days in the way people were thinking. I think they had this idea that religion made it bad to come in. But when you come in that gate you're in another world. It's a *different* world in here. Very relaxed. You come in the gate here and you're completely away from everything. It was so peaceful. You'd think you were in the heart of the country. On a summer's morning you'd hear the birds singing and you were away from everyone and you could just sit back there and the world passed by. And when I came here they had horses and cabs around College Green there. And bicycles all around the place and no one locked them in those days. Now they're getting robbed here every day!

"Oh, being a porter here was a *tradition*. Some of the old porters when I came were ex-army men and they relied on gratuities from students at that time because wages was very small. It was nice with the old porters there. A man called 'The Sarge' was very regimental and used to shout at students and they'd jump with fright they would. He was an ex-British Army man. 'Old Sarge', his bark was worse than his bite and he used to have this moustache. Duty on the front gate was the senior position in those days. That was the top position. In my day it was called the senior porter or the gate porter or book porter. And he would have authority over the other porters on duty. And then there would be court porters. And there was a gate porter that was assistant to the book porter and his job at night was to open the gate and shout the name of the student into the book porter and he'd mark the student down. And if he was out after a certain time you'd put him down in red. Gates back then closed at 9.00 in the winter—but they'd come in over the walls! Oh, that was a *regular* thing, just climb up over the wall or railings along Pearse Street. Ah, but you'd never catch them because they were all very fit.

"We used to wear hats and tails and the buttons would come down and clip in. And we used to wear these black huntsmen's hats, up until about twenty years ago. My wages started at £4 10. 0. a week. My hours was from 2.00 till 10.00 in the evening and on night duty you could come in at 12.00 at night time till 8.00 in the morning. And you only got one day a week off in those days. My title then was court porter because you had to patrol around the courts. And in those days if you came in in the morning at 8.00 you worked till 2.00 patrolling around and ringing bells for services and so forth. You had to ring the big bell in the campanile there in the square. That was one thing they were very precise about, and ringing bells for examinations. And you generally went around and checked to see that there was no damage done from the previous night or that there was no robbing—which in those days there *wasn't*. Everyone was *very honest*. And to see that the students were behaving. And now I never walked around Botany Bay—see, the tennis courts weren't there when I came—but you never walked around the pathway. You went by the back and looked over because the students might be waiting to throw something out the window on you. They'd throw water on the porters. Botany Bay was always a very 'hot' place, a lot of trouble around. Oh, I remember them throwing a mattress out the window on me!

"Back then you always had people that said [of students], 'Oh, well, you're in Trinity, you must be a bit of a snob . . . you're high up.' But I found people who were struggling on. There was one extreme to another. Some people had plenty of money. But in those days the rooms were very primitive, like they had only started to put in downstairs toilets. I mean, to go to the toilet a fella who lived in Botany Bay would have to go to the far corner there, away across the whole square. So things were bad then. And you had no running water up on the landings and there was only a big communal bath house in Botany Bay. That was built by Lord Iveagh, I think, in 1925. He provided this big huge lovely communal bath house with huge vats for washing themselves in. And you'd see students going to the bath house every morning with their dressing gowns on them and their towels to have a good wash. This was in 1953. It's hard to believe. And I had never seen anything like this before.

"And I didn't know what students had to do. It was all like a mystery to me. Some students were very respectful [to me] and some weren't. Some were very privileged and cheeky, but some extremely nice people. But I found that you had to have a sense of humour working in the college after a while. And we had a lot of coloured students in those days, like from Nigeria, cause they'd no universities and they were getting educated here. Had *all* nationalities . . . from India. And when I came in 1953 a lot of students had come out of the war or from Korea or Kenya or Cyprus and all these disruptions. So you had these ex-servicemen in there. And we had all these English people here who had plenty of money and they were on grants. I really got to know a lot of them, I did. Some of them are very famous today like in business and medical professions or professors. And, like, if they were in trouble they'd come to you and ask you not to report them . . . which you wouldn't.

"In those days students would talk to you and you'd listen to them and ask questions about different things and you learned where other people came from and what their customs were like, people in Nigeria and Lagos and places like that, from South Africa. So to come in here was really an education. I learned a lot of things and got very fond of reading and I got an ear for classical music because the examination hall used to be used for concerts. And when they'd have exams, especially the medical fellas, I'd feel very concerned for them. In those days I knew the students by name. I always felt college students worked very hard and if things went against them regards an exam it really went against their nerves. And some had to get medical help. Some could have a nervous breakdown or go berserk. Students used to come into the lodge at night time and talk to you. We used to have this big coal fire and they'd come in for the heat, at the lodge there at the front entrance at the gate. Now they weren't supposed to, but they'd come in for a chat. It was nice. Some of the coloured fellas was away from home and if they were very lonely or homesick the porters might be the first people they'd turn to for help. And in those days the students from different countries couldn't get back home at Christmas time and we'd have a little party with drinks and this and that. Oh, Christmas was a lovely time here then.

"I had to come back in the evening time at a quarter past five to work on Commons in the dining hall. Now this was a thing I didn't know about. I was told about this very vaguely that 'You have to come and work on Commons in the dining hall.' Well, I didn't know what 'commons' meant. Commons was a dinner in the evening and you'd put the dishes on the table. And I had a white coat with my name on it and I had to wait on tables. Now I never waited on tables before. So I had twelve students to look after and set up the big long tables. I had to get twelve dinner plates, twelve side plates and twelve dessert plates, polish them up and set the table with your box of silver. And everything had to be right. It was part of your duty to do this Commons and you were finished about half past seven. With all the shouting I thought it was very jovial. And my fellow porters was there and a lot of other men there that was called 'skips'. Now skips were people who cleaned the students' rooms, the servants. They cleaned the floor, made their bed and probably washed some delft for them. But they were all men because they were afraid of having women in those days for fear that the students would interfere with them. And the skips, they'd earn extra money by working in the dining hall at night time.

"Now it was compulsory for students in residence to dine on Commons. They *had* to. The reason why was the college authorities were sure they'd have *one meal* a day. See, students would starve themselves in those days. They would get their money and spend it on drink, gambling or whatever they'd like. What happened was that students were starving. They wouldn't have any money for food. So this rule was that students had to dine on Commons because they were sure of one meal and they had to pay for this with their dues. And they were fined if they didn't go on Commons. And they had to dress with a tie on and their gowns on. Have you ever seen students in Oxford and Cambridge? And they had to wear a gown when going before their tutors. This all went out round about the sixties. And the professors used to go up and have their meal at Commons and there's a pulpit in the dining hall and the scholar for the college would get up and say grace in Latin and special prayers for the benefactors of the college.

"They had a *great social life* here. Parties and dinners and that. Parties in their rooms and outside in their flats. And, oh, students always had drinking in the rooms. But we were always on the scene. Oh, there was a rule against porters drinking on duty but when I came here first they'd entice you to have a drink at the parties. And, oh, a few of my colleagues might get over-intoxicated. Or you might have a bottle of Guinness if you went to the student's room. They were always generous like that. But there were rules regards parties in college here. Oh, very restricted with women here. Women weren't allowed in on Commons then and they had their own dining room. And they weren't allowed to be seen in a [male] student's room till 12.00 in the day and they had to be out by 6.00. And we were told that this was our job to report it if we seen a lady in the room, which I never done, cause I thought it was silly. And there was a lot of carrying on then with students. To be honest with you, students brought girls in and they slept at night time with them but we never 'seen' it . . . 'What the eye doesn't see the heart won't grieve.' They were very discreet about it. Oh, women were always discriminated against. Terrible discrimination against women in those days, I thought. Then with the parties they brought the rule in that women could stay in men's rooms until 11.00. And it was always more boisterous when women came on the scene.

"And students used to do terrible pranks. No vandalism as you might have today. Nothing destructive. But they got a lathe for cutting keys for buildings, cut copies of keys for buildings, and they'd get into the alarm systems and get into the library, and all these busts in the library, they changed them all around. And they put this thing up on the high ceiling in the dining hall and everyone was puzzled *how* they got it up there. They got in through the attic and bored a hole down with a drill and brought this very fine string up and put this thing up on the ceiling. It was this object they got up there. And then they put a toilet in the examination hall. And one time they put a car up on the dining hall steps. And they brought sheep in the Commons one evening! Brought sheep up the steps and they were going in between the tables. And the English students on Guy Fawkes night would really go mad in here. They loved that kind of thing. They used to get timber and have bonfires. And they always would bring back fireworks from England cause they were banned here in this country. And the professors would go up and have their meal at the Commons but on Guy Fawkes night as soon as your man would say grace they'd start throwing these Jumping Jacks, these fire crackers, and these very old lads would be jumping around the place.

"We had a postman here that looked after the post. He brought the letters all around the colleges. Now he used to have to go around Commons and he wore this blue gown—it was called the blue bottle—and this was part of his job to be on Commons at night time and he had this big huge ledger and he had to mark them down, that they were there. And he knew *all their names*. And he had these letters that'd be sent from the Junior Dean to students for misbehaving, like for being out late at night or if you had a disorderly party or not getting permission on a Sunday night for having a lady in his room for tea. And students used to do things like go into restaurants and take things and the restaurants would be coming back here looking for them. And then there was rows with students, between students. This one fella got sour milk thrown all over him and he lost his temper and he went out to a shop here and bought an axe and come down and *chopped down* the door to get at your man. But your man was a mountaineer and he'd plenty of ropes and so he tied the rope and jumped out the window, climbed down the wall and got away. So these letters sent to students from the Junior Dean for misbehaving said, 'The Junior Dean presents his compliments to, say, Mr Smith, and reminds him that he had a lady in for tea on Sunday and you didn't get written permission. This is against the rules.' And then he might have to go and see him in his chambers.

"Commencements in college in those days was a very riotous affair. Students bought a lot of flour, pounds of flour, which was sold in the Co-op shop. Flour was sold loose in those days and was weighed up in 1 lb bags. And they'd buy a lot of flour and then when their friends came out after being confirmed they pelted them with flour. And they'd throw bags of flour at *everyone*. And some [graduates] were taken up to Stephen's Green and thrown into the pond there. I remember one occasion they had this student in a handcart they got somewhere—those handcarts were quite common then in Dublin—and they wheeled the student up to Stephen's and gave him a dunking in the Green and then they put him back on the cart and brought him down and went into the Dáil, past the guards, and there was a commotion then. And one year at commencement these students made home-made fireworks down in chemistry, for a prank, but one of them went into a girl's boot and burned her foot. She had a fur-lined boot and it was in the wintertime and it burned her leg.

"Now I remember my first commencement and I was in uniform, the long tails and the huntsman's hat. And they were throwing bags of flour and I was dodging them, like all the porters dodged, but you were supposed to go in and get their names to report to the Junior Dean. So then the Senior Dean is coming along, a very nice old gentleman, and he says, 'Now you two porters stop gossiping and get some *names*.' So off we went to get names. Anyway, I seen this student throwing flour and I went over to stop him and the Vice-Provost came and said, '*Stop* that student with the flour.' So I really had to act then and he was going to throw the flour and so I started wrestling with him. And I knew then who it was. I was wrestling with the heavyweight boxing champion of the college! So we wrestled this way and that way and over comes the Vice-Provost then, running in his gowns, the scarlet gowns, and he says, 'Stop this carrying on at once!' And I thought he was speaking to me and so I stood back out of the way. Well, the next thing your man throws the flour toward me, loose, and *all over* the Vice-Provost! And, *oh*, he was a distinguished man with a big bald head and he was all white and I was all white and all my uniform was covered in white. Oh, he was very angry. And he was brought up and severely reprimanded. Now he could have been rusticated. That's the term they used in those days. Have you ever heard that word? In the university you had all these grand names. But he was just fined and had to apologise. But it was all good fun . . . and we became the best of friends.

"I'm the longest porter now on our staff, I am. I've never been bored in here. I always like coming to work, especially at this time of year. On a nice summer's morning I look around and feel the tranquillity of the place. I feel that your outlook on life is young all the time because you're always dealing with young people. And there was a great social life here and I took part in that, the parties and functions, and I've been invited to weddings of students. But I feel myself that working in the college you can't dwell on the past, you must look to the future, cause the college is changing all the time and you have to move with the changes. Like, they carry radios and they have all these electronic and computerised things and this is all part of the scene now. And when they go on Commons now they don't even wear ties, and gowns is abolished. I liked the old traditions. You see so many things changing all the time. Like, skips I knew back then when I came to work here, they're all dead now. It's just a cycle going around. We are the guardians of this place, the people responsible for it. But it's the kind of place that when you retire you're forgotten then . . . like, you just kind of fade away."

LESLIE TAYLOR—BELL RINGING MASTER, CHRIST CHURCH CATHEDRAL, AGE 47

To his mind, all Dubliners within sound of the great bells are part of his "flock". Their mighty chimes can send "tingles up one's spine". Within the ancient cathedral he graduated from choirboy to neophyte ringer to Bell Ringing Master over a thirty-year year period. He possesses a keen sense of history about the belfry and its venerable traditions. Ringing the noble bells on New Year's Eve, with the excited masses huddled below, still gives him a childlike thrill.

"I went to the Cathedral grammar school about the age of 9 and I was a choirboy. And a curious thing, as a choirboy the bells didn't impinge on our consciousness that much. My brother was already ringing and he enticed me into the belfry when I would have been about 12. It was nothing dramatic. And I would have been a bit nervous as my brother took me up the stairs. I had a *real* affection for this cathedral from my years as a choirboy, an affection for the place and a sense of loyalty. And I wasn't the sort of child who followed pop music. I got this particular choirboy education of high-class Church music.

"I was gently coaxed into ringing by Ted Cathalin who was a very nice man who had a very gentle style with people. He was the one who taught me. This happened when my voice began to break and I was going to leave the choir and there was always a requirement in the belfry to get new blood, to get people to come in and ring the bells. With the bells I sort of dropped into it naturally. There was an excitement and a certain *pride* in the bells, the sound of the bells and the ringing of them. They put a rope in your hand the first day but it would be entirely in a controlled situation where there would be no element of danger at all. The first thing that would be told to you at the beginning was that there *was* an element of danger, that *if* it ever happened that your feet *left* the floor you were to let go. And this *is so*. There *is* danger. *Never* let your feet leave the floor. Leaving the floor would happen when the bell ceases to be controlled by you but is controlled by itself, when the bell doesn't stop at its high point and returns but in fact swings more than once and the rope will go up.

"One particular female ringer we had—and this isn't simply because she was female—for years and years her knees used to knock when she was ringing cause she was nervous. The nervousness would come from fear of losing control. It could be very easy to lose control. Recognising that the bells were heavy I was nervous—most ringers are nervous. It's quite easy to lose control of the rope, and also the fear of making mistakes. So there *is* a certain amount of fear for beginners . . . the *tension* . . . in trying to avoid becoming totally and utterly mentally and physically confused. And what can happen is the stay can break and the rope would be taken from your hands and pulled up and you're taught to step back and stay away until it can be controlled, like a bucking horse. A flying rope can do severe damage. I've seen it pull strip lighting out of the belfry and pull pictures off walls when it's out of control.

"When I started I had weekly practice and came on Sundays to look while the ringing was done. In those days most of the ringers were long-established ringers. They'd been there maybe forty years, men in their sixties, and they'd rung together for a long time. But they had not succeeded in getting fresh blood in an art that was difficult to learn. So when my brother and I and several other youngsters started that was the beginning of change. Strength was not important but what did become obvious to me was that what *was* necessary was a very fine sense of rhythm. And I adapted to it quite well. But it took several years before I built up a confidence because I can remember striking badly and being a menace in the ringing, more than being a help, because I would sometimes lose control of the rope. And at first I couldn't really hear my bell. It can take a while for a person to *actually hear* their bell in relation to the others. So there was a certain amount of bad striking caused by my good self. To be a good ringer you must hear your own bell and it can be quite *difficult* to hear that among ten bells, to hear where yours is actually striking. It's very easy to do the job badly.

"It takes a certain amount of stamina but not sheer physical strength, except for the tenor bell. In bell ringing the crucial physical principle is economy of effort. You absolutely *never* pull harder than you need to. Everything is terribly precise, with economy of effort and no unnecessary movement, no tight gripping of the rope. And your hands build up a certain resistance to blisters if you're ringing for a long time, like a peel which lasts for three hours. I remember my first peel which was in a church with lighter bells in Bray as a young chap about 16 and I came away with very many blisters. And I put my hand in my diary and I drew around it to show how many blisters I got from ringing this peel.

"In theory we're in a ring with the ringing of the bells, one after the other in succession. It's called 'rounds'. Ideally, the ropes are in a *tight* circle which makes it easier to follow the other ropes. Ours is a very wide circle. It's a very, very precise art, an old art. There have been new methods invented but everything is based on what went before. There's a terrific sense of continuity. The *methods* that we ring, like the Grandshire which is an old method invented in the 1670s is a system of getting the changes. Now *all* of these methods are there and they're all very mathematical and they've all got their complexities and in nearly every case we're grappling with the difficulties. And you *know* mentally that for a *fact* 250 or 300 years ago people were grappling with these *same* things. This is the *tradition* . . . we ring the old methods.

"The art itself is hard, extremely difficult in the beginning to ring well. This is because the physical act of causing the bell to be struck at the right time requires long training. Striking at the right time means striking after the bell you are following and before the one following, both of which will vary throughout all the changes to be rung. Your bell must strike at a precise time with minimal allowance, or you will clash and cause a bad sound or gap or clip, breaking up the rhythm of all the ringing. This is a mathematical precision. The changes are determined mathematically and the ringer must hold in his head the pattern of all his positions throughout all the changes to be rung. The most complicated are sequences that have long and tricky gamuts of changes requiring a difficult and lengthy pattern to be retained in the brain as a route map and consulted all the time in the mind's eye. We have a particular difficulty in teaching the most complicated sequences because our full ten bells are not the easiest on which to train since the tenor—the heaviest—is two and a quarter tons in weight and several of the bells are 'odd-struck', that is to say, that simply following other bells by looking at the ropes being pulled and pulling directly afterwards will not result in good sequential striking. The ringer has to learn to listen very carefully and to ring by combining rhythm with vision. Bad ringing can be caused by even one ringer performing below standard. The tolerance of error is a tiny percentage. Mistiming will have a devastating effect on change-ringing, one person's error running like a cancer through the ringing. It can only take one person to cause bad ringing, the ripple of defect running through the whole thing, a domino effect and a catastrophe. Now some of the discrepancies we'd notice the public wouldn't notice. But then it is possible for a mistake to be so *gigantic* that nobody but a deaf person wouldn't notice that a disaster had occurred there.

"*Perfect* ringing is machine-like and precise. We're always *striving* toward perfection, if that's possible. When it's done well there's a feeling of a job well done, an elation and satisfaction. Ringers will aspire to the more difficult ringing for the sense of achievement it gives them. And their pleasure will not be less knowing that it makes no difference at all to the listener that the band had rung a very fine sequence of changes of Double Dublin Surprise Major instead of a very fine but simple sequence of Grandshire Triples. Some of us aspire to ring the Double Dublin and if we were then struck by lightning we would die proud! The bells are heard and few can know the hopes and fears that go into each piece of ringing. It's all extremely rewarding. A feeling of aerobic well-being follows ringing, especially when all has gone well and having done an honest piece of work sends us happily to the pub where, strangely, we very seldom discuss ringing. Postmortems on the session's ringing are considered unwise and seldom go beyond a silence following a poor performance or self-congratulations after a good one. We're very convivial. Bell ringers *always* go to the pub after a ringing. You do your ringing and then you go and relax. We simply talk and laugh and most of our talk is *not* about bell ringing. We'd discuss other inconsequentialities like politics and current affairs. And we'd spend a lot of time laughing.

"Now when I was learning with the bells it didn't have to be spoken that there was a history attached to it because this place *exudes* history! Some people go on ringing till they're 80 or more. It's serious. While we all enjoy doing it, it is very seldom you will see ringers smiling while they do their art. You know the tradition is genuine if the participants are not smiling and laughing. The ancient tradition is a *serious* business. We ringers of Christ Church are the upholders for our own time of a beautiful tradition of ringing great and noble bells, bells whose sound can send ripples up the spine. We follow from two men of 1675 whose names we know from a petition they wrote to the cathedral chapter concerning access 'weekly, monthly and quarterly' to ring, Phil Crofts and Mr Dodson. In effect, we salute their memory every time we ring and we remember, when we are nostalgic, the ringers who were senior when the oldest of us started to learn.

"I think it's true that the Christ Church Society is the only society [of bell ringers] that could call itself in any way professional, and that's by our history. We get a quarterly amount of money which has not changed much in a hundred years. So it was a token. And when I was a child this was given out by the ringing master. I might have got two shillings and sixpence in those days for my efforts. And I remember this being a pleasant thing to get. It arises from the history of our society which comes from the 1670s. We are the successors of the society that rang the bells at both Christ Church and St Patrick's. Now in the late 1800s there was some friction that developed because of the poor condition of the St Patrick's bells. I know that some of the ringers had a dispute with the Dean of St Patrick's and they went on strike and refused to ring the bells. And when the dust settled the Dean of St Patrick's called in an Englishman to set up a band of ringers at St Patrick's and this was the beginning of the St Patrick's Society of amateur ringers, while we recoiled and stayed up here and *we continued* the tradition of the society that served the two cathedrals. So the St Patrick Society started then around 1890 as an amateur society. But our own society has been in existence since 1670.

"These bells, more than any bells in the city, are well known and loved. These are famous bells. When I started our bells were very hard going, they needed repair work. There are twelve bells in the belfry. I can vividly remember the front sixth bell and I found that one really difficult to ring. The bells require constant greasing and attention and this is done by another elected officer of the society, the steeple keeper. His duty is to grease and check the bells and tighten and all that. He would learn that as it was handed down. A bell can be cracked by accident but it won't wear out in the normal course of events. It can crack if it's defective from the beginning or, say, if a clapper fell out and struck at an angle. Each bell is inscribed with the maker and the date. We've no names for our bells but one is called the 'great tenor'. Fred Scott was a ringer when I was a child and he died and in his will he left money for the restoration of the bells and the old tenor was recast because it was found to be porous in some respects. It was recast and his name is now on it.

"Now I've *reason* to think that they're some of the finest bells in these islands for sound. Ringers from Canterbury Cathedral were here recently on a visit and they praised them greatly. These are fine ringer bells. The tenor is B-flat, probably the deepest note bell. The sound is *deep* for these bells. It's not a high tinkle in any way at all. It's sort of a majestic and deep sound to the bells. We feel that our bells are the best. Depending upon the atmospheric conditions they can sound absolutely delightful. There *is* a difference. I'm not so scientific that I've worked out *why* but sometimes the bells sound lovely—we get all the value of the notes—and other times it goes thin and we lose it. It's the atmospheric pressure. We send the sounds out into the sky. We are making a noise, engaged in the first mode of human music-making, percussion. And our music is making the loudest music in the city. It stands apart from other music-making because it produces simple music and non-varying rhythm. It is stately and exact. The large louvred windows send the full value of this sound into the streets around and, depending on the wind direction, out to Rathmines or Clontarf, Glasnevin and Cabra.

"I love the New Year's ringing. I *love* it. It's the *only* time we really get an audience in any formal sort of way. Other times we don't know who's listening. But on New Year's they're all out there and they're all listening for the striking of midnight and the ringing after that. Only the best bell ringers would be chosen for that night. A high standard. This is a high point in the Christ Church year. I can remember that great pleasure the first New Year's ringing where we would ring and *thousands* of people would gather outside. And they *still do*, it's continuous. I would have been probably 13 and there was a childish excitement because we were on the radio and all the people outside would cheer. And I must say that while it's a childish pleasure it's one that hasn't diminished. That's when the public impinges on us most, when they're outside there and when we strike the twelve strokes on the big tenor and with the first stroke a big cheer comes up and that overpowers the sound of the bell nearly. And we ring away. That's unique to us in this country. That's unique in Dublin and they only gather around us. And *that* is a tradition that will *absolutely never* die . . . provided that we can do our job which is to keep the thing going, keep training people.

"On New Year's Eve the crowd would start gathering about half eleven. We would ring out the old year from about half eleven. Well, we *used* to ring out the old year from about half eleven. *Now* we start to ring out the old year from about eleven o'clock with the bells half-muffled. A piece of leather is put on one side of the clapper and we would ring the middle eight bells. So you'd get eight open and clear strikings of the bell and then you'd get an echo as the leather hit from the other side for the second stroke and that implies that the old year is dying. The muffled sound is an absolutely lovely sound. It's beautiful to ring the muffled. It gives a sort of sedate taste to everything where you hear the open strokes and then the echo. Then it takes about ten minutes to get the leathers off to make sure we don't make a dreadful mistake. That would be a disaster!

"So we ring out the old year from about 11.00 with the middle eight bells half-muffled for an echo effect and at midnight we strike the great tenor twelve times and then all the bells join in to salute the new year. When we have done our duty we have our party in the belfry around the round table in the centre of the chamber where the ringers for years have spread out sandwiches and cakes. Old newspaper cuttings show the scene in 1938, for example, with a picture taken from above of the all-male band eating their grub off a rough cloth of paper, possibly newspaper. Nowadays near enough to half our group may be female and we have pretty tablecloths. It was grim before the advent of women or female bell ringers. That came in in the fifties and sixties when women came into the belfry. Before that it was very much a male preserve. And women brought in not only their pleasantness but a tablecloth and things like that. The very old ringers might raise an eye about female ringers. In the old books I came across about the ringing of the bells in 1878. In a Victorian style they mention the visit of certain young ladies to the belfry to witness the ringing and there's a feeling that it was an extraordinary event, a typically Victorian attitude. But sitting around our circular table together having our party we put a premium on sociability. And this party around *this very table* has been going on for at *least* a century, if not more. This *very* table. This table is at least 1878. It was made up here, it would be too wide to have been brought up. It had been painted black— it looked pretty miserable—and we polished it up. This party, it's really mostly tea and sandwiches and cakes and all. We sit and turn the lights off and put candles up and we all sit around and it lasts for four or five hours and there's singing. This is after we've rung in the new year and we've done our duty. That can be really very, very pleasant and we've *always* had this party. We come from a long, long tradition that can't be broken . . . unless disaster strikes or the place was on fire.

"Now an ancient rule bans alcohol in the belfry. A rule arising from an incident long lost to memory. It came from some misdemeanour of the 19th century or the earlier part of this century when, as belfry lore has it, the ringers went on an annual outing by horse and cart stopping off at pubs that jumped in the way and the only living creature sober at the end of the day was the horse! But the only people who realised this rule are the bell ringers and recently the new Dean [John Paterson] in his first year in office brought up a gift of a bottle of whiskey and some wine for a celebration. So *he* broke the rule without knowing it existed. And we thought it wouldn't be polite to draw his attention to this—so we drank it! So now on New Year's we have an absolutely lovely party with some wine and beer.

"It feels very special. It's complete in itself. The bells have been rung for the services of the church by a band of ringers since the 1670s . . . we're their successors . . . we are the bell ringers of Christ Church Cathedral, Dublin. We are not famous, most of us like the fact that we are unseen for most of the time. It is, in a way, part of the solidness of the tradition that you get nothing in the way of reward, neither money nor much recognition. Yet you feel you are doing something very special and the *doing of it* is the reward. I am addicted to being a Christ Church bell ringer—not to being a ringer of *any* bells. I feel my duty obliges me to place this ancient art on a very healthy footing in this very ancient cathedral. My duty truly is my pleasure, it is as natural to me now as getting up and going to work. In fact, I jump out of bed on a Sunday morning for my ringing day. I am the elected ringing master, chosen by my fellow ringers who are members of the society. This is a happy coincidence of loyalty and pleasure. I'm one of the people who have in one way or another serviced the cathedral in some way since its foundation in 1038. It's a subtle contribution to make . . . a solid contribution. I'm *part* of the bells, absolutely part of them. I'd quite like to die in the belfry . . . it'd be a handy place to die . . . when you're ringing."

Harry Casey—Phoenix Park Gatekeeper, Age 67

He lives comfortably in a small stone cottage at the entrance to Phoenix Park on the North Circular Road. No one in Dublin had a better site for viewing the motorcades with the Pope, President Kennedy, Grace Kelly and countless other luminaries who passed through "his" gate over the past four decades. Years ago, he wistfully recalls, strolling couples and extended families flocked into the park and it was a special experience in their lives. Today, he laments, people are too busy watching television or keeping pace in the frenetic modern world to appreciate the park in the leisurely manner of their ancestors.

"I was born on the southside but at an early age moved into the park because my father worked in the park. He was a resident gatekeeper—this particular gate. I'm over forty-two years working in the park and over fifty years living in this house. My father died at an early age, 53, and I applied for this position, kind of on compassionate grounds because three in my family were younger than me. At that time I was about 21 and working in Guinness's when my father died. And on compassionate grounds I got the position and this house goes with the job.

"When I started the hours were much longer. I was working something over seventy hours a week on duty. The reason the hours were very long at that time was that the vast majority of employees in the park and certainly on the gates were all ex-British Army veterans who had a pension from the British Army and were not entirely dependent on their wages. And they were the type that in the army they'd always do what they were told, so they liked to be in uniform and be outside and it didn't upset them that much. Actually, the duty of a gatekeeper is to control traffic in the park. When I started you didn't have a lot of motor traffic. More people would come up on the bus and Sunday used to be very, very busy, the crowds coming up on the bus. You'd always have an inspector down at the bus stop there controlling the buses and controlling the queues. And jarveys used to stand just outside the gate and pick up people. You won't see that now!

"The park is nearly the *lung* of Dublin city because the whole area around the park has been built up now. And there's been many attempts of private interests to try and build in the park. Luckily, the control of the park is invested in the government. Now up to a few years ago we had cattle grazing in the park through the summer season. We put an advertisement in the paper inviting farmers to put their cattle in for six months grazing and pay so much for it and take them out at the end of the season, from 1 May till November. There was up to a thousand and that kept the grass down . . . but that died away. Today now you've got vans and trucks, things like that making a sizeable number of deliveries in the park. You've got the depot, the Dublin Zoo, cricket clubs, the American Ambassador's residence, a whole range of places. And the park is used as a shortcut now with traffic going across from one end of Dublin to another. Ah, to see the traffic come hurtling down the main road at sixty miles an hour and three abreast . . . absolutely unbelievable. That's one of the not nice aspects of the park at the moment.

"People used the park a lot more years ago, walking, especially in the area around here. The couples that would go around the park and the gate would close at 11.00 and I have many memories of closing the gates at 11.00 in the summertime and the *crowds* of people just coming down after strolling in the park. I always recognised on Monday to Thursday was always nights when you'd have couples going up to the park. Then Friday, that was pay night, and then people headed into town. It was the quietest night. But the army band used to play there every Sunday, particularly from May on and you'd have something and that would bring crowds.

"Couples strolled. It was just a part of Dublin city. First of all, the number of people around here has changed a lot. I remember on the North Circular Road when they were all owner-occupied. Now they're all let out in flats, so you have a transient population going backwards and forwards. But around Oxmantown Road there's a lot of people who have been there for years and years. All those people were regulars availing themselves of the park. You'd have your head nodded off saying good morning. They were all regulars. They all had their own time for coming up and had their own seats to sit on and their papers. Very regular. I could set my watch by some of the men. A lot of those old fellas had an interest in horse-racing and we'd have a chat about the Derbies and all. There are not many of those left now.

"And you'd see grandparents taking grandchildren up. It was a closely knit community around here. The People's Gardens used to be *packed* in the evenings. Now you go around the park and up to the People's Gardens and once teatime comes you see nobody out. Used to be *crowds* of people strolling . . . now you won't see that any more. A lot of things you could put it down to. I suppose television was one of the things. Television did do away with people walking. But people still living around here now often tell me that if there are a few bad days and they can't get out the first thing when the weather is cleared up they get out and get up to the park. Cause a lot of those houses are very small and you don't have a lot of room to move in them.

"Now when the Pope came here in 1979 there were *rivers* of people flowing in. And Princess Grace came with Prince Rainier and there was crowds for that. But President Kennedy was greeted as a great hero here and there was a holiday atmosphere, like something almighty happening. It was in the conversation in all the pubs and thousands gathered everywhere he was likely to go. He came up the North Circular Road. I saw him standing up waving to everybody. I mean, Kennedy was the clean hero of the world at that time and never denied he had Irish roots and boasted about them and came here and that affected people. I was glad to see him and must admit that I was carried away with the euphoria. Kennedy's motorcade went reasonably slow so people had a good chance of seeing him. But when President Reagan came it was 'there he *is*—and there he *was!*' He flew through and people weren't as interested."

HERBIE DONNELLY—CINEMA USHER, AGE 71

As a young lad he dreamed of being a guard, but he had to accept the "next best thing" which was wearing a cinema usher's uniform. He began in 1939 as a pageboy and soon became a senior usher at many of Dublin's premier picture houses as well as the Theatre Royal. Back then the Savoy held 2,700 patrons who dressed up for the occasion. Before each film the organist would play for about fifteen minutes as people sang merrily to the words projected on the screen. Over his fifty years of duty he met such stars as Bob Hope, Judy Garland, Gene Autry and James Cagney. He is now a familiar and much loved figure to generations of Dublin cinema-goers.

"My grandmother and my mother were involved in the theatres. My grandmother worked in the Theatre Royal. I started in August of 1939 as a pageboy in the Grand Central Cinema at the lower end of O'Connell Street. Cinemas were graded at that time and it was an A-2 cinema. The likes of the Savoy and the Adelphi, the Metropole, the Theatre Royal, they were class A-1. They were the first-run theatres, meaning they had the first choice of the film. And then in the city centre you had the Ambassador—it was the Rotunda—and the Carleton, the Pillar Picture House, the Capitol, the Astor, the Corinthian. The grading did mean a difference in staff wages. At an A-1 cinema you were upper-crust.

"As a pageboy when I started first I got eight and sixpence and I had every second Sunday off. I always felt sorry for pageboys because he was always a sort of 'do-for' or 'go-for'. That's why I did only a very short time as a pageboy. Pageboys were sent out for *everything*. Sent out for a pair of nylon stockings for the cashier. And ushers treated pageboys as lowly. They did *indeed*. I remember as a pageboy I used to be sent out by the manager when I was in the Grand Central to see which cinemas had queues on a Saturday night. Going back to

1939 some cinemas weren't doing well at all. But some marvellous films. You had many of the Betty Grable films of the day, *Gone With The Wind*, *The Man in Gray*, *Mrs Miniver* and some of the Walt Disney stuff. But in those days it was a lot busier right through the day because people then would come along at *any* time and go into a film. Now they want to go in at the *beginning* of the film, not the end.

"Now the regulations with the companies and the unions at that time was that you were a pageboy from 14 to 18. Then you were a junior usher from 18 to 23 and then you were a senior usher. The chances for a pageboy getting to an usher was very remote, the movement wasn't great. But the fact that I was tall I had an advantage and I only spent eighteen months as a pageboy. See, to be an usher in a city centre house you had to be five foot ten in height, because it looked better that a five foot six man. It was *impressive*. And it was the style of uniform that you wore at that time. It was impressive. You wore a uniform cap and a frock coat and brass buttons down the centre and patent leather belt and yellow gloves. Oh, you were turned out! So if you were a tall man you were out *front*, you were the impressive looking person. In any case, I decided to have a go for the junior usher's job. This was at the Phoenix Theatre on Ellis's Quay. I went up and was there for two years. And I knew I was sort of breaking regulations a bit because of age. And in 1943 there was an usher's job going here [Savoy]. There was a vacancy and I came down and interviewed for it and I got it. And I was only 19 years of age when I came here as a senior usher and I got £3 10. 0. a week. That was good money, excellent money. There was a bit of a hullabaloo about it with the union—but I stood my ground and I fought it.

"Back then the Savoy held 2,700. From 1929, when the house opened, until 1962 you had the organ. And the organ made its appearance about twice or three times a day. The organ would come up and he'd be playing there for about ten or fifteen minutes before each film and there'd be slides on the screen showing the words of the song and people'd be singing. And many times they'd be whistling them. Albert Chambers, he was the first organist that came to the Theatre Royal in 1935 and then he was transferred here for a number of years. Oh, I enjoyed it because in any part of the house you'd hear it and it was most enjoyable to hear people singing along . . . and we were having a bit of 'la la' ourselves. You could go down to the front and look up and you'd have your grand circle, centre circle, back circle, stalls in front and back and you'd see 2,700 people there. The interior here was originally designed as a 'Street in Venice'. Lighting was *beautiful*. The ceiling was of blue and it was a starlit ceiling and it was like you were looking out at the elements. Very impressive. Beautiful it was. It was more of a special occasion years ago to go to the pictures. They would treat it as a special thing, much as people now would going to the theatre at night. They dressed up, for coming to the likes of the Savoy, the Metropole, the Adelphi. And I'd say they'd talk about it for a few weeks after. But during the war years everything was rationed and you'd no sweets, no cigarettes, no nothing. That all came back in the fifties when rationing ended.

"An usher in those days, you were more like the guardsmen outside Buckingham Palace. You were very impressive, *very impressive*. You were checking on the doors, you could be on patrol, could be standing in the hall there. I was more inclined to be doing something than standing around. Now patrolling the queue you'd get that type of person [sneaking ahead] and you might stand off and say 'End of the queue down here!' Now I'm not playing to the gods but people around would say, 'Your man is right.' They'd appreciate it. When there's queues outside I'm the person in charge and I will see that *everyone* is treated fairly. Now courting couples years ago would go for the back row. There was nothing wrong with it if they weren't doing anything objectionable. Rarely did we have any trouble. Teenagers misbehaving, you'll always get that. Like on Hallowe'en you might have some teenagers come in with stink bombs and you'd get a terrible smell off that. Very unpleasant. It can become an annoyance to other people who have paid the same amount of money, maybe a little bit more. And they have the right to sit down and see the film uninterrupted. It's my job to see that that happens. If anybody's kicking up it's up to me to do something about it. And if it means 'out', you're out. And if it would mean force usually two of us would move in.

"I was here [Savoy] from 1943 to 1947 and then I was transferred to the Theatre Royal. I was there for two years. The Theatre Royal held 3,410. And you had a much bigger staff back then. You'd two cashiers in the centre and two to the side. So you'd four cashiers going. Speed was the essence. And there was different prices with the circle and the stalls and you had the royal circle. When I come up the prices was a shilling, one and four, one and nine, two shillings, and two and six. In yesteryears some people felt out of place. Today they don't. The Theatre Royal was a beautiful building and you got wonderful entertainment. You got the stage show and you got the film. But what I didn't like about it was you had the bars. Now I'm not against a person taking a drink but you'd be there till 12.00 and afterwards *clearing* the bars.

"Now the stage shows here in Dublin, there were some marvellous stars here before and after the war. But during the war years you couldn't get cross-channel artists at all. We had to survive on Irish artists, which done exceedingly well. Jimmy O'Dea, Maureen Potter, Noel Purcell, Eddie Byrne. They were marvellous. Louie Ellemin was the managing director of the theatres here in Ireland and after the war he brought over all these big stars and he used to entertain them to a meal and an evening in the Georgian rooms of the Metropole. And some of the film stars that have come here were marvellous people . . . Gene Autry, Roy Rogers, Bob Hope, Maurice Chevalier. And many others I met, like Gracie Fields, Judy Garland and Danny Kaye. And I was at the Metropole from 1948 to 1969 and we'd be in the hall and these stars, they'd come in and you were in close contact with them and they'd chat and talk to you. Very, very nice people. Maureen O'Hara—my God, what a beauty! Oh, the camera never done justice to her, and the lovely colour of her hair. And I remember James Cagney. Now you would *swear* you were looking at him on the stage, on the screen . . . the little quick walk, the sharp little man, a *thorough gentleman*. Oh, he was a lovely man.

"When I was at the Metropole I was constantly outside and you were well prepared for the weather with raincoat and gloves. The weather was often that bad that I had two pairs of gloves on me. You could be out from 2.00 to 5.00 and then your tea break and then back out again from 6.00 till the last of the queue went in around 9.00. People have said to me that I just have a way with the queues. And people remember you for the nice things you do for them. I always have this soft spot for expectant mothers. I never like to see expectant mothers on queues. Never. And I always liked to discreetly get them in without causing any embarrassment. On one occasion I happened to stand in a shop doorway and the woman in the shop says to me, 'Aren't you the man that's at the Savoy?' And I said, 'Yes, I am.' She says, 'You worked at the Metropole. I never got the chance for thanking you. I remember when I was expecting my son, you got me in.' And she made me a present of forty Number Six cigarettes. And after sixteen years! People remember.

"When we got our own [Irish] television station here it didn't make such an impact on us. But what did make an impact was when we got that multichannel along the east coast that we could really get BBC 1 and 2 and UTV. People were seeing the BBC stuff and there was no blurred screen or snow falling. That *did* have an impact for two or three years. They thought the theatre was finished. But people will always want to go out, a night out, and the bigger cinemas will always be here. Oh, I didn't want to come into this job. I had wanted to be a guard. It just didn't materialise. So I had to go for the next best thing and this was it. But no regrets. It's been a good life."

PADDY FOGARTY—CONCIERGE, GRESHAM HOTEL, AGE 70

He began as a pageboy at age 14, proud of the twenty-eight brass buttons on his jacket and delivering messages with white gloves and a silver tray. But he resented the class distinctions among the hotel staff. During his half-century of lobby duty he met all types of guests, from World War II American soldiers to General Eisenhower, Elizabeth Taylor and the Beatles. He got along great with them all and treasures the memories.

"My father was a tram driver and I left school at 14 and came here. A friend of the family was the head porter then. His name was Frank Johnson, and he got me in as a pageboy. I had two brothers and four sisters and things were very hard in those days. There were about ten pageboys at that time, on different shifts. I was paid eight and six a week. The Gresham was *the* hotel in Europe with the best name then. But it was a small hotel then, we had only about eighty rooms. And when I came here first it was all horse cabs at the door and only a few taxis. Oh, it was more romantic all right and the big drays going out to the Phoenix Park races.

"I was a pageboy for three years. We used to have to come in at half past seven as a pageboy. When we first came in we had a lot of cleaning to do: clean the lounge, clean the ashtrays and light the fire in the residents' lounge. Big open fire and mostly turf during the war. And the residents' lounge was called the writing lounge. In the morning when we were doing our work we had a straight jacket and your own trousers. And in the mornings you'd always wear your waistcoat and apron when you'd be doing your work, setting up functions and bringing down linen. But from half past twelve in the afternoon you wore a uniform and that's when you'd be on duty really in the hall. So in the afternoon we wore the buttons . . . the jacket with twenty-eight brass buttons down the front. Oh, I was proud of that. And we always had a little pillbox on our heads.

"One of the duties when you came in first was to go for the post on Pearse Street. I went on my bicycle with a carrier on the front. Letters mostly in a leather bag which was locked. Then the girls in the office sorted that out. We'd get the post three times a day. For phone calls you'd page the person by calling out. You'd go into the restaurants and bars and that. And we always wore white gloves then. We couldn't give a person a letter or anything by hand. You had to give it to them on a silver tray. Tipping was part of our wages in those days and we got a very good type of Americans in those days and the Americans were the best tippers. And the Americans couldn't understand us working at 14 years of age and not going to school. And they'd go over and give you a tip to page them, just to page them.

"We had a barber shop back then and shoe shining. The night porter had to do that. The guests would leave their shoes out at the door at night time and they were cleaned and put back at the door the following morning and pageboys had to collect the shoes and it was a night-time job and I was more or less nervous up on the floors at night time on me own. I was only a child of 14 years of age and the doors rattling and that, you'd be nervous going down the corridors. And there was supposed to be a ghost down in the residents' lounge, all right—some people from the 1916 Rising. There was supposed to be somebody shot here.

"The Americans we got had the huge, big trunks and they were travelling for weeks at a time in those days. We got an awful lot of Irish Americans. They'd appreciate what you'd do for them. They're not demanding. The only demanding people were the Germans. And in those days we'd get a lot of people from the Cunard Line. And then we got a lot of American soldiers. And I'll tell you, years ago if a girl and a fella checked into the hotel and they were single—two separate rooms! And if the man was caught in the lady's room he'd be thrown out the following morning. If the night porter saw that. I had to carry out that duty several times. Oh, the reputation of the hotel was a very great thing in those days. And the Shelbourne was always one of the top hotels. I'd say that the Shelbourne went in mostly for the English people but we went for the Americans and the home market. The English lords and ladies stayed at the Shelbourne. And then we got an awful lot of people from Belfast during the war and they'd come down every weekend and you'd get to know them.

"People would stay for a longer period of time then and we had a good few permanent residents here. This was their home, more or less semi-retired. We had an art and diamond dealer. Count Taff was his name. He was an Austrian. Then we had a French lady. Ah, different types here. And a man from Hudson Bay in Canada. And when I came here first they used to dress for dinner. The men would come down in their evening suit. Then that died out . . . I suppose after the war, in 1945. And we had all the big balls and dances and that and we had to set up the ballroom for functions. Dances were 700 or 800 people. It was a great source of income for the hotel in the wintertime cause at that time you'd have very little residents staying here.

"So at 17 I graduated then to a porter carrying luggage. There was a luggage porter for each floor. We had trolleys and the lifts. There was a bit of class being a porter here, or even a waiter. Take, for instance, in the restaurant, there was a wine waiter and a waiter looking after the tables and then a head waiter at the door and a second waiter. A lot of pomp attached to it. I think it's gone from all hotels now. As a porter our day was normally from 7.00 in the morning and we normally got a break from 3.00 to 6.00 and then back till 9.00. But in the wintertime if there was a function we could be back until 3.00 or 4.00 in the morning. And then you'd have to be back at 7.00 the following morning. They were very long hours, very hard work. But yet everybody seemed to be happy doing it. To be a good porter you have to have a good personality in the first place—and plenty of patience. And when an American asks you a question you have to have an answer for them. It mightn't be the *right* answer, but give them an answer and they're happy. But you *can't* say you don't know. But once you give them an answer they go away happy.

"At Christmas time we'd be booked out, mostly with English people. And there'd be a staff party. But now the common staff wouldn't be allowed then to go out [socially] with the officials as they called it. The porters, we had to address the girls in the office as 'Miss'. And we had to clean the manager's shoes. I'd be resentful of that, doing that. And maids was classed with hall porters. House porters and maids could mix, they were classed the same. We were domestics. The official staff was the girls in the office, down at the reception office, and the housekeeper and the girls in the account office. Well, you had to address them by 'Miss'. We were looked down on, actually, in those days. It was observable, all right, because they had a separate staffroom and they wouldn't dine with us. Ah, no. But they'd address us by our first name. But we couldn't call them by *their* first name. I resented that in me younger days. I didn't like the class distinction when I was younger in the hotel. But now today on the continent I think the head porter is even classed above the manager.

"Anybody of any importance stayed here in those days, Count John McCormack and Margaret Bourke Sheridan was another famous singer that was here a lot of times. And every famous person and film star stayed here. Princess Grace, she stayed here, and Laurel and Hardy in their later years. And Victor McLaglen. And Eisenhower. And Richard Burton and Elizabeth Taylor stayed here for four or five months. They were lovely people . . . they used to have their moments but they were great, very friendly, both of them. And they were very good to the staff too. And then the Beatles stayed here when they were only starting up. But I remember when I wasn't very long here and Count John McCormack, well, he was a favourite of mine even as a child, and I brought him up in the lift and he was going to a function on the first floor and he gave me a ten shilling note. That made a happy day for me."

5

Putting the Dead to Rest

JOSEPH FANAGAN—UNDERTAKER, AGE 67

Fanagan's is one of Dublin's oldest undertaking firms, dating back to the 1850s. As a child he liked to play in the coffin loft. When he came into the business in the 1940s there were still wakes and horse hearses. Tuberculosis was rampant and the firm did about 1,500 funerals a year. He is proud that Fanagan's conducted some of Ireland's greatest funerals including those of W. B. Yeats, President Childers and Patrick Kavanagh.

"This is the family business going back to the grandfather. I'm third generation. My grandfather started the business in 1853 on Francis Street but we were on this site in Aungier Street since the 1880s. Then my father took over. My mother died when I was 7. Then my dad died when I was 14 years of age, that was in 1943. Dad was only 49, very young. Both of T.B. T.B. was rampant in Dublin at that particular stage. My eldest brother, Billy, was 8 years older than I am and so when Dad died he took over the company. Now at that time we lived on Wainsfort Road on a farm of thirty-five acres and there was just my three brothers and my sister and we lived in the house there. It was three miles from here [Aungier Street]. The reason we lived on a farm was, of course, the horses. In those days it was *all* horse funerals. So the reason we had the farm out there, really, was for the hay we cultivated for the horses. We had forty-two black horses. We got those from Cooper's of Queen Street.

"When Dad was alive and I was only 14, on Sunday mornings—Dad used to work on Sunday mornings—I used to come in and be up in the coffin loft and we'd get into the coffins, you know. But I came into the business at 19 as soon as I left school. And you didn't have to do any exam, no apprenticeship. I was instructed by my brother when I came in. I just watched what was done and you took it up and did all the work. I remember when I was 19—and I didn't like bodies—and I get a ring from Billy that a plane had crashed over in Wales. And we had to fly over in a private Aer Lingus plane and go up in the mountain in Wales. That was a harrowing one. We were up in the search party and they took over the school house and Billy and myself had to do the identification. It was so bad that you were only getting bits of arms and legs and torsos, you know? Billy gave me a hipper, a flask, in my pocket but I didn't have to use it.

"In my father's time all we did was supply the coffin and the habit and the transport. And the family used to have to go and order the grave themselves and put the notice in the paper themselves, go to the church and arrange things. That was in the old days. Then we started making all the arrangements. We did everything. We went from just an undertaker to funeral director. When I started in the forties a funeral cost about £45 for everything. In those times we did about 1,500 funerals a year. See, the city was *full of people* when we started. And in the funeral business people had great loyalty to the firm. There's no doubt about it, tradition dies very slowly as regards the families repeating with their funeral directors.

"And when I came in here there was a depression and people didn't have heat, elderly people had no one looking after them. The poverty in Dublin when I came in here, in the late forties and early fifties, was *unbelievable*. Oh, I went into some of these [tenement] flats down here and, really, the smells and lack of furniture. I mean, literally, you'd go into some of these flats in the City Quay area and they'd just have a kitchen table and a few wooden chairs. Because in those days people would ring you and you'd have to go to their homes to arrange the funeral. And then T.B. was rampant in the country. If anybody lived above 55 it was 'old'. Everyone in my family had T.B. I was the only one who didn't have it. And we were reasonably well-to-do but still it developed in the family. And in the wintertime we'd be doing up to ten or fifteen funerals a *day*. See, the winter months are up 20 per cent, there's an increase of 20 per cent in the death rate. And in the old days I'd say it was 25 per cent higher. And in the old days I'd say 75 or 80 per cent of people died at home. I'd say that was more comforting, and people didn't like hospitals. And the family circle was much closer then than it is today and they felt that the person would get more comfort and nursing at home than they would in the hospital. And the priest would come along to the house and he'd say the rosary and prayers.

"Now in my father's time with the wakes here in Dublin the first thing people did was go down to the grocer and order food and the drink before they'd order the funeral. Then you'd get a ring and you'd go up and the body would be laid out in the bedroom with white sheets and then the relatives were called and told that there'd be a meeting for the rosary for tonight. The body would be washed and cleaned and shaved. A neighbour might do it. Or we could send a man from here, if necessary, and he would wash the body, shave the body, and clean the body before putting on the habit. And the body would be laid out there and they'd come in and, oh, they'd drink all night. See, in the old days they didn't want to rush the body away, to give relatives and emigrants time to get there, cause transportation took much longer. And there'd be a vigil at the bedside until the body was removed, maybe in two days time. Or more. The wake depended on the preservation of the body, naturally. See, in those days there was no embalming in the country, so they couldn't keep them that long, especially in the summer. In the winter maybe longer. And depending on the cause of death. A person who's been in good health and dies of a heart attack, the decomposition comes in much quicker in that case. I don't know why, what the particular reason for it is, but the skin turns quicker. And especially a stout person, they get a heart attack and in twenty-four hours the colour of the skin would go black. So they'd have to take that into consideration.

"So all we did back in the early 1900s was we supplied the coffin, the habit and the transport. The habit was in three colours. The brown habit was the old tradition and it died very hard in the sense that traditionally it was *always* a brown habit. I think that it had something to do with the monks. It was for men and women both, generally with a figure of the Sacred Heart or the Blessed Virgin on the front. I'd say it died out about forty years ago. It changed from brown to white. Brown is very drab! It was a dark brown. Then they became white and blue. The blue and the white was the Society of the Child of Mary. There was blue with frills of white and that was for women and for men basically white with a figure of the Sacred Heart or just the Sacred Heart sash. Nowadays you get people who are buried in their own clothes. About thirty years ago that started to become acceptable. I suppose that more or less came from the States, really. You know, people coming back, being repatriated from the States to Ireland and came back in the casket with the clothes on. I suppose the people saw that and thought it was very nice and that's what they did.

"In the old days we had eight horse-drawn hearses and about twelve mourning coaches. Now a mourning coach was much larger and two horses. So, the first would be the hearse, then the mourning coach and then the carriages. The hearse just carried the coffin, then the mourning coach was for the immediate family and then the carriages were for the rest of the relatives. In those days it wouldn't be unusual for a hearse, a mourning coach and ten carriages on funerals from certain areas like Ringsend and City Quay which was dockland. They were always big funerals around there. Everybody knew one another in the area and funerals and weddings were the big things, the occasions when they spent their money. Now you could have a hearse and *six* horses. But you'd pay more. Basically, it was a poor funeral with a hearse and two horses. Four horses was basically the usual. They could request six but it was only for show. But it was the man in the street who was more liable to have six. You know, people say that the rich people get the best funerals but that is not true. No. The man in the street is more liable to have the six horses. And it wasn't unusual to have a hearse and eight and ten carriages in a funeral. Nowadays the average funeral would be a hearse and one car.

"The hearses were wooden and oblong and glass in the side panels and then the driver used to sit up on top. Four horses pulled the hearse and white plumes were used for a single person and black was for married people and others. And white plumes for children. Hearse drivers, they were marvellous men. Removals from the house to the church took place up till 9.00 at night. That means the men wouldn't get in until 10.00 and then he'd be back in here at 7.00 in the morning getting his horses ready and washing his carriages. Removals and funerals were done seven days a week at that time. And the men worked in the winter out in the snow and everything. And with the horses, if there was snow and ice they'd have to go up to the local farrier and get the frost nails on the shoes. They might be getting up at 4.00 in the morning and getting home at

10.00 at night. But they were never happier. Extraordinary!

"They had to climb up to get into their seat on the hearse and carriages. They wore their ordinary suits and they had these huge coats with chrome buttons, big buttons. And then they would have the capes as well to go over their shoulders, and if it was wet they had a waterproof cape. Oh, it died very hard. Now one of the traditions was that when the hearse man got to the house he went in and coffined the body and then left the lid off and then he went out and the family came in and said the rosary or said their farewells with the body in the coffin. But then as soon as they did the coffining somebody would be allocated to bring the hearse man into a side room and the bottle of whiskey would be put there. That was the tradition. But they needed it for out in the cold and at night and sitting up on this thing about fifteen feet up. Ah, the drivers were *hard* men and they'd drink it straight!

"Oh, and there used to be a tremendous fear of a pauper's funeral. Oh, a tremendous fear that you'd be buried without a decent funeral or a Catholic burial. They hid money under the mattress or under the floorboards and you'd know it was stale money. Stale notes . . . you could smell it, literally. And it would lose its colour. The green would fade into a sort of orangey colour. You had the insurance company that would run the life insurance and that's what most people had. In the old days he [insurance man] would call every week to them. It was a penny policy in the old days when I came in and that would cover you for about thirty quid, enough to cover a funeral then. Then insurance agents naturally advised people that the penny wasn't enough, they had better make it two pence or four pence, so they'd have a security. That's why traditionally funerals are not paid for until *after* the funeral because people couldn't get the money until they got a death certificate for the insurance company.

"It was a tradition that on the evening of the removal of the body from the house to the church the family walked behind the hearse, even in my time. They'd walk up to half a mile. Or sometimes they didn't want a hearse at all and they'd carry the coffin. And it was a tradition in this country that the body stays in the church overnight. It's tradition. The next morning the Mass would be at 10.00—that's the usual time—and mourning coaches and carriages would be brought to the church. And you always ask the family when they go out of the church, 'Would you like to go around by the house?' That still goes on. But now funerals in Ringsend or on City Quay, not only would they go by their house but they'd go by the pubs he drank in! Oh, yes, they'd go by it several times. Because all these dockers, they spent all their time in the pub. They were all to themselves and they all knew each other from their daily work and they drank in the same pubs. The wives never saw the husbands at all except at night because they'd be straight into the pubs after work and they'd be there until closing time. And then they'd go home and get up the next morning and be out on the job at 6.00. So sometimes it was three times around the house and pubs and sometimes it was twice.

"Mourning, they don't show it any more. I mean, when my parents died we were all togged out in dark suits and black ties and sons would wear the black tie for a year. It used to be that everybody wore black. Absolutely. Up to about forty years ago, the women especially. And they'd go for about a year in black, the widow or the daughters. Oh, very much so. Certainly for six months they wore black. And, oh, there would be wailing. Somebody starts it and it creates it among the rest of them. There's no doubt about it, it's contagious. You don't get it much really now. They don't go into mourning now. And there were certain traditions in the different stratas of the well-off people and the working class. When I came in the well-to-do people, the women, wouldn't go to the cemetery because graves used to be filled in in front of the people. And that was a very harrowing thing to watch, a grave being filled. Not only the 'thud'. So the wealthy women used to go to the Mass and when the funeral would take off, one car would bring the ladies back. But that was only in the upper strata.

"But the poor people were all there, the men and the women. They all went and would stand and watch this performance and they waited until the grave was fully filled in. It could take twenty minutes. And in lashing rain. And we used to supply a coffin pad, a sort of cloth in coffin shape, padded wool or wood shavings or straw or hay to reduce the sound of the soil going in on top of the coffin. A lot of people now throw in maybe a single red rose but in the old days they just threw in a handful of clay on top . . . you know, 'Dust to dust and ashes to ashes.' But that died out. But then [later] some extraordinary requests come in to be put in the coffin with them. Golf clubs! A putter. 'He was a fanatic golfer.' You name it. Even a bottle of whiskey has been put in . . . to support him on the way! 'Oh, he was a good drinker'.

"Artificial glass wreaths were used extensively in the old days. They didn't have fresh flowers so much then. Only the well-to-do got fresh flower wreaths. But the man in the street ordered artificial flowers. They were made out of porcelain and a big glass dome went over them. But the well-to-do didn't like these artificial wreaths. I think they're horrific things, I never liked them myself. Oh, they were ghastly things, all different shapes and colours, in shapes of crosses and hearts. And they'd get broken and they looked ghastly. And even the glass got all yellow and it was a nuisance for the upkeep of the cemetery.

"Now funerals around the City Quay area and the docking area, they used to have the Mass at 10.00 and the family would walk to the Mass but the funeral would take place at 1.30 in the afternoon and then on the way back they would pull into a pub around Dean's Grange and have sandwiches and drink and God only knows what time you'd get your carriages and mourning coaches back! We used to have to be ringing the pubs because our equipment was left standing outside and we used to have to send the men in to get the family out of the pub and tell them that they're due back. And that was *regular*, every day. Oh, there's no doubt in the old days the funeral, like the wedding, the family all got together and it's the one time they hadn't met for so long and naturally they get over a few jars and chat about the old times. Very much the same as a wedding really.

"In the funeral business tradition dies very slowly, no doubt about it. We kept the horses until everybody else got rid of them. We were the last and that was 1952. It was a dwindling number of people who requested them. And coffins

1 O'Connell Bridge, the hub of Dublin street life, circa 1900. (The National Library of Ireland)

2 Horse-drawn hackney cabs on Westmoreland Street, circa 1890. (Chandler Collection)

3 Dublin quays were a hive of activity during the days of sailing ships, trams and horse vehicles, circa 1890.

4 *Dockland provided manual labour for thousands of men before the introduction of mechanisation.*

5 *Open-top trams and horse vehicles coexisted for decades on Dublin streets. (Chandler Collection)*

6 *Guinness barges on the River Liffey, circa 1904.*

7 *The Custom House with Guinness barges loaded with casks of stout in the foreground.*

8 *Cigar and tobacco shops flourished in Dublin during the first half of the century. (Chandler Collection)*

9 *Fire brigade man Jack Conroy (right) in full fire-fighting gear, 1939.*

10 Buckingham Street fire station brigade with Jack Conroy second from right, 1938.

*11 Henry "Ginger" Kelly, World War II
soldier and survivor of Dunkirk.*

12 Dublin seaman Paddy Launders in Bombay, India, 1941.

13 *Jimmy Dixon, concierge of the Shelbourne Hotel.*

14 *Charles Webb, head porter at Trinity College.*

15 Bell ringers at St Patrick's Cathedral.

*16 Leslie Taylor, bell ringing master
at Christ Church Cathedral.*

17 Paddy Fogarty, concierge of the Gresham Hotel.

18 *Jack Mitchell, head gravedigger at Glasnevin Cemetery.*

19 *Horse-hearse drivers at Fanagan's Undertakers, circa 1930s.*

20 *Ellen Ebbs (second from left) with some of her pals from the tailoring factory days.*

21 *Harry Brierton in his early days as a Jacob's Biscuit Factory worker.*

22 *Harry Brierton as retired Jacob's Biscuit Factory employee.*

23 Staff of Mitchell's Rosary Factory, 1940s.

24 May Hanaphy who worked at Jacob's Biscuit Factory for most of her 87 years.

were always made on the site here, always. We're the last ones here who make coffins on the premises. And we've always had the tradition that there's always a Fanagan at the funerals. We spend most of our time, really, out attending funerals because people like to be assured that there's somebody there if anything goes wrong. But very few people die at home now. It's mostly in hospitals. Now I just *dread* hospitals. And I hate visiting people in hospitals. But the marvellous thing is that I don't have to because we cannot [ethically] visit people in hospitals. It can be construed in the wrong way. I mean, even friends, I just don't visit them. They realise the position you're in. But there was a friend I knew from my golf club and he was an old friend and I went in to him because he was an elderly man and the *first thing* he said to me was, 'Oh, you've come to measure me!' That was the first remark he made to me. So we just don't go.

"People say, 'Oh, it's a very morbid business you're in.' But basically we look upon it that we're giving a service at a time when people are looking for help more than at any other time in their life. And there's great satisfaction in doing that job well. But now 'undertaker', I think, is a *terrible* word. I never liked it. Like the undertaker in the films was with a long, drawn face and a bowler hat and the dark suit. Oh, people have said to me, friends, 'Joe, you haven't the funereal face for it.'"

TOMMY HOBAN—COFFIN MAKER, AGE 73

He began his five-year apprenticeship in 1939 making coffins of solid timber, heavy nails, pitch, and linings of straw covered with calico. After nearly a half-century he retired as Dublin's last handcraft coffin maker. He is a smallish man with a wide, toothless grin who now lives in Santry and tends his garden.

"We lived in Parnell Street, a lovely area, real Dublin. My grandfather was an agent for an undertaker. In the thirties there was a very bad depression so my grandfather got me the job. I was 16 and I started about three months before the outbreak of the Second World War, in 1939. I'd have to guess that there was about thirty coffin-makers in Dublin at that time. It was kind of a closed shop for fathers, brothers, sons, that type of trade. As I said, my grandfather got me the job with the undertaker's he was an agent for. They had two coffin-makers at that time and they were older. I did my apprenticeship with them. We were working on the premises. But, see, going back to about 1910 and 1920 on Cook Street, that's where there used to be coffin-making shops there. On Cook Street back then it was mostly families making them. And then an undertaker name of Joe Hendricks over on High Street discovered it was *cheaper* to make their *own* coffins on the premises. So there was people leaving Cook Street and starting off with different undertakers.

"Where I worked the shop was at the back of the undertaker's premises. It was closed in. I was the only apprentice. Them two men was on what they called piece-work and they'd come in and out when they'd like. But I was on a straight wage, got ten shillings. They were very good to me regards showing me how to do the work. They showed me the front and back of coffin-making and said, 'Right, work away.' But they'd supervise me. One man was *very* good. My apprenticeship was five years. Each man had his own tools, that was always the way. My father served his time to a cabinet-maker but when he finished out his time he didn't stay in it and he gave me the tools. I had a jack plane and a smoothing plane and a screwdriver and two hammers. Men wore bibs and aprons, kind of a hard canvas cloth, and dungarees. Oh, some people would say, '*Stay away* from me!' They would. See, the elm used to *smell*. It'd get into your clothes like if you were smoking. Like me aunt used to say, 'Get away from me, I can smell coffins on you.' I'd take me aprons home and me mother'd wash them. They'd only last a few months, cause handling timber was very hard on clothes. Rub up against it, wear it down, you know.

"Then I was about forty-two years working at Fanagan's [undertakers]. There was four other men there, all older. There was a father and two sons and another outsider. They had been in Cook Street. They was on piece-work. For about two years at the beginning I was on time-work but then they switched me over to piece-work. But I didn't rush. It varied how fast a man could make a coffin. I could make two coffins in a day. In the forties coffin-makers started to associate more. Ah, we all knew each other. Like, we had union meetings, the Irish Transport and General Workers' Union. We had our own branch, it was No. 15 branch. They considered us a semi-skilled trade. Carpenters and cabinet-makers was skilled. But *we* was skilled. Now you couldn't take a man off the street and say, 'Make a six foot coffin or a five foot coffin.' See, you had to work out your own measurements and they could easy be out of proportion. Each man had his own system. You mostly kept the measurements in your head.

"We got the timber, big boards about two foot in width, and cleaned it up ourselves by hand. Ah, callouses on our hands. And the skin would crack. Your hands got tough. It was native elm and native oak. We'd bring in American oak, and that was *hard*, and chestnut. Chestnut was the nicest to work with. It was all fresh timber and we'd stand it out in the yard, let them air dry. Then in the winter months it could be on the damp side and then we stood them around the fire. We used the timber cuttings for a wood fire. When the war broke out gradually things got scarce. There was no foreign timber at all coming in. You had to kind of improvise. All native stuff but we were fortunate that we still had enough to keep going. You had to mark the timber out by hand and cut them by hand. Cut the bottom and the shoulders by hand and then put them together. Mark it out with a straight edge and T-squares. We'd make them from five foot up to six foot four. We kept stock. Sometimes you'd get a man or woman who'd be sixteen or seventeen stone weight and you'd need the *width* and the *depth*, a very big coffin. The largest one I made was about sixteen inches deep.

"When we were mounting a coffin we used to waterproof it with pitch. We'd boil it and pour it into the coffin and seal off any cracks. Boil it up in a big bucket. A strong smell. But the timber was nice smelling. We'd put it on with a waste piece of timber and we'd run it around the sides, the joints and shoulders. Pour the pitch, smooth it out. And it'd splash on your hand and burn your hand. Got it off with linseed oil. Then we lined coffins with straw or hay padding and covered that with calico cloth, white calico cloth. It came from Japan. The cheapest calico back then was three or four yards for a penny. But the dearest calico was a penny a yard. And you could nearly make shirts out of it. And you could tear it straight. And we used to tack that over the straw, about three inches thick, and cover inside the lid with the calico, but no straw. It was quite nice . . . like a little private room. More personal. When the lid was put on it was sealed with brass screws by the hearse man.

"They'd send me out to measure the remains, to houses. And I measured them. I used a measure that opened out in six inches to two foot. Some men used a three foot measure. A lot were buried from their homes—they'd have a wake—just laid out on the bed with a white sheet and a pillow and a shroud. Some people'd give you a drink when you went to measure. I didn't like going out to measure on the children . . . always sad. But when I was making children's coffins I got to know the ages and the average size. Like from a month to three months is was a two foot coffin. From a little over three months to about five months it would be two foot four, and so on. Experience taught you. Sometimes people'd say, like, for a 6 year old, 'He's big for his age, so send out the next size.' And during the war there was an [Italian] boat, a freighter, torpedoed off the Donegal coast. Then after the war when they got the money people exhumed the bodies of the Italian seamen and sent them back to Italy. And we had to make bigger coffins so the older coffins were put in it, a kind of outside case. But some of the seamen is still buried in Donegal.

"Oh, there was some characters. Joe Duffy, he was a character, and he'd bring porter into the shop. Usually the boss would be gone out to his lunch. There was a pub outside there by the gate and he'd go up there and put it under his coat and bring it back. And he'd go to the public house on the way home and wouldn't pay them [putting it on the slate] and he owed them money and they'd pull him in and say he owed so much. The younger crowd of coffin-makers didn't drink so hard as the older crowd. But it was a routine, monotonous type of work and we'd talk of football—Gaelic football—hurling, soccer, anything. Some would bet but they weren't heavy backers, probably a shilling on a horse. They'd send me down to the bookmakers. And now I often took a bit of a rest in a coffin. Oh, it's more comfortable than a bed. Good for the back. And when I was serving me time there was a French polisher and she was kind of a high-strung woman. See, French polishers was employed to polish the outside of the coffins, some with oak stain and some with dark stain. So when she come in this day this other man says, 'Here's Nellie, get in that coffin, *quick.*' And he put the lid on it. So I got into the coffin and she put her bag on the coffin and I just shoved back the lid and 'Aaaah!' And she *jumped* back. Just went 'Booo!' And she was home for nearly a week with the fright she got.

"Back then you could buy a coffin for a few pounds. The average price for a funeral around that time would be about £20. Ah, today it's thousands. I had a brother died in 1945 and we had the coffin, a hearse and two horses, a mourning coach and two carriages and removal from the church and then a hearse and four horses and it only cost us forty-five quid. But there was paupers' burials and the Dublin Council buried them, buried them in a pit at Glasnevin or Mt Jerome. And you'd get the maternity hospitals or home births and the child maybe died at birth. They'd get an undertaker and they were put into a mass grave, the same pit, small coffins for children. T.B. was very prevalent at that time and we was very busy around November. Started to build up around November and then after Christmas it kind of built up again. Mostly in the winter months people died, and you were busy up to about March.

"Sometimes something unusual would happen . . . then you'd get stories. One time they buried a young girl, a girl about 18, and they were burying her and when they were going to put her into the grave it caved in. And they had to take the coffin back out and shove it back. *Three times* they done it, caved in, while they were putting the remains in. And the hearse man *swore* that that girl was *still alive*. He'd been into the church before and she was still a bit warm . . . before *rigor mortis* set in. She was still warm. He knew that cause he coffined her. He put her in. And handling the remains he could feel the heat. He didn't think much of it at the time, but then when the grave caved in, then he thought of it. He thought that was a *sign*. See, a person might go into a coma and they'd say, oh, he's dead or she's dead. And *bury* them. You'd hear stories like that . . . long ago.

"I was forty-four years at it. I made coffins for me brother and grandmother and grandfather. For me brother, that was hard. Oh, I probably made thousands of coffins. You took pride in your work. There used to be an art to it, but not now. Now *anybody* could do it. Coffin-makers were really craftsmen in their own right, like a cabinet-maker or carpenter or wheelwright. I was one of the last of the original coffin-makers. Coffin-making is *dead—real* coffin-making. Most coffin-makers, the old ones, dies poor. No pensions then. When they finished that was *it*, didn't get a ha'penny. Some died from just being wore out, just wore out from the hard work. Died poor."

JACK MITCHELL—GLASNEVIN GRAVEDIGGER, AGE 70

He is the head gravedigger at Glasnevin Cemetery, having heaved mightily with pick and shovel for nearly forty years. Digging nine-foot-deep graves in the old days was "slaving" work but men had a way to smuggle in porter from the adjacent pub to sustain their strength and spirits. He is surrounded with history and takes special pride in having dug Dev's grave (de Valera).

"My father-in-law worked here for over forty years as a gravedigger. I came here in 1955 when I would have been 27. Before that I was in the Royal Navy for a number of years and when I come out I was in steelwork. And one night my wife said to me, 'My father said there's a vacancy up at the cemetery, would you work at it?' I knew *nothing whatsoever* about gravedigging at the time. I only used to come up here as a young boy with my parents when the grandparents died. That's all I knew of it when I came here in April of 1955. Now the cemetery was opened officially in 1832. A young boy called Michael Carey from the Cornmarket was the first person to be buried here. Now Catholics used to have to pay a toll rate to get through for to bury their dead here. That particular tower, that's 164 foot tall, and Daniel O'Connell is right under it, and his relatives. There's terrific history in this place.

"In them days you were a year in before you'd be made permanent. You were known as a 'leveller'. The leveller, he'd be at a plot and if he seen a mound of clay he'd level it down, keeping the plots tidy. You can visualise men opening graves and there's clay here and clay there and it was up to you to level it down and wheel it out so that the horse and cart could take it away. You were given a barrow, a shovel and a pickaxe and a spade if it was necessary. But the pickaxe— we call it a 'hack' in the cemetery—was your main tool. So you done a year at that. And as you were at your year of levelling you would always be somewhere near somebody that was opening a grave and you'd watch him. If a foreman came he would say, 'That's all right, you can keep an eye out and know what you're doing.' Because he'd know that it wouldn't be too long before you'd be at it.

"When I started here I think it was £3 or £4 a week I got. We had a brown uniform here, moleskin trousers and overcoats and boots. You wore that opening graves and things. They were moleskin trousers for hard wear but now you took off your coat and if it was summertime you'd be down to your shirt. Now our old boss would not allow you to open a grave without your shirt on because in them days the public gave out. And men had their own tools. We never shared . . . Oh, God, that was taboo. When you were made a gravedigger you were given a hack, spade and shovel and they're yours until they wear out, and then you're given another one. Now your shovel becomes very sweet to you. So does your spade, and even your hack, but your shovel in particular. Because you get used to it and it gets used to you. Believe it or not, it gets used to you and so do you to it. And it becomes very, very shiny and you keep it that way because if you get a mucky grave it would slide off it. Whereas if it was roughish it'd keep sticking and would build up and you'd be putting more weight on your arms than you should be. And so you'd just be flicking it and it'd slide off like that. Your shovel became worn all around here and it became very, very sweet to you. And your spade was similar. And you'd *really clean* them. Most of us carried a penknife and an old scraper to scrape off the muck and then we'd clean them with a bit of grass before we'd put them up for the next day's work.

"When I came here first graves were nine feet deep. Everything was dug by hand here up to about 1972 when the first machine came in. But, well, you see, if you just look in there, left or right, can you visualise a big machine trying to get in and out of these plots? So only in odd places could we get a machine in among the headstones. So a new grave would be dug down nine feet and seven foot [long]. The nature of the ground would determine how long you would take. And it depends on the human being himself. If you were hacking it most of the way it would take about four hours and it was hard. But the more you done it the better you got at it and then you sort of worked out your own system. Oh, there's an art to it. Like now I could show you a grave where you see a man opening it and he had it all shaped lovely. And if it stands that way it's lovely. But if it doesn't it's a bit ugly. And you could get into [digging] a grave and murder yourself because you haven't got the experience. Now we had a strike here in 1965 for about five weeks and we agreed that relatives of whoever was buried was allowed to open the grave. And we had people from all walks of life in here. But some people, it used to take four and five of them to open a grave, because they just *didn't know how*. It was no fault of theirs.

"Now when you'd reopen a grave you'd come across the coffins. Some of them were very, very good coffins and they would be totally intact. Sometimes you might open one, two or three years after and the coffin would be intact but you would get some smells, but that grew on you. Now when it was a new grave two men opened it. And if it was a reopening of a grave, anything over seven feet, you had to have two men. It was for the safety of the men in the grave. It was a help to it caving in on you. And that was to do with insurance, if anything happened. See, the second man would be there to help and you'd be able to get down much quicker and put what we call brace boards down in the grave which keeps the banks from falling in. We've got a gravelly ground that'll fall all over the place. You could go down six foot three on your own and it's quite safe at that. You might have a little subsidence but in general terms it works out. Oh, I had a grave cave in on me. It's a danger but it's the reaction of the person in the grave when you're opening it. When a grave does subside you hear noises and moves and you start to see little dribbles and you watch and go back as far as you possibly can so it doesn't bowl you over. You try to get back to what we call the headwall or footwall. But whatever happens your feet seem to end up in a way that you can't pull them out. I don't know why. So then the lads come across and they'll dig you out. We always keep an eye on each other. I was buried up to me chest before. It *is* frightening at the time.

"We'd start at 8.00 in the morning, till 5.00. The only day we're actually off of work, that we do no grave work, is on Sundays and Christmas day. Otherwise, it's a six day week. And we worked *hard. Really* worked hard. If you opened that grave and got finished you could have yourself a rest and a smoke. We had one man here who drank water in a terrible hurry cause he was roasting and he collapsed. I never drank water till I was actually finished and I'd only barely sip a sup, not a great deal because of what had happened to that older man. And we had another man here and he used to suck a little stone. You get very, very sweaty in the summer but you also get sweaty and wet in the winter. So you get confused which is the worst. You're getting wet even on a dry day because the sweat is steaming out of you. And it might be lashing rain. Now on frosty days the ground is very hard. That's where your hack comes in handy. You hack the top off it. The common saying is, you hack the crust off.

"The old gravediggers were characters in their day. Some gravediggers had names, like one was called 'The Lump' and another was called 'The Swanker'. They were all elderly men and they were characters in their own right. And they were long at it. Like when I first came here I could never see meself being that amount of years here and all I could hear was, 'I'm forty-five years here' and 'I'm fifty years here.' And, let's face it, they had all gone through an awful lot in the old days, with the horse hearse and all. Now this is the only cemetery that I know of with a pub on each end of it and the older lads, even in my time when I started, they'd go down there and through the railing they'd get a pint of porter for seven or eight pence. They *weren't supposed to*! But they were characters. They'd just knock on the side wall of the pub—Josie Kavanagh's as it's known— for the barman to come out and they'd get their pint through the railing during working hours. It was well known it was done. And they'd drink it and go back to work. But if they were caught they'd be in terrible trouble. If they were caught they'd be *sacked*. They were characters.

"When I came here first we used to have a trolley, a big long trolley, just like a small horse cart—and *we* were the horse. In my day you'd put the remains into this trolley and you'd then have to pull that trolley off to the grave with the people walking behind. There was no hearses allowed in. The hearses went as far as the chapel but they couldn't get down on the ground because of the trees and bushes. It just wasn't the thing to be done in them days. So the remains would go into our chapel and after the prayers the remains would come out. Four men would walk in there and take out the remains and put the remains into the trolley. You then put your bar up. And one man would take that trolley. There was two handles and it was difficult. And sometimes you'd have round floral wreaths pushed on to the handles which didn't help and sometimes on the top of the coffin as well and you'd be pulling that at a terrible slant. You'd then have to pull that trolley off to the grave with the people walking behind. You mightn't have liked it but the fact is that that was your day's work.

"Now in my day you filled in a grave there with the people standing over you. There was a sadness to it. You put grass over the top of the coffin to stop the noise and you filled it in there and then with the people standing around. Like you can picture four men, after lowering the coffin, a big heap of dirt here and though there'd be grass down on it you'd hear 'thud, thud, thud', a dull sound till it actually became covered. That was the tradition. In my opinion it was a little on the slave side . . . now that I look back. It was all in front of the public, the mourners. And it was *all speed*. And then you were off to the next one. I think it was like slavery, as I look back on it, because of the amount of work that was involved and you were doing it under pressure, because the people would not leave till that was filled in. That was the tradition. I think the way it's done now is more dignified. Today we just place an artificial cover and the people go away and then the men start filling that grave. You try to do your utmost to be dignified at the situation and not upset the chief mourners any more than they're already upset. So you do everything as dignified as humanly possible, because you're dealing with the public at their lowest ebb. They're down . . . sad.

"It's an emotional thing. People do cry now at the graveside but not as much as they did when you used to hear all that banging. And in them days you'd get a lot of that where they wouldn't want the coffin put in the ground. One time four of us were putting the coffin down, lowering it, and this young man keeps saying, 'You're *not* putting my mother into that grave.' And all of a sudden he really went berserk and threw himself as if to dive in after it and he outstretched his hand and he was suspended over it. He could neither get up nor down. And we had to get him up. And one of the lads said to me, 'If he's that foolish, let him in on top of it.' It was only a jest. And they'd throw roses in. A single rose seems to be the 'in' thing at the moment especially if there's a young family. An odd time you'd see a little bag being thrown in but you wouldn't know what's in it. And one person threw their false teeth in! On the top of the coffin. Now you might remember the hippie era with all the long hair and the funny hats and that. Well, they were just burying someone here and this young man steps out of the crowd and he went around with a hat. And, Good Lord, I'll be honest about it, I said, Oh, Good God, we're going to get a right few shillings here for a pint. That's what I said to meself. And he got quite a lot of money. And the next thing he got his hand in there and he just threw it in the grave and said something, I don't know what he said. And he threw some in there and then he told me to hold out me hands like that and he emptied out what was in it. I think I got something like £2. I thought that was very funny. Of course, I shared that with the other three men that was involved.

"We have a 'poor ground' and an 'angel's plot'. A poor ground is for people at a very nominal fee and the undertaker just pays a small fee to the cemetery. And the 'little angels' are mostly stillborns or a day old or whatever. It's sad . . . I never really liked it, cause you always see your own children. It just hits you. But you get over it. It's something you have to live with. Now, thank God, in today's world the younger women and the young men are *appearing now* with these little coffins. In my day they *didn't*. In my day they'd just come up in a hearse and you'd be told, 'Take that down and bury that in the angel's plot.' And off you'd go . . . nobody'd be there. Nobody with it. The parents didn't come. But now a good lot come. But in my day they just didn't. Sometimes I'd imagine that the mother would be too distraught.

"Digging a new grave today is the same. Nothing has changed. What could change? I've buried many a famous person. I helped to put Dev [de Valera] into it. I'll always feel part of that history. My official retirement is coming up. Oh, but I'll drop in. Now we've had other staff that went out of here and never came back except when they were dead. Now I call this the bad side of progress because, see, you used to have to come up here and collect your pension. And seeing the likes of me here we'd have an old chat and maybe a bit of slagging and it'd be great stuff. Then all of a sudden they decided to send them out cheques. And I never seen them again. Till their wooden overcoat . . . that's what I call it."

STEPHEN BRACKEN—TOMBSTONE CARVER, AGE 78

A sixth-generation carver, he proclaims, "We're stone mad." He began his rigorous seven-year apprenticeship sixty years ago in a damp, dusty, unhealthy stone yard. His ability to do intricate carving soon earned him the reputation as one of Dublin's finest craftsmen. He produced magnificent Celtic crosses, delicate interlacing and angelic figures. Today, still chipping away in a centuries-old stone shed that was once a forge next to Glasnevin Cemetery, he laments that most people no longer appreciate or can afford his ancient skills.

"All the stone people, they came to Dublin from all parts of the country just after the Famine years, about 1856. My people left from Tipperary. And that's when the English firms came over, at the same time. There was Harrison's, Sharpe's—my father served his time in Sharpe's—and my brother who was 16 served his time in Emery's. They are all English names. And there was Smyth's. They all came at about the same time, about 1856, because the country was sort of getting on its feet and money was being collected in the Catholic churches all over the country and they were building new churches. So there was a boom at the marble trade for all the altar work.

"My father was born just off Pearse Street, by Harrison's [monument carving firm]. I was born on Dominick Street and I was only 2½ years of age when we moved out of the heart of the city. My sons are seventh generation [stone carvers]. Oh, we're stone mad. *Stone mad!* So when I left school at 16 I tried Harrison's where my brother worked and they said, 'Oh, yes, we'd be delighted to take you on.' That was around 1936. And I was a bound apprentice at that time. Seven years. I was nearly thirty years in Harrison's. Carving came natural to me. When I was an apprentice they assumed that I was going to be an engraver as our family specialised in engraving. And since my brother was there I was put under his charge. And *he* was stone mad! And he took great pride in me cause I was good at football and hurling and he was lame from the time he was only a kid. He broke his leg and it was badly set. And he finished with a bent knee. But he was a wonderful, gifted carver. All the architects of Dublin went to him.

"I was even able to do little bits of carving and engraving at home before I even started at Harrison's, because he did work at home and we had a shed, a workshop. And my father was a first-class tradesman. My father did the engraving on the foundation stone on O'Connell Bridge. It was done in stone originally. See, our family specialised in engraving. But when I started I was able to do my own carving. The apprenticeship was hard work. It was from 9.00 till half five. I started out just engraving letters that were already marked on. My first main job was doing IHS monograms on stones. And I did interlacing. At Harrison's there were all different sections of the trade. There were stone cutters and monumental stone cutters and then there was church work set out for marble for altar work. I'd say that there were nearly thirty men there. I got training in all aspects and I was lucky to be able to get that. I was doing carving, engraving. I got small headstones and put maybe a chalice in the centre with some vine leaves coming out both sides. Every headstone I did had carving. It's mostly the carving that sells the stones. And I done Celtic crosses. I did *everything*. There was an *art* to it.

"When I started first the wages were extremely bad. It was before anything [unions] was organised. And I got five shillings a week for forty-eight hours. *Five* shillings a week! And within three months I was engraving as good as most of them. There was a man there, Jimmy Dunne, and he was on the wet saw and he told me, 'You're getting on marvellous, you're terrific at lettering.' And I told him, 'I'm only getting five bob a week.' Now my brother used to just say to me, 'You just stay where you are, and that's that.' But Jimmy told me to go in and see the manager and tell him that you're doing nearly a man's work and you felt that you were worth more money and you were looking for so much more an hour extra. So, I took up courage—and didn't tell my brother—and I saw the manager and he was an ex-British captain who used to talk through his nose. He came back at the end of the week and said, 'The Governor'—see, Mr Harrison was always called 'The Governor'—'You must have a great knack with the Governor. He's giving you an extra ha'penny an hour.' But I was only a year there when we had the big strike in Dublin, a big building strike. And all the men were taken out of all the building trades. But I couldn't go on strike because I was a bound apprentice. There were two of us. The strike was very hard on the men. But when the strike finished they made new regulations for apprentices as well as for the stone cutters and tradesmen and I was given nine pence an hour. *Nine pence an hour*—I was a *millionaire*! That was something, nine pence an hour. Now I was doing work that deserved it.

"Conditions were very bad . . . conditions were *really* bad at that time, and very unhealthy. See, the workshop was under the railway bridge [on Pearse Street] and it was made of blackstone and blackstone weeps. It doesn't have to be raining for blackstone to be wet. If it's clammy weather the blackstone weeps. All the machines were worked using water pouring down on them and the roof itself was in very poor condition. Poor conditions and very unhealthy. It was hard work and it was all dampness and young men could get rheumatism around about 40 or 50 from it. It was *always* dampish. A *very* unhealthy place and quite a lot of the younger people died with T.B. And when I was 22 I got pleurisy and pneumonia and it was very bad and I was ten weeks in the hospital. And we got all the dust. Today, with the dust you'd use fans and a mask but in those days you'd no fans or anything. And in stone-cutting the back was always bent so you developed a hump if you were in any way tall. It wasn't good to be tall. Most men, they did get a bit hunched. And no such thing as fires whatsoever in the old days. It was only when the Health departments started and it was essential then in factories to have fires. But we had an open coke fire in the middle of the big shop. But they got away with murder because it wasn't enough to keep everybody warm. Oh, your hands would be very cold in the wintertime, especially doing carving and engraving. There was a tremendous amount of slavery in it, I think. I mean my father *never* got a holiday. And I worked for years without holidays. And you could be sacked like that! But the men, they liked their work and got great satisfaction out of it. Very proud men.

"I was doing the carving and then the engraving [on headstones] and I'd mark all the lettering by hand with the V-cut in it. And you'd get satisfaction from looking at my work. And afterwards as a young man I was able to do fixing work, erecting stones in graveyards. We all had to do it. It was part of the training. So I travelled all over the country. Basically I was at the engraving. But I was a fit young man then and we'd have to go out to the country early in the morning, dig foundations, fill in the foundations with concrete and then erect the monument. Three of us did that, the lorry man, the labourer and myself. If it was a big Celtic cross you'd have to get more men. For years it was my job to go out in cemeteries and do the lettering. The idea was that you had to get level with where you were putting the letters on the stone. So often I had to dig very deep, about three or four feet down into the grave . . . as long as you could get your feet comfortable. And the important thing is to keep the back straight or you'll get humpy in no time. Oh, you'd be sitting down *in* the grave. But I'd have straw or I'd carry what we called ground sheets, tarpaulin with straw underneath to keep the dampness from coming up. And sometimes you didn't have to be digging holes, you had to build up to sit at the stone. You'd use your tool box to sit on.

"There was a blacksmith used to come over into Harrison's, an old man, and my brother, who never learned how to sharpen his tools because he was too busy, used to give him two dozen tools every week, to sharpen. He went around the stone yards in Dublin sharpening tools. But this was mostly for charity because this man, he was a great man during the troubled time here, and when everything was settled he wouldn't take a pension—on principle! That's the way he was made. And he was a very poor man. But I learned from another man, Jack O'Donoghue, who was an engraver in Harrison's at the time. He was a good engraver. *Slow* though. One day he was sharpening and I said, 'Would you mind, Mr O'Donoghue, if I have a look at your sharpening?' See, the way it was with the men years ago, if they saw a lad *interested* in something they'd go out of their way to show him everything they knew. So Jack showed me how to sharpen. And afterwards my father showed me how to make the tools.

"When I started first my father told me *never* to volunteer the loan of a tool. And you *didn't*, cause you'd never get them back. I inherited my father's tools and all my uncle's. And you made your own tools, the mallets and chisels. You made those specially and that fitted into your hand. So if you were making tools for yourself you made them to suit yourself. And now I made special tools when I was a young man, very light stuff and if I was doing a face, around the eyes, I had special tools I made. I still have them in the shop. I had a special little tool for rounding the eye on the stone and to give effect on the nose and lips. I made my own tools. My father showed me how to do that. The tools were made from steel. I'd get the steel bars and do it over the bellows and on the anvil and temper it. I made hundreds of those . . . and most of them were pinched on me!

But I have a lot of them left and I have them wrapped in a bit of a cloth and the cloth is nearly as old as meself.

"The dust, it was a natural thing to drink because of it. See, the men in those days had no money for drinking every night and they were paid on Saturdays at half twelve and they'd have a few pints on a Saturday and maybe Sunday but the rest of the week [very little] . . . and they were better off for it. But carvers were fond of the drink if they could get it. It was only a natural thing. And it was quite cheap. I mean, the people at our trade who didn't take a drink did it because they were too mean to drink, and possibly tried to save. But they never looked too well. See, I think if you're working at a trade like carving or stone-cutting you're *concentrating* on one thing all the time. So when you're finished work you must concentrate the other way, on pleasure and relaxation. It's most important for you if you want to keep young. See, the people who didn't drink, did it for *meanness* sake. That's a fact. But I think they were all drawn looking and they didn't seem to have the same gusto and appreciation for life that the man who took a drink did.

"O'Neill's of Pearse Street, now that was known as the stone-cutter's pub. All my uncles drank there but my father didn't drink much because he hadn't got the money. But stone-cutters, that's the only pleasure they had, in the pub. And they were always talking stone. This was one problem. And Mr O'Neill was a gentleman. And I drank there myself . . . drank too much there. I always tried to forget about work. It's the same as the old stone-cutters of years ago who didn't have the money but they'd meet somewhere and they didn't need to have a drink but they sang and they danced and it was a complete opposite of work. Oh, they could all tap-dance. You see, tap-dancing came into the trade years ago around the country. Oh, my father was a tap-dancer as well. See, going back years ago if a church was being built in a certain town the stone-cutters from a large area would converge there for work. And they were like itinerant workers. And in those days with no radio or nothing they could all entertain in some way or another. And most of them took up the art of tap-dancing. Don't ask me why! But all my uncles could tap-dance and my father was even on the stage here in Dublin.

"I did Celtic crosses. I have two Celtic crosses to do now, one in granite and the other in limestone, with interlacing. Oh, I still do quite a number every year. And if we're asked to clean a stone [headstone] if it's small we can bring it back into the workshop. And last winter I brought back one of my first jobs and it was a young couple that got it made then and they had a little child who died, about 5 or 6. And they asked me could I do something in the way of carving an angel. So I came across a beautiful book with paintings from the Bible and there was a painting of an angel. So I decided to do that, the angel with the arms outstretched with the flowing robes and the clouds underneath. I don't know, maybe it's corny . . . but it's just what they wanted. Well, I brought that stone back and had a look at it and, my God, I was very *proud*, even with the wear on it. About twenty-five years ago I carved that. It's lovely.

"I've had a very happy life and been lucky. It wasn't making any money but it gave me great satisfaction. Unfortunately, the work nowadays is really terrible—but the old work was wonderful. Ah, it was all hand work and they got great enjoyment, fulfilment. I don't think today anyone would ever get the same training I got. Years ago you *had* to get that training. But people can't use their hands today. Oh, it's a dying trade. It's all machinery and computers. Using machines, it has to be done. To me, the work today is *terrible*. But people today are only concerned about price. They have computers now that can make letters on a rubber stamp or stencil and put their rubber stencil on the stone for inscriptions and they can sandblast it. Anybody can do that. And the public wouldn't know a bit of art from a dog's foot! It's a fact of life. It's accepted and what can you do? It's a terrible pity. It's dying out . . . it's very sad when I see so many chancers in the business today and they've a different outlook. They're in it to make money. I've no money to show for it . . . I never worried about money . . . my younger son now is 28 and gradually he's taking over here."

6

Activists and Idealists

FRANK WEAREN—IRA VETERAN, AGE 94

Born in 1902, he joined the IRA as a young man, encountered the dreaded Black and Tans, participated in dangerous raids, was imprisoned and survived an excruciating twenty-seven-day hunger strike. He knew Maud Gonne MacBride and Countess Markievicz and admired both. A proud patriot and active member of the Socialist Workers' Movement, he still attends weekly meetings.

"I was born 8 October 1902 in Gloucester Street. Around the Diamond, that's what they called it. They was all big tenement houses. There was a convent down on Sean McDermott Street, the 'penitentiary' we called it, cause girls in trouble were sent in there instead of Mountjoy. Young girls caught on the street, 17, 19, or maybe 16, they were *shoved* in there and the nuns would look after them. They was left there for maybe a year or two years till they were cured or purified [of prostitution], some of them from the Monto and some operating around Grafton Street and York Street. Now when this Free State was formed the first thing they done was to try and *purify* the city and abolish all this prostitution. They done away with the Monto by forcing the Corporation to build flats for to accommodate them and try to purify their lives.

"I was 14 when I come out of school and the first thing I done was went to work on a messenger boy bike for five shillings a week. I was working for a man named Foley and he had a big grocery shop. Doing groceries and a few potatoes and vegetables, maybe a pound of bacon, a pound of sausage, a pound of butter. The bike had a carrier, a basket, on the front and I'd just go to the door and deliver it. I done that for about twelve months. Then I worked for a man called Connolly that used to own the Refuge pub and I got seven and sixpence a week pushing a handcart with beer, bread, groceries and what have you.

"And when I was 14, I got mixed up in the boy scouts, joined the Fianna on a Friday night in Harcourt Street. I joined there under Sean Heuston and the two brother Hoolihans and another man called Sean Burke and the Countess Markievicz. She used to come there inspecting the boys in their training. I met her time out of number and I knew her as well as I knew me mother, cause she was there looking after the welfare of the children in the Fianna. Because she says, 'The boys of the period will make the men of tomorrow.' Which she was perfectly right! She was a *lady*, that's all we knew. And she was of a very wealthy family. Now she took part in the '16 Rising. And she was in command of the garrison of men that was in Stephen's Green. So, of course, when the surrender comes she was arrested. But she was a British subject, of course, and she was detained for a while and she got out on probation, sort of. But she *still* carried on with Sean McBride's mother, Maud Gonne, until death took them. I saw Maud Gonne time out of number. Oh, a very perfect featured woman and had a beautiful shape. And dressed to the modern clothes. Now after years the Countess went sick and she was put into the private nursing home on Grand Canal Street. And she deteriorated. And she had to *pawn her jewellery* and *sell it* to pay for her attention in the hospital. That's the way she finished up. She finished up with *nothing*. And when she died her husband come over, the Count, and her son and so we marched in her funeral and brought her to Glasnevin and that's all I ever seen of the Count himself. He was a big, strong, robust man. Oh, when she was getting buried . . . history was around.

"We used to generally parade on a Friday night and on a Sunday morning, parade or march up to the mountains. Now for the Rising about seven or eight were picked out of the scouts to do their job, whatever was to be done. I wasn't picked cause I wasn't 15. I just missed it. So I carried on against the government and I knew a lot that was mixed up with the Movement . . . dead and gone now. But, oh, everyone then was afraid of the Black and Tans. Because if you were walking along the path and you sort of looked at them they'd come and give you a boxing. Give you a box across the back of the neck or the side of the head and tell you to keep going—for *nothing*. For only *looking*! That was the sort they were. Oh, you couldn't get worse! But the British soldiers were gentlemen. Oh, they were gentlemen because they were the sons of good English people. And they only joined the army to become a soldier. But now these Black and Tans were all recruited out of the long-term prisons in England and all the bloody big gaols. Fellas in doing a life term or maybe ten and twelve years. They were recruited, especially if they had army experience. £1 a day was their wages. £7 a week. That was a terrible lot of money. The manager of Woolworth's had only £5 a week in them days. The Tans, they'd raid a grocery or a public house and they'd fill theirselves. Oh, that was their dish.

"Now I'd an elder brother and he'd be 100 if he was alive. And he was in the Movement as well. So the Black and Tans got a contact [information] somehow and came to *raid* for him. They came to the house to look for him, to arrest him. And he wasn't there. I was in the bed upstairs. And they called me father and says, 'We want your son, John.' 'My son John isn't here. He's away down in the country, that's all I know about him.' 'How many sons have you?' 'I've Frank and I've John.' 'Well, let us see Frank,' says they. So he brought the officer up to the bedroom and he says, *'Out of bed*, boy,' says he. *'Hop out.'* And I put on me trousers and when he seen me standing he says, 'Get back to bed.' 'How old is he?' says he. Says the Da, 'He's fifteen and a half.' 'Put him back to bed,' says he. So *off* they went. They only came to arrest me brother but they never got him. He finished up with the Free State Army.

"A few nights I'm out late—now this was *curfew*—and me mother and me father is in a sweat. And I was a half an hour beyond the curfew and I could smell the fumes of the cars and there was a *bloody tank* there as well. So I went into this garden and hid under a bush. So I escaped. Another week we heard the cars and me Ma says, 'There's another raid somewhere,' says she, 'hop out the back.' So I went out into the lane and hopped up over a wall under the arches into a dairy yard. And I kept listening and they were walking with their big hobnail boots and their rifles and two tenders. That was life! Another time I was down in Portmarnock with a pal of mine and we were ferreting for rabbits and the next thing we seen was eight or nine or ten tenders coming down the beach and the tide was out. It was the Black and Tans. This was in the month of August, or September. So we got our rabbits and went off and hid in the big high dunes. We was afraid to show out in front of them because we didn't know what they'd do with us. So we hid there for an hour and they were in their skins running up and down the beach with bottles of whiskey in their hands and leaping into the water and coming out again. They spent an hour or two there. And when they were gone we went over picking up half-bottles of whiskey and bottles of stout and bottles of ale. We got something like twelve or fourteen shillings for what we collected . . . along with our few rabbits.

"Now I carried on with the Movement and I was getting trained when I was 18. I got transferred with two or three other boys into the IRA, into 'K' Company of the 2nd Battalion. And we took part between the Belvedere Hotel and Barry's Hotel. I was called the 'Shadow' because I was so light and small and thin. And I was known in the early stages when I was active in the Movement as 'short Mauser.' That was me rifle, it was only 5 lb weight. When I was getting trained I was very active with the short Mauser rifle and it only held five [cartridges] and the Enfield held eleven and it was 7 lb weight and I couldn't balance it accurate. When I got the Mauser I could get a bullseye. And being active with the IRA then we worked to get a press, which is *the Irish Press* today. And we, as IRA men, solicited our friends for subscriptions every week. You went to their doors to collect it and you handed it to a trustee. They started the *Press* on collections of money from here and there and everywhere. And they got a big grant from America, from the Irish people of America, and that's what started the *Irish Press*. To start our *own* Fianna Fáil national newspaper. So the paper started up and it was *flourishing*. And it's flourishing yet! [1989] But it's not as good as it used to be. It's gone down.

"I seen a few actions. We done a raid on two strongholds on the North Wall, the Shell-Mex and the Anglo-American Oil Company. At a meeting it was decided that we'd make a raid on them two particular holdings. There was eleven Free State soldiers in one and nine in the other. We had the meeting in the kitchen of Paul Moore's house in Marlborough Street and decided to have a raid. And I was told, 'You're listed for the raid.' There was sixteen of us there and every man was detailed to what he was to do. So another man was with me and we went to Shell at five to eight with our lunch in our hand as if we were looking for a job. And I'd a .38 [revolver] in my pocket, ready for to pull out the gun. It was nice and light. The .45 was very big. The first man we meet is a soldier sitting in the box as we walk up and so we go in and '*Hands up!*' says the two of us. And the man was reading the paper. 'Keep your hands over your head,' we says. And we grabbed his rifle, and stepped back about six feet. We were told to always keep back about six to eight feet from a man when we were holding a gun, so he could never make a grab *quick* at you. Or he could use a big long leg to give you a kick. So we had him. We led the way and they [other raiders] had the other soldiers under control. And when we went in first there was a soldier in his long Johns cooking his breakfast and the rest was all in bed. Well, they nearly died! We got them all out, standing in the long Johns. So we took that garrison. They couldn't get over it. They were *shocked*. Never opened their mouth. Well, one man says, 'You're not going to shoot us?' 'Do what you're told and you won't be shot. Turn your back and face that wall there.' So the five or six of us all got a rifle or two each and carried them out. And outside there was a van waiting for us. So we shoved all the rifles in the van, got in and never stopped till we got to Drumcondra.

"Then I was working as a messenger boy at Woolworth's downstairs in the basement. 1922 this is. Then this officer says, 'Frank, we're going to have a job. Would you take a bomb and keep it for a day or two?' 'Yes,' says I, 'I have a way of hiding it.' So I took it. It was a number nine, about the size of a mug. 'Take the detonator out,' says he, 'and put it into something nice and dry. Don't let the sweat of your palm on it,' says he. So I put it into me pocket and brought the bomb into Woolworth's and I hid it. Now listen to this! Two days after, about ten to ten in the morning, the boss comes down with three detectives, like the Special Branch men now. 'Frank,' says he, 'there's three men want to interview you.' 'All right,' says I. I knew one of them and he says, 'We're going to arrest you, Frank. Don't ask questions, we're taking you away.' 'Wait till I get me coat,' says I. So I put me coat on and I put me hand in me pocket and it struck me that I had put the bomb into a big match box and I thought to meself, 'Jesus, I'm *done*!' And I says, 'Harry [boss], there's your matches', and he took the box. And I was saved! I was brought out back into the tender and brought to the Bridewell [police station]. I was interrogated every bloody half-hour and I said I knew *nothing*. 'We'll *make* you talk.' So I was left there for about two days.

"In any case, then I was brought up to Mountjoy in a horse caravan, two horses. There was two of us brought in and we was put in with all sorts of thieves. I didn't know the second man but he was an IRA man from some part of the country and he says, 'Were you ever in this place before?' 'No,' says I. 'Oh,' says he, 'I believe it's tough.' 'Ah,' says I, 'we'll have to wait and see, but there's plenty of our pals in it, plenty of comrades in it.' So we was brought before the governor, Captain Monroe was his name, and he wore a monocle. And I was locked into a cell for a couple of weeks. We were all political prisoners. They wouldn't put two in the one cell. You got the prison food. That evening I heard the bell ringing, the triangle, and then the lags came up serving out the food. Lags we called them. They were prisoners in for a small distance. Our fellas wouldn't handle it. The warden opened your door and they handed in your mug of tea or cocoa and a loaf of bread about the size of me fist with a little pat of butter on the top. I said, 'Is that all we get to eat?' And in the morning a man came along with a big container of porridge and scooped it up on your place and you handed him your enamel mug and he filled it up with a ladle of tea. And then he handed you in your little loaf of bread. That was your eggs and rashers!

"Then I was shifted to Kilmainham and I met a lot of me friends in it, prisoners. We were put up in the old part of Kilmainham, locked upstairs, and the bosses were locked separate but you could *shout down* at them over the balcony, down to the other IRA men. I didn't realise the danger at the time. There was another fella down below, Sean Hayes, who was in the company with me and, says I, 'Sean, what are they going to do with us?' 'Jesus,' says he, 'you'd better say your prayers, Frank, we're all praying here.' 'For what?' says I. 'You don't know what's in front of you,' says he. The third day this soldier come up opening the gate and he stood looking at me. 'Jesus,' says he, 'is that you?' Now he lived near me. 'Does your mother know where you are?' 'No,' says I. 'Will you tell her?' 'Of course.' And so he made haste to tell me mother. So me father and some of me relations came to see could they get an interview [with me] but they wouldn't be let past the gate. They'd just say, '*No visitors here*—they're prisoners of war', and they were pulled aside. So I was there November and Christmas and January and February, and March came and there was a terrible lot of shifting here and this officer comes up and says, 'Yous are all getting transferred to Mountjoy and youse are going under arms. Remember, bullets don't go around corners.' It meant you'd be shot *directly* if you made any attempt [to escape].

"So I was in Mountjoy and before Easter this priest, Father O'Donoghue was his name, he comes up and says to the man in charge, 'Any of your boys wants to go to their Easter duties we'll be serving Mass here on Sunday morning, and Communion. And there'll be Confessions here Friday and Saturday all day.' So a few of the boys was religious in their own way. And I went first cause I was the youngest of the group. So I went in and knelt down in front of him and he was in uniform. And I says, 'Are you a priest?' 'I am,' says he, 'and I'm a soldier. Did you come in to argue with me cause I'm in the uniform?' 'Well,' says I, 'I don't trust it.' Says he, 'I want to ask you a question before you make your Confession. If I give you a form now this minute—and I have them here—would you sign a declaration that you wouldn't take up arms against the constitutional army and the government?' 'Oh,' says I, 'I'll sign *nothing*.' 'Well then,' he says, 'go on out! Can't hear your Confession. You're eligible to commit sin or murder tomorrow. That's in your mind.' And when I come out they says, 'What's wrong? You weren't long.' And I explained to them. And Peadar O'Donnell says, 'Comrades, right turn—*to your cells*.' And we all marched to our cells. And nobody went to Confession.

"After Easter we were all rounded up in Mountjoy at half past two in the morning, told to get out of your cell and get dressed and pack up. The officer in charge was Paddy McMahon and he says, 'We're going to the Curragh.' That was an internment camp. So we marched under arms, four deep, with a soldier between each four and an armoured car in front and an armoured car behind. So's if you made a burst you were done. Now McMahon says, 'There's no way of escaping . . . unless you want to die instantly.' So we were marched up and put into trains and brought to the camp and put in huts or into the riding school that was all turned into beds. Now there was 37,000 of us locked up and interned all over the thirty-two counties. Now there was 700 in my camp. And we all had a meeting out in the open and the man announced, 'There's a general hunger strike on. We're on hunger strike in Mountjoy, they're on hunger strike everywhere and *we're* going on hunger strike.' There was some of them there that didn't go on hunger strike. Didn't feel like it.

"On that hunger strike all we drank every day was salt and water. But that kept the bowel free, it kept your kidneys flushed and kept the stomach expanded. And that's how we survived. The first three days and four days was *dreadful*. One fella went on it with me, a fella called Killee. I thought he'd die after the third day. And I was thin, but, Jesus, he was *worse*. He was the colour of that quilt! Yellow. He got yellow. But he got over it. I had headaches, *dreadful* headaches. And if you had bad teeth that was the first thing that deteriorated. You got no end of pain. Get up in the middle of the night roaring and bawling . . . '*Oh, doctor*, get a pair of pliers and pull it out!' You'd be that frantic. Some went so frantic that our own doctor, Dr Jim Ryan—he was there as a prisoner —he used to tell them, 'If you can't stick it, *give it up*!' Some of them did give it up. But it never come on me, never. I was *determined* to either come out on me feet or come out *dead*. That's the way I felt. But I was getting weaker. For the first four or five days I was able to get up and put on me clothes and walk around for a couple of hundred yards. And I was doing that up till the tenth or eleventh day. And the eleventh day I got light in the head and I fell. And Dr Ryan says, 'Now don't get out of bed, you're too weak.' But I was *thinking* [clearly]. But I'll tell you what was *terrible, worse* . . . ah, *dreadful*. You were *dreaming every night* only of fancy food . . . cake shops, ice cream shops, fish and chip shops, restaurants and meals that you were having at home. The dreams was dreadful and you'd wake up *roaring* and *bawling*. It was pandemonium . . . Jesus, it was dreadful. A *hell* it was, a hell on earth. And there was big strong boys and men there and they lost their mind. There was two of them lost their mind. One was called Hobo Kavanagh and another fella from Dun Laoghaire, he was a blacksmith by trade. They went delirious.

"So I finished there on hunger strike and got out in November 1923, after doing twenty-seven days hunger strike. But there was some of them done thirty-five days. Oh, there was. Men there seven and eight days after us. See, it was published that there was so many on hunger strike and there was no end to the demonstrations in the city and in Cork and Limerick and Waterford and everywhere. With the result that the government called a general amnesty to let them all out in batches, thirty or forty or fifty of us a day. They started with the weakest of us. And I *tumbled* out of the bed and the soldier and me own comrades gave me a hand. And me sight had deteriorated cause of the empty stomach. And they wanted me to go on a stretcher. And I says, 'Right, I'm not able to walk.' So they carried me over to a reception committee we had in Newbridge. They brought me over by tender and handed me over to a few of our own confederacy and they took me in. There was eight or nine of us. And the first thing I was put down on a sofa to lie down. And a doctor came and tested me heart and everything. And he says to this lady, 'Bring him a little sup of lukewarm milk.' So I got a glass of lukewarm milk. And about an hour after this fella come over to me and says he, 'Frank, have you any milk there left?' And he took out a bottle of whiskey and poured a drop of whiskey in and 'Drink that,' says he, 'it'll put life into you.' It *did* . . . and I sat up. I sat up!

"Then there was seventeen of us put on the train for Kingsbridge to be received by a committee there. And, Jesus, I sat on the train wanting to get sick and I couldn't get sick. So yer man opened the window and I tried to get sick out of the window and he was afraid I'd fall out and he dragged me in. And when we got to the railway [station] it was *packed* with people waiting to receive their friends and relations. We were all *cheered* and everything. And this man talks through a megaphone, 'I have a list of the names and when I read the names I want you to locate your sons or your uncles or your father.' Well, Jesus, me mother and me father and my aunt was there. They were *delighted* to see me. The Da says, 'To the hospital!' 'No,' says I, 'I want to go home.' But he brought me up to the Mater Hospital first and I was brought in and two or three doctors come down. 'We've a bed for you.' But I said, 'No, Mammy, take me home.' So the doctor gave her a list for my diet. And I was fed like a child. I was on baby foods for two or three days and then I got a bit of porridge. And then I got soups to eat. I couldn't eat any solid food for seven or ten days. And I could feel meself getting me energy back and I could see me sight was even getting better.

"I was married in 1928. Me wife was in the IRA. I don't think I'd have lived so long, only for it. I took an *interest* in the whole machinery of me country. I even *learned* and become more intellectual. When I left school I could hardly write me name and I couldn't spell Dublin. That's no lie. I was active in the IRA up till 1955. They only wanted young men in from 18 to 20 or so on. And that's how they started the Provos up in the North. The single fellas here was *mad* for action and so they amalgamated with the North of Ireland Brigade. You could volunteer to go up. And if you were going up they'd tell you to try learning a little bit of the lingo. They'd learn you their way of talking before you went to mix with any of them in the pubs, try to make you more Northern in your voice, because if you were talking real Dublin you were under suspicion.

"I reared six boys and four girls. But none of me children took part in it. The eldest fella'd say, 'Dad, you were a mug' . . . meaning that I was foolish. And I didn't even trust me brother because he was in the Free State Army. Oh, I did *not*, cause we were *drilled* in that. Jesus, I could write a book on it. But for what? Now, when I'm looking at them up in the North what *thanks* will they get? They'll be the same as we were! What should they care about you being a veteran of the IRA? No one wants to know anything about you. They don't want to know about you. Oh, not at all. I'm not a bit ashamed of what I did. I'm in the Socialist Workers' Movement now. We hold our meetings every Wednesday night. There's forty or fifty of us there. We have a room for lectures and all the rest. I told me daughter, 'I want a plain funeral. No elaboration, no flag . . . only one flag, the Labour flag, the stars and the blue colour. Yous can throw that on me coffin.'"

DANNY GLEESON—WORLD WAR II INTERNEE, AGE 85

As a young lad in Tipperary he joined the IRA and later carried a gun. He came to Dublin in 1930 to work as a barman in Tommy Moore's Gaelic pub. But soon he had to go "on the run" for nine months to avoid arrest. After being captured in Dublin he was sent to the Curragh internment camp. He later became president of the Dublin Barman's Union and in 1955 led 3,000 strikers through the streets of Dublin in a protest march.

"I was a boy in Tipperary and one hundred yards from where I was born and reared in the town of Nenagh the Volunteers from 1916 met twice a week in the square and paraded and then went out about three miles where they had some manoeuvres outside of town. And I followed them out. I was attracted to them. My father had an old pub down there in Nenagh and he wasn't so politically active. I'd say my mother would have been more interested from the point of view of the history of the movement. My father was struggling in the old pub whereas my mother had a background of a mountainy district which was, I would say, seventy-five to ninety per cent Republican. It was twelve miles out of the town of Nenagh. It was a place where even the British military wouldn't go without less than four lorries. Now that was back in 1920. And, oh God, the Black and Tans, they were taken out of gaols. They had half a uniform, a khaki trousers and a jacket. But their numbers were drawn out of gaols in England, for serving gaol sentences, *not* for politics.

"So when the Volunteers used to drill in the town square I always went up to see them and this [interest] continued and I even followed them out with the other lads. Of course, we were too young to be taken in at the time. I suppose 9 or 10 years of age we were. So I grew up with that and it was very popular at the time to be anti-British. And it was easy to get people to follow it. So I was with the Volunteers *mentally* from the very start because it was a popular movement at the time. And I had the blessing of my mother. The resurgence of the Volunteers or IRA was started again at that time and at the time of the Civil War I used to help the Volunteers taking [money] collections, on market days particularly. I remember offering myself to the Volunteers and they looked at me and says, 'Danny, you're too young.' But I became known to be associated with the Republican movement, like I would sell flags on market days. This was one of their means of raising money. This was for the Volunteers that were in gaol, that had been arrested. And some of these men were very hard hit family-wise and they used to take collections for their families. So I grew up in that atmosphere. Afterwards I was *glad* to be in the Republican movement and I got the training and all and they taught me how to use a gun. Afterwards I did carry a gun, for protection.

"I came to Dublin in 1930. A cousin of mine was working out in Dun Laoghaire and he told me that there was a vacancy going for a barman at Walter's public house. After that then I started in Cleary's pub of Amiens Street. Now I was an active member of the IRA at that time. Then I was working at Tommy Moore's Gaelic pub and then this crisis came during the start of the war, 1941 I think it was. Now I arrived at work on a Monday morning at Tommy Moore's of Cathedral Street and there was three fellas standing at the far side and I didn't know them but I got a very quick rumble that they were G-men. Evidently they had my name because of my association with the Republican movement. That was the reason, cause I was active then in the IRA. They were standing outside by the gate and I didn't go into Tommy Moore's. I walked on. My digs were up here in Frederick Street and there was a lad that was in digs with me and we knew that there was a round-up going on politically at the time. And there was fellas standing just opposite our digs. And the fella in the digs with me says, 'Danny, you see those guys right opposite? Well, you know what they are?' And I knew cause this was the morning of the big round-up in 1941. And he says, 'You know what they're waiting for—not to take you on holidays!' So on the Monday morning he says, 'Danny, you'd better *get out*.' I got out the back way anyway and disappeared as far as they were concerned. So I just got an old bicycle and went away out into the country where I had contacts and relations. And I was about eight or nine months on the run. See, I was active in the IRA and there was always friendly houses . . . and I think there always will be. I was in different parts of the country, in the north and in part of my old county of Tipperary. So I bailed out and went out into the country and was about nine months on the run before they caught up with me.

"But they found me out and I was arrested in Dublin and I was sent out to the Curragh. Now I wasn't active at the time but those that *were* active, I was a supporter of theirs. So I was interned myself during the war. Just internment, no trial or anything like that. Oh, no, there was no trials—you were just interned. Although I wasn't involved [in any IRA actions] but they *knew* about my association with them. I was in there for a year and three months. And that was *that*. Maybe according to the government I deserved to be interned. We were in huts, army huts, that housed roughly thirty men. There was a couple of thousand men there, men who were younger and older. It wasn't that bad. The huts weren't that bad. Just timber huts and you got a mattress and a couple of blankets and in each hut there used to be two stoves. But the greater number of men that was interned weren't tried. They had nothing positive that could put them through a court. You were just interned. And now I wasn't charged. But a number of men at that time were actually charged and *sentenced* and they were kept in gaol, but we were kept in internment camp. Now we had a trench and wire fence all around and it was virtually impossible [to escape]. But we had a couple of huts that were *near* the fence and men had gone down under the boards and dug a tunnel over to the trench. But they were caught cause there was stool pigeons inside. Well, they *tried* anyway. It was just when they reached the wire fence that they clamped down on them. But you had to be very careful because there'd be stool pigeons around.

"You became kind of reconciled to it, that you were severing your connections [with the outside world]. After you were there for a spell you could get an odd visitor. You could write a letter but you couldn't put anything in it. The letters, they were all checked, of course. Every letter that went out had to go through the military office. The military [soldiers] weren't bad. And we were virtually in control of ourselves. Some fellas, their background was very well heeled whereas other fellas had nothing. Some men were very bad prisoners and others were OK. It depended on your own mind. Most of them thought, 'OK, I'm here until I'm let out but I'm *not* signing anything.' That was kind of it, you know? Oh, and we had sports, we had football matches. We used to be very keen on football matches. And now we had men that were well educated and we had lessons. See, there was teachers and all interned in there. I'll tell you, we had *very* good lessons with qualified teachers. There was a couple of university men in there in the huts with degrees and they were in charge of the lessons. Irish was the principal subject. There was Irish classes going on all the time. Nearly everyone had to do an hour or so of Irish [per day]. Oh, and we had some very good artists. We even had what I would call theatre groups, some very good lads.

"There was an old wash-house, a shed for washing, and you'd go down there once a week. So there was a chance of a bit of a shower but they were very limited. There was never enough [facilities] to meet the demand. The food wasn't too bad. 'Twas fair enough. The food was plain enough. You got your tea and a ration of bread and a small little taste of butter and maybe a bit of cheese in some instances, just enough to sustain you. There was a canteen there if you had the price of cigarettes but the men that had money for that was negligible. There'd be money sent into them from relations outside. A package of cigarettes was a hard thing to get. Some men, they'd rather get a smoke than a feed. And at Christmas maybe you'd get a little currant cake.

"I was in for a year and three months and you were glad, of course, to be going out. See, they thought that after we had a period in the camp that the movement outside had gone very dead and there was no great danger. You were called out of your huts about 7.00 in the morning and brought down to the [railway] station to go back to Dublin or out in the country, wherever you were picked up. You'd take the train back. I was arrested in Dublin so I went back to Dublin into digs. I went into digs up in North Frederick Street which was known as a Republican house. That's where I had been in digs some years before I was arrested. And I was brought to Kingsbridge by train. I went back to Tommy Moore's Gaelic bar. He brought me back the second day I was out."

DEIRDRE KELLY—URBAN ACTIVIST
AND PRESERVATIONIST, AGE 60

Since her college days she has been one of the leading activists and preservationists in the
inner city. The preservation battles of the sixties and seventies were a significant chapter in
the city's social history and have become part of Dublin's urban lore. She played a pivotal
role in the famous "Battle of Hume Street" in 1969. As she confides in retrospect, "It's a long
story in itself . . . full of dramas and scares." But little has been recorded about the real grass-
roots activities behind these preservation battles. Hers is the definitive inside historical
account, never previously chronicled. Today she is the head of the Dublin Living City Group
and author of two books on Dublin.

"I was born on Upper Leeson Street. It was a great street to grow up in. People
all around us were from all classes and backgrounds, never any feeling of class
distinction. Our home was in a Georgian building and there was a great
community living around there. There wouldn't have been a house that didn't
have some kids in it and a lot of it was in flats. Even in our house there was great
community because upstairs there was a couple from the Liberties and their five
children. My parents made me conscious of my surroundings, always. My father
was a mixture of things, a painter, a bus driver and he ran this little bicycle shop
up near UCD and always full of students and that's why we never made any
money because he spent all his time talking.

"Now just across from us was Sarah Purser's old house, a beautiful old
Georgian house, and the plasterwork in it was absolutely beautiful. It was the
four seasons done in plasterwork on the ceiling. But I remember when that old
house was knocked down. I suppose I would have been around 10. I remember
my father called me to this window and said, 'Watch now', and I looked out and
this was the first time I had ever seen the ball and chain being used. And there
was this huge big cloud of smoke and suddenly there was no house. And then
the lovely trees were cut down and there was nothing left! Just this space. And
I was really very upset about it . . . I just knew that something good was gone.

"Then when I went into my teens I went into the College of Art and got to
know a lot of the artists in those days and it was a whole new world this art
world. And then I graduated to McDaid's [pub]. McDaid's was something on
its own. It's all changed now . . . dreadful . . . modernised . . . Yuppy. But you
used to have all little groups and they knew each other. They stayed in their own
corners. There was the literary group which would be people like John Jordan
and [Patrick] Kavanagh and people like that. And another group that I suppose
you could call literary lay people. They weren't writers but they were very
literary. And then there was a group of oddballs like myself who didn't really fit
into any group but I knew them all. I remember Brendan Behan being carried
out once feet flailing. Kavanagh was going in there and we differed on our likes
of the city. He was raving about how great London was and Belfast and giving

out about Dublin. So we didn't hit it off terribly well in the conversations we had. But things would be discussed and discussed and discussed and it had a great atmosphere.

"Then in my mid-twenties I got involved in politics. I joined the Labour Party. I didn't stay in it very long because they brought in this coalition thing and I didn't agree with it. But I was a great admirer of Noel Browne. And from that I got involved in housing issues and actions in Dublin. There was the ESB [Electricity Supply Board] building issue which I really felt very strongly about. Fitzwilliam Street and Merrion Square were always lovely places and full of life when I was a kid. There were families in all the houses. I often remember going down Fitzwilliam Street on a Christmas and all the Christmas trees in the windows and just *full* of life and people going in and out of all the doors. And now [since the Georgian homes were demolished or converted into offices] if you go down Fitzwilliam Street, especially at night, there's no lights in the windows because it's all offices. It's like a tunnel of darkness. It's *dead* as can be. And I think that's a terrible reflection on us that we let that part of the city die. It should never have been allowed to happen. It's our planning laws . . . and corruption. So with the ESB thing I started getting conscious of Georgian houses and then the canal issue came up. They were going to cover in the canals and build a motorway. That caused a very wide protest in the city. I think it was the first time stickers were actually used—'Save the Canal.' And filling in the canals was stopped.

"Then in 1969 the Hume Street thing started and I just remember thinking to myself that no matter what happened, I'm *not* going to sit by and let those houses go this time. I was involved very much in the Hume Street battle, the occupation. We were there for six months. There were eight houses involved in it altogether, four on each side of the road on two corners. And when you looked down Hume Street, at the very end was Ely House, a beautiful Georgian house, and it *framed* the end of the street. It was a *perfect* Georgian streetscape. Now developers applied for demolition permission for both sides of the street and they got it. There was a lot of legal protesting and Haughey was the Minister involved but all the time behind the scenes it was progressing towards the demolition of the buildings. But the next thing, just before Christmas, we were passing by and realised that there were demolition men inside knocking the buildings down from the *inside*. Then myself and a couple of students and a few other people got in and stopped the workmen. They had a scaffolding and all up and we sat along the boards. And we refused to let them back in the door when they went out for various things. And bit by bit during the day there was a terrific swelling of people coming. By then they had knocked the roofs off. They were working like lightning inside. The actual roof beams were still there but they'd taken the slates off and had broken the floorboards, actually got axes and chopped the floor and some of the joints, and ripped out staircases. So we took over the houses and occupied them for six months. It's a long story in itself . . . full of dramas and scares.

"We had all sorts of people at the time coming in and helping us. So this—

the 'Battle of Hume Street' [as dubbed by the media]—was a most publicised thing. This started at the end of 1969 and went into June of 1970. We actually got *whole pages* of newspapers at the time, particularly when they broke in at the end of the six months. Funny enough, the Shelbourne [hotel] staff were always great with us. They used to let us have our baths there. They were great to the students who were scruffy and they could go over for a bath. They were very co-operative. Now they usually refer to it as a student occupation but we *couldn't* have kept going without people who were working and would come in and keep the morale up. So, strictly speaking, it wasn't just a student occupation, it was about half and half, a good mixture. Then we had a lot of visitors. We had regular visits from TDs and visiting dignitaries, Dr Spock being one of them. And schools used to bring their classes in and show them around. Oh, yes, to show them around. And some of the architectural students set themselves up studios there and worked from there. And that helped a lot. Some of the students actually failed their exams over it. But we were very well organised and a very good security system set up. And we had a couple of people in there who really did a lot for us. One woman, she was the mother of a teacher who'd come in and help us, she would appear *every* morning with little scones and tea and she'd clean up the place. She was always there and helped keep the morale up for everybody. And she was always there for a shoulder to cry on . . . because some of the students actually failed their exams over it.

"So we had all sorts of people at the time coming in and helping us and we were there for Christmas. And Haughey eventually agreed to meet with us and we went in to see him. And it was really only a publicity stunt on his part to see us because he had no intention of budging really. And he said, 'I can't think of why you want to save these old Georgian houses. They're not even nice looking.' So I pointed out to him. *You* live in one yourself!' And he couldn't get away from that. But he said, 'I really don't want to see you sitting in there over Christmas. On Christmas Day you should be in your homes. I'll send you a hamper.' So we just said, thanks very much, not really thinking that one would arrive. But, *sure enough*, on Christmas Eve this huge hamper arrived. And the hamper had everything in it including a bottle of port and a turkey and hams and biscuits and everything else. He sent it to us, the occupiers. So, anyhow, it was a very awkward position to be in, you know. *Half* of them wanted to give it back and half of us felt if we did this we would finish any chance of him helping us. Eventually, anyhow, as this discussion was going on, the sweets were being eaten and the port had been drunk and all that was left eventually was the turkey and the ham. And then suddenly they all started standing on their principles that they were going to go on a hunger strike rather than eat the turkey or the ham. So eventually we sent the turkey down to the nuns and my mother took the ham. And then Desmond and Mariga Guinness sent in a big thing of wine and we had the *most marvellous* Christmas Day!

"Now as the occupation was going on and on and on the summer was coming in and students were having their exams and people were going away on holidays and most of the people we had there had dwindled away and we were down to a handful. It was getting to a crucial stage and we were really desperate. And they [developers] must have realised this because they'd had a security man watching us for about ten weeks. And the morning of 5 June, it was a Sunday morning at 4.00, we heard this banging on the door and we went to the balcony and looked out and there was this big *sea* of yellow helmets and men with pickaxes. And they hammered down the door and came up. Now we had it well organised in case this happened because we were *always* expecting it to happen. And we had this huge big school bell that somebody had given us and we said that whoever was here, if they break in, get out on the balcony and *ring the bell* and shout for all you're worth! And this is what we did and *every light* in the Shelbourne went on! People were even coming around in their dressing gowns.

"And I had gotten a list of people who all said that if this happened [an assault] if we rang them, *no matter what hour of the day or night,* they would come. Among these were people like Garret FitzGerald and Maurice O'Connell and people like that who *promised* that *no matter what happened* they would arrive. So I typed out this list of those people and it was always beside the fireplace. And I'd given copies of the list to people who were on the list so if we got word to them they'd help do the ringing. So when the men broke in, this little girl, Rosemary, ran under the stairs and as soon as all the men went upstairs she *ran* out. And Rosemary went flying down to make the phone calls but every phone box in the area was broken. The phones had been pulled off the hooks. There wasn't a working phone between Stephen's Green and Leeson Street. And the staff at the Shelbourne—which had always been very co-operative—*wouldn't* allow Rosemary to make any phone calls that morning. So she got a taxi and went to Margaret Gaj's house and *banged* on her door and when she opened the door she said, 'They're breaking in . . . *they're killing us!*' And she got on the phone and, sure enough, by twenty to five there was Garret FitzGerald and Maurice O'Connell and all the papers and RTE. They didn't expect this would happen, that we would have the television and the radio and everything down there that quickly.

"Now the breaker-inners were a gang of heavies with a lorry and we counted seventy-seven policemen as well, so they knew they were going to do it. I mean, they'd never have seventy-seven spare policemen. And there was a *most* unco-operative inspector with them and he was *completely* on their side, so they must have picked him. And the next thing they tied these chains from the lorry to the front of the building and they were going to pull off the front of the building. Now they had already pulled my sister and a friend down the stairs through the broken glass and out—cause they'd broken all the windows out with pickaxes— and they were *pouring blood.* They were *dragged* out. They were really damaged. So when the lorry started to pull the front off, Aiden, my husband [to be], flung himself on to the lorry and wrapped himself around the yolk underneath and then my sister got underneath the lorry. And the next thing, one of the men came over and started *kicking them* in the ribs. Now I had a broken arm at that time but I went over and started pulling him away. And the police were standing around doing *absolutely nothing.* And I started kicking your man on the shins.

And over comes the inspector and says, 'Now you move away from there or I'll have you up for assault.' And they were kicking Aiden in the ribs, and punching my sister! But in the end they couldn't move the lorry, cause there were too many people wrapped around the innards.

"Anyway, next thing my sister was trying to get back in through the window but there was this big drop by the railing. And one of the security men got her and was *actually trying to push* her over the side. And I got a broken-up orange box outside and with it tried to push him away. And the next thing all I can remember was a sort of *roar* and with that I got this terrific thump on the back and was knocked flat on the ground and I was completely winded. And it was Kavanagh [head of the security men] himself. Unfortunately for himself he did it in front of very important people from *The Irish Times*, and others. And I took him to court. And I won! He appealed to the high court but I won. The judge could see through Kavanagh. He had witnesses who'd never even *been* there! And he was trying to say that I had picked up this *huge beam* to hit his men with. And with my broken arm! I couldn't have lifted *anything* with it. And it took two men to carry in the beam I was supposed to have used. So, there was a *yell* of laughter in the court—including the judge! But when it went into the next court there was a judge who was very geared toward property developers. And except for the photographer who had taken photographs of me on the ground and Kavanagh just after hitting me—you can *imagine* the photograph—if I hadn't had that I wouldn't have won. I didn't sue for damages. I just sued to have him found guilty. So he was fined a shilling damages. But it didn't do him any harm because he's now the biggest security operator in the country.

"Anyway, on this morning of the break-in it was coming on about 8.00 and there were literally *hundreds* of people around. And there was a change in shifts and a new inspector came on. And from the time the new inspector came on the tide turned. He wouldn't let them *touch* us, but he didn't side with us openly. And then there were three days and three nights of this holding out. And at this stage the house is in bits. I mean, when they got in for about that hour they knocked the chimney off the house . . . and with no regard for safety as the chimney is coming down. And they broke all the floorboards and really cut through the joists. And we had spent all those months painting and carpenters had come and helped us. Now when we were under siege during the last three days we had all sorts of people in there with us, like Conor Cruise O'Brien and Nick O'Leary and Garret FitzGerald and Declan Costello who became Attorney General. So we certainly had plenty of free legal advice! Then the second night of it we were up all night, you see, and all these people who came to help us stayed in the street. And there were *hundreds* on the street all night. People brought along their sleeping bags and they stayed there. Everything went against the developers. And it was the most *beautiful* June night. It was daylight up till about 12.00 and then it started getting bright again at about 5.00 in the morning. And it was *warm* and beautiful. But all this time in the pubs near by the developers, with these heavies, were gathering and were getting drunker and drunker. See, they had gone along the docks—this all came out in court—where there was a lot of unemployment and they gathered men on behalf of the developers. The heavies were big, tough men, sitting there all day in the pubs drinking. And everybody was getting worried because they were making these threats that they were going to gather and come at us again. And we started getting worried because there was rumours going around the crowd of guns.

"Now an interesting thing was that this group of dockers came up to us and said that they didn't want a stigma attached to dockers because it had been said that it was dockers who were these heavies. And they said that they would stay all night and protect us. And they *did*! And then bricklayers came along and they offered to help. And a lot of the fellas who'd been out there doing the demolition were actually ashamed, I thought, of what they were doing. And I said to one of them, 'Look, if I could get you the money that you were going to be paid for this, would you stop?' So I made an appeal for money from the crowd saying that we should pay these men and maybe they'd go away and realise that they were destroying part of the city. And this man came over and handed me £100. And £100 then was a fair amount of money. So I met with these men in O'Donoghue's pub and we had this big long talk and they agreed that they would stop and leave. So we were able to get enough money to actually pay them off and that was a great coup for us.

"The third night we were getting worried. And Haughey was gone now, he was no longer the Minister for Finance. And we had been trying to get in touch with George Colley who became the new minister. Eventually we told him what was happening and he got on to Jack Lynch. But they couldn't get Corcoran, the developer. But, anyhow, the long and short of it was that about 2.00 in the morning we were told that Colley wanted to meet the people involved and with An Taisce. They wanted to meet the people involved to discuss the situation with them and they said they'd stop working [doing demolition]. So we were able then to go out and tell the crowd about 2.00 that the Minister for Finance had said the work would stop—no more demolition—that he was calling in the architect and the developer the following day. And we agreed to go home, to leave the building the following morning. And the people outside were to go home.

"So we stayed there until after the meeting with the minister and developer and we were told that they agreed that they would cease trying to demolish the buildings and they would submit new plans. And that was more or less the end of it. But now the end result wasn't as happy as I would like because the buildings were in *dreadful* condition at this stage and there was already dry rot in two of them. And they were all demolished . . . within months. And they put in very bad mock Georgian exteriors. I suppose we saved having a big modern office block on each corner but we weren't really satisfied with the results. But at least we made a developer do an about-turn. And I would say that it caused people to stop looking on Georgian Dublin as something that had been given to us by the Brits, the idea that this had been built by a foreign power. But it made Georgian facades respectable. And from then on, really, there was a rash of these awful facades on Harcourt Street and Leeson Street and places like that. I think that was the most sinister aspect of it. And then we started the Dublin Living City Group that same year because these *marvellous* old communities were being broken up and it's very traumatic for the old people when they're moved out. So we were concerned with trying to save these communities. I take pride in being a participant because we actually got in there and gave up our time to get something done."

7

Dockland Alive, Alive-O!

WILLIAM MURPHY—DOCKER AND PINTMAN, AGE 87

He was born in Ringsend where as a lad he had many encounters with the British Tommies and feared Black and Tans. At age 12 he went to work barefooted on the docks where stevedores ruled like dictators and demanded bribes from men hired. Like other dockers, he became a hardy pintman, imbibing pints of porter to dispel fatigue and renew energy. In 1925 his father joined the dockers' strike and when scabs were recruited his family went hungry. It taught him that unions offered the only protection for the working man. After fifty-five years of heaving mightily and earning paltry wages he confides, "It was no life."

“I was born in 1909 in Thorncastle Street in Ringsend. Me father worked on the docks and me grandfather was a ship's carpenter. I had three brothers and two sisters . . . they're all gone, I'm the only one that's left. We lived in an ordinary tenement house. My father worked so hard on the docks that he done two coal boats a day. He started at five and six o'clock in the morning and finished up around eight. My father was six foot three and sixteen stone weight. He was a boxer. His nickname was 'Bendigo' because he had a little bit of a bend in his legs.

"Ringsend was like a little village and the British were here at that time. The British military was on the streets patrolling. I was about 9 years old and in me bare feet and I was passing a big fruit shop and I seen an apple and says, 'I'd like that apple.' And I went in and there was a lovely man behind the counter, about six foot or more, serving two or three women. And in comes the sergeant of the British troops and he says, 'Hands up!' And the chap behind the counter goes on serving the women. And he says, 'I said *hands up!*' and he hit him a box. And the soldiers behind him had the sergeant covered with their rifles. And the chap behind the counter says, 'Will you drop that rifle and come outside and have a fair fight?' And he hit him *another* box. I pitied the poor chap. These were the British Tommies. Some of them were bad enough. They never said anything to me cause I was only young.

"But I had dealings with the Black and Tans. *Bastards* they were. One of them chased me down Pearse Street. He was chasing me cause they were holding up and searching everyone and I run and he couldn't fire into the crowd and I knew where to run down Garden Lane. But I done a foolish thing though cause I shouldn't have run. I was putting meself in danger but I was strong headed and I could *run*. He couldn't open fire because of all the people. He was running and he kept shouting out, 'Stop, you bastard, *stop!*' Finally he got tired but I heard him shouting at me. And I lived in Abbey Street with me sister for a while and there's a laneway there and there was whiskey stores and I heard them at night time with the butt of their rifles breaking them doors down to get into the whiskey. It was terrible. When they'd get whiskey they were worse. Oh, they went mad altogether. And one time my father stood in a read for a boat in Ringsend and the Tans come down and they seen the crowd of men and they jumped out of their lorry with their revolvers. And my father was a strong headed man and the Tan that held him up—he was robbing him—he was trembling with fear and me father says, 'I think I'll clout this fella.' And all the men said, 'Christy, *don't*, for God's sake, don't.' He'd have been shot. And they held up a brother of mine on Shelbourne Road when he was out after curfew hours. Oh, they were the *scum* of England. They were *murderers, rapists*. They opened all the prisons in England and let them all over, sent them over to either kill or be killed.

"When I started on the docks I wasn't even 13. The way I got a job was accidental. I was after rambling around the city and I was going home for me dinner and I seen this crowd outside the gate at Wallace's [coal merchants] and I says, 'There must be trouble here', and I went up to have a look. And he says, '*You.*' A read was going on and I didn't know. I thought it was a row. And he says, 'C'mon you'. And I never backed out of anything. And I got a loan of *one* boot. Some chap lent me a right-footed boot. And we worked from 5.00 till 8.00. That was me baptism. And as young fellas we were running in and out with [hand] trucks [unloading fruit]. 'Greyhounds' we were called, we were flashing in and out. And you had to watch the back of your heels in case a fella'd run into you with a truck behind you. Oh, it'd take a lump out of the back of your leg. The boss'd be saying, 'C'mon, c'mon, c'mon!' Oh, if you said anything [back] you need apply no more. Slavery!

"Stevedores, they had the power of the docks and if they had anything agin' you you were out—*out!* Stevedores would get up on a wall or get up aboard the boat and sometimes there'd be about 200 or 300 men and some of them went into the river with the shoving and pushing, all trying to get a job. Went into the river, but they were saved. But that's the way they picked you out. He could pick out one gang or three gangs or six gangs. Sometimes they'd pick over a hundred men. A timber boat could take well over a hundred men. And when it was getting late and you had an idea that you weren't going to get a job in this read you *dashed over* to the other read. I done that. And they paid you in pubs but Jim Larkin finally done away with all of that. The stevedores, they'd mix with theirselves, they'd keep their distance. Cause if you were seen drinking with a stevedore . . . you know what I mean? Now there was one man who was a picker-out, a stevedore, for a few coal merchants and 'Daddy' Byrne was his name. And men'd say, 'There's a cigarette in that package for you, Daddy', and along with that cigarette there'd be maybe two half-crowns. And some'd say, 'Daddy, do you want an apple?' And there'd be another two half-crowns stuck down in the centre of the apple. That's as true as God. It'd be done so me or you wouldn't catch it, but you *knew well* what it was. And he'd call them then when he'd pick out. You knew what was going on . . . but what could you do?

"My God, we got it hard on the docks. I worked boats of coal and slack. You had to put a silk stocking over your mouth with the coal but with the pitch you had to put it over your *eyes*. Yeah, cause if the pitch got into your eyes you were destroyed. I knew a man who lost his eye, but it didn't stop him from working. And I seen men killed on the docks. I seen a man and his head getting beat off the wall. His legs got caught in the rope and the wheel kept going around. It was an awful death. There was no protection then at all. Before the union. And when you were working a coal boat you'd keep sucking on a piece of coal to keep your mouth from getting dry. And when I worked on the docks there was no concrete, it was setts, all cobblestones. I often had to walk all the way up to the northside and down back to Ringsend. There was no buses running then to the North Wall. Coming up that North Wall at half past three in the morning after working a boat of grapes and me missus, the Lord have mercy on her, she was standing at the hall door when I come down. And I'd come home with grapes cause you could take as much as you liked.

"Now we got the 'beero' [break] at 10.00, it was half an hour, and you went for a sup of tea or to the pub. There was two canteens on the docks then and you could get a mug of tea or an egg and a rasher. But most men went to the pub for a pint. I always went in for a jug of tea and a rasher and a sausage. The pubs, there was Dooley's on the quay on the southside, there was Tobin's, there was Kennedy's up at the Butt Bridge and there was the Sugar Loaf and there was Bergin's pub and his daughter had another pub that's called the Ferryman now. Bergin's daughter run that but she was caught diluting the whiskey and she got a heavy fine and gave it up altogether.

"Publicans knew all the men, knew all the 'coalies', every one of them. Pubs had sawdust and spittoons and you'd spit into that. And you'd wipe yourself [after working coal boats] before you'd go into the pub as best you could, rub a handkerchief around your face. The men that I knew would put down over a dozen pints a day, easy. They were that dry. I drank all porter, I never liked whiskey. The pint used to be lovely. It was made from barley and at that time the pint was pulled with the pumps and you had to wait nearly ten minutes and when you'd go to lift it off the counter the tumbler would be *stuck*. Porter strengthened you all right. It's all chemicals now. But I wouldn't touch whiskey. Whiskey drinkers were nearly all blocky men, nearly all countrymen, like farmers. Oh, they'd love their whiskey. You'd know by their faces that they were whiskey drinkers because their faces nearly always goes red, flushed. And they might drink it hot with a few cloves in it. And in Ringsend every publican knew who he was dealing with and if you were short and stuck for a pint he'd *give* it to you and you'd pay him when you got a job. Put it on the slate. But he wouldn't let it go too high. Publicans were very united with the men. Definitely.

Like help with funerals, they were very good that way.

"When there was no work on the docks we all went over to the markets and I drank in a public house at 7.00 in the morning in the market. And there were *gentlemen* drank in the market. And I got drunk one day with a gentleman. He got talking with me, a big shot with plenty of money, didn't cost me a penny. Just to get in conversation with you. And at 10.00 in the morning I fell outside of that shop, drunk. And I struggled up and I crossed over to the far side to Moore Street and got *another* pint. And there was one pub in Werburgh Street and there was musicians and you were merry in the morning till the last thing at night. Singing and melodeons and fiddles and everything. They were very good, lovely singers and musicians. And if you went in you were leaving the musicians a pint. Oh, great sport. And dancing and all on the floor, waltzing around on the floor. It was a lovely pub. In the summer you'd be sitting outside and the house'd be full and you'd be listening to the songs. There was a fella, he was an ex-British soldier, and, by God, what a singer he was! The owner of the pub wanted him to go away and get his voice trained, but he wouldn't go. You could listen to him all night. And now shebeens, they were after hours, till 3.00 and 4.00 in the morning. Same thing as a speakeasy, you don't let the guards hear your voice. There was one in Marlborough Street. Once you had the money they'd close down and keep you in. And on Marlborough Street there were prostitutes in it. That was an awful pub with the prostitutes. He was an American run it. He was a big powerful man. The prostitutes would be drinking in there and a lot of men would go in there for that purpose, pick them up in the pub.

"In Ringsend in my time you'd hardly see a woman in a public house. No. When I was only a young fella I knew a woman and she used to call me every time and say, 'Go over and get me a pint of stout.' She didn't call it a pint of stout, she called it a pint of 'X' and she'd give me a big jug. And that was a penny for me when I come back. And I played around her door every time when I knew she wanted a pint. A lovely woman, a granny. I played around that door and *never* left me eye off that door. She used to get a pint but my mother drank a gill, a half-pint, and she'd put a red poker in it and stir it around and then drink it. They called it 'mulling' it.

"In the 1925 strike me father went hungry. It started over looking for a raise and the employers wouldn't give it. Now there was a man who worked in Ted Castle's [coal merchants] called O'Toole. He was a docker who only worked coal, and he had a pair of hands on him as big as shovels. And a man named Foran, a big shot in the Transport Union in Liberty Hall, gave O'Toole orders to go down to Bray, Wicklow, Galway, anywhere, and bring up scabs. And he went down and brought them all up here. Some of them slept in Wallace's stables, some of them slept in Liberty Hall—under police protection now. And then the drivers delivering the coal, they were scabs too. Yeah, cause the drivers all come out on strike. And they went around delivering coal with two armed policemen behind them. They were escorted everywhere.

"So me father was on strike. My father could have been with the scabs and he said, 'No, I'll never work with scabs. I *never* scabbed.' Oh, I'm telling you, he was a hard man. Families went hungry. And a lot of them scabbed it. The dockers, even up to the day they died, they hated the scabs. They're nearly all gone now. Scabs wouldn't mix, they were afraid. They'd drink with a fellow scab. They went a distance to drink, out of the way. They were no good, they were all countrymen. Well, there was a few Dublin men. There was one man down in Ringsend scabbed it too and he had to sleep in Wallace's stable. I know a man who got six months for hitting a scab. He pulled him off the lorry under police protection and the police arrested him. Six months. Pulled him off the lorry and hit him a few punches and he got six months in Mountjoy. And I'll tell you what happened in a pub I was at on Spencer's Dock [years later]. There was twelve of us men and one was a [former] scab and we finished the boat and was getting paid and one man got the whole twelve men's money to give out to the other men. He gave the money out to the men and then it came to the scab's turn and he says, 'Where's my money?' And he says, '*There* it is', and he hit him a *box*. Ah, he put the scab flying and you'd want to see that scab fella running.

"Now that union, the Irish Seamen and Port Workers' Union, I'm a founder member of that union. You needed a union to protect you and fight for you. We were lost without a union. That's how the employers could do anything they liked. Then things were a long way better. We got two new canteens, you got certain hours you could work, you wouldn't work till 2.00 or 3.00 in the morning without a break, like, before the union when there was no protection at all. But then the buttons come out in 1947 and they were the worst thing that ever come out. The union brought them out, the union we formed, and there was bribery in that. Ah, yes, all bribery, the buttons. That was the worst thing that ever come out and at a meeting I *stated* that because you need other men as your fellow workmates. And if he had no button and he was your workmate and if *you* were a button man there was always a bit of bad feeling. I said, '*Do away* with the buttons. Sure, when I started on the docks there was no buttons and me father never had buttons. Let every man take his chances, let it be an open read and there'll be no enemies.' But, no, they turned it down, they wanted the buttons because there was a lot of bribery. I've known men that never done a day's work on the docks. One of them was a boxer and because he was a boxer and had this [money] he come down to the docks with a *button*. There was about 500 or 600 buttons. You had to go to the union for a button. They knew your background and you mentioned your father's name. I had no trouble getting a button. But I said it should be done away with.

"Now if I seen there was a good bit of work on the docks I'd say to the non-button fellas, 'Get in there.' And some of them got in and got jobs, they did. And I mixed with them non-button men and I showed them how to do it—I learned them. And I never regretted it. And when I went into a pub a couple of times uptown it never cost me. And I didn't know where the pints was coming from till one man come down and says, 'I was with you when you were learning me on the docks.' They remembered it. And I'll tell you what happened to me another night. I was coming out of a pub one night in Gardiner Street and I was going down Marlborough Street and there was a pub, it was a shebeen. But all these non-button men drank in it and they were all outside this night at closing time and I could hear one fella saying, 'Oh, here's another so-and-so button man.' And I said to meself, 'Oh, I've *had it* here.' There was only one thing to do, keep walking and put up with it. And one fella stepped out and says, 'Youse don't put your hand on him. If all the button men down there were like him we'd be all right. Go ahead, William. Good night.' They never forgot it.

"I worked fifty-five years on the docks. But my wife died after sixteen years [of marriage]. It was T.B. Very prevalent. It took me months to get meself together and every time I got a job after that me mind wasn't on it . . . I used to be thinking of her. And when I'd no one I used to work late till 9.00 at night and when I'd come in there'd be no fire lighting, no dinner. It was disheartening. I was going into a pub when I was done, staying there till 10.00 and maybe bringing home a fish and chips . . . and me clothes half wet. It was no life."

TOM BYRNE—A DOCKLAND CHILDHOOD, AGE 80

He was born near the docks into a family of seafaring men and dockers who retained a strong oral tradition. Dockland children swam in the River Liffey and played on railway coal wagons but such dangerous activities meant losing chums in fatal accidents. As a young lad he was terrified by a drunken Black and Tan who aimed his revolver at him. But dockland was an exciting place, alive with thousands of men swarming to and from reads and in his home James Larkin was a "Messiah". He spent his life on the docks working for shipping companies and warehouse firms and had great admiration and compassion for the old dockers as they laboured so nobly to survive.

"My parents, one was born on Oriel Street and the other was born on Emily Place, off Sheriff Street. They lived within a hundred yards of each other. It was a parochial atmosphere at that time, nobody went outside of the parish to get married. It was the parish of Laurence O'Toole. I was born off Oriel Street on Canning Street. There was nine children including a set of triplets. There was nine of us and it was pretty hard going. Four died at an early age. At that time child mortality was very high. The triplets, two of them died before they were 2 years old. And another sister, Bridie, died at about 3 . . . she was lovely. She got pneumonia. And the doctor at that time told my mother, 'Let the window down and get plenty of air into the room.' And my mother, naturally, accepted the doctor's word at that time and I think he was actually responsible for the child's death.

"When I was young most members of the family were at sea, me father and me uncles. And when they went away you'd say, 'Well, he's gone', and it'd be eighteen months or two years maybe. It was always a reasonably long trip because they'd be going out through the Suez Canal and maybe off to Calcutta, Bombay. And for a fair while me father was trading from Portland, Oregon, to

Australia. They were hauling railway engines and tracks to Australia from the west coast of America. My father was a seaman all his life. He went to sea at 12 years old. And his father was a seaman. He was the skipper of a schooner. When my father went to sea at 12 they were on schooners and his uncle was the skipper of the schooner and they would educate him, if they were members of their own family. You'd be amazed how intelligent he was and well read. He went off on a schooner called the Lapwing. That's a sea bird. He was described then as a cook and he would peel the potatoes and get the galley going and the fire. And when there was a bit of rope hauling he'd be called out. And in fine weather he'd be put at the wheel. Schooners used to carry everything, like house bricks, chimney pots.

"My father got married at 27. It was dreadful for my mother with him at sea. He was getting twenty-six shillings a week and she would collect the money here at the agents. When me father and me uncles would come back they'd be sitting around and as kids we'd be drawing them out and me father'd start telling us the stories. And they were really *very, very* good storytellers. They seemed to have good retention and they could paint sort of a mental picture for you when they'd be telling you about it. So I suppose in that way I might have inherited a little of that. Like, my father'd be telling you about when they were being coaled in India and there were *massive* heaps of coal there. And they'd have planks up from the quayside up on to the top deck of the ship, one up and one down. And there'd be a continuous chain of women, Indian women, walking around this heap of coal that had been discharged from the colliers and they'd have these baskets, like saucer-shaped baskets, wicker, and they'd have them on their heads and they'd go around in file. And there was a man there with a shovel and he'd scoop up a shovelfull of coal into the basket and she'd put it on her head and move on. And then they'd go aboard the ship and when they'd pass the bunker hatch they tipped this into the hatch and filed around. And some of them would have young children and they'd be nursing. And he'd tell us how in Calcutta you'd see somebody getting their teeth out and they were sitting on the kerb and the dentist was pulling out their teeth. So we'd always be waiting patiently for my father to tell these things and I could actually *see* it happening. Then when the children started coming along he decided that he'd have to look for something closer to home and he went into the cross-channel shipping. Looking back now on those seamen, they were a race apart. There was a sort of staunchness about them. As a boy I used to go backwards and forwards with them and I used to sleep in me father's bunk on the ship cause he'd take me on a voyage with him during me school holidays, to England. I enjoyed it and Liverpool was a great place at that time. It was a great treat for me lying out at anchor in the Mersey looking at all the liners.

"There were a number of people in our area who were involved in the Republican movement at the time and the Black and Tans used to come around and raid the houses at night. I was only a child about 6 years old at the time. The tenders would come around and they'd hop out and surround the whole place. Looking back on it now I see that a number of them must have been 'head cases' that were hospitalised out of the army and this kind of business—and it was all right to put them in *here*. Cause the things they did were *barbarous*. Like, on Seville Place there was the Gaelic Football Club and they raided that place on one occasion and took one of the men out and dragged him behind the tender. They made him run and then you're going to run out of breath, of course, and then they dragged him. His two hips were broken and the man hobbled for the rest of his life. At that time they weren't great at patching up hips. I remember the man well. They took out people and they'd look for information. If they got the idea that the people *had* information and didn't *give* it—which very often *was* the case—the people were just taken out and they were found the next morning in a ditch on the roadside or up some alleyway. Oh, that happened on a wide scale. A drunken Black and Tan frightened me as a kid. I was outside and this Black and Tan came along and he had a pair of those black canvas-rubber shoes on him and he had two revolvers in his hands. And there was no one in the street, only me. So I was out there playing and he just did this to me [pointed revolvers], a bit of a joke, you know. Of course, I was frightened. Hearing the tales and all, you thought he was just going to pull the trigger.

"When I was 8 or 9 years old we were living down on Seville Place and kids used to swim down in the River Liffey. I swam in the Liffey *meself*. Oh, yeah. Some of them used to swim across the river to the southside and then come back again. And there was a number of boys drowned. And some of the young fellas used to jump into the river that *couldn't swim*. So what they used to do, they used to take the lifebuoys on the stand and they used to let the line go and they'd take that line in their hands and they'd jump into the river with it and haul themselves over then with the rope. But they couldn't *swim*! It took a bit of courage, you know. I remember one fella and he had the rope too short and when he jumped in it was like a pendulum and he banged off the wall and the poor fella was drowned, the Lord have mercy on him.

"Now they discharged coal into railway wagons [on the quays] and they'd have all the empty wagons backed up this incline and they'd have the brakes on them. So on a summer's evening the kids would get over the wall at the dock and they'd be in swimming and some of them used to get up on the wagons and other fellas would let the brakes go and the wagon would run down the incline and hit the bumpers at the bottom. That was great cause they'd be sitting on front of the wagon going down. So this one fella was sitting on the front of the wagon and he dropped off it and the wagon went right across his back. And I *run up* cause a bit of a commotion had started and I thought it was some child after falling into the river. But when I went up they said, 'Don't go near him, he's finished.' And I looked and you could still *see his* back rising. It was nerves probably. He was dead, he was finished. The clothes were holding him together, he had his little jacket on. He would have been about 10.

"As a young lad I started as a messenger boy and then I worked in a brushmaker's. It was Varian's on Talbot Street. I worked on a sandpapering machine and then I was promoted around age 14 to the spindles where I was putting squares of timber through and they were coming out as brush handles at the other end. It was a modern machine that came from Germany and it was *out of this world* as far as I was concerned. Oh, there was hundreds working there, about 300. And men sat around a big round table with a pitch pan in the centre and it was heated with a little gas ring underneath and the pitch all melted. Any money I made there I turned over to me mother and it gave me great pleasure to do that. And she'd give us some back for the cinema. We used to go to the tuppenny rush on a Saturday, only two pennies. That was the Saturday matinee. Westerns, like Tom Mix, and Charlie Chaplin. And you had to queue early to get in. And just bare wooden seats. And we used to have a little bag of treats from Conroy's sweet shop, lovely little mixture of sweets. And the toffee bar was lovely. We used to go to the old Electric Picture House, it was by Amiens Street Station. It was called the 'Elec', it was an old fleabag. They used to say that you'd walk in and you're carried out—the *fleas* would carry you out!

"Then I went to sea when I was 15. I was in Coast Lines running around the coast of Britain from Liverpool to Plymouth to Southampton, on British ships. It was all cargo we carried. I liked it but I was *permanently* seasick. So I was only about eight months at that, but I gave it a good try. Then I went into the shipping warehouse for the same company, it was B & I. I was a storeman looking after each ship's cargo that came in. You segregated cargo and checked it in against the manifest. I was most of me life at that. But I did dock work as well . . . I did nearly everything. When the war started I was in Birmingham at the Austin aircraft factory. Then I came home and was working in the dockyard with shipwrights at a variety of jobs. I did nearly everything.

"My grandfather was a docker and a coal porter and he was handy with horses. And he was a *big* man, about six foot six and twenty-one stone weight. But he wasn't a *fat* man. He was active on the docks long before Larkin came. And when Larkin came they looked upon him like the *Messiah*. What he said was law, that was it, they accepted it. He had a great gift of the gab, Larkin. So you couldn't say anything [negative] cause 'Larkin was a great man.' And we grew up listening to this. And he knew Larkin well and Larkin knew him well. There was great antagonism over the 1913 strike. And when Larkin went away to the United States to seek funds for the workers of Dublin the British Government got the American Government to haul Larkin in and he was interned in Sing-Sing at the behest of the British Government. Oh, yeah, it's on record. While Larkin was away and interned the British Government was still in occupation here. So while he was away the employers here, behind the scenes, there was a group organised to work with the employers and there was a lot of *scab* labour brought in. They wouldn't employ the old workers. The scabs were actually sleeping in the shipping sheds on the North Wall cause they were afraid to go out. The police would come along in large numbers and escort them up the quays. There was a number of them injured and thrown into the river.

"Then they went into the Irish Transport and General Workers' Union which was the union that Larkin formed. So when they took over the Irish Transport in Larkin's absence they elected him *out* because they knew if he came back that he certainly wouldn't have them in occupation. So then he formed his own union, the Workers' Union of Ireland. And the union office was in Marlborough Street and that's where the Workers' Union Hall was there and he used to have boxing there, used to form boxing clubs for the youth in the area. And he used to have dances there. Larkin organised that. And there was Larkin's band formed and they used to call themselves the Suffering Ducks, the bandsmen. See, there was an old Dublin saying at that time, they used to say, 'Oh, suffering ducks, look at who's coming!' The band was very prominent at that time and they'd say, 'The Suffering Ducks are going out tonight', maybe to an electioneering meeting. When my grandfather died the band played for him down from the hospital to the church when he died and we had to walk behind. Oh, my grandfather was very prominent at that time with Larkin. The band marched behind the remains all the way down.

"Ah, and the animal gangs was about in 1936 or 1937. There was some dockers involved. They were tough customers and there was some fellas there and they would have made a good living if they had got into the boxing. Cause they were good and they had plenty of guts and all. But the row would get out of hand and there'd be pitched battles with weapons and all. Now guard '123', his name was Byrne, he was very slight built, he was a Clint Eastwood type, a fair complexion fella. And he was a *loner*. And he used to prowl the rough areas. Other fellas would go out in the squad car to pick up a fella and there'd be maybe four or five of them in the squad car. But if he wanted to pick anyone up he'd walk in *himself* and he'd bring them out! And if a fella was inclined to be a bit rough he'd say, 'Now, look, you're *going in*. I'll *bring* you in. I'll tell you what I'll do. We'll have a go here [in the street] and if you beat me you can go ahead about your business. But if I *beat you*, you're going in.' And the fella'd be brought in and he wouldn't say that he resisted arrest or anything. He was famous at that time and the fellas seemed to respect him. All had kind of a respect for him . . . they were afraid of him.

"Dockers had a hard life. I seen a number of fellas killed on the docks. A hard life, their conditions were very bad. It was physical and they weren't terrible well paid for the job. The money was small, like they got six and eight shillings for working a ship. They were paid each day then. And they went home and gave the wife so much and it meant that they had something left for a couple of drinks and a package of cigarettes. A package of Woodbines was two pence, with five Woodbines in it. But the conditions under which they worked were *shocking*. They were out in all weather and no holidays, no sick pay, no nothing. The fellas that worked the coal boats, they had big shovels and it was a peculiarly shaped shovel called a No. 7. It was shaped and went down to a point at the bottom. Well, when they'd be digging it into the coal their one foot would be digging in and the boot would wear. So when they'd be getting their boots repaired they'd tell the local bootmaker to put digging bits on them. This was a piece of leather that they used to get tacked on there. The whole thing was built-up, like, and it saved wear. Because boots were a *costly item* at that time out of the small money that they had, so they had to protect their footwear.

"In bad weather in winter the dockers would put a black scarf around their neck and sort of half-knotted. And they only got a half an hour off for their meal and someone [family member] would bring down a billycan and you could have tea or soup in that. And they always had a clean woollen sock and they'd put the can into the sock and it'd keep it warm. They might get some soup or stew or maybe they'd just send down tea and sandwiches. They just sat down on the dockside where they were. And dockers believed that drink was their nourishment. Cause the *quality* wasn't like today. It's like dishwater what they're giving in pubs now. And stevedores had the power to hire and fire and some of them used to take advantage of it and they took a backhander from the men in the pubs. See, they used to pay the men in the pubs and then they'd be getting drink back from them. Some of these dockers felt *obliged* to give him the drink cause they wouldn't get work otherwise. And there was great company in pubs then with dockers. They had conversations on politics and you'd be amazed to listen to their political discussions. And there'd be trade union discussions. It wouldn't be just trivial stuff. And then they might finish off with a bit of a song and there was some lovely singers. And when some of the fellas, seamen, would come home after being away on long trips they'd be singing these emigrant songs and their relations would all be with them. Some *beautiful* singers, like Johnny Cullen, he was a tenor. And another fella, Pat Bradshaw, he wouldn't sing unless he had a few drinks and then he'd go out and sit on the doorstep and he'd sing. And people'd knock off what they were doing to go out and listen to him.

"When I was young there was *thousands* of men working down on the docks. And at 5.00 there'd be *hordes* of men going from work. And when the Angelus in church would ring the men'd stand and take off their caps and say the Angelus. They were very religious. And when we were young there used to be annual missions and the church we used to go to was Laurence O'Toole's church and I was an altar boy in that church. And during the mission the men would knock off from the coal carriers and just throw water on their face from the open horse troughs on the way. Just go along and *throw* the water on their face and take out a handkerchief and they'd have a black scarf around their neck and they'd knock off from the job and go into the church for the mission. It'd start sharp at 8.00 [evening] and the church would be full and it'd go on till about half nine. And they'd sit there and some of them wouldn't have had anything to eat. And you'd look down at them, men that was after working *all* day, *physically* played out, and there they'd be going to the mission. As an altar boy I used to look down at them and I had the height of sympathy for them. Some of them was *tough* customers. And the mission would go on for a fortnight. They got Saturday night off to go to Confessions. And when a docker died all his mates would be there. The hearse would go around his house and it'd go down around the docks and as he'd be passing the ships the fellas would stand and lift their caps and just stand there until the funeral had passed."

PADDY ROBINSON—STEVEDORE, AGE 88

At age 14 he began work on the docks as a "singer-out" on coal boats where he saw men crushed to death by the huge swinging tubs. After digging coal himself for twenty years he became a powerful stevedore in control of men's lives and their families' welfare. Despite efforts to be fair, he made enemies and sometimes had to resort to using his boxing skills. In an age when many stevedores were tyrants he was respected as a "decent fella" who treated dockers with dignity.

"I'm a Dublin man but I'm coming from the Aran Islands. There was a picture made, *Man of Aran*, and all my people were in that. They used to use a curragh and they'd put a line on their cattle or their horses and they'd tow them across to Galway. My father was one of seven brothers and he was the youngest and they wouldn't let him go to sea. The other six went to sea. But me father was born here in Dublin because me grandmother come up to Dublin. Her husband was a deep sea captain and she married him and they come up here to Dublin. And me grandmother had a shop by where Butt Bridge is and she had two windows, one was rigged out with oilskin hats and boots was in the other window, long high boots that was for seamen. And me other grandmother was making the Aran sweaters. She was in Peterson's Lane. She'd go aboard the ships and sell them to the sailors.

"Me father had a horse and dray and he delivered coal all around the city. Now he didn't deliver coal all his life, he began to work for a stevedore and he worked the ships from then on. He was digging the coal out of the ships, a docker. When I was 3½ me father picked me up in his arms and the 1913 strike was on, Larkin's gang. And there was a bit of a kick-up here over the children being brought away and they was supposed to be getting taught Protestantism, which was all *wrong*. The Larkinites done that. Anyway, my father cut all that out and he wasn't going to take any chances, so he threw me on his shoulder, walked the North Wall, went into a pub and called out the steward of a Scotch boat and gave the steward a letter and said he'd be paid in gold if he took me away. And he was to take me halfway up the Clyde [River]—they used to discharge the cattle there—and he was to meet this woman with the money there with the letter and all. She was me father's sister and I'd be safe with the uncle as well even though he was a Protestant. She was a Catholic woman from here but her husband was a Protestant. He was a shipyard man. He had a great skill for building ships. Oh, she was well-to-do. Do you know what she came [to collect me] in? A coach and four horses.

"I went to school in Glasgow at St Anthony's and I was in the boys' choir as a boy soprano. And then when I was about 14 me father wrote me a letter that he wanted me back here to help. And I hardly knew me father. Only a very odd letter me father'd write to me in Glasgow but they knew that I was safe with me Aunt Kate. I was 14 and after starting serving me time in the shipyards learning how to build lifeboats. I got this letter from him that he wanted help, for me to get a job [in Dublin] and help to give him the wages for me mother. He was working on the docks but he wanted *extra* help to rear the others. There was fourteen in our family, seven boys and seven girls. And I didn't want to come back but I did, because they had been very good to me. But when he appealed to me I couldn't let it go. So I came home here and got a job in Heaton's [coal company] telling the crane man what to do. I was a 'singer-out.' A singer-out was to protect the men in the hatch. First of all, he'd shout out to the men in the hatch to 'Look out below!' That's telling them to get in out of the way. And then the crane man would come in with the crane and lower it [coal tub] and they'd pull it where they wanted it and then when it was full up the crane man would lift away. Singer-outs were mostly old men but there was no other job for me. The boss made me a singer-out and he took the responsibility. And there *were* accidents. For instance, there was a young man *crushed* between two tubs. You should *never* go between two tubs, especially when you put the hook on cause that tub is going to lift and it'll swing there and God knows where it'll go.

"I remember O'Mahoney our boss and he was like the gangster Edward G. Robinson. Oh, he had the trilby hat and all. He was the manager of the coal company. He had power. He called me one day and I think I was about 16 and I was getting an odd job [digging] on the ships. And he walked behind me this day and he says, 'Robinson.' And I looked back and says, 'Yes, sir?' And he says, 'Is it a fact that you don't smoke and you don't drink?' And I said, 'That's right.' I didn't drink for twenty-six years. 'Well,' says he, 'I have you marked down in the book and you're going to get promoted sooner or later cause I know that you have a bit up there [head].' He predicted a future for me.

"But I dug coal ships for twenty years, with the No. 7 shovel, a big round shovel with a sharp eye like an ace of spades. Whitehaven was the best shovel, made in England. And they used to call us 'Whitehaveners.' Some of the companies provided the shovels and they'd put holes or something in them to mark them, but they were still knocked off. Steal them and bring them home, keep it for themselves. We might earn thirty shillings. And coal men'd be black all over. It was always only your teeth and your eyes showing. And when you're down on the docks you'd get *all* nicknames. I was known as 'P.R.' That was me initials and they called me 'P.R.' down on the reads. When I was a stevedore I hated to call them by their nicknames. No, I thought it was degrading on a man being called by a nickname. But I *had* to do that because I didn't know his name, but I knew his nickname. I mean, you got a christening for your own name. Like, there was a man called 'the dummy' cause he couldn't talk.

"And one thing that struck me all me life was the fact that you'd hear a man uptown, say a respectable guy thinking he was great, and he'd say, 'He was using docker's language', and I *hated* to hear that because I knew that dockers *respected* women and it got me down, got me annoyed. They were uppish. *One* thing about the dockers was that if a girl was knocking around with us *nobody* would curse while she'd be there. *No* bad language at all. The docker believed in that. They were the best in the world, take their money home and take very little back for tobacco or to go to a football match for a shilling. But dockers never went to picture houses. They *never* had time for picture houses. I never went to a picture house. No, I'd go into the Abbey [theatre] and see the acting.

"Now years ago sometimes we were paid in pubs. And that was *wrong.* Years ago the stevedore used to make money that way. He'd go into the pub and pay you and then you could leave him a half a quid that wasn't noticed. And then there was other times that the stevedore got money in a cigarette box or a matchbox. Oh, yes. And then another thing in the pubs, a fella'd go in there to have a pint himself and he'd say to the publican, 'Leave a half for such a fella', and the half was a little piece of coal that size and it was put up on the shelf. If there were two halves it would be one pint. It was according to the size of the coal put up on the shelf, a little bit of coal that would constitute a half of a whiskey and a bigger piece, that was for a pint. And then the stevedore'd go in and was told, 'There's something here for you.' My father used to *dread* it because he believed in standing like a man to get a job and if he didn't get a job he'd walk away, but other fellas would be *pleading* with the stevedore, crying up in his face. Some of them'd believe in that . . . but me father would walk away.

"Eventually I took the job of stevedore. I was about 35 when I got the job. But I wasn't terribly keen on the job because you make enemies. I give you a job and leave him out and I'll make an enemy of him. I always wore a white shirt. I was known as the man with the white shirt. Always. I put on a collar no matter where I was. Because me missus would do it up real nice. That shirt would be washed, starched and pressed. There was a reading time from 8.00 to 10.00. I'd stand up on anything. I used to stand up on to a [railway] tip car cause the crowds would knock you down. Oh, fighting for work. Could be 100 to 200 men. You'd get to know them. You'd have to know the ability of the men. Like, you could pick the biggest men and they were the worst workers. The big fellas were no use. We used to call them 'elastic backs' because they'd be so tall.

"I was able to pick the men for *hard* jobs that the others couldn't do. Like, if you had a coke boat you couldn't get anyone to take jobs on a coke boat because it was so tough. Because you'd have to hand pick it sometimes and your hands would be bleeding. Coke is coal that is burned in a furnace and the foundries here would take that. Oh, yes, it was very crusty and your fingers would be all scraped. Oh, God, you couldn't get *through* it. And I'll tell you, I done one or two pitch boats and that's *all*, and I said I wouldn't do any more. Pitch was terrible cause the pitch burns your eyes and the ear. You could never guarantee your sight. You got a powder, an ordinary powder for, like, making you cool, like a talcum powder, and you spread it on yourself and you got a lady's stocking and pull it down over your chin and it'd stop the pitch from penetrating. But then you could hardly breathe. I knew two men that was working it up in the yards to make briquettes and them two died with cancer. Yeah, cause the pitch brings cancer and you'd get cancer sores.

"Once you didn't pick a man you'd know the fella was disgusted . . . and I was often disgusted meself. A fella'd come and say, 'You didn't give me a job', and I felt bad meself. You wouldn't feel right at all. One time there was a fella and he was corrupt and he come down after a read for a big ship and I was after employing nearly 120 men. But I wouldn't employ him because he was a lazy son of a bitch and I just said, 'Leave him there.' So when I went down to the ship after sending the men down there he was ranting and raving and calling my name. And I went down the gangway and walked up to him—and he was a big fella about six foot two and he was a waster—and I walked over to him and says, 'Are you looking for trouble'? And I took off me coat and I'm looking up at him. 'Well,' says he, 'I don't want any trouble with you. You know how to use yourself', and he got lost. That's a fact. I had no fear of any man. Me father taught me that when I was young and he was a good boxer himself. They put me down as a lightweight, but I could use meself. In fact, I was attacked in the house by three fellas because I didn't employ them. They were drunk and they come up to me in Townsend Street and I wasn't drinking and they came up shouting and all and I just said to the missus, 'You just stay there', and I come down the stairs and I made a run at them and smashed the banister and we all fell down. And I went to town on them and threw them out of the hall. I done the *three* of them, cause I had a bit of boxing experience. I said to them, 'Go home and get sober.' And then I was never challenged cause when I put them three fellas down the stairs it went around like wildfire.

"Now there was a strike in 1925 and they threw a bomb into the Custom House where the scabs were sleeping. In 1925 the dockers declared war on the [coal] merchants. Then the likes of Heaton's [coal company] brought the scabs down from Rush and the North of Ireland. Men that wanted a job, they come down and scabbed it on us and we called them scabs. There was even two schoolmasters from the North of Ireland came and scabbed it. Yeah, cause the money was there. But they couldn't dig properly and they had to be trained for that. They came up and just put shovels in their hands. They were there in the Custom House, locked in, and there'd be thirty or forty scabs in there. And wherever the ship would be they were escorted down there by the police. They'd be escorted to their work and *dare you* put a finger on a scab! That was a real charge and you were brought up before the magistrates. And some of the fellas forgot about them scabbing it, they'd [scabs] buy them off. There's men that'd forget their own religion for a few shillings or to get a pint or two from the fellas. I had no rancour against them, never, cause I just said to myself, 'They're *ill*, there's something wrong with them, they're a low type.' That's what I thought.

"Dockers drank around the docks. They always got a plain porter. And you used to be able to get a half and half, half a stout and half a porter. And some of the pubs would sell pig's feet. Coal men'd be black all over. Pubs were open from 7.00 [morning] cause the justices seen that these men were working so strong and they needed a bit of a meal in the morning. It was just a sandwich or something. But the bit of a meal gradually faded out and then it was just drink. Oh, there was men that *lived* on pints, no dinner or tea or nothing. 'Beero' was at 10.00 till half ten. Then you knocked off at 12.00 for your lunch. And then you knocked off at half past three for another beero. Now I didn't take any pints when I was working. I took milk, a big quart of milk at the time. So we'd get our beero break, but my beer was milk. But the other fellas was into the pub for a drink. They had an export stout in Guinness's one time and we knew the barrels cause they were all painted blue on the rims. They were export going to India and Africa and all. They called it export stout. Some of the sailors that was aboard the ship tasted it and it was strong. And there was hoggers that would spill one barrel on the top of another one with the red raddle [around the rim] and their mouths and all would be full of this and they were called hoggers. You knew that he was a hogger when you seen him with the red on his face.

"There was a pub over on the northside there and it was called the Kind Lady. A woman used to run it. It was called the Kind Lady cause some of the sailors they'd be tapping her for credit and the kind lady would look after them, so they christened it the Kind Lady. I'd say she was between 50 and 60. It was a speakeasy and it was 'shhh!' if you heard a noise outside. At *all* hours of the night. Two o'clock. Also, McCormack's pub in Townsend Street, he was a great big fat man, an ex-policeman. He used to look out the window and if you come along he'd come down and serve you for what you wanted. All you had to do was go along and stand there and he'd look out the window and he'd come down for you. You didn't have to knock or nothing. He'd come down to the door and give you the drink outside and he'd keep his eye out for policemen. And he'd get a telephone call when they were going to raid. He'd get tipped off.

"Now Kennedy's wasn't a docker's pub. Do you know why? Because the dockers found out that he used to let women in, *wrong* women, into the pub and therefore they didn't like Kennedy. He was supposed to be a great Catholic and he had a son going into the priesthood and so they called him a hypocrite cause he was entertaining these women to get money off them. Prostitutes. Yeah, he was taking the money that they were getting in the wrong way. He done that. And no other publican down there would do it. He was the only one that would take them girls in. They'd be met outside with the sailors and they'd make the appointment to go to Kennedy's and then they'd meet in there and it was a business deal. They'd be in a snug and then they'd go into the nearest laneway. Oh, the place was littered with these [laneway] places. Oh, it was terrible down there. The women'd meet with the sailors and get them drunk. And they deliberately used to put the [street] lamps out, with stones, so there'd be no light. And Kennedy was getting the cash for the drink he was selling them and they'd always take bottles of wine away with them and that was more cash for him."

JOE MURPHY—SHIPWRIGHT, AGE 70

A Ringsend native, he became a fourth-generation shipwright apprenticed in the ancient craft. From the old masters he learned everything there was to know about building sea-going ships. Some of his coveted tools, especially those inherited from his grandfather, are now museum pieces. When the demand for fishing boats declined he turned to making elegant yachts. After more than fifty years at his craft he is proud to be one of the last genuine shipwrights in Dublin.

"I was born in Ringsend. It was a little community you might say, a very close-knitted type of people. One helped the other. It started off as a fishing village and then the Tar Bays, these Protestant people from England came over. They were a different persuasion. When I was young we had a company here that used to import salt and coal, then we had the ice factories and we'd four rowing clubs there on the River Dodder and there was three boatyards there on the River Dodder. Oh, Ringsend was a very lively village. Ringsend men would very rarely drink outside of Ringsend. And another thing, if you married 'over the bridge' they wouldn't speak to you. When the rest of Ireland was on its knees during the war years from 1940 up to 1945 Ringsend had a very good time of it. At that stage uptown they were paying £1 15s. a pound for tea and they couldn't get sugar. They were using saccharin. And we were going around with pillow cases full of sea-logged tea and sugar. It just 'floated around', let's put it that way . . . it just got to Ringsend.

"Me father and me grandfather and me great grandfather were all shipwrights. And I'm the last of them because neither of the two sons I have are following the trade. They built the fishing smacks and then the sailing ships and there was a *tremendous* amount of work for shipwrights. And my grandfather's father, he had our own boatyard there and it was the second biggest boatyard in Ringsend. The yard was very, very successful . . . it held out to 1951. Bernard, my grandfather's father, he had blacksmiths there and nail-makers. There was no such thing as buying nails in those days. You had to make your own nails. And there were sail-makers. We made our own nets and our own sails and our own ironwork, cut all our own timber. Girls used to make the sails and the nets. I have the receipts in there from about 1820 or 1830.

"I lost me father when I was 4 years old. I believe he drowned out in the bay here. My grandparents reared me and I think that was an extra bonus because what my grandfather gave to me you couldn't buy it or teach it because he was giving me experience of years and years. And I was way ahead of everybody else. I mean, he'd more up his sleeve in ten minutes than a fella'd learn in a lifetime, cause he was a boatbuilder *and* a shipwright. And my grandmother, she used to send me over to 'Baldy' Fagan's pub for her gill. Now a gill was an enamel jug that held about a half a gallon and you went over and put this thing on the counter and sixpence and you carried this gill back for your grandmother. And she'd have the fire roaring red and she'd take this poker out about two foot long and it'd be red with sparks flying and she'd stick it into this jug and the *smell* off it . . . I used to run out the door! It mulled it, mulled the beer by putting this hot poker in it and then she drank it when it was lukewarm.

"My grandfather, he was a father to me. And he was a small man and he had badly burned hands and face. What happened was this. A very, very uneducated boatman in Ringsend came in one day and put a can of tar and pitch on the stove in the kitchen and it boiled over and went afire and set the house on fire. And when the house was blazing little Esther, my mother's sister, was *in* the house and he *charged* in to get her and got badly burned to such an extent that he was eight years in the hospital. And he was woefully disfigured. And when the house burned down it was discovered that the child was behind the door he went into! She was *just* behind the door. And a surgeon in Baggot Street Hospital patched him up with skin transplants. People who knew my grandfather had the highest respect for him.

"Myself now, I served me time under H. G. Smythe of Ringsend. He was a boatbuilder. You started at 14, a seven year apprenticeship. Under the shipwright's profession in those days you *couldn't* serve your time under your own father or grandfather. No, that wasn't allowed. You had to serve your time elsewhere. So, as a result, I was put in H. G. Smythe's yard for two years and then I was sent to the Ringsend dockyards for three years, then I was sent back to Smythe's for one year and I finished the last year in the Dublin Port and Docks Board. It was hard work, very hard. There was no let-up. You started at half past eight in the morning and you finished at 6.00 at night, working under one man. He was a naval architect. He was a very strict man. Now I remember on the first year of my apprenticeship he asked me how many rivets we got in and I said, approximately three hundred, and I forgot to say 'sir' and I was sent home. Yeah, I forgot to say 'sir' and I was sent home for one day to learn manners. So one day's pay, that was seven and sixpence, that was a lot of money. Then I always said 'sir.'

"What he taught me basically was woodwork and sheet metal work. And in those days a boatbuilder was expected to plumb the boat, wire the boat, put the engines in them, do the lot. So any apprentice that served his time there had to be a plumber, an electrician, a sheet metal worker, a woodworker and a painter. Apprentices were the most versatile characters you could ever come across. I wore mostly dungarees. Your lunch break was from half twelve to 1.00 and you had it on the workbench, a can of tea and a few sandwiches and that was your lot. And no smoking. And no bad language. Oh, the weather factor didn't come into the picture at all. I mean, it was nothing to be working outside and sweeping the snow off to find where the screw holes were that you bored the day before. Mostly outdoor work and you'd no protective clothing. You'd work in the rain to a certain point and then you'd be shifted into the shed. And no fires, because of all the dust and shavings. Your hands would go hard. It was very tiring work because in those small yards you'd nowhere to hide! I mean, when you went to work you went to work! And no tea break in the morning or the afternoon. You could drink water.

"The older shipwrights mostly kept to themselves. Basically, they were like most other craftsmen, they went to their work in the morning, had the ability and calibre to do the job, and they went home in the evening. Very rarely would they ever lend tools. Some of the men were very cold and distant, they didn't want to *tell* you anything. And this used to *baffle* me. You'd ask them a question and they'd give you some petty excuse and this used to annoy me very much.

Most of them, due to the foreman, wouldn't tell you anything because they couldn't be seen talking to you. Oh, God, no. Cause they'd be wasting the employer's time. And men wouldn't part with their secrets, under no circumstances. What they feared was the young boys coming up. They had this opinion, 'When I go it's going to die with me.' This was it. But some were good men and they'd tell you where you were going right and where you were going wrong.

"Then after your seven years apprenticeship you had to do three years as an 'improver' before you got full pay. So it was a full ten years. The improver was that you were a young shipwright and basically you got three-quarters of the wage. After my seventh year me wage was fifty shillings a week. My grandmother reared me and I gave the best part of it to her and the cinema then was only four pence. And me grandfather, God bless him, he used to take me to the Olympia *every* Friday night. Take me up in the Gods and he'd buy me a big bag of fruit, apples and oranges and bananas and a bar of chocolate. And he'd be more often in the bar than looking at the show and he'd leave me sitting in this seat. Oh, I was happy enough. Then about an hour before the show would be over he'd appear alongside of me.

"Now the boatyards *originally* were catering for fishing boats, smacks and trawlers, and then the sailing ships. And drifters, they were fishing boats that used drift-nets. Then in the early 1930s they came along with these big steel boats and they were huge to us. They would be 600 to 800 tons. Then most of the smacks and drifters faded away. Now there's a difference between a boatbuilder and a shipwright. A boatbuilder strictly builds boats, mostly of timber in those days, and they could range from six feet to a hundred feet, yachts, fisher boats, work boats. Now a shipwright, on the other hand, works in a dockyard where he's dealing with steel *and* he's dealing with timber. The first platers in the world to plate a ship were shipwrights. Shipwrights would *frame* the ship, *plate* the ship. A shipwright was *the* man in those days of my time, and even during the war. And we had a very strong union. It was a British-based union, funny enough. Yeah, because, see, we were never a shipbuilding nation. The union was the Shipwrights and Ship Constructors Association, British based but all over the world in Australia, Canada, America, Spain. And I was a member. It was handed down. And there was *tremendous* conflict between shipwrights and boiler-makers in the ship-making industry. Oh, and many a strike. I remember them well because they were moving in on an industry that was thousands of years old, with this modern material called steel or iron. And years ago all ships carried a shipwright and he was an officer and he was regarded as the master of arms as well. Lloyd's [London insurance company] demanded that ships over a certain tonnage carry shipwrights. This was after the war and well into the sixties.

"When you served your time as a boatbuilder or a shipwright your tool box was very heavy, *mighty* heavy, because you had everything in it, from a quarter-inch chisel up to an inch and a half chisel, the full range, and bores for wood bits from a quarter up to an inch. And you'd three or four hammers on top of that and then you had the adzes and then the maul and gouges and all that. The basic tool we had then was the adze which is the oldest tool in the world—Noah had to build the ark! And that's still used by ship-builders today. And I have an axe here that belonged to me great grandfather and it was bought in Quebec. During the war when you wouldn't get timber we got these telegraph poles and you had to chop these down to make spars out of them and we used to use the axe. It was a marvellous sight to see them using those axes. You used the axe and if you missed, of course, half your blinking leg is gone! Oh, it'd take a slice off you. Cause the axe had the silver steel in the middle of it and it was forged with the 'V' and it was like a lance.

"On Saturday morning everything in your tool box had to be cleaned, oiled and sharpened. And in those days we used to have a sharpening stone called an Indian Red carving stone and the old one that I had now you'd sharpen a chisel and it'd be like a razor. The sharpening stones now aren't the same quality. You'd leave your tools in the workshop locked up. Each man had his own tool box. Where I served my time there was one hour every Saturday morning given to sharpening your tools, between 11.00 and 12.00. You'd sharpen *every* instrument in your tool box and *dare you* be seen sharpening tools during the week! Everything had to be *razor* sharp for the following week's work. In those days the chisels were silver steel and it was forged under iron and when you sharpened it, it was like a *lance*. But the tools nowadays you buy are melted down condensed milk cans or something like rubber. They hold their edge for about ten minutes and then they're gone blunt.

"I remember an old man that I knew for years and I always admired this man. He was one of the greatest men I ever met in me life. I've never met one like him since, a man named Bill Tracy. Now Bill Tracy worked in our boatyard with us for years, for *years*. But we were sitting in the yard one day, sitting in the yard on a block. And I asked him how did he ever come to learn to splice wires and ropes and that, me being a young boy and he an old man. And he gave me this story which I never forgot. It appears that when he was a very young boy at the age of 12 or 14 he came out of school one day with his little bag, and instead of going home he walked across the Grand Canal to Rogerson's Quay down here. And there was a pub down there and there was a big Norwegian bark there that was finished unloading. And to make a long story short, this man got hold of Bill by the scruff of his neck and brought him aboard the ship. And Bill was screaming his head off, crying and roaring, and there was two redcaps, like the Black and Tans, English police, and they were standing outside the pub and actually saw this man skull-dragging him across the road and putting him aboard the ship on the gangway going up. And they done *nothing*, never lifted a finger. So they took Bill away—*shanghaied*!

"When he arrived back in Dublin he was 29 years of age. And he came back to Dublin in a sailing ship and when he came back he got drunk and there was two policeman in Ringsend, one was called 'Lousy Shoulders' and the other fella was called 'Leatherneck.' They took over while Bill was away. So these two policemen decided to rough him up in the pub and Bill was a small man and he put the two of them to sleep like a stroke of lightning. He *detested* policemen. Anyone that wore a uniform, he detested them. I actually seen him meself years later in the Yacht Tavern in Ringsend, a pub, and a young garda came in there one Friday night and Bill scattered him all over the place. He bounced him off the four walls like a rubber ball—and Bill was an old man at that stage. It was the way the garda approached him or handled him on the shoulder. Bill didn't like anybody pawing him. And Bill put him out the door. It was all bare fists in those days.

"Oh, back then Ringsend was riddled with pubs. Tradesmen mostly drank with themselves but the shipwrights and the dockers were thick as thieves. They'd go into the pubs on a Friday or Saturday night and they'd get talking and a whole hooley would start up, a sing-song and the whole lot. The Dublin dockers, by God, they were terrible hard-working men. And when they went to the pub all you'd see was their white eyes and white teeth and red lips and red tongue, but the rest of them was just *black*. And when I say black I mean *black*! And when they'd spit into the dust it would be black. You must remember that the pint in those days was a *different* type of drink. See, in those days you had the pint of porter and then Guinness brought out stout. But it was mostly porter and the dockers would knock back anything from ten to fourteen pints of porter in a shot. Oh, God, yes. On their way home from the boat. They'd go *straight* into the pub before they'd go home and they knocked back pints hand over fist. Guinness was a food . . . at least we called it food. And anybody that was sick or invalid, they used to have a Treble X stout in bottles and that was the superior Guinness's drink of the whole lot. If you drank that you'd live for ever!

"Hooleys was mostly Saturday nights, all sing-songs. Now mostly people ate fish and that was why it [Ringsend] was called 'Raytown.' But on a Saturday night there was tripe and pig's feet, crubeens, you know. Oh, God, yer man would come into the pub with a white enamel bucket full of cooked pig's feet or mussels or prawns, but mostly pig's feet, and they'd eat them with their porter. And men had handkerchiefs then and they used to be red, a big red or white dots on them, and they'd stretch them out on the counter and put the pig's feet on top of it. And they'd count the bones in the pig's feet and there had to be thirty-two bones or there'd be *war*. Because that was a full pig's foot. And they spit the bones out on their handkerchief. And there was about a foot and a half of dust from the edge of the bar out on the floor.

"I always admired the Dublin docker. They had it tough, they must have been made of flint. Back then we had a football team there called the Shamrock Rovers in Ringsend and that consisted of a lot of local dockers. One in particular, Bob Fulham, he'd a woeful kick. He had such a good kick that he'd be at one end of the field at the goal post and he'd kick the ball straight through the other goal like a *rocket*. And he made a shot one day and the goalkeeper caught it in his chest and that was the end of him. Wiped him out. Nearly killed him. And imagine now at that stage digging a coal boat and coming out from work and playing a football match and still black with coal. They were hard men. They must have been made of cast iron! The shovel alone now, the blade, was about a foot and a half wide. I'd say each shovel would be about two stone and loading coal tubs with that all day. Each fella had his own shovel and dare you go near it! Had their names carved into the handles and everything. Take them into the pub alongside them. When I used to go into the pub for me grandmother for her gill you used to see this shiney thing like a sheet of armour, their shovels. They were great men.

"The stevedore'd drink with the docker but he wouldn't move around, he'd stay in the one spot. The dockers would go to *him*. The stevedore used to sit up at the top of the bar with a big hat on him. To me, he was always the biggest man in the pub because he always had a big velour coat and a big slouch hat on him. A lot of the stevedores were well-to-do fellas, well dressed. Now you'd go to reads here years ago on the North Wall and the stevedore got up on this wooden platform about ten feet up in the air with steps up to it and you could have six or seven hundred men all around in a circle and he'd have the paper in his hand and the men that was left then would just go away very downhearted. You could see them putting their heads to the ground and putting their collars up around their necks on a winter's morning in the lashing rain and their hands in their pockets and walking away. I've seen that meself. I'll tell you, they were *hard* men. And there was a thing called consumption which was known in later years as T.B. and that was rampant for a long time down there. And any docker that was a victim of it, the Ringsend people looked after them. A loaf of bread was sent in or a bag of sugar or bag of tea. That's the type of people they were. And the publican, he used to help them out, mostly with burials. In Ringsend now for a funeral the whole village would come to a standstill. Shops, pubs, grocers, the whole works would just shut down dead. Then there'd be a wake that'd go on for about three nights. Then they'd go back to the pub after the funeral and sympathise as they used to call it—and get *scuttered drunk*. And the arch enemies of one another would be the best of friends!

"When my grandfather died he left the whole lot to me as a young boy. And our boatyard in Ringsend held fifty-four yachts and that yard was very successful. As the fishing boats faded away boatyards moved into building and repairing yachts for yachtsmen. Even during the war when things were bad we managed to make a living out of it. Of course, in 1945 when the war ended it really boomed altogether. What caused the boom was this. Before the war working-class people hadn't got much money to spare but after the war with the *huge* amount of gratuities from the British and American Armies the average working lad that came back from the war had money to burn as we called it in those days. With the result that the ordinary middle class moved into the yachting circles. You had boats all over the place, as a sport, a relaxation, pleasure. With the result that it boomed and you couldn't build them fast enough and so they got boats built in England and brought them over here to finish them. In 1946 the only day we stopped work was Christmas Day.

"Then when the recession hit here in the fifties a lot of the boatbuilders and shipwrights went to the building trade. I built the last ocean-going yacht in Ringsend in 1951. That was the last big yacht that was built in Ringsend and then our yard closed down. And that was the end of the boatyard. And then I used to draw boats for the fun of it and I found meself getting entrenched in *designing* boats. Then I went to the Dublin Port and Docks Board to work as a shipwright and then the vocational people here at the technological school asked me to give boatbuilding classes throughout the country. But I'm the last shipwright because my sons are not following the trade. I've ended up now as a senior technical supervisor in the Dublin Port and Docks. It's still nearly all hand work. Very little has changed. But where we used to use a cross-saw we have a chain-saw now which goes through timber like a scissors. And where we used to bore two inch holes by hand with an auger we have a pneumatic drill now. And now there's power planers and electric drills and electric sanders . . . with the result that most of the hand tools became obsolete. But in my time a shipwright was *the* man . . . but I'm the last one because my sons are not following."

MARTIN MITTEN—DOCKER, AGE 81

All the menfolk in his family were dockers, going back to "ancient times". His father was a personal friend of James Larkin and a union man to the core. He remembers well the 1925 strike as a bitter clash between dockers and scabs, as men battled in the open streets and women poured scalding water from tenement windows down on the hated interlopers. When he began work as a docker at age 18 he felt like an "animal" waiting in reads hoping to be called by the stevedore. But life on the docks was always hectic and exciting. When containerisation technology first appeared he clearly saw the end in sight for old dockers. Today he is visibly sad as he walks the lifeless cobblestones along the quays.

"I was born on Townsend Street. Me father was at the docks for fifty years. And *his* father before him. And *his* father *before him*! And I had five brothers on the docks. You were reared up to it. You were born on the river. Sure, where I was born you could throw a brick in the river. We had to bring our father's dinner down to the North Wall. Our mothers would make up their dinners and put it into a bowl with a can of tea and we'd walk to bring down their dinners. So you were around the docks when you were about 10 years old.

"On the docks me father done everything, drove winches, dug coal boats, tipped coal, done everything—same as I done. My father now in his time, he was mostly trade union and he was a great admirer of Jim Larkin. He was a personal friend of his. Oh, indeed, I spoke to Larkin meself. Oh, he has a great reputation, old Jim. Now me father was a founding member of the Transport Union—that was in 1907—but when Larkin formed the Workers' Union my father changed to Larkin's union and stayed with him till he died. And I was in Larkin's union. And at that time if you stood up for your rights and argued with your boss they used to blackball you. They *wouldn't employ* you, so my father would sometimes be left out. But the women of the dockers, they were marvellous women. Oh, they'd get a feed [for the family] no matter where they'd get it. They'd always make out a grub for the home. My father never missed his breakfast in his life. Sometimes when things would be bad he wouldn't come in to his dinner, he'd wait till evening. But mother'd get something for us. Ah, she was great.

"When I was getting reared in the twenties I was never hungry and I pay tribute to me mother for that. She was known as Mary Kate, a big woman of twenty-odd stone and six foot tall. Yeah, and she was as broad! She was very much a local character. She used to wash the dead and if a woman would be in labour Mary Kate would be sent for. Oh, she was very popular but she didn't drink much. But *all* the women drank at a funeral. Like when someone'd be getting buried, that used to be like an excursion. Mostly people'd be getting buried at 2.00 in the day up at Dean's Grange. And all the [horse] cabs would be all lined up and the women would have a day out then. The women were fantastic, marvellous. When things would be rough they'd go to the Jewman to get money to get food for the home. Like my mother. The Jewman would come around selling holy pictures and then he'd start lending her money. You'd get the lend of a £1 and you'd pay five bob interest. Pay a shilling every week for your interest. And if times were rough, women had to go to the pawn, so you'd have your grub. The pawn was a part of life. Oh, there was great gas at the pawns. One woman, the pawnbrokers knew her so well, she used to put two bricks in a box and take it to the pawn and she'd say, 'A pair of shoes.' That's true. And she'd get four bob. And he wouldn't open it. He knew . . . but he'd get the interest on it.

"I left school at 14 years of age and at that period the economic war was on in Ireland in the 1930s. I hardly worked at all, worked a couple of weeks here and there as a messenger boy. Around 16, I used to go down on the docks and spell me brothers. Maybe go down and fill a coal tub with me older brothers. Work for about an hour with a big No. 7 shovel and that was breaking me in for when I'd start meself. Soon as I come 18 I went on the docks. Oh, the docks then was *full of life*. In the mornings and in the evenings when they were knocking off from work you'd see *hundreds* of men walking along. Dockers, we was all in the one area. And you knew everybody and their families and their histories. Now Ringsend and the southside, there was rivalry with the northsiders, always a bit of rivalry. Oh, sometimes it'd break down into fist fights. Some very bad fights. Oh, it was about who was the toughest mostly. Now most of the coalies, the men who worked coal, they come from the southside where I lived. The southside fellas, they were more flexible, they were able to do nearly everything. There was a lot of good dockers on the northside as well but they were more used to cargo, just taking cargo, timber, boxes, containers and loading cattle. But they didn't like shovel work at all. No, most of them wouldn't go *near* it.

"But we all used to go around to all the different reads. We all ended up in the one place. Then we had just one place to read and that was at the North Wall gates. That was a reading space for *everybody*, coal, cargo, you name it. There was three stands erected and they'd have to wait their turn to go up and read. Oh, there'd be up to 2,000 men sometimes. See, some days there'd be up to 1,500 or 1,600 men working on the docks. Now Palgrave Murphy's *always* used to read at the North Wall. And men would keep pushing forward trying to get work, trying to get picked. But the bosses mostly knew who they wanted. And some men was better known than others. Some men was *good* workers. So at the docks you'd have to wait every morning, had to stand in the read where they'd pick out the men, the foremen or stevedores. The big companies like George Bell's and Palgrave Murphy's had what you called foremen. But a stevedore was his own boss. Now the Carricks, they were stevedores. They were middle men between the shipping agents and the dockers. Then there was the Nolans, they were stevedores. Some of them used their power very hard. Dockers more or less had to toe the line.

"When I was 18 and starting, it was very hard, cause you weren't known at the docks. When you started you mostly got work through your father's name. But they got to know you gradually. Hundreds would be there for a read in my time. *Hundreds!* When I was starting it was terrible. Each firm picked outside their own door. And you had to *run* from that read to the next read. It was terrible. Had to run from that read to the next read if you didn't get a job. Ran *all* up and down the docks. Some of the men used to get bikes. Carrick's now, he used to read for work sometimes at twenty after seven. And he'd call all his relations first. At a read you just stood there and took your chances. I always felt we were like animals waiting for the foreman to call us. There was a fight one time and I seen a foreman giving the docker a dig. Oh, he was a huge big man.

"Stevedores, some of them used their power very hard. And some dockers used to leave drink for them. This really happened. They'd leave a couple of drinks in the pubs for the bosses and some of the men used to give a baby Power's whiskey to a foreman so that he'd call his name. And men would get angry with one another over that. Oh, the stevedores had practically the power of life and death over you. They employed you when they wanted you and if they didn't like you they didn't want you. After a while you'd get known by certain stevedores. The bosses knew who they wanted and one fella, he'd pick the men but never called out the name. He called them *all* by their nicknames, maybe call a *hundred* men by their nicknames. He was a foreman at George Bell's. He was *fantastic*, this fella. Now some of the nicknames was 'Lax', 'Scouts', 'Bunter', 'Lucky Bar', 'Rollo', 'The Deviler', 'Saddler', 'Salt Box', 'Jam Face', 'Rabbit', 'Joker', 'Lights out', 'Hairy Eye', 'Spit in Pint', 'Pee Wee', 'Guzzler', 'Hookey', 'Lordy', 'Slim', 'Stumper', 'Never Wrong', 'Joxer', 'Nudger', 'Tricky', 'The Blind Fellow', 'Pegleg', 'Shoulders', 'Yank', 'Sailor'—called them *all* by their nicknames.

"You were never bored on the docks, always different work. Maybe you'd be on a coal boat today digging coal and on a bag boat the next day and then an iron boat or timber boat. And dockers used to do work on Guinness's boats and most of them was drunk in the hold of the ship! They had their own gear, their own tools to open up the barrels. So then Guinness's took it over and done their own work. Now in the olden days the men would be working very hard. They used to carry sixteen stone bags of cement. And there was a lot of grain work before the silo went up around 1934. You used to fill the grain with bushels with two handles on it. You'd fill that and another man would hold the sack and you tumbled that in. And shovelling ore, that was hard work. It was very, very heavy and you'd have a smaller shovel, a No. 3 shovel. And phosphorous or pyrite ships, that was terrible dry work.

"Mostly I was connected with coal work. Oh, you'd be filthy. Just trousers and shirt mostly. I never took me shirt off. And boots. A ship of 400 tons, there'd be sixteen men on that ship in the hatch and four tubs, four men on each tub. We'd all be digging down and putting it into the tub. Ah, there was accidents. I was knocked out five times meself by the handle of the tubs, cause you'd tip them up and they'd come around as you'd swing them out to empty them. They'd hook them on big cranes and they'd swing the empty ones in and swing the full ones out. And I lost the top of my finger on a cargo ship. I was trying to steady the hoist and I had me hand around the rope and the rope ran and caught the top of me finger and pulled it off. There was two ropes looped through each other and it was running and burning.

"With coal you got paid on tonnage, so much per ton. And your hands got hard. You were told to do your water on your hands to harden them. Just put your urine on your hands and that hardened them up. Oh, that's *true*. It got your hands hard. And afterwards nothing would bother your hands because they'd be solid welts. Now some of the old coalies would put a little bit of coal in their mouth and suck it and that'd keep moisture in your mouth. And the coal dust was a way of life. One class of coal that'd come in for the steam engines was *filthy dirty*. Wet steam they called it. It used to come in for the railways. And sometimes you'd get out of that coal boat and you'd go home and take off your trousers and it'd nearly stand on its own with the sweat and the dirt. And then you'd get into an old bath and scrub yourself down.

"With the coal merchants you always went to the office on the docks to get paid. But sometimes we'd have to be waiting in the pub to get the money from the stevedores. And the pub would be giving us a gargle on the slate. That was credit. Sure, we often got up out of a coal boat at 10.00 in the morning and we'd break to half ten and we'd go over to the pub and some of the fellas would drink four pints. At ten o'clock! And, see, we got paid *daily* in them times. No weekly pay. Some dockers was first-class boozers. Most dockers were big drinkers—it was very hot, thirsty work. Businessmen and maybe retired men, they'd come down along the docks, rambling down for a day, and they'd go into the pubs to look at the dockers drinking their pints. Go in *just* to see them drinking their pints. They used to enjoy looking at them. Oh, some of the dockers would put down ten pints [in one session]. Now Mulligan's pub on Poolbeg Street, my father used to drink in there. We all used to drink there. We'd go in there and most of the time you drank five or six pints before you'd go home. That was *normal*. And some dockers was big betters. One particular man had terrible trouble gambling. Once we had hard work, five days at it, and we got a lot of money at that time—£29. And the average week's wages then was about £5. And I met him the next morning and he hadn't a *penny*. He hadn't even gone home to his wife with the wages. He was after going to the dogs in Shelbourne Park. Not a penny left.

"Oh, there was some fights in pubs. There was often a docker's boxing match. I seen some men killed. But they used to fight very clean, you know, just stand-up boxing, bare fists. I seen some of the younger fellas kicking one another but the older dockers didn't do that. There was some men that was great boxers and they'd get work cause the stevedore would be afraid of some of them. And I seen two families, a clan war, on the side of the docks. Two families boxing one another. And the *women* of the families was boxing as well. Between two docking families. Over some argument or something. The fathers and the brothers got involved and then the women got involved. That happened out in the street where I lived. Oh, a clash . . . it got very bad and some of them got hurt. And they all came together after years.

"Now the 1924-25 strike, that was a *bitter* strike. That caused terrible trouble among the traditional docking families. Ah, brothers split over that and some of them went to Larkin's union. The old dockers mostly went with Larkin. But the bosses recognised the Transport Union and they wouldn't hire Larkin's men. If you wanted a job you had to be sent down by the Transport Union. And there was what you called the 'big six', they were docking families that worked for the coal companies and cement boats. And them 'big six' was called 'scabs' by the likes of my people. They brought men up from Wicklow and got them to join the union and got them employed on the docks and showed them what to do. They was known as the 'big scabby six.' And the coal merchants, they'd have their horses in the stables here on Poolbeg Street and they used to come down to yoke up their carts in Townsend Street and they was called scabs. And I seen me mother and all the women in the big [tenement] houses then and they was throwing scalding water down on top of the scabs. And some of the older fellas was running along with whips lashing the horses to make them jump up. And then detectives out of the Pearse Street Station, they come down and firing shots in the air to try and stop the people attacking the scabs. They had guns. To stop the scabs from getting bashed . . . murdered. Oh, and that went on for years afterwards, that bitterness in families. And afterwards the sons of these men [scabs], when there'd be arguments you'd say to them, '*My* father never scabbed it like yours!' You'd stab them with that . . . you never forgot about it. In later years then the union brought in what you called the 'button system' for the older men that was there all their life. You had a union button, a badge. And they were the button men. And I was one of the first. The union forced the foremen to call the button men first and men that come after that was casual. You had to wear your button in your coat. There was a battle royal for to get that, cause they were above the casuals and had to get preference.

"Now containerisation, they got that idea from the last war, the idea of roll-on and roll-off ships. The beginning of the roll freight service. That was the beginning of the end. In the fifties they wanted to bring containerisation into

Dublin. I knew it was going to be detrimental to the port, because it was less men that was going to be employed. Oh, there was terrible battles in the union. But men like meself knew that if we didn't move with the times we'd be left behind. Now just imagine 150 men doing all the dockers' work—and doing more tonnage! And on a given day I often seen 2,000 of us doing the work. When containerisation came in the gangs was all shortened down. Like, timber, it used to come in loose but now it was all stacked in *bundles*. It used to be that there'd be up to a hundred men and it'd take them five days to do that ship. Now there was twenty-four men doing it in seven hours with the new technology. Oh, some of the men were kicking up murder . . . wanted to *stop* it. Oh, sometimes the [union] meetings would become very hot. And this man says to me, 'Martin, the dockers are like the small farmers, they'll be getting cut down.' Says he, 'The day will come when a hundred men can operate the whole docks where there's thousands working today.' And he's proved *right*. Oh, the writing was on the wall. But it was a terrible interesting life, I'm telling you. There was no time to be bored. When I was there it was *full* of life. I miss the *activity* . . . like it's *so silent* . . . no life."

8

At the Bench: Jacob's Mice and Rosary Beads

At age 14 she became one of the young "Jacob's mice" at the biscuit factory where she remained for nearly half a century. Despite the strict discipline, hard conditions and small wages, it was a coveted job at the time. One could be sacked for stealing a few biscuits or being discovered pregnant. Managers were Protestant and there was no promotion for Catholics, who simply accepted it as their lot at the time. But she loved the jolly camaraderie with her pals as they sang away to pass the time. Then the 1922 Civil War disrupted Jacob's trade and workers had their hours and wages cut drastically. After the war ended she delighted in dashing home to give her mammy the eleven shillings earned, with a few bob returned for the pictures and sweets. Though she "loved working there", she retired in 1970—having never once been late—without "a penny . . . I had to go on the dole."

"I started when I was 14. Jacob's always took on girls at 14. We were called 'Jacob's mice'. Actually, they preferred Whitefriar Street pupils—that's the Carmelite school—because it was near the factory and they were good scholars there. When you were 14 you wrote in an application. We all applied. We were taught how to write to make an application . . . 'Dear Sir or Madam, I am 14 years of age. I am leaving school. I would be very pleased if you would accept me to give me a trial to work in your factory. I would be very grateful for a trial.' And I always remember my teacher, Mrs Simpson, saying, 'Now always make it short because they don't be bothered going into details.' And at the end, 'awaiting the courtesy of your reply', I thought that was beautiful.

"Then they sent you a card for an interview. So you lined up at Mrs Gill's office and then she called you up by your name. And being youngsters you'd be all excited and pushing one another and all . . . a kind of fear, kind of excited fear. You were brought into the room one by one. Now the interview was a wee bit personal at that time. Children wouldn't accept it now, of course. It was all very militaristic the way it was done but we accepted it. At first the lady supervisor would look at your head to see was your head clean, your hair. They went through your hair with a pencil, they wouldn't touch you. With two pencils.

Just part the hair and look. And they looked at your nails and at your feet and they'd make you walk across the room and back. And they had a doctor and a nurse on the premises and the lady made an appointment with the doctor for you. And you were all aquiver with excitement, you know. You needed to pass the doctor's examination of your chest and your ears and your eyes. Then they had their own dentist in Jacob's as well and you opened your mouth and he went through your teeth. And he'd say, 'Oh, you have to have that tooth out.' And you had to do it if you wanted to work there. Oh, you were just like little animals. Some girls had to get teeth out and that's the reason some never went back. They were afraid. See, the dentists then were butchers actually when we were children. Only little rooms some of them had in the tenements. And they just put a bit of cocaine with a syringe into the gum and just pulled your teeth out and it hurted you. Oh, it was most crude. But Jacob's had their own dentist and you could go to him. But some of them still wouldn't come back. They'd be terrified.

"After the doctor examined you, you were told to start on Monday morning. And you got your little card and your name and address on it. Oh, I was *delighted*! I went home and said, 'Oh, Ma, *look*!' I started at eleven and six and gave it *all* to Mammy. *Every* penny. I was delighted to give it to her. And she'd give you back sixpence or a shilling. You know, Kevin, we didn't know the value of money. We didn't want money . . . we didn't *need* money. We only wanted it for our parents because we played in the streets all day and we didn't buy anything. Now if you were fond of sweets or fruit, fair enough. So anything you had you gave it to your mother. Except when you got older and *then* you didn't give it [all] to your Mam. Oh, many a raise went into me pocket, I'll tell you that, and I wouldn't tell me Ma. Maybe a raise of half a crown. That was fair enough.

"Now the first morning I started my mother had a lovely blouse on me, a little red blouse and skirt and dressed up lovely. And all polished up. And two little ribbons in my hair, up like two little drumsticks, two little plaits. Your hair was divided in the back and combed and you were plaited with a big ribbon at the end. I started at 8.00 in the morning. There was a horn that went at ten to eight and at eight. Now I only had to go around the corner and into Jacob's. Oh, my mother was a little general . . . 'Are you not up yet? Get up.' And Mam would have the fire lit and we had fried bread and tea. We had wonderful drippings at that time. Mammy would put the dripping into the frying pan and had it steaming hot and it was beautiful bread then and she'd put the bread in the frying pan. We got two cuts of fried bread and a cup of tea, but that was a substantial breakfast at half past seven.

"So at 8.00 we went in the entrance and Mrs Gill had this little office and she was very bossy and very tall and you were afraid of your life of her. And she had a big clock. And after eight the doors were closed and you were late. That was a bad mark against you. Now they'd tolerate anything but bad timekeepers. They'd say, 'We'll tolerate bad workers, slow workers, dirty workers, but we will *not* tolerate bad timekeepers.' You were *gone* if you were a bad timekeeper. When you started you got a number. My number was 534. They were called 'checks' and they gave you that every night at about a quarter past five. About the size of an old half-crown and about as thick. I think it was brass, you could polish it. You'd get that every night and you daren't lose that. When I'd come home I'd always put my check up on the mantelpiece where nobody'd touch it. So in the morning there was a big clock there and a big bowl and you'd put your check in that. And then Mrs Gill collected all them checks and if there was no check for you you were *out*. Then you could come in at 10.00. They gave you that privilege, but you'd be afraid for your life.

"When we went into Jacob's they supplied us with nets—caps came in later. Oh, they were very keen on hygiene and you could be sacked for that. You had to be spotless. The nets were put over your head, a fine net, and your plait was put up in the net. And you got a blue overalls with a big square neck. Good linen. And a belt sewed in the middle in the back to tie in the front. No pockets. They had a laundry. Discipline was absolutely a little bit too much. Each foreman had a whistle, like a policeman. We got a tea break at 10.00 and you brought in your own glass jam jar. And it was Shell cocoa, purple or blue—it was *awful*. You got ten minutes. And you weren't allowed to smoke either. Oh, no. Now a lot of girls in those days smoked. We called them 'fags'. Now there was five toilets and the foreman had a toilet check and you'd hear the girls saying, 'Oh, God, I'm dying for a smoke.' And they went up and said, 'May I have the check?' But they could be sacked for smoking. Oh, yes, that was a terrible thing. So you're working, looking at the clock, and then the whistle at 1.00. You covered your benches with grease paper and you got only an hour for lunch and I'd dash home. Oh, like *lightning*. And maybe just time to boil an egg or something—and *dash* back. And now there were five or six floors in Jacob's and they had a lovely veranda up at the tip, tip top of the tower and after your lunch you might have a few minutes there. You stood out in the sun and it was lovely up there.

"Now in 1922 there was a civil war going on here. I was in Jacob's and I was 14 then. I remember the Civil War. At that time it was brother against brother. Oh, civil war is a *dreadful* thing, a dreadful thing for a country, with one half on one side and one half on the other. Now they were called the 'rebels' then, which was much nicer than the IRA . . . 'Oh, he's a rebel', they'd say. Buildings were levelled in the Civil War here and the recession was bad. And we had only been over the other war, the 1918 War, and just over the Rebellion in 1916. So we were born in the years of wars. In 1922 we had a shortage of materials in Jacob's and we went on short time. The foreman would say, 'Sorry, girls, *off at 1.00* today.' It did disrupt our lives moneywise. I only got about five or six shillings. Your wages went 'bang'. That went on for a good few years now, until de Valera's government got in. Then Jacob's export trade with England went down but the home trade came into its own . . . great, marvellous.

"We were put into a training school on the top floor and we had a forewoman called Mrs Hudson. A little woman she was, and very nice. They wanted tall girls for putting the tins up high, to pile tins, and if you were short then you would be accepted for wrapping or messages, going around as a messenger. Everyone stood at their work in the factory. Oh, yes, you stood packing and wrapping and tissueing. I was very small and had to stand on a little box made in the carpenter's shop. No seat, no chairs then. And we'd steel floors, all steel, and every window would be open. In the training school you were trained for everything. You could be a sweeper, a cleaner, and if any department needed wrappers you were well trained.

"Now at the beginning I started only wrapping little packages. There was a big trade for England at that time. Their biggest trade was exports, to England and the dominions. Ah, there was a great export trade. Oh, *all* the British dominions were supplied by us. And you wrapped very slow because you had to be very careful with your folds in. If you wrapped fifty for the morning that was very good and that was marked down on your sheet. Some people were on piece-work and some on standard wage. And you had to crease your folds perfectly. That pack had six biscuits in it. You put your wrapper down first and then you put your little folder inside the wrapper, beautifully done, very clean, and your biscuits then. And you had to examine your biscuits—no broken biscuits, or no biscuits with specks on them. And no high baked or low baked biscuits—not too pale or too burned. They were put aside. They were put in a box beside you and they were put into little bags afterwards and you bought them at the end of the week for two pence a bag of broken biscuits. It was *great*. But now if you were seen taking biscuits out you were sacked. There was a saying, 'Eat all, pocket none, if you do, you'll get the run.' You'll be sacked! But we'd take a few biscuits and put them in our pockets and we'd eat them. You wouldn't go *out* with them, because there was often searches on. You'd hear, 'There's a search on tonight.' But Jacob's was very good cause you could buy [flawed] biscuits for little or nothing and they were beautiful. You could buy a bag of biscuits that size for three pence and it'd do a family. It'd do four families, really. And then you could buy broken chocolate for four pence and it was gorgeous. And you could buy broken chocolate sweets. And you could buy broken cakes. It was a good idea because it kept you from stealing anything. It was better to buy it for a couple of pence than to steal it. But in our time *fear* would keep you from it . . . and your *religion* would keep you from it.

"Anyway, then I was called out to be a messenger. And I was delighted. Oh, a messenger had great great freedom. Now if I hadn't been a messenger in the beginning I'd have known nothing. So I was made a messenger and had a medallion around my neck on a string. I was a messenger for my own department, like, I'd go down for some wrappers or seals. Anyway, you came off the messages at 16 and you didn't know where you were going. And now they had a school and Mrs Cooper ran the school. Funny enough, they never sent me to school there. I don't know why. They went for about an hour and a half. And it was a great relief from standing. I think that was the idea, too, to give the younger children a little break. I wish I'd gone. She'd teach you how to stand and how to walk and how to talk properly. She was a great drill mistress on how to stand and walk and how to talk. I would *love* to have went there. But I was sent to the stock loft where all the tins was finished and girls laid out the tins for different parts of the country, for the orders. So many tins would be put on the wagon and the wagons were sent down to the loading platform. We had canvas conveyors and the horses and vans were outside.

"When I went into Jacob's we had a thousand and three hundred, but only a sprinkle of men. There'd be men to help with the *hard* work, like in the bake house and in the mixing loft for mixing the dough because it was very heavy. You might have had ten or twelve departments full of girls and you might get two men in each department, for the hard work. That'd be all. But in the bake house and the mixing department and the carpenter's shop it was all men. Men and women *did* mix. But you weren't allowed much freedom. You couldn't walk around the place or leave your bench. Very strict, disciplined rules. But they'd meet their boyfriends in Jacob's. Oh, lots of marriages were made in Jacob's. Plenty of girls came in and they got married at 21 or 22. Jacob's gave you a cake and £3 if you were getting married—and you had to leave. And then they could re-employ again, more juniors, for less wages. Actually, you were delighted to get married and get out. You took a load off your back.

"Now if girls got into trouble [pregnant]—and it did often happen—they'd be sacked immediately. Eventually they'd be found out. You know, Kevin, the girls were very innocent then. I was innocent myself, actually. You knew nothing. Our mothers told us nothing. And I think many a girl just fell to knowing nothing. We had these big aprons, like a big sheet, that'd go right over your head with the square neck and if any girl got into trouble she could fasten the belt so that you wouldn't notice it. And sometimes the parents wouldn't let the girls get married. Mothers wanted their wages and didn't want them to leave. But eventually it'd be found out, and they'd be sacked. Now there was really a lot of charity then and I don't mean actual money, but a lot of charitable people. Everyone helped each other. Like, if you knew a girl who was in trouble that way you just shielded her completely. Everyone kept their mouth shut. They were very loyal. Many girls there carried their babies nearly six or seven months. And then they'd have to leave if they were found out. And a lot of girls did come to grief, God love them. So we were always sympathetic and we blamed nobody. If it happened it was, 'Oh, God help her.' . . . We were very charitable in our own little way.

"Now the Jacobs, they didn't talk to you. They were the directors, George Jacob and Charlie Jacob. George was very, very tall, very gentlemanly. Charlie Jacob was a small fussy man with a beard. They came from Waterford. They started it in Peter's Row as a penny biscuit factory. They didn't look down on us actually but we were always the peasants. We were more afraid of the manageresses than the directors because they had the power to pull you down, the power to give you a job or get you sacked. You watched yourself and wouldn't incur their wrath. The managers and manageresses were Protestant but the workers was mostly all Catholic, but we got no key jobs. There was no promotion for you. I remember I was once told, 'Once a factory girl, *always* a factory girl.' A Catholic got no key jobs. But it didn't affect you . . . I think we were ignorant of it. Now that was broken down later in Jacob's and it did come to pass.

"It was all men in the bake house because it was very heavy work. What they used, it was like a miniature cement mixer. You could see the things going around and the noise would be deafening. And the dough then would fall on to a canvas in the shape of a biscuit and they would move on then slowly into the oven. And it would come out baked at the other side of that big machine. Every window would be open and birds would get into the bake house. It was like an aviary in Jacob's in the bake house. You'd hear them singing all day up in the roofs. *Always* birds in the bake house. You'd see the birds flying around under the glass roof and they'd say, 'Oh, that's all the old men coming back that died, they didn't want to leave.' They used to call the birds the old men, coming back in the shape of birds, the old lads.

"Then there was the wash house where they washed the tins out and the tin room where they made the tins. Oh, the wash house, everyone *dreaded* the wash house. See, when you were taken in, if you were robust and big, you'd be selected for the tin wash house. And another thing. If you were troublesome or a bad worker you were always threatened with the wash house. We used to dread it. Even if you weren't robust you could be sent there. When I was a messenger I was often up there. Big tanks in the wash house and the girls would wash the tins that'd come back from the customers. They had rubber aprons and clogs and when they'd wash the tins they'd hang them up on hooks and the drips from that would go down on your head or shoulders. And they had big heavy gloves and they'd wear out in no time. *Physically* hard, the work was *extremely* hard. If I was ever sent up there I would have left. I definitely wouldn't be able for it.

"The tin room was another place everyone dreaded. They made the tins in the tin room and the tin came in in big sheets, huge big sheets. And the *noise* was *absolutely* cruel as they crashed down on the tins to cut the tins by machine. And the women all had cut hands. And you had to shout to be heard. There were about six machines or more. And they put all pictures of Ireland on the tins, shamrocks and O'Connell Bridge in Dublin. Now there was a machine and the lids that was crooked was put into it and you had a small lever. It was to straighten out the lids. Now my friend May had lovely hands and one of the lids went crooked on her and she put in her hand for to fit it and *forgot* that she had her foot on the lever and she pressed the lever, the little pedal, and there was a piece of metal with spikes on it and that came down for to straighten out all the bumps on the lid. And she brought down the thing on her hand and her hand wasn't severed but it had to be severed afterwards. They couldn't save her hand. God love her, it had to be amputated from the wrist. They fixed her up with a glove and she was given a nice little job going around.

"We used to make lovely cream crackers then, and lovely cakes. Exquisite hand decorations. There was the cake room and the icing room. And in the 'Five o'clock Tea' room they did the *beautiful* little cakes, tiny little cakes and different colours on them, little icing and little cherries and maybe a little green tree. And that was all done by hand. See, there was a cake room and there was a Madeira cake, an Oxford Lunch cake—oh, that was *the* cake. It was sophisticated, it had the richest of materials. And then there was the 'King's Own' department and the 'Fairy Cakes' department. They had a lady called Maggie Davis and she had beautiful hands and she made cakes. I've *never seen* anything like them . . . Chateau, Plum, Oxford Lunch, Madeira, Chocolate Walnut. Gorgeous! The Chateau cakes were iced all around like crystal glass and it was absolutely out of this world. It was pillared icing. You'd just think it was crystal glass, so beautiful. And her department made the jam puffs. They were lovely. They were biscuits, fluffy, they'd fly away in your hand. And Maggie made special wedding cakes for some of the big shops in England. And we all got our wedding cakes made there. Jacob's gave you the cake, a two-tiered wedding cake, and you were asked if you'd like to buy a third tier yourself. The third tier was only small. And at Christmas you put your name in for a cake a week or two ahead. It was only four shillings. And every Christmas Ma would say, 'Don't forget to leave your order for a 4 lb Madeira.' Oh, that was beautiful. It was just that thick in milk and eggs. Oh, you could just lap it up . . . the eggs and milk. When the prices started to rise they had to give up all those cakes, they were too expensive. The 1939 War broke that up and the cake room had to be abolished. Then the troops had to be supplied with ordinary biscuits. They got a little, hard, round biscuit that could keep for years. It was for the soldiers. So the 1939 War finished all the cakes. But there was fun all the time. Oh, girls would sing at their work . . . the old songs. All the songs of that period, the grand old songs. We knew *every* song that was going. And the pictures then was very much in evidence. We went to every musical years ago. And we went to the Gaiety, saw *every* show at the Gaiety. And we got a week's holiday when I started and there was a holiday fund of £5. A man named Mr Hannan got up the holiday fund and took our money. They stopped the money out of our wages and sent it down to him and he put it in the bank for us. And then when my holiday came around I'd say, 'Mr Hannan, may I have my money?' We had no Christmas fund and on Christmas we never got any bonus. They were tight where wages was concerned. At Christmas you might bring in a bottle of wine underhanded and then serve a little sip of wine, if you *could*. But some of the forewomen were very strict and you couldn't in some departments. But we'd sing among ourselves. I loved the factory, loved my work. Oh, I really *loved* working there. I was never late. But when I retired in 1970 and came out of Jacob's I hadn't a penny. I didn't get anything coming out . . . and I had to go on the dole."

ELLEN EBBS—TAILORING FACTORY, AGE 86

She began work at age 14 making tweed caps and soon moved to a tailoring factory specialising in gentlemen's suits. On the piece-work system she preferred hand sewing to the machine which once drove a large needle completely through her finger. Saturday dances with pals provided welcome diversion from the factory routine. And Christmas parties in the

factory were great fun as the boss even joined in the singing and dancing. A skilled tailoress,
she still enjoys making beautiful clothing for her children and grandchildren.

"I was born on Townsend Street. My father was a foreman in a coal merchant's
way over on the North Wall. And I had six brothers and three sisters. And I'm
the last of the whole family left . . . the *last* one. We were always pretty
comfortable when we were young. I never had a poor day until I got married.
My husband was a house painter and when there'd be a slackness, like some bad
weather, there wouldn't be work and he'd be knocked off. But thank God he had
a very good mother. She was very kind and very generous to us. She got us
through the hard times.

"I came out of school when I was 14 and went to work straight away. First of
all I worked at cap making, finishing the hand sewing on them. Tweed caps. It
was a Jewman's shop over on Parnell Square. But I wasn't there very long and
my other two sisters worked at tailoring and they said, 'Here, we'll get you into
our factory.' Which they did. It was Baker's, another Jew. I was about 15. It was
quite a big factory, anything up to fifty people. They made gentlemen's suits.
But, see, nobody made a complete garment. Like, you made a lining and I made
a sleeve and somebody else made the collars. And then there was one person
that'd put them all together. I done anything and everything. The boss, he called
me his 'sundry hand'. He used to give me the special work to do. I did the
finishing work by hand. When I started at the factory I put on what they called
the crotch, that was a piece of material just at the fork of the trousers. I hemmed
that on. From then on I went to finishing sleeves and things. We were called a
tailoress.

"The factory was on Cornmarket Street. It was pretty comfortable. It was
real bright, lovely big windows, and plenty of light in the winter evenings. And
plenty of heat. We had our own stools to sit on and we used to bring our own
bit of cushion and sit on it. You just wore your own clothes. We had to be in at
half eight in the morning and we worked till 6.00 in the evening. And we got a
tea break at 10.00 in the morning, ten to fifteen minutes. And we'd bring in
maybe a couple of biscuits or a cake. From 1.00 to 2.00 we had for lunch. We
brought a lunch with us. There were three of us, meself and two other women,
and I'd bring in one thing, maybe rashers or sausages, and another'd bring in a
potato. One woman, she'd half-cook the potatoes before she'd come in in the
morning and then we'd put them on a little electric thing with two burners on
it, in the factory. Anyone who wanted to use it could. And we'd have a proper
little meal. Oh, and we'd sing to our heart's content! *Singing* at the *top* of our
voices. Yes. Someone'd start a song and the rest would join in and we'd all sing
together. To pass the time. We made enough noise that you'd hear us over the
machines. Oh, we'd sing every day. When you were singing you wouldn't feel the
time going by. And people'd go by the factory with the windows open and hear
us singing at the top of our voices.

"It was all piece-work and the more you did the more money you had. The minimum wage was thirty-three shillings a week. And, well, if you earned over that, good luck to you. And we did work overtime, mostly in the summertime when you'd want to be out and going places. I gave my mother her share of my money. Oh, gosh, she needed it cause my father was dead at the time I was working. A stroke. And she only had a small widow's pension and I was the last left in the house. But I didn't care for the piece-work system very much because I didn't earn an awful lot of money. I was too precise doing my work. Some people working there were *flyers!* You know, do the work real quick. But I'd take me time and do it neat. You had a book and every bit of work you did you had to enter it into the book and then at the end of the week that'd be all added up and that would be your wage. But I didn't earn an awful lot of money to tell you the truth. But I managed.

"Now I done most work by hand. We had big industrial power machines, a big row of machines all along and everyone sat at each machine and done their own work. But I did the finishing by hand. I was frightened of the machine when I started because I had never sat at a power machine. Then I was taught the machine and I got used to it, to regulating the foot [pedal]. You press this thing and the machine starts. A foot pedal. And if you hit it too hard the machine would go *flying* off real quick. The foreman himself was standing there telling me what to do. But I preferred the hand work because I wasn't so keen on the machine. Because one time I got a needle through me finger, went down through me finger and the needle, believe me, was that size [three inches]. That was with the padding machine. The needle went down through me finger and one of the men, he got some kind of instrument, a pinchers, and pulled it out. *Right through* me finger. Oh! I was in a panic and I kept screaming cause it caught me finger *in* the machine. Just put a bandage around me finger and I had to keep on working. That's a fact. I wasn't sent home or anything. It healed up afterwards. I was a bit careless and I must have turned me head away.

"Oh, I went to every dance in Dublin and then on Monday at the factory we'd tell one another who we saw, what they gave us and how we got on. There was the Pally up at Parnell Square and then there was the La Scala off Prince's Street. And there was small dance halls all around. Loads of dance halls around. We went with our own companions that lived down beside us. And we used to go over to the Workman's Club over on the quay, that was another dance hall. And we always met up with fellas to buy us some minerals or ice cream. The fellas weren't a bit shy, not the ones we knew anyway. We used to have what you called a ladies' choice. You'd go over and ask this fella, 'May I have this dance?' and you'd get chatting with him. Then it would be a 'gent's return' and then he'd come and take *you* up. This is the way it went. But in the summertime it'd be very hot in there.

"Now Mr Baker was a very kind man, everyone liked him. His name was Isaac Baker. But Mr Baker wanted you to do your work and he'd chastise you if it wasn't right. He used to walk up and down and have a look and see if things were right. And Mr Jimmy Browne was our foreman. He was a jolly type of man but he wouldn't take any nonsense from you. If it was done wrong it was brought back to you and you had to rip it out and do it all over again. Oh, but Mr Baker was a great man and he used to give us a party every year at Christmas time and it'd go on through the night and he'd be up dancing with his workers. But the following morning he didn't *know* you! This is the funny part of it. That's true. The party would be on a Saturday in the Christmas season, in the factory. We used to empty out the store rooms. All the bales of cloth would be all pushed aside and there'd be plenty of room. And plenty of food, all sorts of sandwiches and cakes and drink. And the funny part of it was that Jews are not allowed to eat meat from a pig. But, by God, he had plenty of hams. Oh, he *ate* that, that's a fact. And we had music, we had a piano there and he'd bring in somebody maybe to play an accordion. Oh, it went well into the night. And at the party Mr Baker'd come and dance with everybody and you'd have great sport with him—but the following morning he didn't know you and he'd pass you by. He was a lovely man though.

"Now Mr Baker, he kind of lost his memory or something and then he got this other man in named Fisher—he was also a Jew—to take over as the boss. But we didn't like him at all because he was always nosing down at you, following you around. And at that time the war broke out and we said he run out of England because he was afraid to be conscripted. He had lived in England and he should have *fought* for England. I'd say England fought for them [Jews]. I feel sorry for the Jews with what happened out in Germany. It was terrible. Oh, he was watching every little thing you'd do and you couldn't *talk*, believe it or not, when he came around. If he saw two of you standing talking together he'd tell you to get back to your work. Oh, you could still sing but you were doing your work at the one time. But you couldn't talk to another person, even if you were going to the toilet. See, the girls that smoked used to go in regular to the toilet to have their smoke. And we often laughed because they used to come to the end of their cigarette and sooner than throw away the butt they'd stick a pin in the bottom of the cigarette and they'd be puffing until it'd be gone to the very end. We used to laugh . . . keep puffing at it until there'd be nothing left but the pin. That's the truth.

"I was 32 when I got married and I went back to work after I got married. The reason I went back to work was, as I told you, my husband used to be in and out of work. At this particular time he was working and I was working and it was a bit awkward for to have a dinner ready for him when he'd come in. He used to be in before me and I'd get back home from the factory and he'd be sitting waiting for me and I'd have to start to cook a dinner for him. I was tired but I had to do it just the same. And this started a bit of an argument and he said, 'Either you work or I'll work. I'm not going to sit here waiting for you to come in to cook a meal.' So I gave up the job. Now he wouldn't get away with that today. Every woman works now.

"I had a flair for sewing and I *liked* it. I'm still sewing, believe it or not. I was always fond of the sewing and I started sewing at home for me own. I made me own wedding clothes, I made me daughter's wedding clothes, I made me two daughter-in-law's wedding clothes. I did. And all the bridesmaid's clothes. And

I never got one shilling for anything I made. I done it cause I liked doing it. They gave me little presents and things. And I made Confirmation dresses for some of the little girls in the street where I lived. And my granddaughters have had babies and I sat down and made all their christening robes . . . I was always fond of sewing."

MAUREEN BOYD—SOAP FACTORY, AGE 77

She left school at age 14 to work in Lever Brothers Soap Factory. Filling packets with soap powder left her hands so raw and sore that they had to be bandaged on weekends to heal. And working with harsh scrubbing detergents could severely burn one's nostrils and eyes. During peak periods workers had to put in twelve-hour shifts. Still, she was "quite happy" in the factory because it provided a weekly wage. On Founder's Day the boss took all the employees on a day's outing by train to Belfast for lunch, sightseeing and tea. In later years she joined the Women Workers' Union and gladly did picket duty during a strike for better pay and conditions.

"I was born on Summerhill in the tenements. Six children my mother had. My father was in the British Army in the First World War and then he joined the Free State Army here until he retired out of it. When we lived on Summerhill the barges used to go along the canal with all the grain and I can remember the locks filling up and the horses used to draw the barges. And the water was *clean* at that time. A lot of children were in their bare feet when I was young. And kids used to dive off that bridge, it was that clean, and in the summertime you'd be standing there watching them. They used to swim there and used to go under the archway to dress. And the swans used to be there and it was lovely, and the ducks. And there was the lock man's cottage.

"And then we moved down to Tolka Road when I was 14. I was the oldest and there was five after me so when I was 14, I went to work at Lever Brothers' Soap Factory down on Castleforbes Road. They made soap powders, soaps, cosmetics, perfume. It was an English firm. I got the job in Lever's through school, the parish priest, Father Kearney. There were six or seven of us through him got the interview. I think he knew the nurse. And you had to be well recommended. And you got an interview. There was a nurse there and you had to be examined before you went to that job. Had to have an examination and see that you had good teeth and hair and everything had to be clean. And if you were sick she was a qualified nurse. I got ten shillings a week and I handed that up to my mother and got sixpence back. And the pictures then was only four pence.

'You had to work very hard now. You started at 8.00 and finished at half past five. When you'd come in in the morning you got your card stamped and going home in the evening it was stamped. My clock number was 196. And there was always a man timekeeper there and if you were late a minute, a quarter of an hour would be stopped on you [from wages]. You were allowed a cup of tea in the morning at 10.00, just the women. The men didn't have it. And you only had five minutes for your tea. And you couldn't eat and if you were caught eating, like bread, you'd be sacked. We could talk and we could sing the latest songs and that—as long as you didn't overdo it. Sing all the old and new songs and we'd join in. And when there was slack time you got cleaning floors and windows to do and scrubbing. But we were delighted that we didn't get a notice that you were getting knocked off. Everyone was happy to do that so that you wouldn't be sacked. So you were told to do cleaning and you got aprons and buckets, scrub brushes and cloth.

"Now my job was all hand-filling the packets with soap powder and, oh, it used to cut the hands off you. You were supposed to wear gloves but your hands would get sweaty and you'd do better without them. And you had to have a mask on your mouth. Your hands would get red and raw and then they'd get cut from washing them with the coarse sodas. We used to go home and rub a kind of gel into our hands and they had a kind of white vaseline that they'd give you for to rub on your hands. At weekends you'd have them bandaged up and your hands would heal on weekends and then you'd be fresh for Monday. Then I was filling cardboard packets with Vim. Vim was a cleaner for scrubbing things. There was potash in it and you had to have a mask because that got into your lungs. The mask had a square of cotton gauze and you'd tighten it at the back of your head and you had to have a hat and your hair had to go up underneath the hat. And we wore white overalls. And with the mask the *sweat* was *dreadful* and you had to keep changing this pad. They called it a respirator and you could change the cotton wool pad. You *had* to change it with the sweat. You would change it about every hour. It would swell out and the nose part would be black, from whatever it did to your nostrils . . . it'd turn black. It'd come from your nostrils. And one time I got Vim in my eye and I had an *awful* eye for about a week. Oh, it was dreadful. But workers up in the cosmetic department, they used to sit, making toilet soaps and perfumes. When work was slack you might be sent up to the cosmetic department. I did that. It was lovely clean work and all the toilet soap was hand wrapped.

"The bosses were behind the scenes but they'd take the odd walk around, just stand there. The bosses were all English, Protestants, but we all got on, we were all the one. And we always had a Founder's Day outing, until the war years. A Founder's Day, they used to call it, for the founding of the factory. We used to get a *lovely* outing. We went to Belfast and to Cork. Oh, yes, by train. The *whole* factory, men and women, went. It was a good factory to work for. You were brought to a hotel for your lunch and sometimes you got it on the train and you got your tea coming back. And when you got there you could go around yourself with your friends, sight-seeing and that. We'd get the train at 9.00 in the morning and then get back about 9.00. A great day and they provided everything. And at the Christmas party you got a tea and there was dancing among the workers. It was in the canteen. There'd be decorations and all and people, if they were game enough, could sing and dress up and do their party piece. But there was no drink. But many of the women met their husbands in the factory. Oh, yes. And the women didn't work after they were married. No, never. And if you were getting married they always gave you a present of a clock and it was stamped with an engraving from Lever Brothers and with so many years' service. For a wedding gift. It was like a Westminster chime clock, lovely, and every quarter-hour it'd strike. Either sex got that when they were leaving to be married. And if you were widowed you were taken back.

"We had to work standing all the day. Standing and bending over. And summertime was the busy time and we were in at 7.00 in the morning until 7.00 in the evening. It was non-union at that time, there was no union. And when I'd get home and have my tea I'd fall asleep at the table. It was too much, such long hours. No union when we first started but we joined the Women Workers' Union and you had to pay your union [fees] every week. The Women Workers' Union was over in Fleet Street. Oh, everybody had to join that. And there was a strike for about six weeks and you had your time to picket. I didn't mind being on the picket line for a couple of hours. You were young. It was for more money at the time. And before that we got a week's holiday but with the union we got two weeks' holiday and you were paid for your holidays.

"Now I was on Tolka Road when the bomb fell. I was 21. We were all in bed and my mother and father was in bed and I was the last of the children and I was saying my prayers and I heard this engine with its [droning] sound and I looked out my window and seen all the searchlights. And the next thing this big, big flash. It happened over on the North Strand. And *all* the windows rattled and I got all the children out of the bed. And my daddy was deaf from the First World War and me mother said, 'Eddie, Eddie, *get up*, they're dropping bombs on us!' 'Oh, will you *lie down* now,' he says. It was a landmine they dropped on the Strand. I saw the flash, like a bluish flash it was. And we all got under the stairs. Oh, *everyone* was running and the *doors open* and people *roaring* and *shouting* and *screaming* and all going to the Strand to have a look. But the following morning we went out and it was a *beautiful* morning and this big crater in the road and all the shops and houses were gone from both sides. *Crowds* of people, they came from everywhere for to see. The local defence forces were all around with helmets on and you wouldn't be let too near it. This was all new to us in a neutral country. People weren't expecting the likes of that. It *really* was *dreadful*.

"Oh, we were quite happy in the factory. If you done your work there was no one to bother you. They were simple and happy days . . . you hadn't a lot but we were far happier. I had a very good mother and father and it was homely and happy. All my sisters and brothers had to go to England, there was no work here. And I have four of them buried over there. And I went over too cause it went slack in Lever Brothers and you were getting a week on and a week off. I worked in a munitions factory making bombs. We were working with T.N.T. powder and making round detonators. It was £3 [weekly wages] we were getting and we thought that was a lot now, for the time. I was about three years in England."

CHRISSIE MCADAM—MITCHELL'S ROSARY FACTORY, AGE 70

Upon leaving school, she was employed in Mitchell's Rosary Bead Factory where her mother worked as a forewoman. Fancy rosary beads were exported in all shapes and colours around the world. Although the work was dusty and tedious the factory was one of the better ones in Dublin at the time—but there was no pension system. Mr Mitchell was a much-loved fatherly figure to many of the women workers and after his death factory life was never quite the same.

"I was born on Sean McDermott Street. My father worked in the Dublin Corporation as a night watchman. At that time he had T.B. and he wasn't too strong of a man. And my mother had to take up work in Mitchell's. My mother worked all her life, forty-odd years, in Mitchell's and she was a forewoman there. She dyed the rosary beads different colours. We lived in tenement houses and there was just my sister and me. And the toilet was out in the back in the yard. I remember that Sean McDermott Street was great, the *atmosphere* with the people. Very friendly, very homely people. It was wonderful. We'd be sitting outside the hall door on the steps and we'd all gather together and be sitting there and be singing or playing. You knew everybody. It was wonderful. Now we'd be 16 or 17 and we'd go out on the street and play at skipping with a rope. And *married* women and all would get out and be playing. Oh, yes. Oh, it was marvellous, honestly.

"Now the convent here, back in those days it wasn't a criminal convent but they used to have some girls in there. And I had a cousin in there and the nuns reared her because her mother died and she had twenty-one children. And she was the youngest of them. And she was very wild and so the nuns helped out and they took her in and they reared her up. And years later the convent then took in criminal girls and girls off the street, girls in trouble. And they were made to work hard in the laundry doing curtains and bed clothes.

"I went to Rutland Street School for a while and then to Marlborough Street School. I come out of school when I was 14 and went into Mitchell's straight away. Your mother would just automatically bring you in. Mitchell's was on Waterford Street. At that time I'd say there was maybe fifty people and most were really old people. There was a lot more women than men. I enjoyed going in. Started at 8.00 in the morning and we worked till 6.00 at night. It was very hot there sometimes when you'd be working, cause you'd have to wear a hat. Oh, yes, your hair had to be up under a hat because your hair could catch in the machinery. A kind of elastic hat. And we wore a white smock. We could chat with each other cause we were all sitting there. But the noise from the machines would be a lot, you'd hear the noise. But we'd be sitting close to each other and we'd have a little chat. And the place would be full of singing. They *all* sang while they were working. And you could have your cup of tea and in the winter he had a big boiler in the middle of the room and when it'd be too cold we'd all take our turns and go stand around it. And, of course, we'd forget ourselves and stand around it for half of the day. And when we'd see Mr O'Neill [foreman] coming we'd all run!

"And a crowd of us together from the factory used to go dancing. We had a great time. At that time the Americans, the Yanks, would be over and I was going with one of them. I met him up at one of the dance halls and he was coloured, not really dark now. I remember his name, Vincent West, and he come down to me mother and I was going with him and me Ma was very strict about religion at that time and she'd say, 'Ah, no, she's Catholic and that wouldn't work out.' Cause in those days all the people around Sean McDermott Street married one another. And he went away then and wrote to me and then I stopped and that was the end of that.

"The rosary beads were made out of the cow horns. Mr Dunleavy'd cut them. He used to be at the back and he used to open the cow horns and flatten them out. He'd have to heat them to soften them to cut them. And he'd *flatten* them out, dead flat, and then they'd be put in bags or maybe thrown in a big heap outside in the back and we'd all go out with our buckets and collect them. And we'd come back in and sit down and get on the machine and shape all the beads out on this thing. And then you'd turn it around the other way and press them and they'd all come out then. And there were different shapes. Like, some were heart shaped. Oh, *all* different shapes we'd have, all shapes and sizes. There'd be tiny ones and Communion ones and bigger ones, and little round beads with a little shamrock on them. A variety, cause a lot would be going to the United States. The rosary beads were sent to all foreign countries. So the machine would cut out the beads just like you'd drill into a piece of wood and the beads would pop out. And then we had a sort of griddle thing and we'd shake that and all the shavings would come away and all your beads would be left. Then you'd put all your beads into a box and in the evening we'd go up to the foreman and we'd have our beads in a box and he'd weigh them and see how many pounds you'd have and he'd mark that down in your book. It was piece-work. And at the end of the week he'd add all that up and you'd know how much you had. I used to come out with a fair bit of a wage.

"Doing the beads was very dusty. Oh, there'd be dust all over you, in your hair and everything. And sometimes we used to cover our mouths cause of the dust. Oh, there used to be terrible accidents there. I remember a young girl there, she was working with me, and she bent down to pick something up off the ground and she cut the scalp of her head on the [machine] belt. Oh, her *whole scalp* was gone and they had to take her away.

"A cousin of mine used to join the beads and make the whole rosary with a wire. And I used to do it at one time. You'd do it with a wire and the beads had to be polished first. My mother used to polish them and dry them. You polished them on a big buffer machine with electricity and that'd go around and polish all the beads. And for dyeing them you had to put them into a big tray and leave them all on a tray to dry. Oh, God, they had *every* colour. A natural colour, just a plain light woody colour, and then you'd have an oak colour and green ones with a little shamrock on them. They'd be special. My mother was the only one that done all the dyeing. And the crucifix was shaped out by a machine. The cross was made out of an Irish cow horn, they pressed them out. And then the figure had to be put on the horn cross. The figure was metal or tin and they used to cut them out and some of the girls used to have to nail them in. A girl would be pressing a lever and they'd cut out all these little figures. And *I* could do all that.

"Now it happened that I was 16 years old when my mother became pregnant, after sixteen years. Oh, she was into her thirties. And Mr Mitchell wanted to know why she wasn't in that day cause she was working up till the time she was having the baby. And he didn't know. And she was carrying these huge trays of beads. She worked very hard. And he wanted to know where was Dolly, cause they called her Dolly. And someone said she was home in bed having a baby! And then she went back to work again. My mother wasn't out long after having the baby. She went straight back to work. She *had* to, cause my father wasn't earning much money and she *had* to get back to work. She worked *very, very* hard. Me aunt used to look after the baby. And when she was born, my sister, she was *black*. And my mother, her body was all discoloured. It was like getting a brush and splashing her with colour. And the baby was coloured black, a mahogany colour. Me mother went to a doctor about it cause they couldn't figure out what it was. But she thought it was from all the *dyeing* with the beads, that she might have got discoloured. I used to see her body all splashed with colour.

"Mr O'Neill, he was the foreman, he used to look after all the girls and do the knives when they'd get broken. He'd fix the knives for the machines. See, sometimes when you'd pull your cutting machine too hard the knife would break and he'd repair that. But he'd give us a telling-off, I can tell you. Oh, we used to be half afraid going up to him. They used to be terrified, some of them. But he was a good foreman. And there was one girl there so afraid of Mr O'Neill that she actually would shake with fright. Now Mr Mitchell was very, very good. He was a *lovely* gentleman. He was a huge big man and he used to wear these navy pinstripe suits and always had a big red rose. Or he'd have a pink one. And, oh, my God, the minute they'd see him coming in in the morning *all* the heads turned and he'd walk over and say good morning. You know, a lovely gentleman and very homely and very friendly.

"Indeed, sure me mother used to go out to his house in Mount Merrion and I used to go out with her. She might do a little turn-out for him in the house and she'd bring me with her and he'd get all the apples up [from the orchard] and give us a *load* of apples to bring home. Oh, he had a beautiful house. He was a proper gentleman. And when I was younger we had great parties in Mitchell's. On Christmas Eve we'd have a great party. There'd be singing and dancing and Mr Mitchell's sons used to join in. At that time they were at college but they'd come in and join in with us. We had a few drinks and the lot. I used to look forward to that cause I was only a kid at the time.

"And I had a cousin from Galway and me mother got her in there to work and she got a kind of a limp and wasn't it T.B. of the hip she got. And Mr

Mitchell used to give her a bottle of milk a day and he'd tell her, 'Take that, drink that', because she'd be going like that [limping] and she was delicate. He was a gentleman. He was like a father figure he was, a great man. When Mr Mitchell was dying I was up there with him. I went up to the Mater Nursing Home to see him and I was very sad. I was crying because he was *so kind* to me and me mother. And his son Alex was there. And you'd see Alex cutting the bread very tiny to give to him, like a baby. And then he took him up in his arms like a child and walked him all around the room. It was very sad. I cried now when I seen him . . . cause we were very close. I liked working there. I worked from 14 and I was about seventeen years there. But they had no pension. My mother come out and never got nothing. And she worked there *all her life*, over forty years. When Mr Mitchell died his son took over . . . and the place wasn't the same then."

ARTHUR MURPHY—WINSTANLEY'S SHOE FACTORY, AGE 80

He is an outspoken man with strong convictions about the exploitation of workers in the old days. As a young lad he was badly treated by shoe repair men for whom he worked. Then at age 14 he went into Winstanley's Shoe Factory working "only" forty-eight hours a week for eight shillings. Conditions were "primitive" as workers had to endure deafening noise from the machines and dust which clogged lungs and caused serious respiratory illnesses. He eagerly joined the Workers' Union of Ireland and participated in a bitter twenty-seven-week strike in 1934. When strikers were bullied and threatened by the owners they turned to their hero Jim Larkin for advice and support. After fifty-one years he retired in 1984, receiving "nice words" which he felt were empty. Afterwards he walked home feeling downhearted about how he had spent his working life.

"I came out of school at 13 years and 10 months and went to work in a shoe repair shop. It was a man named Grennel. You looked and seen advertisements in the evening paper—if you were fortunate enough to *have* an evening paper— and then you went and applied for it. I went to work for him for little more than a year. The hours were too bad. Half eight in the morning to half six. But Thursday, it could be till maybe half twelve the next morning. Kids were exploited in those days . . . all workers were being exploited. I had a little push-bike and on one occasion I came home here at ten past 1.00 in the morning after working and me father was sitting here waiting for me and he says, 'You've done your last day in that place.'

"Then another shoe repairer down on the Coombe was looking for a boy. At that age you're ambitious and I could visualise meself maybe in ten years' time owning me own shop. Ah, we all had our dreams! Anyway, I went down there and made it clear that I wasn't going to work outrageous hours. His name was Gartland and he *assured* me, 'No way, no way.' Well, that was all right for a while. He started me off ripping off the old soles and heels. Then you progressed to putting on layers of leather 'build up' where the heel was worn down badly. And then you learned hand stitching and how to make threads with hemp. Now I lasted not very long because he started the same thing again. He used to keep me in the shop for *company*. Now I was working for seven and six a week and I wasn't getting any overtime. But he kept me there for company for himself till half ten and eleven o'clock Saturday nights. And there's boyos coming out of the pubs intoxicated and they'd be shouting and brawling. Oh, his door was open. Because they were all tenement houses on the Coombe and women, they'd be running down getting their family's shoes to have them for Sunday morning. This is why he remained open so late.

"Anyway, I was getting a bit fed up with it. So this particular night I knew he was *keeping* me and I says to him, 'I want to go home.' But didn't a young girl come in with what we termed a bluecher boot. Dairy men and men on heavy manual work wore them. Very heavy. The uppers were made of kip, very hard, tough leather. And they were nailed and screwed, the soles, with hobnails. Now this fella was a dairy man and his pair was *caked* with cow droppings. They didn't even bother to *clean* it. And he threw it to me and said, 'Would you stitch that heel on for me?' And it was a quarter to twelve at this time. Oh, that was the straw that broke the camel's back! I finished the job because this man wanted his boots to go out and milk the cows at 4.00 in the morning. I felt I'd be letting the man down if I didn't do the boot. So the boss gave me the seven and six and I says, 'I won't be in on Monday.'

"So then I got told by somebody that there was a chance of getting into Winstanley's in Back Lane. Oh, this was a step from hell to heaven! Because it was 8.00 to a quarter to six with a half-day on a Saturday. You only worked a forty-eight hour week. And that was that. So I went up and seen the manager and I told him that I had experience, that I wasn't going in red raw, and he took me on. He put me at very menial jobs, fitting out lasts for shoes. Boys starting there were 14 years of age. No apprenticeship, you went straight in on the production line. And management at that time was *very quick* to say it wasn't a trade. They didn't want to pay tradesman's rates! Oh, but it *was* a trade. It was. When I went in it was eight shillings a week. At age 21 you qualified for £2. Actually, we had all tradesmen, all shoemakers, it was one of the oldest trades.

"At that time we were doing nail and screw boots, like the bluecher boot, for Guinness's brewery workers and we made them for the army. All the labourers then wore those bluecher boots. It was a very labour-intensified job because it was practically all by hand. Oh, they'd last for ever. Now my father was a brewery man and he used to wear them and he'd be sitting there at night time whistling an old tune to himself and he'd get his penknife and scrape off all the dirt and mud off that boot. Then he'd brush it *thoroughly* before he'd apply Cherry Blossom boot polish. That was the thing used at that time. And he'd always get a good shine. Then new technology came in and we started to make what was called the welted shoe. The welted shoe was a better product, not as big nor as cumbersome, nor did it entail as much man hours to make. I'd say the bluecher went out around 1934. Then we started making women's shoes and we made mostly the Cuban type heel shoe. People didn't go in for all fancy shoes at that time. They made what they called a court shoe, a flat-heeled shoe. And another one had a strap across. Very simple shoes at that time. Now also at that time here we had tanneries in Ireland. They made leathers, like O'Callaghan's in Limerick. But they weren't producing leather cheap enough for the factories here. And we started importing stuff from England and all our tanneries *folded* up. Now I was an active trade unionist and I always queried, 'Why shouldn't we buy Irish material if we're making Irish shoes?' And they said, 'It's a matter of economics.' It was a stand pat answer.

"I'd say there were about 150 people working at Winstanley's. It was mostly men but women worked at the cutting and tapering. And the women got less [wages] than the men, always did. In the morning a little man named Dick Woods used to come out at five minutes to eight and he'd ring a hand bell. A small little grey-haired man with a hard hat on him. We'd be gathered outside and he'd ring the bell and then he'd go in. Some men'd leave at five to eight and others would hang on till the last. The second bell was *funny*. See, when he'd ring the first bell if you were down at the end of the lane you moved up near the gate, but you still didn't go in. And then he'd come out and ring the second bell and then you *ran*, because if you didn't run he'd go in and shut the gate and you were locked out. And you lost a half an hour [wages]. Then he'd come out again at half eight and open the gate again and ring the bell again and you had to be in like a *flash*. But you look back at those times . . . and they were a source of annoyance to us.

"You brought in your own apron, a cotton apron. They didn't supply it. Oh, conditions were very primitive. It would be hot in the summertime and quite cold in the winter. There was a big boiler and they'd stoke it with coke. And there was pulleys off this boiler that drove the power in the factory. It was *steam* power driving the machines. And they had gas mantels that would be lit. And the men worked on their feet. But the management and office staff was all Protestant. Wouldn't *oblige* a Catholic in the office. We sort of accepted our lot. And no smoking in the factory. And tea breaks were forbidden—*forbidden*! You had a toilet where there were two toilet pots and a urinal about three feet away from those. Oh, it was terrible small. If there was four men in it, it was overcrowded. And men would be standing in there having a smoke [secretly] and chatting and if you were a lad you wouldn't be allowed to stand and converse with the men. Men wouldn't tolerate it. One of the men'd get you by the ears and you'd be throwed out.

"Oh, and the factory was very dusty. When I went in there they were stone walls, whitewashed, and very rough. And all wooden beams across, say about ten feet high. And fanlights in the roof, but no windows in the walls. Just light through the roof. Now there was a *three* to *four* inch layer of dust on these wooden beams. The dust would come off the leather, from people scouring. In those days there was an inadequate extraction of the dust. Oh, I finished up with acute bronchitis and I suppose many, many men before me came out of it with the same complaint, leather dust clogging up their lungs. Very fine dust. And the noise from the presses, cutting out leather, was *unbearable*. And nobody put things over their ears. That was unknown. And it was one of the more risky jobs. Most of them had fingers missing . . . or bits of fingers. It was accepted, it was a job and you done it.

"You know, it's a strange thing . . . human beings are funny people. There were those who thought they [O'Neill's who ran the factory] were great people, 'Oh, they're keeping the factory open. They're keeping us working.' Then there were the others who said, 'They're screwing us, *exploiting* us, and we're just getting the minimum of what we're entitled to.' And a large percentage of us had that attitude. But people were *afraid* to express it. Fear of being sacked or sanctions taken against them by management. It happened. Oh, it did. One instance happened to me. I had this run-in with this managing director and he was the son now, Denis O'Neill. I had a hot and heavy argument with him in the office. I was representing the workers.

"I was the chairman of the factory committee. The shop stewards were with me and I had some very hot things to say to him. And the next morning I was walking down in that direction and he was coming along and I was going to say 'Good morning, Mr O'Neill', and he turned his head like that [away] and put his nose up in the air and walked away. And he done it for six months, deliberately. And the managing director was a man named R. J. O'Neill. And at Christmas time he used to come and stand at the gate and as we came out he'd say, 'Happy Christmas, happy Christmas, have a nice time.' But we *got* nothing. And there was this old man, Johnny Madden was his name, and Johnny was after having a couple of jars at dinner hour, you see, and Johnny was walking out and he [director] says, 'Happy Christmas' and Johnny turns around and says, 'What have we to be happy about?' and walked on. He caught your man by surprise. And that was the last time he appeared at the door saying 'Happy Christmas.' Never again.

"Sometimes we had short time. You'd work for about three weeks and then bang, you were thrown out for a week. And it happened at a moment's notice. So we became members of the Workers' Union of Ireland. And I met the famous Jim Larkin. He was a wonderful man. And then we had a big strike in Winstanley's in 1934. We were out for twenty-seven weeks. Very bitter. Oh, we done negotiating. Now there was a shop steward, Paddy Grant, and he done *fifty-seven* years' service in the factory. He went in as a boy at 14 years of age and had to climb a barricade in 1916 to go up the lane to go into the factory. They had barricades during the Rebellion and Paddy had to climb over the barricades to get to his job. And Paddy got us to join the Workers' Union of Ireland. And there was a lash-back—management *sacked* him. And there was a vote taken and we came out on strike.

"Now when we were out a couple of days we went down to a place, an old building in Fishamble Street, called Mallon Hall. The WUI had that as their hall and we went down there and had a meeting. And it was agreed to go [stay] on strike . . . a vote. We were only a couple of days out and we all received letters to our homes telling us if we *didn't* resume work on the following Monday at

8.00 we could come up at 9.00 for our cards—we were *sacked*. That was their attitude. So we went up and seen this man, Jim Larkin, and we asked him what to do. And he says, 'Do what you think is *right*. Yous have the conscience, yous have the ability. You say yes or no. I'm not going to tell you what to do. It's entirely up to yourselves. You can go into work as that letter tells you or you can go up and get your cards at 9.00 and *fight* on.' So we had a picket on the factory, a huge picket. There was about a hundred of our people on it. And this was at 8.00 in the morning. Then Dick Woods came out and rang the bell at five to eight. And half the picket line disappeared. *In* the gate! Rang it again at 8.00. And another half of the picket line went in! *Fear*! The threatening letter. They went in for that. We were left with twenty-eight men and we were told to go up and get our cards. They went in and scabbed the job. Oh, the unity broke. Oh, there was *murder* over it. Oh, a couple of them was roughed up. Workmates. It was never the same afterwards.

"Now they went in and worked for two and a half days and *then they* were sacked. The firm had to lay them off, because key personnel were out. See, among the twenty-eight of us were the key personnel. And these people couldn't work without us. So they were laid off. And the firm told them they could go to the unemployment exchange and get their unemployment. So Jim Larkin told us, 'Yous go sign on the labour as well. If it's good for them, it's good for you.' So we went down and signed on. So they disqualified the *whole lot* because we were signing on. We were told, 'You're on *strike*.' Incidentally, I wasn't a member of the union at this time. I was too young, I was only 16. But I was out with them on strike. And Paddy Grant said to Mr Larkin, 'Jim, we have a young lad here and he's not a member of the union but he's out with us.' And I can remember Jim Larkin's words. He says, 'He *is now*! He's a member of the union now.' And he says, 'You'll get a half a crown a week strike pay.' And that's what I got.

"But it was a hard time. As I said, we had twenty-eight of us and we had to picket seven shops and the factory. Seven shoe shops. They called their shops 'Denisons' because the eldest son was named Denis. So we had seven shops to picket and the factory. With twenty-eight people. And we had to picket these shops for eight hours a day, which was very hard picketing. Now all this started the second week of August and we were out from then to February. Right through to the third week of February. And *that* Christmas was a very hard time for most people. There were married men out. I was a boy and I had me father working and me mother was only worried about me going out and getting wettings on the picket. But come Christmas the message was getting around that these people have *nothing*. I remember Jim Larkin and a man named Charlie Phipps who was connected with a butcher's section of the union and on Christmas Eve they went around the whole city walking. They had no transport. And they went around *begging* the butchers and they got about nineteen or twenty-three *shoulders* of bacon to give to the men who was on picket, the married men. That's true. They *begged* the butchers. It was for their families. That was their Christmas dinner. I come off me picket and we were all told to meet at Mallon Hall at quarter past six. And when he got back they were handing out these parcels to the married men. Ah, I felt like crying . . . the significance of the whole thing. And after that, on Christmas Eve, Jim Larkin didn't even have the price of the tram fare for himself and he walked home. He was a *huge* man in spirit. That made an indelible impression in my mind. And later on I read about him.

"I worked from 1933 to 1984 when I retired. They brought me up to the general manager's office. I meekly walked behind me foreman up to the office. And the manager behind his big desk. And then they started to sort of talk to one another, reminiscing about all my virtues and what I had done in the factory and how I had put factory first and I was always a dedicated worker, but from time to time I have caused them a little bit of trouble with me activities in the union and we didn't always see eye to eye but we always agreed to differ. You know, a *lot* of pious platitudes. And I was getting a bit uneasy and I started to sweat around the collar. Ah, they gave you all this nice phraseology, all these nice words, but it was only words. *Deep in their heart* their attitude was 'them and us.' And I just said, 'I done me duty as I seen it.' And then he stood up and handed me this little parcel and wished me a happy retirement. They gave me this clock in a box with me name on it. And me heart was down in me boots. I said to meself, 'There's fifty-one years wasted.' I was terribly upset. But I didn't say it to anyone. I just took it in my stride. And I still feel a bit of resentment. If I had me life to live over again I wouldn't have went in there. But great men . . . fellow sufferers! Ah, they were marvellous."

HARRY BRIERTON—JACOB'S BISCUIT FACTORY, AGE 81

When he was a young lad working in Jacob's they had a school, swimming pool and recreation hall with billiards. But the intense heat from the steel floors caused him to feel weak and lose weight. He began rolling dough and later worked in the bake house. He especially enjoyed the annual Christmas party in which talented dancers, singers and comedians from the factory performed. Eventually he joined the union but resented the shop stewards who greedily sought power. After forty-nine years of service he retired with what he feels is a paltry pension.

"I was reared on Mercer Street and was 14 when I went in. I had three sisters in Jacob's. You just applied for it and with a bit of luck you were taken on. There was over 3,000 in it at that time, when they were in Bishop Street. It was next to Guinness's. You had to pass the doctor, they had their own doctor in the factory, and a nurse. And you had to pass an intelligence test too, written. And then there was a school in Jacob's. You went for a couple of hours each day. The schoolmaster, Mr Taylor, was the *best* man that was ever in there. He'd no pets, everyone was the same to him. He taught *everything*, arithmetic, carpentry. The school was from age 14 to 16 and different times for girls and boys. And there were vats in the centre of the factory about twenty foot by thirty and you were taught to swim and taught life saving. Sometimes you'd be brought up to the zoo and you were even brought out to visit other factories, for education. Like cigarette factories and chocolate factories to show you how everything works. And you were taught woodwork. They had a night class there for woodwork and they had furniture-makers there teaching anyone who wanted to go. Some chaps learned to make their own furniture when they were getting married. That's a fact. The like of me, I started drinking young and I never bothered about going to it.

"We worked from eight till half five. And we worked on Saturday too, eight to half twelve. At ten to eight you'd be standing outside having a smoke and at three minutes to eight you'd start rambling in. There was boards inside with hooks and you had a little check, about the size of a ten penny piece, just metal and your number was on it and you hung it up on your number going in. The timekeeper came along and checked all the numbers and anybody without a check was absent. An awful lot of people had bicycles in them days and we had a bicycle shed there in Peter's Row. They were covered. And that was a job for another man that'd look after the bicycle shed. There'd be a couple of hundred. As a boy in the factory you got a kind of khaki blouse and trousers and a red canvas belt. The girls had blue smocks. You bought your own shoes but it was very warm in the factory and when you come in everyone'd take off their shoes and wear an old pair of slippers. You brought in your own slippers. And after the war sandals with the open straps became very popular. One man, he come up and says, 'I was down at the bake house and they're going around like San Francisco monks!' Like them sandals the monks wore.

"Oh, it was *very hot* at that time, cause it was all steel floors. There were five lofts. The lofts were like storeys in a house. The bottom part, that was the bake house. It was hard to put up with the heat. Sure, the steel floors used to get hot. Heat all over the place. You could open up your shirt. I know when I went in first I faded away and got very thin from the heat. Very uncomfortable there in the heat and then they didn't want you opening the windows in case birds would be flying in. See, birds used to fly in and be picking at the dough. Not much fresh air. I seen many a person nearly collapse from it and then brought up to the surgery.

"When I started at 14, I think it was fourteen shillings a week. Now at 14 young boys would put the dough on the table and we'd roll out the dough and there'd be men cutting out the biscuits by hand. And then you had steel pans about three foot square and we placed the biscuits on this and then put the pans on a rack with wheels on it. And then shove it up to the oven and a man'd put them in. Other boys would have the job of greasing the pans so the biscuits wouldn't stick. You done that with a kind of cloth and you smeared it over. If you put too much on it the biscuits would spread. And if you didn't put enough they'd stick. Had to be just right. Then at 16 you might be put down on a machine that used to cut out the dough. The dough would run along in a big strip like the carpet there and that'd go under the cutter machine. The machines used to work very fast. You'd have to be very alert. The shortbread was all cut out by hand but other biscuits like Arrowroot, they'd be all done by machine and had to be iced or sugared. But then all the boys were sacked when they were 19. See, they were coming to men's wages. That was the idea. At 19 it'd be about £2 odd wages. So at 19 you knew you were going. There was some kept on. I don't know why some were kept on and others were sacked, cause there was good lads, good workers sacked there. Now I escaped that because I was sent out on the vans as a van boy at 17. Then I got driving after that. So I escaped being sacked at 19.

"The girls had the hardest jobs in the factory. They were kept going all day. It was mostly women. I'd say there was three women to every man in the factory. Now when the biscuits would come out baked the pans were emptied on to a canvas [conveyor] and girls used to pack them into boxes—and you'd want to see their fingers going! Stack them up to their elbow and put them into boxes. Ah, it took some doing and they were going all day. Ah, the women had it rough. Doing the *same* thing. But the girls would be as happy as Larry, all singing when they'd be working, whatever the latest songs would be. They'd all be singing together. Breaks the monotony. But all the tins that came back from the shops, they all had to be cleaned and the girls did that. And where they worked it was a draughty old place. And they had these rubber aprons in front of them. Some of the tins coming back from the shops were disgraceful, grease and everything would be in them. Used to be *filthy*. And they had to have them all spotless to be used again. Very bad job it was.

"Men and women could mix. Oh, that's how many a fella got married in there. It all started in the factory. And girls knew it was the rule that if you got married you left. You'd see that a couple was getting close to each other and there was something brewing. But in them days they didn't do it openly like they do it now. The canteen was for both and you could buy your dinner and all. The canteen was up at the top of the house and you had one hour, from 1.00 to 2.00. There was one old lad used to go up there in the canteen, the 'Jigger' Murphy. He was driving a horse. Well, he'd go up and sit at a table, sit down and get his dinner, and no one would get near him. And if some new young ones—girls— would come into the place, fellas would say, 'Oh, there's a seat over at that table.' And Jigger would sit down and next thing he'd take out his teeth and put them beside the plate. Couldn't eat with his teeth in.

"And they had all trades there, like a cooper. And when they had horses a blacksmith up on Camden Row used to look after them. The horses used to pull the lorries with boxes of biscuits and go down to the quays with them, big wooden boxes, crates. And the stables was down here in Cuffe Lane. I'd say they had eight or ten horses. And Jacob's had a football ground up on Rutland Avenue. And in the recreation hall you had billiards and things. You could go over there in the night time and play billiards, play solo, different games. And you had a gala in the vats every year. A swimming gala. All kinds of races. It'd go a couple of days. It was in the night time. And there was a temperance club in Jacob's. Nearly everyone joined it when he was a boy. It was two pence a week. And you got a free excursion and you got little benefits out of it in the summer. Ah, but a van driver got me put out of it when he found me drinking. I was about 19. Ah, but there was better drinkers there than me.

"I went out on the vans. They were motor cars at that time. Five hundredweight Dodges and then these big three ton Albions. Now the Dodge had only the driver but the bigger vans had a helper. I was a helper. Helped to load it up and then when you went to shops you had to carry the stuff in and carry out the empties. Now it was pretty rough because there was places where you had to go upstairs to them. And you'd be tired at the end of the day. We used to carry five of the large biscuit tins at a time. I was at helping for four years and then I went to driving. When the war broke out I joined up and I was out of the factory for about six years. And when you joined up they gave you half pay. Now I was married and my wife got the half pay all the time I was in the army. That was a help. I was in this [Irish] army first but the pay was *hopeless*. I'd five children at the time. So I got out and went up north and joined up with the RAF in Belfast. And I come home the end of 1946. And when I come out I was back on the vans again. And, as I told you, I was fond of the gargle. So I was being watched. There was a fella trailing me on a bike and I didn't know it. Oh, I was finally sent for and he told me he wrote down every pub I went into. They were making all kinds of threats. So I says, 'I'll go into the bake house', and then I finished up there.

"Now when I went into the bake house you couldn't get a smoke in there and couldn't make tea in Jacob's at one time. If you got caught making tea you'd be sacked. But then [later] you were allowed ten minutes in the morning and evening for a tea break and we had a place we used to call the Green. It was an old graveyard, the Huguenots' graveyard. That was in Peter Street and it was in the middle of the factory. Oh, there were headstones there. And seats all around where we used to sit. And the building was a mortuary, that was still there. And we used to sit in there when it'd be raining. And that's where you made your tea, in the mortuary, in big metal containers. You'd bring your own mug. And you could smoke. But in the factory we used to be slipping away to little nookways trying to have a smoke and others would be keeping a watch out cause if you got caught you could be sacked. Finally I just said to meself, 'I'll just chuck it altogether.' That was one good thing when I went into the bake house, I gave up smoking. But now that graveyard in there, well, Jacob's were going to build on that and they had to get special permission. And that graveyard was dug up and *every* bone, even the smallest bone, was all re-buried up in Mount Jerome.

"Now George Jacobs and Charles, Charles was the small man with a big white beard and George was real tall. They'd come around and pay their visit around the place—and if you saw the older crowd in there they'd be *bowing* to them. Oh, it was awful. And they used to refer to them as 'Master' Charles and 'Master' George. They used to make terrible little of themselves, the older people. But with the younger crowd there was no bowing and scraping to them. You were there to make them rich, that's all. Anyone that got employment there had to earn what he got. And you worked up till Christmas Eve and years ago you couldn't even put up [decorative] chains or anything. They wouldn't have it. And Protestants got more benefits. When you'd apply for a job they'd ask you what religion you were. It didn't stop you getting into the factory but it stopped you getting promotions. You just accepted it. You were glad to have a job and that's that. There was a time when a Catholic wouldn't get a job in the office. Oh, yes, that was in my time. Now my eldest sister, she had a job up on the director's lobby and it was a bit better like than most girls would get in the place and everyone thought she was a Protestant *because* she was there. And I remember meself when on a holy day Jacob's [workers] would all go to half seven mass on Whitefriar Street. And I remember one time there was a bloke out of the offices, a big tall man with a moustache and everyone at the chapel was watching *him*. Couldn't *believe* it! Cause he was a Catholic and working in the offices. And the *only one* he was. He must have been the first Catholic ever got a job in the offices, cause anyone with a good job was Protestant.

"In them times there was actually no union in the place. And then when they did form a union the fellas that became shop stewards done a lot of mouthing and all them got promoted. And most of them were taking the jobs of shop stewards just for the sake of getting promoted. They never done it for the sake of the *workers*, done it for their own sake. The factory was full of them. I *had* to join the union. I knew fellas there and they hadn't an ounce of intelligence. One fella, when he'd be on overtime, he used to ask me to make up his wages for him. And he was put in charge of me! A shop steward belonged to the union and looked after collecting the money for the union and going to the union meetings and all. They'd go mad to get voters cause there'd be elections and we'd vote for a shop steward. And a fella'd get his cronies and say, 'Make me the shop steward.' They done it for their own sake. The union would be a good thing if it was *worked right* cause you would need a union for to get better conditions. There was a few strikes. It was mostly over pay. Then you had a few stoppages over some fella who'd be treated wrong and all the rest would walk out. It never lasted very long.

"We used to get one week's holiday and then it was made two. You got your wages plus your holiday fund. See, they used to have a holiday fund and you paid two shillings a week into that. Then that was given out August week. And it used to be £5 4s. or something. And £5, that was *money* then, all right. And the fellas would be saying, 'When are we getting the lump?' There'd be a gas. Very few would use it for a holiday over to the pub as soon as you'd get it! And now every Christmas they used to put on a pantomime in the recreation hall on Bishop Street. It was all workers out of the factory. And it's surprising the talent that was there . . . singing, dancing and comedians. God, they were *very* good. And there was a bloke there and he'd go around the factory all day with a face on him. He wouldn't smile and he was real miserable and he'd talk to no one— and he was the *director* of the pantomime! He'd a brilliant brain! The way he'd organise everything. But very solemn looking and he wouldn't talk to anyone. You wouldn't think it was in him. But people used to come from near and far to Jacob's pantomime. Oh, it went on for weeks, every night, like what you see in the Gaiety.

"Now in Jacob's, up to some years ago, there was no age limit. There was one man there, Harry McCloskey, he was sixty-four years in the place and he was 78 years old. And when the men would go out they'd all be ancient, over 70. And they didn't get a pension out of it. They used to call it a gratuity. And it was fifty shillings [per week] at that time. And if you got anything [work] to do outside and they knew about that they'd cut that off. So men stayed on and they kept them there till they were no use, you know? Now there was one man, he was well over 70 when he went out, and he lived up near the football ground. And people used to go to matches on their bicycles at that time and he was minding a few bikes for people and they'd come out and give him maybe tuppence. But some 'brilliant' person wrote in to the factory about him, said he was minding bicycles, and the welfare manager sent for him and told him to either give up the bicycles or his fifty shillings. Oh, whoever wrote the letter was a *bad one*. Cause it'd only get him a bit of tobacco. They never treated the workers fair. You never got a fair deal. I'd forty-nine years' service and when I come out I got £10.33 a week. Now I have £18 a week. After forty-nine years' service! You'd think they'd show more appreciation to workers."

CATHERINE CORBALLY—TAILORING FACTORY, AGE 77

One of thirteen children, she grew up in a tenement house on Clanbrassil Street adjacent to "Little Jerusalem". She began working as a tailoress for Jewish neighbours who owned small factories. Advancement to a large English firm offered the piece-work system and higher wages. Sometimes she and her work pals would pawn their shears to get money for admission to dance halls. During the war years it was off to England to work in an aircraft factory. After surviving curfews, air raid shelters and bombings, she returned home and got married.

"I come from Clanbrassil Street. There were thirteen children, I'm the second youngest. My father worked at the pigs. He had an old stable down the road from us and had a horse and cart and he used to sell bags of coal. At that time they were ten stone bags. He used to be down to the docks every morning very early to meet the [coal] boats coming in and he had a few men working for him and my mother used to have a big breakfast for them when they'd come back from the quays. She'd have rashers or sausages, pudding, fried bread, cause they'd been all morning down on the docks and they *needed* that for a start. And then they'd be off selling the coal.

"We lived in a big old tenement house and the Jewish people owned them in them days and it was only five shillings a week for two huge big rooms. Our tenement house had been a nunnery and there was eleven families in the house and you had to come down the stairs for to go to the toilet out in the back yard.

And I had to go down every day to the stable to milk the goats. We had two beds for the boys and my mother had a curtain right across [the room] and the girls was on this side. This was a division we had. Four boys in the one bed. The mattress on the bed was straw and the straw would get old and we'd have to go and get bags of straw. The boys, they'd have a candle and they were really educated with comics. We had an aluminium vat [bath], big oval shape with two handles, and my mother had to fill that and boil water off a coal fire for our bath. And when she'd fill that the youngest would be done first but there would be one at the bottom and top of the bath on a Saturday night. And for washing clothes she had a washboard and the vat would go up on two chairs and she'd be paddling away there hand washing.

"Now from our door up it was all the Jews on both sides, up to the South Circular Road. That was called 'Little Jerusalem.' There was a good few hundred Jews, could have been thousands. They were great and I always worked for the Jewish people, at sewing. They used to go around on Tuesday morning and their arms would be packed with satin scarves with fringes on the end of them and they'd knock on your door and they'd sell them for so much and you'd pay them by the week. And they sold holy pictures. And they used to lend money. Oh, God Almighty, of course they did. If you were stuck you'd go to them, up to Wolfson's or Goldwater's, all those people. And you had to pay five shillings [interest] on the pound. That's how they made their money. And they'd come every Monday and collect, they had a little notebook. It would be about a shilling at that time and you'd pay each week. But some people wouldn't answer the door when they'd come to collect. Oh, and the Jews were house mad, property mad, and bought tenements. They used to buy up tenement houses. And there was a synagogue in St Kevin's Parade, a little old synagogue, very small synagogue, like an ordinary house like this. We used to swing on the lamps outside, a rope around it. And when the Jews would be going to church they dressed beautiful, first-class style, like Paris fashions. It was a sight for sore eyes. Cause they were all at the sewing factories. They had beautiful clothes. But now the Jewish ladies, they were the bosses really. The Jew men were *terrified* of their wives. Oh, yes. The wife was the boss.

"They used to buy fish in the street from the dealers. They were fish mad and Friday night at 7.00 they'd start their Sabbath until 7.00 Saturday night. And *every* kid in the road used to run around and knock at their doors, 'Do you want your fire lighted?', cause they couldn't touch a light once their Sabbath started. They'd pay a penny or a ha'penny to the kids. And up about two blocks from us there was yards for animals, like horses, and they used to have their chickens flying all around and they'd pick out the chickens they'd want for the weekend and their necks would be rung. And come the weekend that was their meal, the chickens. And we'd be standing there and we'd get a penny for plucking them.

"At school we learned Irish, English and maths and drawing, cooking. Oh, yes, cooking every Tuesday. And hand sewing with just needle and thread. Many a hiding I got at school. Oh, they were very hard on us. Like, if you laughed or anything or talked or pulled the plaits on another girl and we'd be caught and the teacher'd say, 'Wait until Mother Ignatius comes in!' And she'd give the report to her and we'd be called out and our back to the chalk board and we'd have to hold out our hand and we'd *pull back* when we'd see the thing coming. And then she'd make it worse for us. The Reverend Mother would get a report from the teacher when you'd do wrong and she'd come out and she'd *fling* back her long sleeve over her shoulder and she'd a long mahogany stick and she'd get her hand up in the air . . . and I went home one day with blisters from there to there [wrist to elbow].

"I left school on a Friday and Monday morning I went to work in a Jewish factory. It was Baker's on the quay. I was a very good sewer. I was four or five months at it. I'd say there were roughly sixty workers. My mother knew somebody who got me into it and she took me down [for an interview]. Mothers led you everywhere, they were very careful. I started by hand sewing but I was mad to get at the machines. We made all gents' clothing, suits and overcoats. In the olden days if you went and bought a ready-made suit there was a ticket on it that showed you the size and the material and the price and all on it. So I was only sewing on these tickets in the beginning. And then I was called a cleaner, clipping off all the threads after the machinist. You know, you had to creep before you walked. I started at half past eight and worked till 6.00. My wages was five shillings and ten pence. You got that in a little brown paper packet and it was sealed and writing on the outside, so many hours and me rate of pay. And I'd take that to my mother and I couldn't open it and she'd give me four pence back.

"Now I was very clever and one of our managers, Ginger Davison, he left when Polycroft's was built. Polycroft's, that was an English man and he built a big factory in Rialto and there was hundreds in it. So a good few of us packed it up and went up on our bikes and he took us in immediately. Polycroft's was a big sewing factory that used to do dresses, ordinary everyday suits for all the big shops in town. The minute Mr Polycroft saw us in the office he said, 'You can start tomorrow.' We got two years to learn the trade and I was going in for full coat-making. I'd nothing to do with the trousers. See, there was different departments. I picked it up very well. Then we went to piece-work and I remember for a gent's military trenchcoat we got a half a crown from *beginning to end* making those. Made the *whole* complete thing. I made them with the machine. I loved piece-work cause the more you worked the more you earned. I was a *flyer!* I was left on me own and the first week I come home with me pay packet and my mother was very holy and honest and I said, 'Ma, look at me wages this week', and she looked at it and there was twenty-seven shillings. It was *fantastic*. She was a real lady, like a saint, and Monday she went up to the factory to the office to know if that was correct. Was there a mistake? And they said 'No, she's on piece-work now and it's *entirely* up to herself to earn what she liked.' She was a *very* honest lady.

"There was hundreds worked in that factory and the hand sewers always sat up on a table. There was clocks when you went in and you had to punch your time. And punch when you'd be going out. A hooter would go in the morning at half past eight and we had to be in. And at dead-on 1.00 we'd all *rush* from the factory to our bikes, *home* for our lunch. We had one hour for lunch and me mother'd have it on the table, maybe cabbage, potatoes and a rasher. And I'd wash my hands and face before I went back. And then we'd hear the hooter to get us back. From our house in Clanbrassil Street we used to hear the three short hooters. It was a beautiful factory because we had been in other little factories and the rain used to pour in on us. But it was nearly all glass and it was hot. In Polycroft's each section had a different colour overalls. We were in the coat section and they were green. We didn't get a tea break in the morning but the staff did and we used to smell their breakfast in the canteen. They had a beautiful self-service canteen. And we'd pretend to go out to the toilet and when the matron wouldn't be there we'd just put our heads in [the canteen] and *run* and grab a cake or maybe sausages or something and we'd run in the toilet with them.

"Now say I should have been in at half past eight and I was a *minute* late, I had to wait until half past nine. And if you were caught smoking in the toilet you were suspended for six weeks. *Six* weeks! And if that happened we used to get up on our bike and go off into another factory for the six weeks. It depended on your own wit to get another job. If the sewing was in you, you got it. I was excellent. But then we'd go back into Polycroft's because there was better pay there. And they'd their own dentist and doctor for you. Sure, the matron would press the button and the dentist would be there on the spot. We were sitting working and you could talk. Oh, and you could *sing* your head off. We always sang, all the old songs. Now Mr Polycroft himself, he used to come over [from London] so many times a year and if you done anything wrong, caught smoking or anything, you were suspended for six weeks, and you were sent up to the head office. And now he was only a little man and his office was magnificent. It was like a beautiful sitting room. And he was a very *ignorant* man and he'd have his feet up on the table and he'd be giving out and he'd say, 'How *dare* you! And yous are getting your bread here. The next time it won't be suspension, it'll be the *sack!*' He was very rude, the boss himself. And if a girl became pregnant and there was talk, she'd be sent for by the matron and she'd get the girl examined and she'd be sacked for that. Oh, yes, she was sacked. And we were all very open-minded and we'd say, 'Sure, God help her, she's mad about him.'

"They had a club for holidays. We had two weeks' holiday and we had a savings club and they'd take out so much each week. And *once* you made that pledge you had to keep it, you couldn't go up to the office and say, 'Don't stop me holiday money, me money's low this week.' You couldn't do that. We used to go to the Isle of Man or Blackpool. The *whole factory* would go. At Christmas there was a little party with tea and cakes and sweets, streamers and we'd shove back our stools and we'd dance. And then the bosses would have their party with drink and everything in the office. And Polycroft's had a swimming club out in Blackrock and we used to go straight from work. We used to have our togs under our clothes. We'd go out on our bikes and as we got good at the swimming we'd dive off.

"And we were dance mad. On Sundays in the afternoon we used to go to the Ormond Hotel on the quay. That was an afternoon tea and dance. A whole gang of us would go. There was about ten of us used to cling together. We were terrors for dancing. And at the Metropole on Wednesday afternoon there used to be a dance and I became forewoman at the factory over two big benches and we'd say, 'Are yous going?' and they'd say, 'But we've no money', and I'd say, 'Right.' And I'd put me hand on the [machine] wheel and press my foot and we used to break down the huge motor by doing that. And then we'd all have to go home, cause it'd have to be repaired. The mechanic was on the job. Oh, *deliberately* we'd do that. And then we'd take our shears with us, cutting shears. We got our shears in the factory, we paid sixpence a week until they were paid for. They were seven and six, I think it was. So we'd take our shears into the pawn office, to Kilbride's, on the South Circular Road [to get money for the dance]. And when we'd go into the factory the next morning we'd say, 'There's no shears', and he'd say, '*God damn it altogether*!' And he'd [foreman] put his hand in his pocket [for money] and send one of us down to collect the shears. We pawned the scissors only the one day, on the Wednesday. And we'd be sent into the pawn to get them the next day cause we couldn't work without them. He used to lose his head. He'd give one of us the money to go back. He'd pick somebody trustworthy to get the shears out and she'd get up on her bike and go down to the pawn, hand in the ticket and the money and she'd bring them all back to us. And his heart was broke cause we wouldn't give it [money] back to him. We'd say, 'No, *you* got it out, *we didn't want them*.' See, cause there was plenty of work everywhere at other factories for us. So he used to *have* to pay for that.

"In the war years there was no work here. We weren't getting the work in and we weren't earning any money. People didn't have the money. So I packed it up and went over to England and got digs and worked in the Austin Motor Company in Birmingham. And after that I worked over there in the sewing factories as well. I was over there about three years. At the motor company I worked on huge big machines making parts for bombers. We had to do night work in the blackout and you couldn't even light a cigarette in Birmingham at night. Oh, no, you'd be fined and brought to court the next day. *No lights* showing cause that'd be a signal for the planes coming over. Bombing raids *all* the time, night and day. Even when we'd be coming home in the winter in the evenings you couldn't see where you were going because everything was blacked out. And we used to sit at night time listening to Lord Haw Haw. And Hitler, he was the devil himself. And Vera Lynn used to entertain us. She used to sing in the canteen. She was a lovely lady. During our lunch hour she'd sing for us and play the piano up on a stage. And I met Edward G. Robinson, he came over. I shook hands with him. And then you'd get an air raid siren and everyone'd run down into the air raid shelter. They were underground and often the water pipes would burst with the explosions and we'd be in water up to here [knees]. The German planes used to come down nearly on *top of you*. When the planes came down so low you could nearly see the pilots in them! We more or less got used to it. But I'd get fed up with it cause maybe you'd just gone to bed and tired and the siren would go off. And I got fed up and said to me landlady, 'I'm *not* leaving here any more. I'm tired and I'm not going down to any air raid shelter.' And she'd say, 'Cathy, you *have to* because when the night is over you'll be dead up here', in the house. Just a few doors down from us a whole family was killed. It was life! After the war I came back here and met me husband and got married."

9

Battlers and Champions

JOHN "YOUNG SPIKE" McCORMACK—
BOXING CHAMPION, AGE 52

His father, "Spike" McCormack, was one of Dublin's greatest street fighters, boxing champions and legendary characters. Upon his death, journalist Adrian McLoughlin hailed him as a genuine "folk hero" to inner-city Dubliners. "Young Spike" grew up in his father's huge shadow and became the Irish and British light-heavyweight boxing champion. As a young lad he was sent to Artane for mitching from school and had his first fight with a bully. Upon returning to his tenement home on Gardiner Street, he witnessed his father's bloody street brawls with mortal enemies. But everyone respected Spike for his courage, kindness and generosity to the poor. Although he idolised his father, young John knew his heavy drinking and street fighting caused his mother much suffering. When he captured the coveted British boxing title, father Spike was filled with pride. Their close relationship is poignantly portrayed in Spike's deathbed scene as John murmurs, "He was a lovely dad . . . I loved my father."

"I was born on No. 7 Sean McDermott Street, on the corner of Gardiner Street. It was a tenement. I have five brothers and eight sisters. We lived in this one bedroom and there was a very small scullery in the corner. They just called it a cooker and a wash hand basin and a gas stove where you just put a penny in the gas meter. My grandmother lived in No. 6 Sean McDermott Street and my father's sister lived in No. 2. And my father's brother Willie lived at the top of Gardiner Street and his brother Jimmy lived in Gardiner Street. So the family *always* stayed together in the inner city. In the tenements it was always looking after other people. My father travelled all over the world for about twenty years on ships, Kevin, and he used to say to me, 'Dublin is the greatest city in the world, no matter where I went in the world. America is the place to go but they haven't got the feelings that the people in the tenements have.'

"Now when I was about 4 or 5 years of age, when we lived in Sean McDermott Street, I used to come around to play in Gardiner Street. But it was a small world and kids would be saying, 'You don't live around here, you go back into Sean McDermott Street.' And I'd say, 'I can go where I like. *My dad's* Spike McCormack!' See, I was always Young Spike. People would walk past and say, 'That's young McCormack, that's *Spike's* son.' Spike knew *everyone*. And everyone knew *Spike*. Everyone! He was a Kerry man, a Kerry man with a Dublin brogue! He became a legend in the inner city. As a young man he was a great footballer, a great hurler, a great handballer. He was great at everything. He started fighting amateur about 1928 and he was professional for about seven or eight years. To anyone who met him, Spike was God!

"We'd be all living in the one room. *One* room. One bedroom, and the little scullery. So my mother and father slept in one bed and we slept out here. There was four beds in one room. But there was no room to move the beds, you couldn't move around. There was thirteen of us. The girls would go to bed before the boys cause we weren't supposed to see the girls. There was no bath in the house. The toilet was down on the next stairs. And you'd a slop bucket beside the bed. Your father and mother had one and we had one. Every morning your mother'd say, 'Go and slop out.' And we'd say, 'Ma, there's a spunker down there', cause there'd always be a spunker living in the toilet. In them days, Kevin, a spunker was a person who was always drinking and there was a smell off him. And there was always spunkers living on the stairs of the tenements. Now when we wanted to go for a wash we went to Tara Street baths. And I remember the kids taking me down to the Liffey at 6 years of age and just *throwing* me off Butt Bridge and several of them jumping in after me. Imagine standing up by the rail and throwing me in. They were teaching young Spike how to swim!

"When I was young I always used to say to me mother, 'I don't want to go to school.' I wanted to be home all the time. And she said, 'If you don't go to school I'll send you to the borstal', a reformatory. Everyone from the inner city, we all went to the reformatory. Oh, yes, it was never any great problem going to the reformatory. Just for mitching, if you didn't go to school. I was 9 when I went there, in September 1954. When I went to court the second time the judge, he said to me, 'You're not going to school. You haven't been to school for a year and a half. This can't go on. You're *continuously* missing school.' Now today, Kevin, they can get away with *murder* but in them days just by mitching from school, a *simple* thing like that, you were sent to the reformatory. Oh, I went to Artane Industrial School till I was 14½. Christian Brothers . . . straps. Oh, it was very, very hard, Kevin. *Very* hard.

"I have very bad memories of it, cause the *way* they treated you. There was about 800 boys when I went there. The Christian Brothers indoctrinated them. It was like 120 in a dormitory. Bad memories of it. Like you had a hobnail boot with forty-eight studs but if one stud was missing you had to report it to a Brother. And if the stud fell out you'd say, 'It probably fell out playing during the day', and he'd say, 'You *should* have reported it—go to the boot room!' The boot room had like pigeon holes where you put your boots at night. And we'd go to the boot room and we wore a night dress that came down to here [ankles] and he'd say, 'Take off your night dress', and you were in your nude. And he'd say, 'Why didn't you report that stud missing out of your boot?' And I'd say, 'I didn't know it was missing, sir.' Everything was 'sir'. And, oh, he'd *punch holes* in you! Some Brothers would slap you across the face and others would take great delight in beating you more and make *sure* you were crying. *Everyone* broke down and cried. But if he wasn't getting any satisfaction out of you—if you were stubborn like I was—he'd be hitting you with a thick leather strap, in the cold of the night. And you're standing there in your nude and he's cutting away and I didn't cry for him. And as I'd come back from the boot room the guys, they'd say, 'Young Spike won't cry.' Very bad memories.

"But some Brothers were very nice and you got a trade and they had the Artane Boys Band. You've heard of that. I played the trombone. And I learned how to read, where I couldn't spell 'John McCormack' when I went into Artane. They were very, very good teaching. They would put you in the lowest class, they were *real dunces*, and they'd say, 'We're going to teach you to read and write and by the time we're finished with you you're going to speak Gaelic.' And I did! I spoke Gaelic very good. Oh, yes, *genuine*. But you were told, 'You're out of the inner city. You're never going to make anything of yourself cause as far as we're concerned you're a lost cause.'

"And there were bullies in there. Oh, yes. I remember my pal and he got beat up by this bully. The bully says, 'I'll see you around by the trees.' The 'trees' was a place by the toilets, huge big oak trees, and when it was in foliage in the summer it *hid* anyone that was behind it. So any time you wanted to go have a fight you'd say, 'I'll see you down at the trees.' And my pal says he was going to fight this bully and we all walked down. And this was a fist fight, fair enough. Now I *never, ever* had anything to do with boxing [at this time]. And they [the Brothers] used to always bring these [newspaper] clips and put them up [on the bulletin board] with 'Spike McCormack is fighting in the streets of Dublin' and it was very embarrassing. My father was a boxer in the ring and I was very *proud* of that. But my father retired in 1948 and this was 1954 and I'd see about these fights on the street where the police took Spike in. I was embarrassed cause he was always fighting on the street.

"Anyway, this fight, this friend of mine went down to the trees and the crowd naturally formed a ring. Now this bully was big. I mean he was obviously big compared to me. This would be 1956, two years after I went there. This bully put up his fist and says, 'I'll do a wallpapering job with you.' That means he's going to plaster him. And my pal broke down and started crying. And I remember, through *no reason*—I can't remember even understanding why I *attempted* to do it—but I remember stepping out and saying to him, 'My pallyo can't fight.' And he says, 'What has it to do with you? Are you going to take his place?' And now he was *much bigger* than me. And my pal says, 'No, Johnny, he'll kill you, you're too small for him.' So I just says to Leo [my pal], 'It's OK, Leo.' So I took his place. And I just stood there and put my fists up, just like John L. Sullivan. That's the way I started. I didn't know anything about it. So yer man makes a move and I hit him—*bang*! I just gave him one smack. And yer man is crying. And then everyone runs in, they *all* take part in it, it's a big Donnybrook, all the fellas hitting each other. And this Christian Brother runs in and blows the whistle and everyone runs then. Anyway, this boy comes up to me and says, 'I want to shake your hand. I didn't know you could fight.' And I says, 'I *don't* fight, I can't fight.' I was afraid of my life now, Kevin. I was trembling. But whatever it was . . . Leo was *my pal*. And no one would go *near* me then! Because they'd say that I was able to use myself. So, of course, I got *great* mileage out of this. So consequently one of the Brothers said to me, 'Would you join the boxing club?' And I said, 'No, I don't want nothing to do with boxing, I don't want to be a boxer.'

"I remember one time saying, 'Where does the fighting come from, Da?' Cause a reporter came to the family and says, 'How come you're all fighters?' And Spike told him about his father, my grandfather, and they called him 'Toorah' McCormack. There's a saying in England when people are going away they don't say 'goodbye' or 'good luck', they say 'toorah'. My grandfather came from Kerry and when he was with the British Army his lungs were gassed and he come up to Dublin with a British Army pension. Now my grandfather was only about five foot two. He was a nice little man. But, unfortunately, when he came to Dublin at first they said to him, 'The culchie's coming in', and he *hated* that culchie name. But he'd go up to Killane's pub and drink then was about six pence a pint. But one time he was in the pub and someone called him a culchie and he took umbrage and says, 'I've lived up here all these years and you *still* call me a culchie, you lousy Dublin bastards, you lousy Jackeen bastards.' And this fella said something to him or hit his hat off him and me grandfather said, 'All right, step outside the door.' So they were all laughing in the pub cause they were saying this fella would make mincemeat out of him because of his bad lungs and all. And this big fella went outside with him and says, 'Do you want it straight?' And my grandfather says, 'I can manage you.' And my grandfather only hit him once, but he hit him *some* punch and he was rolling in the street and me grandfather says 'toorah!' And they were all saying, 'Jesus, he can hit *some* punch!' And, consequently, from that night they called him Toorah McCormack.

"My father was the professional middleweight champion of Ireland from the late thirties to 1948. But he was a great man for fighting on the street. He started fighting amateur around 1928 and then he was professional for about eight years. Kevin, he was *very* impressive. Now he was only five feet seven. Oh, he was only a little man. But he was gorgeous when he stood up. He had a barrel chest, a *wide* chest. And he'd big arms on him and a left hook and all big knuckles on him and he'd just hit them once. It was *amazing* the way he'd throw that punch. He had this fighting spirit. He was *bred* to fight. The man was a pit bull! The man was bred *specifically* to fight—although he was a gentleman. Oh, *could* he fight! He was *unbelievable*. His constitution. I seen him on the street fighting myself, Kevin. And he was ambidextrous, he used both hands. Cause when he came from Kerry when he was young they wouldn't have him writing with his left hand in school. You must write with your right hand. They kept slapping him on his knuckles until he wrote with his right hand. He fought initially as a southpaw but they switched him around and his left hook was always his best punch. He had a *great* left hook.

"He would work out when he was boxing but he wasn't a strict disciplinarian as regards training and he always went over to the pub afterwards. He would *always* be drinking. He did his boxing [training] in Gardiner Street. It was an old kitchen in a tenement, underneath the house, and *all* the fighters, when they finished training, they all got washed down with that one bucket of water. Peter Glennon [another Irish boxing champion] used to say to me, 'Your father had a *naturalness* about him, he didn't have to train. John, you were bred to fight. You came from a great pedigree, you're like a race horse. You *had* to fight, coming from where you came from.' All the boys fought. My father used to say, 'Any McCormack that's born and can't fight, you ship him out and send him to the other side of the world and tell him to change his name cause he's not a McCormack if he can't fight. *All* my sons can fight!' He was very proud of that. And I won the British championship and my brother won the British championship.

"Gardiner Street, that's the street of champions. The likes of my father and Blackman Doyle and Mickey Gifford and Peter Glennon all went away to Chicago in 1937 and took on the [US] Golden Gloves champions. And they all came out of Gardiner Street. And three of them beat the Golden Gloves champions, my father and Peter Glennon and Mickey Gifford. Peter Glennon, he was the 'fighting newsboy'. He's the only one alive still out of them all. My father's last [amateur] fight was here with the famous Jimmy Ingle. Jimmy Ingle was very famous here, from the southside. And he fought me father here in the National Stadium in his last amateur fight. Now me father was in the hospital at the time, in the Mater Hospital. See, he had gotten blown up in the war, the Second World War. But they came to the hospital and told me father that Jimmy Ingle was turning professional and he wanted to have a last amateur fight in the stadium on Friday night. And this is on Wednesday in the hospital. So me father says, 'Well, *I'll* fight him.' And so me father comes out of the hospital on a Thursday and he went up and fought Jimmy Ingle and he collapsed in the ring in the third round. And they took his shorts off and they saw this big hole in his side and they said, 'Jesus Christ, he shouldn't have been able to *stand*.' So Jimmy Ingle turned professional but my father said, 'I'll get him again when I'm *good*.' So my father turned professional—just to get back at Jimmy Ingle.

"And my father was a deep-sea sailor for about twenty years. When he was away at sea he would be gone for maybe a year, to Valparaiso, South America, Canada, for long periods. And my mother used to get a retainer off Irish Shipping here, and there was ten of us in the tenement then. But my mother used to love it when he was away cause she'd say, 'He's not in trouble, he's not drinking.' But then when he used to come home he'd sign off for three months and my mother mightn't see him for four days after he'd come home. He wouldn't come home. He'd go off to Killane's pub in Gardiner Street. Now one time they took a ship out from Irish Shipping to America and in the middle of the ocean they *mutinied*. See, there was a union strike and scabs brought the ship out and my father was specifically put aboard that ship by the union. My father didn't want to be on the ship cause it was what he called 'scabby'. But they said,

'The reason we're putting you on the ship, Spike, is because they want to *take over* and we won't have it.' And so my father went with them. See, my father was put on the ship to keep a rein on these scabs. But they mutinied in the middle of the Atlantic Ocean and they wanted to take over the ship and the captain actually went up to his room and locked himself in. And my father worked as a greaser in the engine room and he went up—and this is *history*—on the deck with a big fire hatchet and he says, 'There's *no way* you're taking over this ship cause you're scabbies and *I won't have* that!' And he *done* about *seventeen* or *eighteen* of them. Oh, he went really amuck on the ship with the hatchet. And when they come off the ship any time my father was drinking and he was in a pub and they'd walk in he'd say, 'Give them nothing, they're *scabbies*, they're keeping *decent* people away from jobs.'

"And when my father used to come home he'd get all his money and bring it up to the fellas that was maybe laid off the ship and he'd buy them food for their children. And he'd always come home from America with clothes [used] that you could turn inside-out and he'd go around giving loads of gifts to the guys around the neighbourhood. So, consequently, he became like a Robin Hood. And he cleared up the pennies toss school when the southside fellas tried to move in. And half the taximen down there, they got their plates through Spike. See, Spike always knew someone down in the taxi office and he'd get taxi plates for them so they could work. So [afterwards] when he'd get into a taxi the fella'd say, 'You OK, Spike? Great.' *No* money. *Everyone* knew Spike. And when my father got drink on him he'd go home at night and he'd be singing coming out into the street and all the kids used to be around him and he'd take out handfuls of pennies and ha'pennies and *throw* them money. He'd be very drunk and he'd waddle down the road and *all the kids* would keep following him, following him like the Pied Piper of Hamlin cause they knew he'd grush. And when he'd get to Sean McDermott Street he'd reach into his pocket and he'd *throw* all the money and the kids would all run. There was no cars around at this time and there'd be pennies and ha'pennies and shillings flying everywhere and he'd say, 'Good night now.' And my mother used to be watching him [from the window]. And my mother used to say to me, 'Go down and get the money, pick up as many half-crowns as you can and let him give the kids pennies.' And he'd always call the kids 'broken nose' and he'd have his arm around them and he'd say, 'Them kids are lovely, they're the kids of the future.'

"My father would drink me under the table—forty and fifty pints of Guinness in one day. Oh, *unbelievable*! Stout. *Forty* pints in one day . . . *no* problem to him. He would get drunk three or four times in one day, Kevin. Really. He'd go out at 7.00 in the morning and come back at 10.00 *so* drunk and go to bed from 11.00 to 2.00 and go out at 2.00 and come back at 5.00 *so drunk* it wouldn't be true. Go to bed till 7.00 and go out and come back maybe at 10.00 or maybe 12.00. Or he mightn't come home all night and maybe be gone for three or four days. But once he'd touch whiskey! Even my mother'd say, '*Leave your father alone* when he gets whiskey on him because there's no one, but *no one*, will tell your father what to do when he gets whiskey on him.' See, he

25 *Spike McCormack, famed Dublin street fighter, professional boxing champion and inner-city hero, clowning with young pugilist, early 1950s.*

26 Spike McCormack (right) signing for a fight with arch rival Jimmy Ingle.

27 Spike McCormack (left) and boxing opponent Tommy Armour.

28 Spike McCormack in his "old gunfighter" years.

29 Spike McCormack (second from left) and his boxing champion son John (second from right) at a family wedding.

30 The late John Read Cowle, Dublin's last genuine cutler, standing in front of Read's Cutlery which dates back to 1670, making it Dublin's oldest surviving shop until it closed in 1997.

31 The late John Read Cowle conducting a transaction on his antiquated brass cash register a few months before his retirement.

32 William Coyle, Dublin's last authentic hatter.

33 David O'Donnell, one of Guinness's last coopers, and his wife Nancy.

34 Dunne's cooperage in Smithfield, Dublin's last cooperage, 1980.

35 *Greene's bookshop on Clare Street, one of Dublin's renowned literary institutions, still with wooden stalls in front.*

36 Peter Comiskey, the doyen of Dublin's traditional barbers.

37 Pioneer women's hairdresser, Vera Nichols.

38 Lauri Grennell, veteran Dublin shoe repair man.

39 The last shoemaking shop in the old Liberties, 1980.

40 *Kearns's Pawnbrokers on Queen Street, one of only three surviving inner-city pawnshops.*

41 *Margaret Doran Murphy, legendary traveller, clairvoyant and oracle.*

42 Terriss Mary Lee Murphy, famed Dublin fortune teller.

43 *Agnes Daly Oman (standing front centre) who survived the 1941 northside bombing as a child.*

44 *Agnes Daly Oman on the coveted bicycle she rode to work at the shirt factory.*

45 *Lynch's stone cottage on the North Strand.*

46 *Maureen Lynch, canal-side cottage dweller.*

47 Michael Lynch, canal-side cottage dweller.

once said to me, 'John, I'm a normal person when I'm having me pint and then someone gives me a whiskey and I change into another man. I *change* into another man. Just remember, son, when someone gives me a whiskey there's another man there.'

"Now he was a *dangerous* man when he had whiskey, *highly* dangerous, and very easy to motivate when he had whiskey on him. He was very easily led. Jim ['Lugs'] Branigan once said to me, 'I had *great, great* respect for your father. But your father was *badly led*, John. It was the people of the inner city that wanted a fighter and he was the Robin Hood. No one could come out and fight the policemen, but Spike would come out and do it for them if he had whiskey on him. They'd feed him whiskey and say, 'Spike'll do you.' And your father would come out. I've seen him on *numerous* occasions coming out and fighting policemen and a policeman had *no chance* against your father.' My father was very easily led.

"There was a family in the inner city called the Corballys and they were all off the ships too. There was Scelar Corbally and Sugar Corbally and another fella. And the Corballys, they hated Spike's guts. They *hated* his guts! Hated the man. *Really.* Now it was unbelievable the hatred they had for him. And my father had this *vendetta* against them and he'd *never* let it go. *Wouldn't* let it go. The mother of all the Corballys, my father *hated* this woman, because he said it was this woman who *started* all this trouble *years* and *years* ago. Years ago she apparently had a row with his mother and she sent her sons around and her sons broke all my granny's windows, throwing bricks through my granny's windows. Now this feud with the Corballys, they wouldn't *look* at each other, there was a needle between them. That's where all the fighting used to start. When my father got drink on him he'd go home and he'd be out on the street and then the Corballys, maybe *they'd* be going home, and he'd spot one of them and they'd say, 'Oh, you want to carry on again?' And he'd say, '*Anytime* you'd like!' So Gardiner Street would be lined with people and me father'd come out in the middle of the street and stand out there with the Corballys. This is true, Kevin. I *seen* it. And he'd kick off his shoes and his shirt would come off. And he had a big barrel chest on him and he'd stand out there and he'd say, 'Right, none of yous are any bleeding good. As *long* as I'm here in these tenements you'll *never* beat me. This is *my* street.' I seen him on the street . . . fighting. He would stand up and he was left handed and everything worked off his left hand. If you offended my father at all he really didn't like an apology, he wanted to chin you. As far as he was concerned, if you were looking for a fight you came to the right place. He was *such* a *stubborn* man. I've seen him when there was four or five of them in a pub and one would get sloppy and he'd walk in amongst them and say, 'If yous want a fight, I'll take you.' But he said, 'I don't roll around the floors. I just hit them *once*.'

"Anyway, with the Corballys people'd line the street and there'd be four or five of them and he'd take them on. In the middle of the street. And he'd stand out there, Kevin, big barrel chest on him and he'd say, 'If yous ever think for one minute that yous will ever get the best of me, I'd die on these streets.' And then the Corballys, they'd *fly* out and they'd be *punching holes* in each other. And then you'd hear the ambulance and the police would come and the police'd say, 'Spike, Jaysus, what gets into you?' And he'd say, 'Them *pigs*, they'll never get me off the streets of Dublin.' I remember one time when my uncle Willie and me uncle Jimmy, they wanted to come out with him [to assist in the fight] and he said, '*No* stay off the street, this is not *your* fight.' Now the place was *jammed* with people and the police and all. And my mother'd be upstairs and I'd say, 'They want to kill him, Mam, there's loads of them down there.' And she'd say, 'Leave him alone, he's all right, he knows what he's doing.' And they'd all stand aside, men, women, children, and the pubs used to empty and they'd *all* come out and they'd say, '*Quick*, Spike's at it again', and other fellas'd say, 'Holy Jaysus, he's at it again.' And he'd take them on, *every one*—he didn't care! They never come up behind him, they always fought him fair, I have to say that about them. They were terrible honest people as far as I was concerned. And after the fight he'd stand there and the blood would be gushing out of him and they'd be all *screaming* and *cheering* and all and maybe the ambulance would come over and they'd be trying to get him on the stretcher and he'd be saying, 'No, I want to shake hands with them', with the *Corballys*! And they'd say, 'No, I won't shake hands with you.' And he'd say, '*You'll* shake hands with me!' And he'd shake hands with them.

"The only time I ever seen anything wrong [unfair] in fighting was at this place called 'the buildings' on Corporation Street. Well, there was big, huge gates there and he went down there one night and something happened. These weren't the Corballys now, but a gang of men. He went down there one night and his brothers was saying, 'Jesus, Spike, *stay out* of that area', cause these were the local coal men and wharf men and fellas that worked on the docks. But he went down and a gang of men, they cornered him and strapped him to the gates and they lashed him out, left him in *bits*. Tied him to the gates and they got *chains* and *lashed* him . . . they *crucified* him. Tied him and he couldn't get away. I think he was three or four weeks in the hospital. He was around maybe 35 then. At the Mater Hospital he had an operation cause he was in a *bad* way. But the *day* he come out, Kevin, *the day he come out of the hospital* he went *straight* down to Mick Killane's, got his few beers and he was given some whiskey. Once he touched that whiskey he went back down and stood outside the gates. And he was [still] in *bits*, Kevin. I think he'd even casts and all. So he stood outside the gates and said [shouted], 'You remember me, *Spike*, now? Yous strapped me to them gates. Now I want you to come down, one at a time, or three or four of yous if you want to, but don't strap me to the gates. Let me fight like a man. Don't think I'm bleeding going away. I'm *staying* here till yous come down and I'm going to be in this city for the rest of me life.' But they never come down.

"When I was about 7 years of age we moved to Sheriff Street, into a tenement again. Down in Sheriff Street I had a few fist fights on the corner. Somebody'd say something maybe about a girl or your mother. I'd always tremble a bit, you'd shake a little bit and 'bang', then when the first punch is thrown that was the end of it. Like, when you get into a boxing ring you'd always get butterflies about what's going to happen and everything flies around in your head. I was 16 when I started amateur boxing. Me father was running an amateur boxing club out in Donnycarney. And when I come out of school at 16 I was going to sea too, as a deck boy on a ship. I'd jump off the ship, go up to the National Boxing Stadium, ask 'em if I could have a fight and they'd say 'Yeah.' And young Spike didn't need to train. They'd say I got that from my father—but *I* didn't drink. Oh, no. I had forty-four amateur fights and won forty-two.

"Then when I was 18 my mother kept saying, 'You keep eating all the time, there's not enough food here for you', with thirteen children now. So I had to get out of the house and I was going to join the army. My father wanted me to join the English Army. He said, 'The Irish Army, they're a waste of time. They're only a Mickey Mouse army.' And I always remember him saying, 'Hitler took Poland by storm and took Ireland by telephone.' So I got a little bag and I went to London,. Me mother gave me a pair of shorts, underwear and a T-shirt and since I had worked on the ship I got on for nothing and went over to Liverpool and went down to London on the train. And my father told me to go and see a great friend of his in London and he said, 'I'll look after you. Would you like to be a boxer?' 'Not really,' I said, because I wasn't really good, but I was *strong*. But I loved boxing then and the speed ball and the double skips, and I *loved* boxing people. So I started off in there [boxing] and I never come home for seven years! I had forty-two professional fights and won thirty-four of them. But I lost a lot of them on cuts, Kevin, cause I was very, very cheek bone. I lost five or six of them on cuts.

"I was better known in England than I was here. And I used to box in Belfast and my father used to come up all the time. He'd get a taxi here and the taxi man would drive him up to Belfast [free] and he'd keep the taxi man up there for three days and they'd get drunk. Really. When me father'd come up he'd be stone drunk. One night I boxed up there, a fella called Bob Nicholson, the Northern area heavyweight champion, and I beat him in seven rounds in the Ulster Hall, and it was the *biggest thrill* of my life cause after the fight they took the microphone and said, 'Ladies and gentlemen, we'd like to introduce you now to Spike.' He didn't say Spike *McCormack* . . . just Spike. And *everyone* in the Ulster Hall stood up and they were clapping for about ten minutes. And I stood there and I was getting a chill and I said to me father, 'I won the fight, Dad, and the ovation they're giving is for you. They all know I'm Spike's son.' And he said, 'I fought up here long before you were even born, son. This is *my* crowd.' And he just stood there in the ring with his cap on and he bowed. And I said, 'Take your cap off, Dad.' And he was going bald, with just his little bit of hair going across, and he took off his cap. They *all* stood up clapping for about ten minutes . . . for the famous Spike. And I just looked at him and said, 'That's my dad.'

"I went on to win the light heavyweight championship a year and a half later. The night I won the championship I beat a fella named Eddie Avoth, in seven rounds. I beat him that night and flew from London straight back to Sheriff Street at 3.00 in the morning and the house was quiet. And I had the Lonsdale

Belt, the British Championship belt. Now they said that the belt stays in England but I said that I wanted to take it back to Ireland. And they said, 'Where do you live?' And I said that I lived in a place called Sheriff Street. 'Is it a good area?' And I said, 'I'ts a lovely area', and I got to take it out. And when they found out afterwards about the area they said, 'Bejaysus, if we had *known* the area that it was there was *no way* you were bringing it home.' So I got home about 3.00 and went into the house and sat down and I had the belt on the table, it's *gorgeous*. And my mother got up out of bed and said, 'Are you all right? Is there something wrong?' I said, 'No, no, I was fighting in London last night.' 'How did you do?' 'I won.' 'That's grand,' she says and so she made bacon, egg and sausage and black and white pudding and fried bread. And then my father came out and he said, 'What are you doing here at 4.00 in the morning?' And I said, 'I won the British title last night.' 'Did you really?' And I said, 'There's the Lonsdale belt.' Now I had to make two defences on that belt and then I could keep it. After three fights, two defences, it's yours. So I said to him that night, 'When I win that belt, it's yours. That's your belt, it's something you never got when you were boxing.' And he said, 'OK.' And me mother said to me, 'You couldn't do that cause he'd *pawn* it.' So I said, 'Dad, you couldn't pawn that, it's *invaluable*. But I brought that home cause I knew you'd be proud.' 'I'm *very* proud.'

"So he got dressed then and says, 'Right, we'll go for a drink.' And my mother says, 'Where are you going?' And he says, 'We'll find a beer.' And we walked all the way up the North Circular Road up to Phoenix Park into the barracks and he knocked on this small iron door and the soldiers was all in there drinking, maybe twelve or thirteen of them sitting around having a drink. And me father says, 'How are you keeping, lads?' And they said, 'Fine, Spike, come in and close the door.' And we went in and there was *barrels* of drink and you just pulled your own and my father says, 'Sit down there and have a drink.' And I says, 'I don't drink, Dad, but I'll have a drink.' *'Here's to the British champion!'* he said, 'I *knew* I had it somewhere in my family . . . I knew you had it, son. I'm very proud of you.' And we left there about seven in the morning. I held that title for two years and I travelled to Australia and America and all over Ireland. Now I got two notches on that belt and on the third one I got disqualified and I never boxed after that. My last fight was in 1970.

"Now the last fight Spike had with the Corballys was this [other] night I got home about 1.00 after walking home from my girlfriend's and my father was walking across the road and he had a hurling stick in his hand. This was the last fight he had with the Corballys. And I said to him, 'Are you all right, Dad?' 'Yes, son, go on home.' And when I got home I said to my mother, 'What's wrong with me Da?' And she said, 'He's gone up to get one of the Corballys.' And I said, 'Oh, Jesus, I'm *gone*', and I *run* out and found him walking up the North Strand and I said, 'What's wrong, Dad?' And he said, 'One of those Corballys has started it again.' My father had been walking home and Sugar Corbally jumped him with a knife and *just missed* his jugular vein. He cut him with the knife. So I went with me father up to Sugar's house at the top of this two-storey tenement. And my dad kept saying, 'I'll die before I'll let these fellas get the better of me. They used to do it years ago when I was fighting and I won't have it now . . . I'm getting old. Look what he did with this knife.' Anyway, we went up and knocked on the door and this woman answered and it was the mother of all the Corballys. And my father, to him, it was like a red flag to a bull because he *hated* this woman because he said it was this woman who *started* all this trouble *years* and *years* ago. Me Da looked at her and she was a big woman, a fine big woman, a good looking woman, very, very dark, like a gypsy, even in her later years. And me father just looked at her and she says, 'Oh, it's you.' And he said, 'Yeah, where's Sugar?' 'He's in bed.' 'Well, you better get him out of bed.' And with that we heard a door open and it's Sugar and he says, 'Ah, you're here.'

"Now Sugar Corbally was huge, physically like a bull, very strong. And I said to him, 'You should never have got near my father with a knife.' And he said, 'Should I not?' And with that I hit him and I knocked him *spark out*, in the bedroom. And they woke him up and I said, 'We have grown up now, the family, and there was *never* any need for you to go near him with a knife. He had forgotten all about you, hopefully. But now that you've started it again I just want to tell you that now *we* do the fighting. I'm the son, I'm John. I am now *Young Spike* and I'll take this on my shoulders. *I'll* now do the fighting cause he's getting too old.' But my father wouldn't have it. He kept saying, 'I just want to get one minute. I just want to get my hurling stick. I'm going to get a belt at you tonight. I haven't long left in this world but when I f_____ go I'm going to take a Corbally with me!' And Sugar says to me, 'We heard all about you. We've been watching your career and we've been rooting for you. We're glad that you never grew up like your father with the drink. You never caused any trouble.' 'No,' I said, 'I only want to tell you that the fight stops with him now. This is now the next generation of McCormacks. You have now taken on the new generation cause he will *never* fight you again. I'll take up the fighting for him.' So he said, 'Give me your hand', and he shook hands with me. And me father says, '*Don't* take it.' And I said, 'No, Dad.' And I took his hand. And he said, 'We've great respect for you and we've always had great respect for Spike. We've *always* looked up to Spike.' And that was the last fight he had with the Corballys.

"One time my father was to do an interview with Gay Byrne on his show. This was back in the sixties. It was the *Late, Late Show* on a Saturday night and everyone heard that '*Spike's* on!' So all the pubs cleared cause there were no televisions in the pubs at that time. *Every* pub in the Sheriff Street area and the inner city all cleared out cause Spike was on the show. So my mother got his suit out of the pawn and we dressed him up nice. So they sent a motor car down from RTE to get Spike for the show and there was two people in the car, a chauffeur and this fella from Telefís Éireann. Anyway, the car comes down and the fella says, 'We're bringing you to the *Late, Late Show.*' And Spike says, 'OK, but will you do me one favour? The first pub we come to, just pull up cause I have to have a pint before I go.' 'We were told *specifically* by your *wife* and *Gay Byrne* that you were *not* to have a drink. He won't put you on the show if you have drink on you. That's one thing about Gay Byrne, he won't have a drunkard on the show.' So my father says, 'Well, I'm *not* going on the show unless I get a pint. You've got to loosen me tongue.' So they went around to the public house and he brought in the fella in the car and the driver and says, '*Have one*, you're *going* to have a drink with me!' And with my father there was no such thing as not having a drink with him—you *had* to have a drink with Spike.

"Anyway, by the time they got out to RTE my father had a good few drinks on him. But there was some sort of hitch and Gay Byrne says, 'There's a bit of a hitch, Spike. Go down to the reception down below and you'll get a drink down there.' And all the technicians are there and they all say, 'How are you keeping, Spike?' *Everyone* knew him. So he goes up to the bar. And this light comes on for the stage-hands [to return] and the show is now getting ready to go on but someone says, 'No, Spike, don't come yet. When that light comes on, come back up again then.' So the others all left their drinks there! And my father went along the *whole* table and he says, 'Jesus Christ, leaving all that drink. That's a *sin*, that's a mortal sin!' So he went along and cleared all the bar! And Gay Byrne says to someone, 'OK, go up and get Spike.' And it was 'Holy Jaysus!' My father told me, 'I slopped out all of that bar.' And when he went down to Gay Byrne he said, 'There's no way under any circumstances will I have that man on this show.' And he *wouldn't*.

"Spike and Lugs [Brannigan] and me was great friends. Lugs refereed, he was an amateur referee. He refereed his last fight in my gym. I used to bring him up in my car to the gym where he'd referee the kids fighting for me. And we always had a coffee first, Lugs and me, and we'd get a big scone. Now he was getting old at the time and a little bit hunched and he always wore a big mackinaw and it looked unsightly on him, rather than a neat jacket. And I said, 'Can I just ask you something, Jim?'—cause he didn't like to be called 'Lugs' cause he'd big ears. You'd *never* call him Lugs, it was Jim. So I said, 'Jim, would you tell me, of *all* the fights that you refereed what was the most *memorable* fight?' 'Let me tell you,' he says, 'the *most memorable* fight I ever refereed was between your mother and father in the house. I was called one night when your father was creating murder in the house. He was really bad on the drink and he broke all the windows and your mother said '*Get Brannigan!*' And I come down in the squad car. Five of us come down when we heard that Spike was at it, even when he was old.' See, you couldn't control my father when he fought, Kevin. He was physically *terribly* strong. He'd the strength of three or four people. He took a washing machine up once full of water and threw it over the balcony—that's how strong he was. Now Jim was a big man of six foot four and he says, 'What's wrong with you, Spike? Have you any money? You can get bloody drunk but you can't bring any money home for the dinners to put food on the table.' My father had a good few drinks on him and he was standing up and me mother went to give him a dig. My mother went to swing at him and she *hit Jim* Brannigan with a left hook! And Brannigan went, 'Oh, Jaysus, Nellie, now *hold on* a minute!'

"My father knew *everyone*. Brendan Behan used to come down to the house regularly. And everyone knew him [Spike] and they were giving him stuff, but they wouldn't give him money. When he'd come home at night he had stuff coming out of the butcher's shops, he'd have legs of chicken, seven or eight steaks, he'd have newspapers under his arm and he'd come home in a taxi. He'd have a *dog* in the car and he'd say, 'I got this from a pal of mine out of the pet shop up the road', and me mother'd say, 'I *can't* look after thirteen children. What in the name of Jesus are you bringing home a dog for?' He came home one time with a *monkey* and my mother was saying, 'What in the name of Jesus am I going to do with a *monkey*? I can't feed a monkey.' And the monkey was jumping around the place and my mother was saying, 'Get that monkey out of here.' And he'd go down with all the fellas to Croke Park when Kerry came up to Dublin and he'd go up and stand at Hill 16 [pub] with all the Dubs with his Kerry accent and he'd say, 'C'mon Kerry!' And one fella shouted out, 'Jesus, Spike, you're the only Dublin man with a Kerry accent.' Oh, he could stand on Hill 16, Spike could, but no one else could. Today a country man couldn't stand on Hill 16. A culchie, he'd get *killed*. But *Spike* could. Spike did it every Sunday with all the Dubs, shouting for Kerry. He was the only one allowed to do it cause he was so tough. No one bothered Spike.

"My father was like an old gunfighter. This is the way he phrased it himself, 'I'm the old gunfighter.' I said to him once, 'What's wrong now? How come this young guy 35 years of age and you're 64 and he's here annoying you?' And he said, 'I don't care how long it goes I'm still the fella there that's to be taken because I'm the old gunfighter.' In the pub once this fella was calling him some names and my father says, 'I don't even know *who* you are.' And the fella says, 'But I know who *you are*, Spike.' And my father says, 'But I don't know who you are, so why are you calling me names?' This is where the old gunfighter phrase came in when the man came up and said, 'I'm talking to *you*, McCormack!' And my father says, 'I'm like the old gunfighter.' So my father stepped up to the barman and says, 'What are you going to do about this?' And the barman says, 'Don't mind him, Spike, he's looking for trouble.' And me father stepped up and *hit* him. Oh, *flattened* him. Now I *mean flattened* him. Oh, he was half my father's age.

"My father was 66 when he was dying. He was in hospital and then we brought him home for about two weeks. Oh, he died at home. So I said, 'We'll go and get him a drink.' Now he'd given up drink ten years before he died. So we got him some brandy cause his mouth was very dry and his tongue felt three or four times its normal size, cause of the radiation and morphine he was taking. It eased the burning sensation and pain in him. And he took it and said, 'That was great, that was lovely.' And we gave him plenty of brandy . . . he wasn't short of brandy that night. Now you'd have to be in the room to realise this, Kevin, cause it was lovely to see. Have you ever seen someone who has convulsed into laughter? It's very contagious and everyone around started to laugh. Now this man is *dying* and we say to him, 'What are you laughing for?' And he says, 'For *forty years* you're trying to keep me off the drink and ten years ago I gave up the drink and *here you are* trying to push it down my throat again!' He thought this was very funny . . . I thought it was great.

"And the next night he died. It was during the night, about three or four o'clock in the morning, and you know the way they hallucinate? I'll never forget this. He dozed off and he woke up again and he says to me, 'Am I still Spike?' And I says, 'Yes.' And I thought it was very sad when he said that to me. Like, for me to think that he didn't know who he was. It was a shock. And I said, 'Yeah, Dad, of course you are.' When you saw a man like that in the bed you thought, 'He's going to be OK, a new day dawns.' You'd say your prayers that this man would be coming back. But that morning he died. And then when he's gone it hits you. I remembered a phrase we had in school, 'God calls any time.'

"I idolised my father . . . and it wasn't the boxing, it was the *person*, he was gorgeous. Like our brother, he's mentally retarded and he doesn't know who we are, Kevin. He hasn't an inkling. And he's a big, big young fella. And I seen my father with the Mongolian young fella, the last of the thirteen. I seen him sitting holding him when he'd have a runny nose and he'd wipe his nose with his jacket and he'd say, 'I'm minding this fella, he's my pal.' He reared him up with my mother and then he used to go and see him in the home. Oh, he was a lovely dad, Kevin. Oh, he was a lovely, lovely person. In *every* way . . . his nature. He had a great nature about him. And Spike's funeral was out of this world. They couldn't get in the chapel, Laurence O'Toole's, down on Sheriff Street. And it was *amazing* the number of people after he died who told me the *help* that he had given them when he was going away to sea and the way he was helpful if there was a bit of trouble. He was very helpful towards everyone. He was some character. They all said, 'He was a *great* friend, your father. He was so different from you. You're so quiet compared to your father. When your father walked into a room he lit it up.' He had this Kerryman's way of lighting up a room and he knew *everyone*. Older people still say today, 'Oh, you're Spike's son' . . . young Spike. I loved my father."

Douglas Cord—Irish Track Champion, Age 93

He and his family survived the 1916 Rising and Civil War during which they tried to remain neutral despite their British origins. As a young lad he found that he could run like the wind. In the 1920s he became the Irish mile champion, setting a national record. A second place finish in Croke Park to the American world champion was a glorious achievement. With little use for serious training, he succeeded on pure natural ability. He could endure the pain of extreme physical exertion and had the heart of a great endurance runner. At age 93 he still delights in recounting his most memorable races.

"I was born in 1903, I had five brothers and one sister and I was a twin. My father was a dairy farmer. I used to drive the milk cart around the city. I'd deliver to different houses and institutions. And I was only a young fella. We had three full churns of milk—and there was no water in it! It was an offence to put water into it. Generally, private houses used to take two or three pints of milk and it was a spout can and a 'little drop for the cat' [extra]. I used to leave about 8.00 and go all around the city and finished up at 1.00.

"Now when the Rising was on in Dublin in 1916 I remember I was coming up Camden Street and I had to stop there and 'bang, bang, bang, bang!' The bullets was flying around me, one was attacking the other, and I happened to get caught in the crossfire. Lucky enough, I wasn't hit. But I noticed that one of the soldiers was hit cause you could see him falling. Oh, and indeed I remember the Black and Tans and they were *no good*. They were the scum of England, prisoners out of gaol and everything. I saw them but they didn't give me any trouble . . . and I didn't make any trouble for them. When I was young I was more interested in young ladies at that time. Politics didn't interest me. But the Tans were only the scum, doing the dirty work. See, the British would tell them to go and get someone but they had no proof, but they knew certain fellas were in the IRA and they'd tell the Tans to shoot them. And the Tans would get away with it. They were a lot of liars.

"And I remember the Civil War well. A playmate of mine was shot in the Civil War. He was in the Free State and the IRA shot him, a young man around my own age. I mixed with both sides in the Civil War. We knew the IRAs and we knew the British and we knew the Free Staters. We knew them *all*. We were friends with them all and they all *knew* that we were neutral, that we didn't take part. See, the *Cords* were neutral, we didn't take any sides, we were glad to get on with everybody. Now down in Rockport House, our farm, there was an IRA man on the run and he came to my father one night and asked him could he put him up for a week or two. And my father *brought him in* and put him up. And he'd always go out across the fields early in the morning. He was supposed to be getting shot if they could catch him. But they never caught him. Now my father done that—and we were supposed to be British! He used to come in late and sleep there. No one knew about him, only the family. Oh, we were taking a risk, all right. And he got a lend of my father's gun off him one day. I don't know what he did with it. My father'd help *anyone*. Actually, the British army were here camping down where we used to play football, camping in the field here beside our house. And my father gave the officers the option of sleeping in a room here, in our house, in the *same* room as the IRA fella slept in. My father was in-between like . . . but he was beginning to find out what the British were. At the *start* he was British, then he was beginning to find out that they were no good. And I know *better* still . . . I know more than I did then. And they're *still no good*! And I used to shake the British flag at one time—*not now*!

"Now I was the Irish mile champion from 1926 to 1929. And I ran for Ireland in the cross-country as well. I was about 21 when I found out that I could run. And, well, I'll tell you about that, it's a funny thing. All the young lads around here was always up around the woods. So I was up there one day and I was coming down through the woods and I seen smoke coming up behind these bushes. So I poked in to see what it was and here it was a lot of pals of me own and they had a fire lighted. It was in the wintertime and they were warming themselves, it was cold. So I went in and had a warm too. And eventually they all drifted away and there was no one left there, only meself, and I was getting the final warm up. But before I was about to go too in came one of the [land] owner's sons, Tristan Massey. He burst in and says, 'What the hell are you doing here?' You know, a big shot! One of Lord Massey's sons. 'Ah,' says I, 'I'm only getting the heat, I didn't light the fire, they're all gone off now and I'm the last here.' 'Well, I'd better go and tell the gamekeeper,' says he. So I just got up real quick and I *shot out* through a hedge and away down a long field. And just as I looked back he was coming after me. And the two of us was running through the field. And I beat him through it anyway but he was still after me, a big tall fella. And then I *shot* through the gate and down towards the river and he was after me but *still* he couldn't catch me. And finally he didn't go any farther. He never caught me. But, anyhow, I found out after that that Tristan Massey, he was the quarter-mile champion of Oxford!

"After that I went down there and joined the Denora Harriers. And there was no one down there that could catch me. Yeah, I could run away from them all, at any distance from a half-mile up. Like there were some sprinters there and I couldn't touch *them*. But from a half-mile up to ten. There used to be local races all around the country and I started entering the half-mile races. And I won the first six half-mile races I went in. Won the whole lot of them. And I knew I could run then. And at sports meetings you'd run a couple of races a day. In my first mile race championship I ran and beat a fella, Queen was his name, from England and he was the champion in England and the champion here. So he held the championship and I took it off him . . . and that was the last of him. Yeah, he was out and I was coming on.

"So then after that I went into the Irish championships and the first time I ran in the mile championship I won it. And it was an Irish record at the time. My time was four, twenty-four [four minutes, twenty-four seconds]. It was the native record. Now they do it in training! And then I went to the cross-country and I ran for Ireland and I was always second or third. To be a good miler you *must do* cross-country because it builds up your stamina. So I ran for Ireland in France and Scotland and England, Wales and all around. I ran from a half-mile up to ten miles. It was the mile I was best at. I ran in the games here in Croke Park and an American beat me in it. Hand was his name, Lloyd Hand. He was the world champion at the time and he won it and I was second. Yeah, I had no hope of beating him.

"And there was a mile race with England and Scotland I remember down in Cork one time. There was a track cut out, mowed out, and outside the track it was long grass. Now I didn't like the rain but, well, I was able to run in the muck actually *better* than most other fellas because I had a quick step and I used to never lift me feet much off the ground. Anyhow, two Englishmen was leading and I was on the shoulder and I was making me sprint for the tape and I was coming up and the second Englishman moved out over on top of me and moved me out on to the long grass—and no one protested against it! *Pushed* me out into the grass. I couldn't run up his back! He should have been *disqualified*, naturally. But there wasn't a single protest. So if the officials didn't protest what's the use of me doing it? Oh, it was a bloody disgrace.

"I had an open air life and we used to be kicking football and running all me life. And I was never very heavy. My running weight was nine stone, nine. The running was just naturally in me blood . . . run, run, run. And I didn't train much, just ran on natural ability. Diet . . . I ate anything I got! I was never drunk in me life, I wasn't a drinker. Everybody else was training night and day but I didn't bother training. Now and again I used to go down to Denora Harriers about once a week and have just a lap around the field and that was it. It wasn't training. I couldn't be *bothered*. It was just natural ability. If I had trained I could have beat the four-minute mile meself. Blooming sure!

"Now I had the final kick. If you haven't the *kick* in running you might as well give it up. And you had to be very cute, too, in certain races. Don't run too fast at the start. If you run too fast you just run yourself *out*. You should know your own rhythm, just know yourself, your own speed. Ah, and you'd want to have heart. And you'd have to put up with the *pain* . . . the pain of exhaustion when it'd be coming on you. You'd have to put up with that because you'd know you were near the finish. There could be pain in running but you had to put up with it. I remember I finished a race in Croke Park one day. I won the race, and when I finished I fell down. I was pumped out, *exhausted* completely. And with the roaring and all I went deaf, went *deaf*. And you must learn to *lose* as well as win. I was winning a race one time, had it won in me pocket, just going to touch the tape and I never looked either way and wasn't there a fella bursting alongside of me and he got the tape before me. 'Ah', says I, 'it's me own fault.' Over confident. I was just pulling up at the tape. You must always run *through* the tape.

"Running was in me blood. I raced over a period of about twenty years. I was in me forties when I was running. It was company, you know? It was natural ability that I ran on and I ran for the joy of it. My nickname was 'Duggie', from Douglas. When I was running in me forties I was running against fellas half me age. I could have been running against me own sons. But the speed wasn't there then."

10

Tradesmen's Tales:
Cutlers to Hatters

JOHN READ COWLE—CUTLER, AGE 90

He is the proprietor of Read's Cutlery shop on Parliament Street. It is the oldest surviving shop in Dublin, dating back to 1670. Originally, the speciality was making fine swords and several of 1600s vintage still hang on the rear wall. In more recent centuries business thrived from the making of precision surgical instruments, gentlemen's razors and elegant ivory-handled eating utensils. Today, business has been reduced mostly to selling imported cutlery and sharpening various cutting instruments. The shop still exudes a Victorian ambience and he is reluctant to retire and sell it to a new owner, but he knows realistically that the day is close at hand. [Mr Cowle passed away in 1996.]

"I was born in 1905, in this house. My family lived above the shop. Now this shop [business] wasn't here when it started. We started in 1670 on the quays. It was called Blind Quay because it was a cul-de-sac. In 1750 we moved from the quays to Crane Lane [which today is at the rear of the shop] and we've been here ever since. But about nine years after that Parliament gave a grant to build a new street out there [Parliament Street] and Crane Lane is parallel to this street and so the back of our house used to be the front. Now the shop was on my mother's side. Hence, my name is not Read, it's Cowle because Read was on my mother's side of the family. My father was in the boot and shoe business and he married my mother and this was a rather flourishing business so he packed up his boots and shoes and came in here and lived here and my mother reared six children in this house. And, very fortunately—and this is rather amusing—they had two boys and then me and they gave *me* the name Read in the middle of my name. It could have been either of the other fellas. But they weren't a bit interested [in the business] and so they picked the right one to give the 'Read' to because I was the one who came into the business.

"I was always in the shop. I loved it . . . I loved it. I loved the workshop cause I was rather good with my hands. My father ran the shop but he died when we were all very young and left my mother with six little children. He was 57 when he died and I was 14. I was still in school. My mother knew all about the business but she couldn't run the business and run a family. It was necessary to get somebody else into the business so I left school before my two elder brothers and came in here. There were two men in the shop at that time and my mother and me. And we had three men in the workshop. We had a manager running it and she superintended it. Now my mother had the good idea that I shouldn't come straight into this business. I should be sent away to learn something about business generally. Very wise. So I went away for three years to another shop here in Dublin, an ironmonger and hardware shop. At the same time she sent me to do an engineering course of one year in the college of science to learn how things were made. I got to know what a lathe was, what a casting was, I knew about machines and drills and got to know one metal from another. That was a great help to me all my life. My mother, she was very well advised, a wonderful woman. I look back on her with great affection and great admiration, to take on six little children and a business. Anyway, I've been here ever since and I love it.

"I was married when I was 28 and my wife was the same age as myself. And she died after only three months, of T.B. Could you imagine anything worse than that? Isn't that dreadful? She had T.B. and I waited for her and she was in hospital for years, in and out. And eventually the doctor says, 'She's all right now', and we got married. We went on a honeymoon, we came back, and the *day* we came back she got into bed and she never got out of it. I got wedding presents after she was dead. Now my present wife was a friend of hers and I always knew her and admired her. She was a very nice, tall, elegant person. And one day she passed the shop here and we had a chat and when she was just about to go I said, 'If I asked you out, would you come?' 'I would.' So I rang her the next day and I asked her out and we never looked back. And I've been intensely happy ever since.

"Now when this firm started they were sword cutlers. Now sword cutlers were *important* people. Swords was the original trade and then they began to diversify after a long time and drifted into making cutlery, dinner knives and forks, and eventually surgical instruments which was a very big trade. We would have been the leading surgical instrument makers and all our old labels and documents have 'Surgical Instrument Makers' written on them, old billheads and that sort of thing. And the thing about surgical instruments—and I'm talking about the mid-1800s—the most eminent surgeons in the world were in Dublin. Some wonderful surgeons . . . Sir William Wilde and a fella called Simpson and those sort of people. Simpson invented a lot of scalpels. And these men would have been doing the original appendix operation and we were making their knives. That's what gave us great distinction because we were making knives for these very eminent men. Now I found this old ledger up there [on a shelf] one day and it was beautifully written in copperplate, beautiful writing. And all these very eminent men were in this book. We were making their instruments. And the entries were day by day in flourishing letters and they wrote down everything that happened during that day . . . 'Dr Reilly called and collected his lances', and there was little sketches in the margins. This suggested that at one time maybe the doctors themselves drew the little sketches of what they wanted, the shape of the blade or whatever it was.

"And we made scissors for barber shops and sharpened their scissors for them. And we always did a lot of business with Guinness. We did business with the brewery ever since it opened. We sold them whistles. They always had whistles on the boats and trains and the cranes. And we'd sell them a lot of scissors. And we made a lot of veterinary instruments. A great thing in those days was 'bleeding'. Didn't matter *what* you had, they thought you had too much blood! They thought this was blood pressure. And their idea of curing blood pressure was to let out some blood and there were things called leeches for bleeding. But we made an instrument here and it was very popular and greatly used. It was called a 'phleams', this was in the mid-1800s. Now phleams were made for veterinary purposes and for ordinary use on people. Big ones were used for veterinary and small ones that were very refined were used for humans. I still have a few of the veterinary ones.

"Now all these instruments were beautifully made with tortoise shell handles, ivory handles, horn handles. All made here. There were some wonderful handles of ivory and old horn, stag horn, buffalo horn. And another thing I should tell you, they had a secret here for staining ivory green. And green ivory became a speciality of this house. Now the ivory was originally white and they stained it green and we don't know *how* they used to stain them . . . the recipe could be somewhere in the house, we don't know. The stain went well in, it wasn't just superficial. We tried all sorts of things [to duplicate it], like copper verdigris and all sorts of things that would turn green. And, if you'll excuse an indelicacy, they even tried *urine*. They thought it might sort of be that was how it was done. But they *never* found out. We *do not* know how this was done.

"Now I want to show you this. This is a street directory for 1778 and it's an almanac they called it and it has all sorts of things. It's quite a valuable little book. Now we were in this book, of course. See, the Reads, they were a very eminent family. There were trade guilds and they were masters of the guild. It was the Guild of St Luke, the cutlers' guild. There's an awful lot of stuff in this shop. Unfortunately, I've lost a wonderful package of old documents that I had . . . they're somewhere, but I can't find them. What was interesting about them was that they had advertisements in them, from newspapers. There was one from the *Dublin Evening Post* for 14 January 1799, or something like that. But advertisements were *the* business. And this fella, Thomas Read, he was a very stuck-up fella and he used to advertise and say, 'Of course, if you buy anything anywhere else you're mad!' That was the tone he had. 'We're the *only ones*!' He put, 'Mr Read wishes to inform the public in general, and his customers in particular'—Wasn't that a lovely start?—'that he still maintains the high quality of products in his shop which are manufactured under his personal inspection on his premises on Parliament Street. These include spurs [for riding], steel appliances for the weak and distorted limbs, callipers for people with crooked legs, a newly-invented instrument for a fine edge on razors and a newly-invented instrument for cutting straw.' I think that must have had something to do with thatching for cottages, a new instrument for cutting straw. I never knew what it was called.

"About the beginning of the century, round about 1902 or 1903 when my father was here, we were badly stuck for men in the workshop. We had two men and one was an elderly man and the other was a man from Cork who was a terrible drunkard and he used to get paid on Friday and we wouldn't see him for days. He went off and drank all his money and then he staggered in on Tuesdays. But he was *very good*, an old fella from Cork, and his name was Fox. But he'd disappear and we wouldn't know where he was and this began to annoy my father who was a good businessman. And in the workshop at the back we had an ex-soldier, a man with one leg. It was a menial job but it was a good job and he was never out of work. It was *manpower*, we worked on wheels that revolved. They were called buffs. There was no motor power available. This was before we even had a gas engine. So the retired soldier was employed to turn a huge wheel, a flywheel, and they drove belts from that wheel on to machines, grinders and buffers and glazers, from this big wheel. And when he came in in the morning they all started the wheel [to assist pushing it in a revolving motion] and they eventually got it going. Now once you got it to go it was going.

"Anyhow, my father started to scout around to try and get a proper expert cutler. And he tried in Sheffield but there was nothing in Sheffield but specialists. A man in Sheffield was a glazer, a buffer, a grinder, putting scissors together, putting on handles—but we wanted a man who would do the whole lot. And he was told to try some of the English provincial towns where there were very good cutlers. And he eventually put an advertisement in a paper called *The Newcastle Times* and a man answered that advertisement and because my father was offering very handsome wages, £2 8s. a week, that man thought it was worth his while to pack up his family in Newcastle and come over and live here. Now this man, he came over here, his name was Overy, and he was a typical north of England countryman. And he brought over his wife and three sons and they settled down in Dublin. This is a very interesting man, a wonderful cutler, and he was an agnostic. He'd never walk in the door of a church. He'd tell you, 'Oh, I have no time for churches.' And his family were the same, which is rather strange in Ireland which, as you know, is a rather religious country. But, still, he was in many ways the *most moral* man I've ever met. I never knew that man or his family to ever tell a lie, under any circumstances. And he was *never* late. And he was never *early*.

"They were a wonderful family, very industrious. And one of the sons, the second boy, came in as an apprentice to his own father. The old man and his son had wonderful hands. Now this old man's son, that boy worked here for sixty-two years! He came at the age of 13 to learn the trade from his own father and he was still doing a few hours work for us when he was 75. He was a remarkable man. Ernest was his name. He and his father could do anything with their hands. In the workshop we wore an apron and the old man, Mr Overy, was always singing, in a high voice. We were always repairing but we did make the odd thing. I remember during the war Ernest made surgical blades for surgical knives, just to oblige surgeons. And he made a most precise instrument for a tonsillectomy that you put down the throat. Now I worked with him in the workshop and he was like a brother to me. And I had surgeons thanking me for the wonderful job this fella did for them. Oh, I enjoyed working in the workshop with Ernest and, in fact, they had a bit of a job dragging me out of the workshop into the [front] shop. Oh, it was great fun. And, as I told you, they were an atheist family. Religion mattered a lot in Ireland but it didn't matter to them at all. And Ernest married a Catholic girl and had two boys who were brought up as Catholics but, of course, he couldn't care less.

"Oh, over the years I've had some very bad cuts. It's a terrible risk but I'm quite used to it and it doesn't distress me. Fortunately, I heal very well, but unfortunately I bleed. And there was a danger to your lungs. See, there was emery flying around and grindstone. And we had gas lighting. Now we used this machine with pulleys and it drives a shaft with buffs. A buff is a wheel. The wheel would be made of wood and was covered in leather, a special leather. We had bull neck leather which was very good. And we made our own wheels in the shop out of wood and then covered them in leather. Then the leather was dressed with emery—and we still do that—and that flies around like a grindstone. The emery is available in different grits, coarse emery, flour emery, medium emery. The grit is measured by so many holes, like a thirty-hole would be very coarse grit and a ninety-hole would be very fine grit. And the finest of all is stuff called flour emery. That's like black powder. And they dressed the wheels with this emery and we'd use that for polishing. There's an art to that. Now the skill in working the emery wheel is a very steady hand. You used to sit on what was called a 'stoop' and they sat like that [stooped] and here was the wheel going around and you were taught to sit with your elbows on your knees, stooped over and with a steady hand you ran the knife backward and forward over the wheel . . . slowly. Now if you didn't do it slowly it would have a very rough finish. But if you had a nice smooth buff and had a steady hand you could get a lovely finish. We were very good at finishing. And we also had wheels that was called glaze wheels made of wood with no leather on them. And they were used for doing the insides of scissors. They were very, very accurate, just a very, very hard wood surface, dressed with emery again. A hardwood like mahogany or teak. It wouldn't warp.

"You had to dress the wheels, scrape off all the old stuff and then cover the wheel in glue and roll it on an emery tray until it was completely covered and became a rough buff. Now after a day or so the roughness wore off it and then they put what was called 'emery cake' on it. Cake emery was stuff like black soap. Now the Overys made their own cake emery and I never will forget when they made it. It was extraordinary. First we sent out and we bought mutton suet, mutton fat, from a butcher. And Mr Overy had a big ladle and he used to put the mutton into the ladle and heat it and it melted. And the *smell* from it was *abominable*! Like burning fat. Dreadful. And he'd start putting the flour emery into the ladle and mixing it up and then put it into little cardboard boxes like little cakes of soap. It would set. And there's one thing about this I've never forgotten—this is very interesting—he had a little secret ingredient he used to put into this. And I'd say, 'Now what are you doing?' And he'd say, 'You'll learn about that some day.' And he *wouldn't tell me* until I undertook that I wouldn't tell anybody else. This was a little trade secret that he had. And he was *so proud* of this. This enhanced the thing somehow or another. And after a long, long time he told me. And do you know what it was? A little pea of bee's wax! It would melt in and added something. Whatever it did, it worked. And the emery blocks were like soap.

"Now razors also used to be a big job. We used to do a couple of dozen razors a day. And we used to call ourselves 'Razor Specialists.' Oh, there were no Gillette razors in those days. You'd only see straight razors. And we carried an enormous stock of razors, running in those days from half a crown—that was two shillings and sixpence—up to ten shillings. And for ten shillings you got an ivory handled razor. *Real* ivory. Of course, that's gone now. And we *made* razors here once. Never in my time. That stopped before any of us knew anything about it. And a good strap [leather] brought a very fine edge on the open razor. We used to get the straps from Birmingham and Sheffield and London where there were some very good firms in the razor strap business but, of course, it's a trade that's gone. Now that shoemaker, Tom Malone, he's still up there in Crampton Court just beside the Olympia Theatre. Well, he still makes razor straps for us.

"At one time this was a very busy passing trade in this street. But the street has declined terribly and we only exist now because we're specialists. Like, we sell hair cutting scissors to the prisons—now that's a funny thing. You'd never think of that. Another thing we do very well with now is French cooks' knives, filleting, carving, chopping, boning knives. That's a big end of my business. We supply chefs with sets of these and there's a lot of catering colleges and schools and they buy a lot of stuff from us. We import [cutlery] mostly from Sheffield and Germany. My workshop at the moment does not really pay. You can't charge a man more than about £1 or £1.50 for sharpening a pair of scissors. It actually costs more than that to do. And when we're busy in the workshop we take a week because sharpening scissors is not easy. They've got to be taken asunder and then you grind the inside and grind the outside edges and that takes a fair amount of time . . . can't make it pay.

"It's a dying trade. There's no money in it. I often think I'm mad to keep the workshop open but I'd hate to give it up because it adds a little bit of professionalism and prestige. If you haven't got a workshop you're not a cutler! And even though it doesn't pay I still wouldn't want to scrap it. My wife wants me to retire now. I have mixed feelings about it . . . I want to go and I don't want to go. I'm very attached to her and would like to spend more time with her. I have to face it very soon, what's going to happen with the shop. Now when I die somebody will have to keep this place going. It's a very specialised trade and you couldn't walk in off the street and start in the shop without knowing something about it. So I want to try and get rid of the place when I'm still active . . . cause if I'd get somebody to take it over I'd stay on with them for a while to break them into the business."

WILLIAM COYLE—HATTER, AGE 68

As the proprietor of Dublin's last genuine hatter's shop, he is fond of saying, "I fell out of the cradle and into a hat, cause that's all I ever knew." In his apprenticeship days men never ventured forth without their hat—it was "part of them". Labouring men wore tweed caps, dashing types donned a fedora, while civil servants and some tradesmen favoured the bowler hats which they coveted and meticulously cared for. Hatters were proud, fussy and secretive about their trade. Over the past century he has properly fitted every type of man from gurrier to government ministers and is unabashedly proud to be Dublin's last true hatter.

"My father was a hatter. And this is an old building. I'm going back four or five generations. In my father's time I'd say there were about twenty hatter's shops. Now we're down to one. My father was born in 1898. He went to work in 1908 when he was 10 years old and he worked in a firm down here in South George's Street called Troy's and they were hatters. He did an apprenticeship there, the *hard way*. Back then you had hats [selling] from 1s. 9d. to 7s. 6d. Caps were sixpence. Now in Ireland, up to 1936 or 1939, *nobody* went without a hat. Everyone wore a hat. In the olden days when a person chose a hat he didn't buy it lightly. He gave some time to it. Hats were very personal to people. Older people loved their old hat . . . it was *part* of them. Now I remember growing up as a young lad, 9, 10, 11, going to the Catholic church with my father. And you always put your hat on the seat in front of you and then when you'd be sitting down you'd take it and put it beside you. But sometimes you'd be engrossed in what was going on and you'd forget about it and someone'd sit on it. *Well*, I've seen him in church and he *would lift* the person in front of him out for doing it. And he'd say, 'Why don't you look where you're sitting?' See, if you sat on a good hat and if you crush it there's creases in it for a lifetime.

"This is the last hatter's shop in Dublin. The shop goes back to 1936. My father was manager down there at Troy's but when he moved up here to open his own shop that man who employed him at Troy's tried to close him up. It was terribly dirty. But this was the way you done it years ago. He rang up all the wholesalers and manufacturers and said to them—and he didn't say '*don't buy*'—but he said, 'Coyle has opened up a shop and I just want to say to you that I've been buying stuff off you for the past twenty years and the devil you know is better than the devil you don't know.' Now that's all he would say. In other words, he was saying to them, 'If you go up there and deal, if you sell to him, you're gone from here.' See, it was the proximity of the shops. He didn't want us having what he had. And he actually *did* that. That was an act of sheer malice. But that's the way they were. But my father, being manager down there for years, he knew all these people. And, funny enough, we found that in a religious capacity those who were not of the same persuasion [Catholic] as ourselves would come in and say, 'We wouldn't go for that sort of thing, we'll supply you, whatever you want, and you needn't pay for it for six months.' A starting-off type of thing. The Protestants, they were the people who would supply you. Your *own* wouldn't! Possibly their definition of Christianity was a bit broader.

"Back then it didn't matter how ridiculous you looked, everyone wore a hat. One of the comic pictures I have in mind is the early photographs of crowds of people, men, on O'Connell Street and all with these big, wide-brimmed hats which they adopted from America during the Capone era when they had the FBI and you had this fedora which was a word which came into the hat curriculum. A fedora was actually a black hat or a dark hat worn by the Federal Bureau of Investigation—he was a 'Fed.' And the old pictures we have of gangsters years ago standing on the street corner, that came over here. It was adopted over here by hatters. And the origin of the hat was America. Oh, yes, the first hat that was made, you go back to that fella that fought in Texas, Davy Crockett, he was the first one. He killed a coon [racoon] and took the skin and dried it and used the coon skin for the hat and with the tail hanging down. And that was the original of the hat. And then from that the American beaver took over and beaver hats came on in Europe.

"In Dublin here there was a line drawn. See, Dublin, back from the Elizabethan division of the country, it became known as the Pale, an area from County Louth down into Wicklow. And that was basically *English* people who were sent over here to colonise Dublin, the Anglo-Irish, if you wish to call them that. And they brought over with them British ideas. Like, the best type of hat we could buy over here in Dublin was an English hat, not an American hat. Because with American hats it was an *outlook* . . . big and broad and like the country itself. It expressed itself in wide-brimmed hats. But over here we had the British Conservative, the Whigs or Tories, and they brought over with them a most sophisticated style of hat. You're talking about the soft fedora style hat and the Italian influence was very much there as well. And the Anthony Eden which was the ultra-conservative of the hats, and the bowler. And from that the racing fraternity took over and came into it, the English Beau Brummel if you like. And he softened the style of hats and made them less severe and more appealing in the sense that they were more 'man-about-town' stuff, the young philanderer type of thing. It was called a slouch hat.

"I started at age 15. I was apprenticed to a firm called Pim Brothers on South Great George's Street. It was a three year apprenticeship and I was sent by them to the various schools to learn. It was comprehensive, very good. It started off with haberdashery where you sold buttons and thread and everything. And then you moved downstairs to leather goods and then you sold silks and wools and all. And then I went into the ready-made department where the hats were and that's where I found a niche, where I liked to be. But with all the training that one would get from a commercial school or a firm, *nothing* would be as good for apprentices—it couldn't *compare*—as the practicalities of learning all about hats from a hatter himself, from a man *steeped* in hats, who knew how to roll brims, how to stretch hard hats. It was a *personal* thing. And I was taught to make hats, my father wasn't. I was taught by a firm called Wilson and Stafford over in

England. They showed me how to make hats. That was part of my training, to know how a hat was *made*. Because if I go to sell you a motor car I've got to know about the engine and all. So if you come to buy a hat I'm the *authority*.

"In most of the multiple stores years ago—multiple stores that sold ladies' and gents' and children's clothing—they had men's departments which were divided into the shirt department, a hosiery department, ready-made suits, tailoring, and then the hatters. Then there were hatters' shops that sold only hats. There was Dunne's up on the Green [St Stephen's] and Collins of North Earl Street and another firm down on Westmoreland Street. These were hatters. *Exclusively* hatters and nothing else but the *best* of hats. The other old hatters are all gone now, dead and gone. I knew most of them. But you didn't mix with them socially. They had *their* customers and there was always a disparagement if one was speaking about the other. I mean, we grow old in wisdom . . . like, years ago if a man came in here to me for a hat and I hadn't got it and he said to me, 'Is there anywhere else I can get a hat?' I wouldn't tell him. I *wouldn't* tell him. I might say, 'There's a couple of hat shops downtown.' But I wouldn't give him a *name*. I wouldn't recommend anyone to him because I was giving business to somebody else. Why should I do that?

"And a hatter was a very *secretive* person and a very *proud* person, very proud of his knowledge which he wouldn't give to anybody else, unless he was giving it to somebody who was going to work in his business. Other than that he was a person set apart. He didn't divulge these things. They were very precise people. There are things I can do with a hat that *nobody* else would know about. And I wouldn't even share it with anybody because that's my trade and it'll die with me . . . in the conditioning of the hat, in tricks that you learned when you were growing up. Hatters are perfectionists. And a critical eye . . . and that's the downfall in life. And in your relationships with other people. It makes you over-critical, over-exact, which isn't the best thing in this day and age. Like, in my father's time you could never walk the street with your two hands by your side. You always had to walk with your hands behind your back. Or one hand behind your back and the other at your side. It was the *thing* to do, that was the *proper* thing to do. And no man would walk the streets of Dublin without putting the woman on the inside and he walked on the outside. In Dublin in the 1920s, 1930s, up to 1948 that was always the thing. And no man would go in through a door unless he put the woman in first and no woman would [have to] stand in a bus or a tram.

"Civil servants here wore bowler hats because if you go to London you'll see that syndrome where the businessman wears a bowler hat and a briefcase. And all coopers wore bowler hats. But now a labourer wore a cap, always wore a cap, made out of basically Irish tweed. It was what they call a salt and pepper mixture, a tweed with little flecks in it. That was a *style* of cap. And it had to have that ding [dent] in the front, that was synonymous. The top of the crown of the cap floated from left to right. They wore them from ten to twelve inch crowns, mostly twelve. And they were big and they hung down. That's where the Dublin gurrier got his name, from the cap. Oh, yes, the cap was *slung down* over the head and pulled to one side . . . he was a gurrier. You'll see it in Brendan Behan's plays. A gurrier means a fella that was rough and tough and would pick a fight quite easily and his language wasn't the best. And he wasn't above a little underhanded in his life, but at the same time a heart of gold. And the cap was heavier because most of the tweed we used then came off looms which were what they called two-by-two weaving. A lot of it came from Irish sheep in the west of Ireland in Connemara and the wool wasn't good. It was coarse. It had nothing of the refinement of the Australian sheep or the American sheep. It was *rough* and it was coarse but it was *hard-wearing*. And the caps, they'd be worn until they fell asunder. There isn't any doubt about it. Because it only served a purpose and that was to keep his head dry and covered from the wind and cold. A man would have one cap. And he wouldn't care for it. No way.

"Caps stayed basically the same until about 1942 or 1943 when they brought out what they called the country-style cap and you got more sophistication. Now they were talking about England. The country-shape cap came about from the English gentry who had big farms down in Sussex and places like that. And they brought out the cap like this that is a stitched peak cap and they reduced the crown from ten or twelve inches down to seven or eight inches. And it suited fellas like me that had narrow faces. And I could put it on and push it down like that and it became part of my head if you like. So this type of gentry cap was adopted by the worker, the working fella here in Dublin. It stuck on his head, it was close and warm and it was small, and gave his face *character*. Different from the gurrier cap which was a big floppy cap with no sophistication at all and nearly all very badly made at that time, and coarser. But now these caps are made of handwoven Donegal tweed. And there's a *proper* way to lift your cap to a person. 'Doffing' a cap—the word we used years ago—or tipping your cap to a person, that was polite, that was *manners*. Doffing was a greeting. Like, most people who worked on an estate would doff their cap when they would meet their employer. Doffing meant taking it off and putting it back on. It was a complete take-off. It was a sign of subservience I often thought.

"Now *fitting*, of course, is *paramount* in a hat. And *styling*. A hatter must give his *considered* opinion on the style of hat you should wear. You had to judge the size, the shape, the height of the man, his width, the shape of his face and the style of the hat *you* would think would suit him best. See, most hats when you buy them, they make them shaped like a dunce's cone. And from that a hatter makes a hat and he has to make a brim, shape the crown and all that sort of thing. The wool hats are made by using what they call blocks and having the block covered in frames which are aerated and all this is pushed in through a machine and there's a suction which draws all this loose hair down on to a finish and then it's taken out and it's combed. And linings in hats and caps years ago were silk. And they were made specially for people with different colours. People asked for their own colours in hats and got them, for the lining. And their initials, that was *most* important. In the old days you practically never sold a hat unless you put the initials in. And they were done with a little machine. Initials were put into the leather. Oh, a person wouldn't buy a hat years ago unless he had his initials on it. That was the big thing. It was a snob thing, like an identity thing, to have a hat with your initials. I think it was psychological, a person identity thing. But caps were different.

"Now the people who cared for their hats were the jarveys, the cabbies, who drove the [horse] cabs. The jarvey wore a fur bowler hat made of rabbit's fur. The jarveys, they were a breed apart. The whole attraction of their business to the layman that used them was the fact that it was a nice cab and the fella was well turned out. That was the attraction. And not alone his hat but his whip was carried in a socket on the front of his cab and looped and tied. Very seldom would he use it. And then all his harness on the horse would be polished and glittering. Beautiful. So they wore the hard bowler hats. Now the jarveys would bring in their hat every week. See, you were in the city where you were getting dust and grime on it and they didn't look after their hats themselves but they would bring them in here. Oh, it was a recognised thing. Back in my father's time I remember him taking in about *forty* or *fifty* hats on a Friday evening or Saturday morning to be steamed and combed and brushed and polished by that evening, so that they could use them for the weekend. It was a hand process. It would be brushed and steamed and you'd dampen it and heat it and you'd shine it and the gloss that would come up on that would be lovely. And they would *inspect* their hat. It was a service of two shillings at the time. And if a jarvey was going to buy a good hard hat he would buy his hat box in a leather shop. Oh, they were *leather*. The box was as much cared for as the hat was. When the hat wasn't being worn it would be put into the box.

"In the old days it wasn't just a passing trade, you had *customers*. Oh, it was a very sophisticated, polished approach. If you came in to buy a hat you were *known*. I mean, people built up their customers. So if you got a person in for a hat you *kept* them. Because in those days you couldn't take what was commonly known as a 'swop' if you valued your life and your job. A swop is a person coming in to buy something and you're not selling it to them. That was considered a mortal sin in the trade. You couldn't take a swop because as soon as the customer would go out the boss would come down and say, 'What did they *want*?' And you could be sacked like that! For not selling. Oh, yes. It was a mortal sin. If they walked out of that shop there would have to be a terrible [good] reason. In other words, when people served their time in shops like this years ago you became a *salesman* and that was the big thing. You were there to *sell*. Not like what we have today in the modern shop where you just work there and a person comes in and says, 'Have you got such and such?' And you say, 'They're over there.' That's the way the trade is now. Oh, but you couldn't do that back then and you couldn't do that in *this* shop. Every person that would come into *this* shop I would sell to.

"It's my whole psychological approach. It *has* to be . . . to know the mind of the person who's coming in. Oh, you get a lot of eccentric customers. You will get eccentrics. The biggest head I ever had was a small little man about that size and he took a seven and seven-eighths in a hat. As you know, the biggest head that ever was was Einstein's and he was an eight. And Americans are very big-headed people. And the countryman here has a bigger head than the Dublin man. And now there was this snob thing that if you bought it in Pim's shop it was *good*. Clery's *couldn't* be the same as Pim's. If you bought it in Clery's it *wasn't* as good. So shops would depend on the fact that government ministers bought their hats in there and it was a step above the fella who was two or three streets away. See, the other fella wasn't as big a hatter because the snobs went in the other shop. And the theatrical people went in there. I can remember many times in this shop around 1930, 1940, when well known judiciary, government personnel, those who were in the ascendancy group—and I'm talking about 'Sir this' and 'Sir that'—who would come into a shop like this and pay one and eleven or a half a crown for a pair of socks where they wouldn't go down into a shop like Switzer's or Arnott's.

"This is the last hatter's shop in Dublin, a shop that is geared towards the biggest variety of hats, coupled with the expertise which I think I bring to the hat trade. Young people know nothing about hats now. You'll only get that knowledge from older people. Hats were very personal to people. Older people loved their old hat . . . just *part* of them. And now the older crowd will always know their hat size and the younger crowd will never know their size. And from my point of view and speaking for the firm and speaking for myself and my own name, I would *not* sell you a hat that I didn't know anything about. I would not impose upon you a sale of an article unless I knew everything about it. Nor would I sell it to you if I didn't think it would suit you. But if you want a hat and you want advice about a hat I'm your man, because of my knowledge of it and my experience of how it would wear. So if you come to buy a hat I'm the *authority*."

David O'Donnell—Cooper, Age 76

Following in his father's footsteps, he served a rigorous five-year apprenticeship and became a cooper in the Guinness brewery in the late 1930s. There were about 300 coopers on the premises and the trade flourished. Back then a job in Guinness's was much envied for the security it promised. But in the post-war years the first metal casks, known as "iron lungs", made their ominous appearance. A decade later wooden barrels were abandoned and the ancient craft of coopering suddenly became obsolete. He found it demeaning to finish out his years making wooden garden seats from cask staves. It was a psychological and emotional trauma from which he has never quite recovered.

"I was born in Blackhall Place and this part of Dublin, to me, always had a sort of 'villagey' atmosphere. In this area I remember saddlers, wheelwrights, blacksmiths, bootmakers, tobacconists and bakers and they all did a great business. And I remember my father, he was a cooper as well, and he always wore a bowler hat and always had his boots polished in the morning before going out and he always used to wear a white stiff front with a flannel shirt underneath. He died when I was very young.

"I started at Guinness's in 1939. Before that I had been working at bootmaking at Winstanley's making a fair wage of about £3 a week. Then I left to go to Guinness's to serve me time and I did my five year apprenticeship. My master paid me because your master was responsible for you and he paid me eleven shillings a week for the first year, fifteen shillings a week for the second year and twenty-two shillings a week for the third year. After five years you came out of your time and had your test, making a barrel, and representatives of the society [Dublin Coopers' Society] would watch you and you had to have two sponsors, two coopers, who would vouch for your work. Then you got your certificate as a cooper and you could work as a journeyman.

"There was nearly 300 coopers in Guinness's in my time. Many were from around here and around the Liberties and from the artisans' dwellings. Coopers were well paid craftsmen. See, we were on piece-work and you could go in to work whenever you liked provided that you could make your own week's wages for yourself. You made so much for each cask. And you could go home whenever you wanted. There was a great feeling of comradeship. And there was the thing that if you made a cask you wouldn't think about the money, you always wanted to make a *good* cask, and have a look at it and get pride out of it. You needed the money, of course, but the pride . . . you wouldn't get a good name making a bad cask. Reputations were important. I became a master cooper. But they were hard times and you sometimes worked fifty or fifty-five hours a week. But it was nothing to us then to really work. And in the summer we'd come home and have a rush of tea, go out for a swim after bicycling seven or eight miles out into the country.

"At Guinness's each man had his own berth with his tool box there. And you had to have your own tools. Tools were very, very important and nobody would loan a tool to anybody else. They would come to fit your hand but some were handed down from father to son. When I was making casks I'd be in by about 8.00 and you'd have to light fires for blazing heads for casks and set out your tools and have your staves cut to measurement. Now we were on piece-work and didn't have to get in at 8.00 if we didn't want to. In fact, it was a rule that you couldn't work before 8.00. Some men were exceptionally fast. We'd make a 100 gallon cask called a butt, a sixty gallon called a hogshead, a thirty gallon called a barrel and a half barrel or kilderkin and that was sixteen gallons and a firkin, eight gallons. Those were the sizes. And now if I was working in the repairing shop and I'd get a cask in I'd smell it and if it was foul it would get an extra cleaning or steaming. Most coopers had to be able to smell a cask to tell if it was foul or sweet. And they'd have another set of smellers before the beer went into that. Now some of the stacks of casks in the yard would reach nearly a hundred feet and in the summertime they had to be constantly hosed down because the hoops would fall off and so they had to be kept wet.

"Now all hard work encourages drinking. You'd be perspiring all the time now from 8.00 in the morning, winter and summer, until the time you'd knock off and you'd have what we called a wet shirt. You'd be so tired and exhausted that you'd really be able to sit back and enjoy it, relax. A man could put away six or more pints of porter in a day and it wouldn't make you tipsy or anything, not when you'd be in the shop working. Now the brewery had a scheme where if you didn't want the beer you could go on 'scripts' and they'd give you the price of the beer. It was tuppence a pint. One day we had the trainer or coach of Mo Connolly [swimmer] come by and she asked us what did we use to replace the sweat. And we said, 'We don't use anything.' And she asked, 'Don't you get cramps?' 'No', we said. 'Do you take salt tablets or anything?' And this cooper next to me, Dick Flanagan, says, 'No, we just take porter.'

"A thing that I noticed from the first day in the shop when I went in was the *smell* of the shop, the oak timber which has a very distinctive smell. It was the first thing that'd hit you, a very pleasant smell. And tremendous noise there all the time. Quite a lot of men would go deaf in one ear because of the banging of the hoops. Ah, and your hands would crack like a horse's foot. At the end of the day they'd be just solid welts. Usually in the wintertime I'd get a crack down along here and it would be quite deep and I often stitched it up with a piece of thread when it would become really open. It was like leather, you wouldn't feel a thing. Then when I came home I'd put tallow on my hands. I think it was a type of goose grease or something. I often took a piece of it home and I'd do it in front of the fire because that's what my father used to do. The first thing he'd do was wash his hands.

"Guinness's was a good employer. We had our beer every day, porter it was. In practice our allowance was one in the morning and one in the afternoon but you could manage to get as many as you liked. But you hadn't really the time for that because you'd want to get your work done and get home. Also, we had an athletic ground. And there was a bar on the grounds where you could get a pint for seven pence. Also, you could have breakfast there in the morning and it was subsidised by Guinness's, a full breakfast for nine pence. And you could have a wash, shower or shave. And you had your newspapers in the reading unit or you could read a book in the library. You could have your lunch there and your tea there and if you wanted to go over there in the evening there was billiard tables and card tables and a library. Some men there, from the country, all they needed was just digs and they'd have their breakfast, tea and dinner at work. Guinness's even had this burial society where you'd put so much into it, into the insurance, you know, on your burial. The premiums were very low but the rewards quite high and the fellas nicknamed it the 'bury yourself society.'

"Life was better back then and the cattle market up on Prussia Street here was every Thursday and that would bring in a lot of farmers from the country and they used to do their shopping. Cattle buyers would stay at the City Arms Hotel and there were little banks beside it. They'd open on market day for the cattle men. Most of the deals were cash deals. You'd see the men in the divided sections like at Mulligan's pub to talk horses and cattle or whatever they sold. Men would find a spot to make their deal and they'd spit in their hand and shake the other man's hand to make a deal and then they'd have a drink. And outside there were buskers with music and dancing. They played the ukulele and concertina and melodeon of course. And I remember on Sunday morning you'd hear all the church bells and a violinist would walk around from house to house playing very beautiful music and people would give him pennies. And then there was a fella named Barney Nugent who rode around on a horse when he got drunk and he'd go into the pub and say, 'A bottle of Jameson's for me and a pint for the boy who's holding my horse.' One time he got drunk and rode the horse up the steps of the old cinema into a cowboy picture. He had an unfortunate end. When he'd get drunk he used to get up on the wall on the bridge across the Liffey at O'Connell Street and he'd walk across the wall, and he fell into it and was drowned.

"When I was in Guinness's there was hundreds and hundreds of men in the cooperage and everybody was busy. And when the metal casks started coming in we weren't so worried because we had a strong guild or union, the Dublin Coopers' Society. We knew that even if they did come in we wouldn't lose wages anyway. I first saw a metal cask after the war and I thought it'd be a failure. Many coopers felt that beer shouldn't be in metal. I think that any beer or spirits should be matured in wood. There's a happier relationship between the wood and the beer, and oak breathes. And when there was the change from wooden barrels to metal a lot of people felt the taste changed, that it was a tinny taste. But I think it was a different brew actually, more synthesised. They pressured it. It's *not* the same by any manner. Even the pint of porter, although it was a very light beer, had more body than a pint of stout at the present time.

"Anyway, the younger coopers were the first to go, some of them just out of their [apprenticeship] time. And they went to the bottling or elsewhere in the factory. Then they closed the cooperage, no more barrels! They had us making garden seats and such, didn't really know what to do with us. Actually, I finished out making garden seats and miniature barrels. It was sad because we were just killing time really. And we had to clock in at 8.00 and clock out at 5.00. I remember a foreman coming over to me and saying when I was making garden seats out of hogsheads, 'For God's sake, take your time in making those things . . . cause we've nothing to do.' I was very disappointed at the end of coopering because I had visions of my own son going to the trade. I had taken him down to the brewery and showed him the casks. So then I bought a taxi and put the taxi on the road. But I had been used to action all the time and I'd sit in the taxi and was irritated, maybe sitting the whole day waiting for a fare. I couldn't understand just sitting down the whole day. Anyway, I got a state pension and today I have a small Guinness pension and they have a recreation room for pensioners and a bar . . . and I get an allowance of two pints a day for nothing."

HERBERT PEMBREY—BOOKSELLER, AGE 87

Greene's Bookshop on Clare Street, of which he is proprietor, is one of Dublin's renowned literary institutions. His father brought him into the trade in 1928 when it was still mainly a lending library. From behind the small counter he daily waited upon—and delighted in chatting with—the likes of W. B. Yeats, Jack B. Yeats, George Russell, Samuel Beckett, Oliver St John Gogarty, Patrick Kavanagh, Brendan Behan and other literary luminaries of the period. To him, they were friends as well as customers and he relished being in the centre of Dublin's vibrant book world. Now, at age 87, he warmly recounts those halcyon days in the small, venerable bookshop.

"I was born in 1908 in Leinster Street West, Rathmines, and my father was English. He came from Oxford, the university town. In 1892 he came to Dublin. And he had been apprenticed with a firm there called Thornton's. They were a very well known booksellers in Broadstreet in Oxford. He came to Dublin in 1892 as a manager of a bookshop called Combridge's in Grafton Street. My grandfather was a professor of oriental languages in the University of Oxford, in the old Clarendon Press at that time. He was an extraordinary man. He could write and read in nineteen oriental languages. He used to read the proofs of the people who wrote the books in Arabic and Hebrew and all those different languages for the Clarendon Press.

"My father bought Greene's in partnership with a lady, Mrs Fotrell, in 1912. Her husband was a solicitor and she was only a sleeping partner. But the arrangement they had between them was that whoever died first the survivor had the chance of buying out the business. Now John Greene started this shop in 1843, in July we think. And he died in 1889. And his son, Godfrey, ran the shop for three years but he died in 1892. People called Quinn ran it from 1892 to 1919 when my father took it on. But we'd never change the name of Greene's. And the trams stopped directly outside the door. The tram conductor would say, 'Greene's!'—it wasn't 'Clare Street!' Anyhow, I left school in 1924 and in 1926 I did a bank exam at a bank here and passed and I was waiting to be called up and in those times you had a long time before there were vacancies. And Mrs Fotrell died on 1 February 1928, and I hadn't been called up. During that time I used to come in here and help and do odds and ends. So when she died my father said to me, 'Would you like to come into the business?' And I was delighted and said that I *would*. So I came in here on 12 March 1928 and I've been coming in ever since for over sixty-five years.

"My father showed me everything. He told me of books he had enjoyed, like the one by that man [author] Prescott who wrote about the history of Mexico and Peru. And he told me that I should *read* those books. Once you started *handling* books and looking at the title it *stuck* in your memory. It just stuck in your mind and it *stays* there. He said to me, 'When you get a book coming in pick up the book and *always open it* and look at the title page, see the name of the book and the author and the publisher. If you look at that, if you're asked about the book in a year's time, you'll *remember* that you *know* the book.' Now in those days we were mostly a lending library. Oh, yes, a lending library, and stationary and printing. With our printing we had an ordinary hand press. It wasn't electrical or anything like that. And that was money-making because the people who were getting the library subscription, they used to get their stationery printed up at the same time. It was *handy* to get the two done in the one place. The lending library was by a yearly subscription. In those days I suppose you paid a subscription [fee] of about £1 or twenty-five shillings for the *whole year*, it was so cheap. I mean, library books in those days were about five shillings or seven and sixpence. Most of the books came from British publishers. In the lending library we had a stock of two or three thousand books I should think, that would cover fiction and non-fiction, books on travel and biography and everything. During the war years things were much scarcer and you couldn't get the quantity of books you wanted for the library. We used to get books from a big distributor in London and from Macmillan's and they'd only give you a *ration* of them. You know, if you ordered a half a dozen copies you might be lucky if you got one or two copies. And we were very old customers of theirs over the years.

"Now there were *two* stands out there and then my father put that canopy up about 1917 or 1918. And he got an extra four stands and we had *six* stands then with books ranging from a penny up to a shilling and people'd come and browse through the second-hand books. It was a browser's paradise! Books were cheap in those days, a penny and thruppence and sixpence. There would be very few biographies and things like that that would be more than two or three shillings. Oh, books were treasured in those days. Oh, no question about it. And there was a man who worked here, he was really a porter, and he used to mind the stands outside, Tommy Breen. He used to mind the stands and see that people didn't run off with the books. His wife died and he had no family, no relations over here at all, they were all in America. He was about twenty years with us. And he was a wonderful piccolo player—but he couldn't read a *note* of music. But if you'd play any tune once or twice he had this wonderful musical ear and he'd remember it and be able to play it back for you. And he was in coat and tie and he'd deliver parcels for us. And he was very fond of the Guinness. He was in here at nine o'clock and he used to carry out the stands. And then at five past ten he disappeared, around to Kennedy's pub for his first drink of the day. And when we asked him why he went at five past ten—when the pubs are open at ten—he said that he'd never drink the first pint out of the pipes. He was a great character.

"Customers came from all around Merrion Square and Fitzwilliam Square, all this residential area. They all took out subscriptions to our lending library and used to get their stationary printed here. Of course, in those days Merrion Square was residential, every house in it was *lived* in. They weren't offices as they are now. The regular customers who lived around the square, I knew them all. Many doctors and I knew them well until they moved away or died. We had a tremendous number of customers who wouldn't go anywhere else, they'd just come in to us. And if we hadn't got the book in stock they'd ask if we could get it for them. The personal touch makes a *tremendous* difference. You'd make chat with them. I knew them by name. It was a different clientele. I mean, around Merrion Square we had living W. B. Yeats and George Russell (A. E.) Very often they'd come in. Oh, I knew them *well*, knew them well. And Jack B. Yeats, the painter, he was in Fitzwilliam Square. Yeats and A. E., they'd come in to browse, or for a particular book. W. B. was a great man, he'd drop in for a chat as well and same with his brother Jack B. Oh, they were very approachable. Just drop in for a chat. Talk about ordinary things like 'How are you? How are things going?' And Samuel Beckett often came over here to collect stationery. I remember him well. He'd come in and have a chat. But he was never a very friendly fellow. He was very quiet, never cracked jokes or anything like that, a bit eccentric. And then later, in the fifties, Brendan Behan and Paddy Kavanagh and others came along. Brendan Behan used to come in with his wife and they'd be looking at the stand outside and Behan would pick up a couple of books and apparently he never carried money. She handled the money. And he'd come in with the books and say to his wife, 'Pay the man.'

"We used to have one particular customer and it was very, very funny. My father was here at the time and at lunchtime people would come in and be browsing around and every day this man came in for about half an hour and he'd take the same book out and he was *obviously* reading it from beginning to end. So my father says, 'I'm going to move it.' And he took the book and put it in another part of the shop. Next day your man came in and *straight over*. And his book was gone! It was so funny . . . little things like that. He looked around a little bit and then he presumed it had been sold. I even got presents from people. There was an old lady and she was a great admirer of John McCormack, the Irish tenor, and he died in 1945. And she wrote here wanting to know did we have any books about him and I had several books and I wrote her and quoted them to her. After that she would write and anything I came across about McCormack I would send it to her. And she was a painter and she sent me a very nice little round wooden tray and she'd painted it with flowers and signed it. And then at a later date she sent me a marble snail. She was quite old. Then about two years ago her son rang me up to say that she'd died suddenly.

"My father died in 1942 and I was left on my own. I was 34. And then in the early 1950s I closed the library completely. I was *very* glad I did because I was able to turn the *whole* shop into books for sale. And the [Merrion] square had started to change and the people were moving out and they were being turned into offices. So we hadn't got the same clientele. And also around that time I closed the printing because some of the big printers started. And then I used to go over to England around the bookshops and buy any Irish books cause you'd get them cheap enough. And there were two famous doctors here in Dublin, a Dr Ball and Dr Oliver St John Gogarty. And Gogarty had written a volume of poetry and he wrote to Ball who was off in Scotland for deer hunting with his family and he said, 'I've just written a volume of poetry'—and it was named *An Offering of Swans*—'and I've been into Greene's of Clare Street and told Pembrey to send you a copy of it immediately. I hope you'll enjoy it.' This was dated in 1924. He had been in to my father. And I *bought* this second-hand book of *An Offering of Swans* in a town called Sutton down in Surrey in England. And this letter was in it! It was the book we had sent and I got the letter in the book, just tucked in the book. Dr Ball kept the letter and put it in the book. A small world!

"We had a staff of about a dozen when I came in. I got on very well with the people we had. They were all very loyal, they'd do anything you'd ask them to do. And at Christmas time for years we always took the whole staff out to some hotel for dinner and had a meal and a great chat with them. They used to enjoy that. All the staff we had were over fifty and sixty years here. Yes! They spent their *whole lives* here with us. Mrs Judge came in here at 15 years of age and she died within the last year at 89. She had left the shop here about ten years ago when she had a stroke. But she'd worked her whole life here. Mrs Rochford came in here at 17 years of age and she actually left here at 5.00 on a Friday and died. And she was 82. And she was *up the ladder* on that Friday and sold a bible to the German ambassador. And she never admitted to being over 64 because if she said she was 65 she would have had to claim old-age pension—and she wouldn't do it.

"I had five children in the family that had to be educated and I found it a bit of a struggle. It meant that I wasn't able to take as much money out of the business as I normally would have. But I've never regretted that I didn't go into the bank. If I'd gone into the bank I'd have been retired seventeen or eighteen years ago and I would probably have been buried by now. I thank God every day that I made the decision that I did. I've reached my age of 87 and I've never had a drink in my life. An Irishman and I've never had a drink in my life! My son now would be third generation [in the business] and his son is the fourth. Oh, I very much take pride in that. And I thank God every day that I'm able to come in three days a week at my age. I'll tell you the truth, there are *so many* people, friends of mine, that retired at 67 or 70 years of age and *without* exception they're all either senile or have Alzheimer's disease or that. They'd no hobby and they're home in the wife's way . . . they've nothing to do. And I feel that coming in here three days a week and *meeting* people, maybe some people I haven't seen for years, and we have a chat and it keeps the mind clear. Now unfortunately I cannot read now for the last couple of years. I've got very bad glaucoma. I can't read at all. My wife has to read the newspaper to me. People have said, and written, that Greene's is an institution. People have written even from America saying that they'd heard about Greene's from their parents and they're glad to hear that we are still here."

PETER COMISKEY—BARBER, AGE 81

He owns the Waldorf Adare Barber Shop on Westmoreland Street, a traditional "Gentleman's Hairdresser". Like the old "Tonsorial Emporiums", it is adorned by a red and white striped pole. In his early days barbers offered face massages, mud packs, facial vibrators, hair singeing and moustache waxing. Back then barber shops were the urban equivalent of the country forge. On rainy days, especially, with its good scents, warmth, company and lively conversation it was strictly a man's domain. Barbers have always been a friendly, talkative breed who could converse on all sundry subjects but tried to stay clear of religion and politics.

"My parents were living in Bride Street and my father was out on the front during the First World War when I was born in 1915. There were eleven children. I was the eldest. My father was an ordinary house painter before he joined the army. When he came back unscathed—he was about three years in France—he went into Guinness's Brewery. Very secure job. I was born in the British time but when we became a Free State and got our own government, well, my mother was one of the first women to have triplets in the Irish Free State. And Guinness's, of course, thought that was a great thing to happen to one of their employees and so they sent my mother away on a holiday with the triplets. And also, my mother got a quart of milk *every day* free of charge from Guinness's and I used to have to walk about two miles at least to go and collect that milk—and I'm sure you can just imagine what I'd be saying about those triplets!

"I was a young lad in the Catholic Boy Scouts and I was approaching the age of 14 and a Mr Daly, one of the parents, was talking to us one evening at a scout meeting and told us that he knows of jobs for boys. That was in the late twenties and jobs were scarce then. So, of course, I grabbed the opportunity. So this man made an appointment for me and brought me down to see a hairdresser on Capel Street and my parents came down with me. So he took me on and I became an indentured apprentice from January 1930 to 1935, five years' time. And all I got was three shillings a week. I lived with my parents and I only got one shilling out of that for my pocket. There was two apprentices, including myself, and the boss and the boss's son and a part-time man. I used to have to come in at half past eight, go to his house and collect the keys and clean the salon inside, wash down the front, do the windows and sweep the pavement out front. Inside I'd clean the wash basins and do the brasses and do the mirrors. And I had to have that done before 9.00.

"It was a very up-to-date shop for the time. The lighting in the shop was ordinary bulbs but no heating *whatsoever*. Just the heat from heating the water, that was all, and that wasn't giving out very much heat, I can tell you that. And it was a very high ceiling and a big fine mirror that almost reached up to the ceiling. And a lot of brasswork and marble. At that time some men had their own brushes and mugs. We had them in a case on the wall. Now the shop, we called it a 'Gentleman's Hairdressing Salon', that was always the term. And on my indenture it said 'hairdresser.' My hours were from half eight in the morning till 8.00 at night and on a Saturday from 8.00 in the morning till *10.00* at night. I'd be going home at 11.00. Our union, it was the hairdressers' union, was composed of voluntary workers and you didn't get paid. You done it for nothing. I was on the committee myself in my earlier days. You only got paid your bus fare to the meeting. That was all.

"I learned to cut the hair mostly from my boss's son. I'd stand there and he'd be cutting hair and I'd stand beside him and he'd explain. Then after a while you'd get confidence in yourself and he'd tell you, 'Just prepare that man. Run the clippers up so far.' And then I used to go at night up to the tech [technical school] on Kevin Street, twice a week, and used to learn and they'd be the guinea pigs. Then the boss would bring in some down-and-outs for me to practise on. He came in contact with a hostel here and would bring some fellas down. It didn't cost them anything and I used to practise on them. Now shaving, I suppose I was shaving myself before I shaved the customer. But I told the boss one day that I'd like to shave a customer and I got through it all right. I had good confidence in meself.

"At that time you had hand clippers, no electric clippers. Every so often you'd give them a bit of oil. And we had brushes to clean off all the loose hairs. I used to hate them because I had to wash them, the dirty brushes, in ordinary soap. There was no such thing as washing powders then. And we had a copper boiler, a kind of tank, it was resting on the gas ring and we'd use this water that'd be going all day for doing shaving, face massaging and mud pack. We'd boil the water and it'd be going all the day. It was about two feet high and about two feet wide. Now a face massage, you'd use hot towels, a cream and you had a vibro, a vibrator. It was electrical and there was a rubber top on it to do all over the face. We called it a vibro and you'd vibro the face. And we done mud packs back then. A mud pack, you'd put hot towels on him and there was what was called Boncila—it was kind of a paste in a tube, a very large tube—and you smeared it all over the customer, every part of his face. It was a very greyish thing and when you put that on it'd get real stiff on your face, very, very stiff, hard. And you'd leave that on for a short time and it'd harden and then you'd get more hot towels and put that on him, over the Boncila. See, it'd come soft again then and you'd get a couple of towels and clean it all off. After that you got cream and creamed his face and got another hot towel and cleaned that off and then a cold towel. Ah, it felt very good for their skin . . . and sometimes they had been on the booze the previous night and he wasn't feeling so good the next morning and that'd pep him up a bit. It was probably just his imagination maybe.

"A shave and a haircut where I was cost one shilling and sixpence. You could get your hair cut for sixpence and maybe a shave for fourpence at a smaller shop. Where we were we catered for a certain clientele, you know, the businessman, a little bit above the ordinary. And we could get that price. And there was tipping. Tuppence was the ordinary tip. The basic haircut was short back and sides—the clipper run well up—and a good bit let off the top. That was the basic haircut in those days. They got it cut about once a month. In my early years you'd get people from the country and they'd tell you that they'd get a better finish on their [haircutting] job in Dublin. You know, it would be just a rough type of cutting in the country. Some people would come to Dublin to get their hair cut. And moustaches were more common. I used to do handlebar moustaches in those days and wax them. 'Hongroise' we'd call that. Hongroise was a type of wax. Trim it first and then Hongroise it. And that was free of charge. That stuff used to get very hard and it was a nuisance, but I had to do it. And we put lotions on their hair and creams, like Brilliantine. Hairdressings and lotions for men has almost gone out now. Everything now is a spray.

"After Capel Street I went to other places and then off to England during the war. Then I heard that this place here was going to be open, from a friend of mine, so I came in here. I'm here forty-two years in this shop. Now when I was away over in England during the war and I was doing hairdressing I was based in a US Air Force base and the pilots used to come in to us a lot. Some of them you wouldn't see afterwards . . . they'd be killed on bombing raids. Now most of those men got crew cuts, that was in 1942, and they always *insisted* that I singed it afterwards. Now for a crew cut singeing gave a nice smooth finish. That was the whole idea of it. And then [later] we done singeing back here in Dublin. A lot of men at that time used to think it was good for their hair but in my opinion it just *closed* the hair that had been cut. See, I got this taper and I lighted it and I run the comb and pick up the hair and run the lighted taper right across and, of course, you were going pretty fast you know. Oh, it was *lighted* and you'd *burn* the hair, so much of the hair, you see. You'd singe the tips right over the whole head after we cut it. It was supposed to stimulate the hair. But, personally, in my opinion it just closed the partially cut tips and sealed it. That was my conclusion about it.

"Now I done ladies' hair as well. See, we had a separate room for the gents and the ladies was done in the back room. We had a whole separate entrance through a hallway for the ladies. Now I was cutting ladies' hair one time and this girl asks me to put suntan cream on her legs, but I said no. I said, 'No, I don't do nothing like that.' That did happen, all right. I said no, a flat no . . . more or less out of fear than anything probably. Now the only woman hairdresser that I knew of that cut men's hair back then, and that was before the war, she had a place in O'Connell Street near Parnell Monument. That was in the late thirties. A friend of mine worked for her. She shaved men and cut men's hair. I seen it meself. That was a *rare* thing in my day. Oh, she done a nice little business though. Of course, men—even now—the reason some men go to these unisex houses is because they have these little girls around them.

"The majority of people here are very nice people, very friendly in every way and also from different positions in life. Some of them go back forty years and I've seen their children come in here as small children and getting married, rearing families, and grandchildren. Sports and weather they talk about, but I try to keep away from politics. I just change the subject. And very rare that wives would come in with their husbands and sit there. But some of them might be that bossy that they'd come down to see that we do it the way *she* wanted it done. In this business now you get customers that tell you personal things because they *trust* you. They know that that's as far as it'll go with you. A customer places a lot of trust in you and wants to get something off his mind and to ease his mind by telling me, his barber. *Very personal* matters, I'll say that. Now it just stays with me, doesn't go any further. Brendan Behan, Ronnie Drew and the Dubliners come in here down through the years and at the moment we have a Chief Justice coming in here. Oh, Brendan Behan always came in here and Jimmy O'Dea and Paddy Kavanagh. Behan was a great character—when he was sober! You enjoyed listening to him when he was sober. If they've too much drink we'll let them fall asleep in the chair and then wake them up when we're finished. That's the best way to do it.

"Early on I used to say to myself, 'I must be mad to go into this business', when I should be off on a Saturday afternoon. I'd be going home at 11.00 at night and my wife, a great woman, and I thought, 'I don't know how this girl stays with me', cause I couldn't take her out and about. Oh, she was a great woman to stay with me . . . and I'll be fifty years married next year. But in the long run I was very glad to be at the job because I think it's a very nice thing to deal with the public."

David McGrane—Tobacconist and Cigar Merchant, Age 45

He is the manager of Fox's Cigar Merchants & Tobacconists, established 1880, on Grafton Street just across from Trinity College. It is the last of Dublin's "Gentlemen's Emporiums" of fine cigars and tobacco. Old traditions still survive here—hand-blending tobaccos, ageing and storing of cigars in humidors and vaults for valued customers. One humidor vault holds a precious treasury of the finest cigars placed there in trust in 1948 by a father for his son in later life. Being situated just across from Trinity's gate, the shop was always accessible to the elite young gentlemen of the country. Many doubtless bought their first fine cigar in Fox's.

"I left school, having done my leaving, and just answered an ad in the paper and came for an interview and got the job and I've stayed here ever since. That was at 18. Most of my relatives never smoked. My father would smoke maybe five cigarettes a day and that would be it. So I knew very little about the business when I came here. It was a shop I always assumed was for those with a lot of money. It was very elite. This shop goes back to 1880 when they started the trade. I think it was a German here before who was a snuff blender. We still sell snuff today, quite a good bit of it.

"When I started here we blended our own tobaccos. There was an old manager in the shop who had been in the business forty years or more. He had left school and apprenticed himself to the trade. I learned directly from him. At that time there was four in the shop. There was another older chap who was responsible for the blending of tobaccos and a lady who did the packing. Cigar smoking and pipe smoking, it's *completely* different from cigarette smoking. Cigar smoking isn't really a *habit*. It's something you'll do because you like it. You really feel it's good for you. Now pipe smoking today, I think it's only one per cent of the smoking public in Ireland. But years ago pipe smoking was completely different, life was at a different pace.

"There was more pipe smoking years ago and it was more of an *art* than it is today. There are still people who regard pipe smoking as an art and they like the tobacco they can get nowhere else and they have their little idiosyncrasies. And pipe smoking is completely different than cigarette smoking because people can give up cigarettes and they'll miss the nicotine or be craving for a cigarette. But when they give up a pipe they feel they've lost a *friend*. It *is* like that. People who smoke pipes always seem to be relaxed. There's a great aura about them that they're relaxed and capable of dealing with situations. I don't know whether that's true or not. Like the poster with 'A Thinking Man Smokes A Pipe.' But there's nothing nicer. Even an old man, although he mightn't be able to get around much, if he's able to sit and you see him smoking his pipe there's a *friend* with him!

"At that stage when we blended our own tobaccos most tobaccos would come in from Virginia and Cuba. This was all for pipes. And we used to bring in some tobaccos that nobody else had, like Perique, an American tobacco, and nobody had it. It was brought in processed and cut and ready to blend. We were just the blenders. Tobacco would be brought in in packs of maybe 5 lb up to a sack containing half a stone. And they would be passed to the chap downstairs who looked after the stock levels. There was a blending table which was up against the wall and it would blend itself coming down. See, you would sort of throw this up on the wall when you were blending it. It was an ordinary table. Say one mixture might contain five or six different Virginia tobaccos of different amounts of moisture in them. So, having cut up all the ingredients it was a matter of blending them in, just like a cake. Oh, it could be stuck together [when arriving]. They'd be stuck together and you'd have to tease them out. And some tobacco would have to be re-moisturised again to bring it back so it would be pliable enough to blend. Otherwise it would just turn into dust if you touched it. We had about eight or nine mixtures and we had to blend them up. Downstairs on the table it was a big effort where we'd blend maybe 100 lb of tobacco. The recipes were written down. The blends were easy. It was just like a recipe for a cake.

"After that was the putting in of the moisture. That was just something you learned. You'd just learn it by touch. At that time it was done by a fine spray pump, a hand pump. It never changed here. Just an ordinary fine hand spray pump, something like you'd use for a garden. And you'd spray the tobacco as it was on the table. Even it out and then leave it for a while, about a quarter of an hour, and then blend it up again and then you would leave it for about a day. You'd cover it over with the old grease paper until the next day so that the moisture would seep into the tobacco. See, if you put it straight into the bins it would go mouldy. It would suffer the heat and the water would cause it to go mouldy. After that it would be packed into tins. We had a compressor downstairs and this lovely little lady that packed them into tins with a tin liner, a paper liner, all packed by hand. She did it all here and at that stage we were exporting to Germany and to the United States and that was all packed by hand. So we'd get an order from the United States or Germany and it would be 'all hands on deck' until that order was dispatched. It might mean that we would have to work late into the evening.

"Customers have their own mixtures. We *know* our customers, we've known them for years. Like, someone might come in here and try our Banker's Tobacco and find that too strong or whatever and then we would either add a little bit of something to it or take out a little and get it to suit your palate. Because there's no such thing as a perfect tobacco. If you like a tobacco it doesn't mean that *I'm* going to like it. Or if you find it mild I might find it extremely strong. So there is a personalisation attached to tobacco. And we have a little book and we write these in. So you can send in for your own tobacco or come in for it yourself and we'll have it in the little book. Oh, it's part of our business. And there are plenty of women who smoke pipes. Oh, plenty! And some of the strongest tobacco we have. I wouldn't even be able to smoke it. All ages. Those, I would say, would smoke at home. I don't think I've seen women around Dublin smoking pipes. I've seen them in the country, yes. We sell small little ladies pipes but some of them smoke the standard, conventional pipes. And at a dinner party or cocktail party it would be accepted.

"It's very hard to define what a cigar smoker is. Certainly a lot of businessmen smoke a lot of cigars. They're expensive enough. Some chaps would go through twenty-five cigars in a week. But then there are some men who wouldn't have particularly good jobs or much disposable income and yet they'd come in and they might pay £4 for one cigar and that's all they might smoke in a week! That is just their treat at the end of the week. They mightn't drink or smoke anything else. Just come in and pay £4 for one cigar and then smoke it on a Saturday night or Friday night or whenever they have the time to themselves. A *lot* of people are like that. They just enjoy that one good cigar a week.

"There's still a sense of power with cigars, possibly because most of the top businessmen smoke cigars and you'll see them with cigars and there is certainly an aura that 'you've made it!' when you see that. And there are some people who smoke cigars because it's the done thing to smoke them, the same way they'll drive big cars. But there's also people who smoke them just because they are the *best*. They really *are* the best. The most expensive at the present time are Lusitania. They're £165 for twenty-five. A person might come in and buy one, for their father or their boyfriend, and say, 'Thank you.' Cigar smoking hasn't really declined, I wouldn't say. The Cheroot market is slightly down but nothing like cigarette smoking. Maybe five or six years ago the half Corona size in the Dutch was the biggest seller. Now it isn't. People are going for longer, slimmer, smaller ones. Tastes have just changed. And you must look at the market and be prepared to change with it. So tastes have changed . . . and a lot of women smoke cigars now. Oh, women will even smoke the larger cigars. Not in any great number, but they *do*, certainly. I can name women who would certainly smoke these cigars at dinner parties or cocktail parties. Why not? There's a lot of people that just like the flavour and aroma of cigars and there's no reason, particularly today, why women shouldn't smoke them. And we've got a very young society and they're willing to try things.

"Now for cigars there's about a three year delivery from Cuba. So we carry roughly three years' stock of cigars in bond in the warehouse. Our cigars don't come exclusively from Havana. We do sell cigars with Brazilian tobacco that are made in Germany. But it's largely Cuban. We did bring in Jamaican and Manila cigars but the trouble is that the price difference is so small between the Havanas and the others that, really, the Havana has the reputation. And it also has the shelf life. A lot of cigars are very nice when they're smoked young, relatively quickly after they're rolled. But Havanas improve with age. We can carry cigars in stock and know that they'll be in perfect condition when they're sold. They arrive in boxes of twenty-five and in cases of from 500 to 5,000. After they're assessed for duty and taxes we put them into bond because we then hold them there free of duty. Then as we need them we draw them into the shop. They were originally held in the Custom House docks. Now the temperature and humidity must be controlled and there was something about the stores down there that kept them *perfect*. There's a special section they use for all tobaccos. They were very old, deep cellars that they were kept in and it suited the cigars perfectly. Whether it was chosen originally by the customs for that purpose I don't know. But it's now been moved to Alexandra Road.

"But because there's a three year wait for cigars to come in from Cuba, if you like a particular cigar, well, we may be sold out of it by the time you come back in again. So you buy what you need for maybe a year or whatever, or maybe buy some cigars to pass on to your sons. Oh, there are cigars in there [humidors] that have been there since *1948*! Some could be *older*, but I certainly know there's cigars that have been there since 1948. They have been stored here. A humidor is a box that cigars are kept in. They're in lockers that are controlled with temperature and humidity. And their [customers] names are on them and we have a book of stock so we know what everybody had and as you take it out or put it in we alter the list accordingly. So you might have a dinner party tonight and you might just come in here and want five cigars to take out. Most have an account but some do pay cash.

"Now the way Havana cigars are sold, they were conditioned, they were dried and they were aged before they're sold and they're quite firm to the touch. Now tastes are changing. The American market always goes for the cigars that are very soft, very wet, as we would regard them. But the English style cigar is always sold drier and it always gives a better taste. But tastes are changing and we're selling more cigars more moist than years ago. And we try to have the cigars here in the country for at least two years before we bring them into the shop. Then, having brought them into the shop, we would hold them for maybe two or three months before we'd bring them up here to sell. See, they were ageing down in the Customs House [or Alexandra Road] and when we bring them up here they're aged but they're soft. So we let them dry and the best way to let them dry is by coal fires. The only heating in this building is coal fire—it's all we use—because it's the slowest heat. It must be very slow. Electric heating is dry and it's bad for cigars. The cigars are then left in their boxes for drying *upside down*. See, when they come to the shop they're the right way up so if you always pack them the right way up the top ones will dry out and the bottom ones won't. So it's to give them a good all round drying. The old coal fire is definitely the best . . . the slowest. There's nothing dramatic about it and it suits the cigars perfectly.

"There's this thing about cigars that you should never roll it up beside your ear to hear this crackling—though they do it in films—but you should never do that because all you're doing is breaking the leaves inside. If you just hold it in your hand and test it. Some people prefer to cut the top off with the guillotine or to slice it in a 'V'. That's personal choice. But the best of the lot is to slice it off because the smoke is coming out of a large aperture, whereas if you restrict it by piercing it with a pin or a match or making a 'V' you're restricting the flow of smoke and that can lodge then in the sides and give a bad taste. And another old idea was to wait until the cigar had heated up sufficiently and then remove the band, for fear that if you pulled it off immediately the glue on the band might pull the leaf off with it. So you'd wait until the cigar was heated.

"And we still sell a good bit of snuff. Most of it is stuff we bring in from the English and it's all snuff for the nose, rather than for the mouth. It's something that you don't see people use, yet an awful lot of people *use* snuff. It's very good for stuffed-up head, blocked nose and things like that. You can buy it in small little boxes. Very cheap, from 29p for a little pack of it, to £3. But it's *always* been used a lot. A lot of barristers and other people would use it on days when they couldn't smoke. Now you wouldn't be allowed to smoke in the courts. So a lot of barristers use some. And not exclusively men. People have the image of snuff-takers as always having to pour it down their throat and that it's a dirty habit. But it's not *really*. As I say, a lot of people now use it to clear their heads rather than take medication which is a lot more expensive. But it's not something that you see people doing. I suppose it's the old image of going in for a penny's worth of snuff in the old days and it always seemed to be old women or old priests that took snuff and it always seemed to be a dirty habit because you always saw it done in front of them.

"I think we're the last *real* gentleman's cigar merchants in Dublin. The staff here has been traditionally Irish, but we have a branch in London now. We still do blending here today. It's a more formal shop than other shops you go to today. The fact that we all wear suits. Yes, we try to keep that image that it has *always* been like this, and it goes with the product. And when people are coming in here to buy the best they should be treated well and whoever they're dealing with should look well and give them whatever attention is required. And not everybody starts off as well-to-do and upper crust and you must encourage people to come in. I mean, there's a lot of chaps in Trinity College who are starting out in jobs and wouldn't have an awful lot of disposable income and they might come in and buy one cigar. But we have to look after them the very same way because they will eventually be tomorrow's people. I see no reason why we shouldn't continue to prosper. I think people are going back to fine shops. In the last few years there are an awful lot of shops that just opened and closed and there's no real character to them. And we get people who have given up cigarettes and smoking and they just come in for a whiff. And we say, 'By all means, walk around and breathe it in.'"

VERA NICHOLS—HAIRDRESSER, AGE 77

She is one of Dublin's pioneer women hairdressers, starting out in 1928 when most women cared for their own hair at home. Early women's hairdressing was a rigorous, complicated "craft" in which she had to learn how to use heated tongs, give Marcell waves and do Inecto colouring and peroxiding. Since lice could be a problem in those days, towels had to be disinfected and the cut hair burned. The little shop in Stoneybatter closed in 1964. She feels that the prices charged in posh hairdressing salons today are "scandalous", especially since the staff have minuscule training compared to her long apprenticeship.

"My sister Lily May and my sister Kathleen May, we were the first hairdressers around this area. Back in the twenties and thirties most women did their hair in the home. Lily May went to America and got her training. She went over to visit relations there and she took the training and had a certificate and all. She started the shop in 1928 but before that she was doing hairdressing in another sister's house because there was no shops then. Then the three of us sisters did the hairdressing. There was no permanent wave then. There was only Marcell waves, cuts and sets. Some women would have a beautiful head of hair down to their back and we'd have to wash and Marcell wave that. Some wouldn't want it cut. A lot of women back then never went to a hairdresser, just let it grow and put it up.

"My sister had to start the shop with just her stove and her tongs and her scissors and that was it—and a chair and a table and a mirror. That's how you started and you went on from that . . . got another table and got another mirror. We were only renting the shop. In 1932 the rent was £2 a week. I remember, because we were figuring that £2 was a lot of money to hand out every week but we'd chance it. We had a square sign outside, 'May's Hairdressing'. My other sister and I trained and then we got our stove and tongs. We had a waiting room and a coal fire and electric lighting. The chairs were like polished armchairs, highly polished wood, nothing like the barbers now—that's luxury! They were movable chairs and the table was in front of you there and we would have to move it to suit big people and small people. Cause if you got a big fat lady and the table was in front of you you'd have to move the chair back to let her fit in.

"We wore a white coat. Oh, we weren't allowed to do hairdressing without a white coat. My sister trained us and we had to watch and she was pretty strict. Now on Prussia Street there were droves of cattle and sheep going up and down and the flies would come into the shop. Oh, you might get twenty or thirty flies but I used Flit, a spray, to get them out. And I'll tell you another thing. There was inclined to be dirt in those days in the hair. They were nice people but dirt was very prevalent. People had problems with lice. Sometimes my sister would say, 'Be careful of her hair', and you'd know what was wrong. But we couldn't offend them. So what we would do, we always used talcum powder on the neck and you used a paper napkin over the gown so that the gown didn't touch everyone's neck. It was very hygienic. You didn't have to wash it after everybody. It was a kind of silk square gown in various light colours. So the gown went on but it would never touch the neck and then we'd hand wash them ourselves and hang them out. And the three towels we used we only used on one person. We always used two towels and a small chin towel and a paper napkin for the shampoo and the Marcell wave. Next person comes in and three more towels. We used to wash them, disinfect them and hang them out, all by hand. We kept the towels packed over the fire and they were always warm. But sometimes a person was *very dirty*, like this one lady. So we'd take the two towels and the chin towel and burn them. You wouldn't even disinfect them. Burn them. And we always burned the hair in an open fire. That was the best disinfectant. We'd usually do it at night.

"Our scissors came from Sheffield. You had to steady your fingers because you had to cut fast. You'd get a welt on your fingers. And if you didn't keep cutting fast you wouldn't keep in the line. Back then a cutting comb cost about a shilling. A good pair of scissors would last five or six years, maybe more. We used to get them sharpened in McGiverney's, the jeweller's, at the corner of Moore Street. They don't do it now. We used to always bring our hairdressing scissors down there and they specialised in that. And May taught us that we always had our *own* scissors, our own comb and our own brush. And we bought our tonics and agents from Eason's. They had a hairdressing department. And my sister, coming back from America, could manicure but no one here could afford that then . . . back then you were almost barely living.

"Hairdressing was fairly severe in the beginning to learn because it was really a trade. It was a *craft*. It's not like now when any young girls can go and do it because they can roll up curlers and put on the agents. Hairdressing then was much more difficult than now. I mean, *now* with the perm we just roll the rollers but in those times you had to square-off *every* square inch, put a rubber pad on it, draw the hair through with a button hook, wind the hair and then wet the sachets and put them on. In fact, the permanent wave *wasn't known*, wasn't known at all when my sister started. It was only Marcell waving and you had to wave the hair with tongs. The tongs was about a foot long and we had two or three for using and we had a small little gas stove for heating them and you had to check them with your mouth [the heat]. You didn't [actually] put them to your lips because once you were trained you'd know by the smell but sometimes you'd lift up the tongs and they'd touch your mouth and if they were too hot you very often got a bad burn from that. We did a Marcell wave all over the whole head. Must have been named after whoever designed it. It must have been Marcell who made the tongs or something. You'd have [at least] two tongs all the time because you'd have one on the heater and you put the other one on. We had to do *every* square inch over the whole scalp. No such thing as rollers. You had to finger wave the hair and roll the curls at the end and put a little clip on it and then dry it with a dryer. It was really a *trade*. And the 'Bob' came in in the twenties. It continued on in my time, youngsters with nearly always a fringe, parted in the middle, a fringe and a bob, straight around. It cost one and six for a Marcell wave in old money and we *earned* it! And a trim was sixpence. And sixpence for a child's trim. But it was very rarely children got their hair done. And on the first haircut for a child I'd save a curl and put it in an envelope for them.

"And we did hair colouring. It was Inecto colouring and you'd get it Inecto'd. It was expensive but it was good. If you were dark and going grey in them days and if you had the money you'd get this dark colour put on. And you could get blonde but you wouldn't get too many in-between colours like they have now. We used peroxide for blonde and you had the *responsibility*, like when you were bleaching you couldn't dare let peroxide drop on them or you'd be in serious trouble. You had to be very careful, so it was a craft all the way. Peroxiding was the only thing then. And we used to put soap suds on the end of their hair so if the peroxide leaked down the suds would soak it up to stop it bleaching too much. They didn't go for any extremes. I remember a lady, a very moneyed lady, and we had the hairdressing shop on 72 Aughrim Street divided up into cubicles and this lady would have to have the curtains drawn and no one was to see her getting her hair tinted. That was it! And we always had an appointment for her and when she was finished we'd walk over and get her coat and put it on her and then she'd go out another back door.

"But all different people would come to us. We had from the highest to the lowest type here. At that time, Peggy Dell—Ireland's Sophie Tucker—she was a customer, and I remember her real deep voice. Summer was much busier because in the winter people would wear hats and scarves, but in the summer they'd be going out. And women would form clubs among themselves, say six of us got into a club, and pay a shilling a week and it'd be your turn this week and your number next week. The women would get their hair done maybe every six weeks or that. Now we worked in the summer very late and we worked for a pittance. Then in the winter we wouldn't be that busy and we wouldn't have the money to go out anywhere—but in the summer we were so busy we couldn't go out! Women would want their hair done on *Saturday* to have it looking fresh for Sunday. Now we would open at 9.00 and close at 8.00, but there were really no regular hours. Like I remember in the summer, one particular lady, and we were open and it was a Saturday night and my sister said, 'Door shut, that's it!' Cause the waiting room was full and you could see that. So I went to this lady [at the door] and said, 'I'm sorry, we can't have you in.' 'It's only five to 8.00,' she said. And I had no pluck now and you daren't be cheeky or anything and I dropped back to my sister and said, 'This lady wants to come in, it's only five to 8.00.' 'All right,' she said, 'We have to let her in if she forces the issue but tell her she could be here until 1.00 in the morning', thinking that that would knock her off. But I was letting her out at ten to one on Sunday morning! Oh, we worked very late hours.

"And people tipped very, very little. I'll tell you one instance. A lady, she said, 'If I win this [Irish] sweep ticket I'm going to America and I'll bring you as my own hairdresser.' Now I never expected anything, never looked for anything ... we weren't allowed and we didn't think that way. But she *won* the sweep and this lady came around after winning and I thought, 'Thank God, I'll have a few pounds, a few bob.' *Do you know what she gave me?* A three penny tip! That was the only tip I ever got off her, before or after. And it was *fabulous money* she got, two hundred and something thousand pounds I think. That was a *fortune.* I was sure I was going to get a few bob. Three pence!

"It was very small money we had. It was very tough. My late husband was a cattle drover at one time and the best job he had was night watchman. See, my husband should have been a cooper in Guinness's. His father was a cooper and fathers always trained sons. But his father was dying and this man said, 'Don't worry, Johnny, I'll apprentice your son.' That was my husband, Joe. But when he died he reneged on it, so there was no way he could get in. So we had idleness and illness with my husband, especially in his late life. I always got only about £3 or £4 per week all our married life to rear six children. That's what we had to live on and there were no handouts. Maybe there was St Vincent de Paul's, but the way we were reared was with *stinking pride!* We were reared with a lot of stinking pride and I wouldn't go! And if I had it to do again I'd probably do the very same thing . . . you wouldn't crawl. I often went down to Leonard [butcher] and got a bone, a big marrow bone, and it'd take me two hours to make a soup of that and it would be gone in about ten minutes with the children. They'd eat their fill of potatoes and soup and that was it. You didn't go out and cry or moan or anything else.

"The shop closed in 1964. But I put everything into life and I'd do it again. We're as long known around here as anyone, I'd say. From around 1928. So we must be part of the history of the area. There's a lot of young people that goes to hairdressing now and maybe they hadn't an education and they'd go to it and they weren't trained. Definitely not trained as severe as we were trained. Today a shampoo and set, they're scandalous! To think that we used to do a shampoo and set for two and six old money. In those days the money wasn't flowing. Nowadays, let's face it, they rip you off if they can get away with it. Funny enough, my daughter never went to the hairdressing but she does my hair now . . . it must be kind of bred into you."

LAURI GRENNELL—SHOE REPAIRER, AGE 64

He served his seven-year apprenticeship under his father who was a master shoemaker. The hands of the old shoemakers in the shop were "nearly deformed" from cuts with sharp knives but they had great pride in their craft. Back then a pair of shoes was a treasured possession, well cared for and made to last as long as possible. Today, after nearly a half-century of labour in his small, 150-year-old shop on Parnell Street, he is one of Dublin's last traditional shoe repairers. When reflecting on his seven years of training, he can only scoff at the modern "quick fix" shoe repair shops which give their staff about four days' training with glue and staple guns.

"My father made shoes. In his younger days he was a shoe repairer for the British army when they were up there in Beggar's Bush. He wasn't in the army but he was employed by them. Then he had his own premises in Lower Liffey Street. He was there from about 1930 onwards. Himself and his brother started it off and they had five or six men working down there. Then there was a fire there in 1947 and we moved to Upper Liffey Street. At one stage we had twelve men making shoes and doing the repairs. And the 'Waxie's Dargle' was a place over in Sandymount where shoemakers and repairers and the poorer classes in Dublin used to go to have their picnics. See, the waxies were the shoemakers. Now there were nine of us in the family and our mother died very young so my father had very grave responsibilities. He worked from 7.00 in the morning till 9.00 at night.

"When I was going to school I used to come into the shop. The men seemed to be old type Dublin people who were at it. Some of the men were on piece-work and others were on full time. But the piece-workers were the men more inclined to get a few bob and go out drinking. In my father's shop you were a benchman or you were a finisher. A benchman was a man who actually took the soles and heels and repaired the shoes, making them presentable. And the men would chat all day long, chatting and working away. And you got a tea break and you'd put on the kettle and be sitting around the fire. And you'd be burning all the old stuff in the fire. Just pile on all the old scraps, soles and everything. You'd have to heat the place, you know. And you'd get the smell of leather all the time. And a man from the Labour Court used to come down to my father's shop and check on the staff and make sure they were all happy. Oh, yes, they used to do that once a year. Yes, the Labour Court used to send inspectors around to come and inspect the premises. And they'd inspect the toilet! And the machinery. And they'd go up and speak to the men and say, 'Are you happy? Have you any complaints?'

"I remember when I was going to school as a youngster and Saturday was always our half-day, till 2.00, and my father'd bring home a load of shoes and I'd deliver them around the area. You know, he'd repair them and bring them home and I'd earn my pocket money delivering them, walking and on a cycle. And you'd wrap the shoes in brown paper and twine then. You had reams of brown paper and a ball of twine. Oh, they had to be nicely wrapped. And there was an *art* in doing it, I can tell you, in wrapping a pair of shoes and twining them. You twined it and made a handle on the twine. And there was an art in breaking your twine, snapping it, as well. And I remember very well—like it might be my job on Saturday—to polish the shoes at home and you had five or six pairs lined up to be polished and they were your [family] Sunday shoes. And then you had a weekday shoe, a tougher shoe. But on a Sunday you had what they called a Sunday shoe. They were light shoes, a good one for going to Mass. And on a Sunday night they were supposed to be put away. But it was a great thrill to be able to sneak into your Sunday shoes and go off to school. They were lighter shoes, you see, and you felt you could run better and stuff like that. And in the summer when we got our holidays from school we wore a very light, flimsy runner. They were canvas. And it was *marvellous* to go around in those. You got as long as you could out of a shoe as a youngster. Even if you complained that they were pinching you, you still got a couple of extra weeks out of them until your parents would have enough money to buy you another pair. I remember you could get a very good pair of shoes at Denis Guiney's for twenty-five shillings and they were a beautiful shoe. But you could get a pair for fifteen shillings. And the ordinary shoe polish was the Nugget polish, that was *the* polish at that time. It was a brand name and it seemed to be the *only* one out at that time. Now you can get twelve, fourteen different brands of polish. It was a good polish, indeed. So your shoes were taken out and polished and your clean socks for Sunday. A Saturday night was bath night and all chores were done. You got out your good clothes and the iron was taken out and your trousers pressed, even though they were short pants. And make sure you had a clean shirt and clean hanky.

"When I started in my father's shop I was 18. You served your time to a machinist or a benchman or a finisher. And I had three brothers in the trade. I don't know if there had been any distinction whether you were a maker or a repairer, we were part of the same crowd. My apprenticeship lasted seven years under my father. Oh, he was very patient. At first you took the shoes apart when they came in. And you'd get a knife and you'd be cutting and trimming away. And then you got the opportunity which you wanted to go to, the bench or the machine. And I seemed to be fascinated with the machine. And I served my time to that.

"Now anytime I have heard of anybody doing the 'cobbling', as they referred to it, doing it at home, I always got the impression that they were country people who came up here to Dublin. I don't ever remember anyone ever telling me of a Dublin person doing the cobbling. Because down in the country they had to do *everything*. They had what they called a three-legged last. There was a heel and a big sole and a small sole. There was three shapes on it. People in the country always had them. You still see them around. Made out of metal. Nearly every home in the country had one. Of course, shoes in them days would last you for years and years and they were handed down from one member of the family to the other because the poverty was there. And there's a misconception about a cobbler, because he was the man who used to do the cobbles on the road. He was a cobbler. Back when all the streets were cobbled. So a real *cobbler* was a man who did the streets and there was a real art to that. But how it hit the shoe repairers I don't know. Now we say it as a joke, you know. Like, when the old people still come up and say to you, 'I'm looking for a good cobbler', and I just say to them, 'Well, we're not cobblers, we're shoe technicians.' But it's only a joke.

"In them days when I served my time they had really good dyes and also the quality of the leather was first class. It was the *tanning* of the leather, that was the real thing. Oh, they had tanneries all over the country here. Tralee was the last one that I saw. The quality of the hide from the animals was better and they'd more time to tan them. They'd put them in the ground with acid and tan them. Put the skins in the acid vats, that was all part of the tanning. The leather was *lovely* to work with. Now all the [Irish] tanneries are closed. And, truthfully, I find that the English nails we use are better and cleaner and better finished. I used to use brass nails cause they wouldn't rust but they went very expensive. During the war years they used crepe rubber, mostly made of petroleum. They made the whole bottom of the shoes of that, for ladies' and gents' shoes and it outlasted everything else.

"The policemen were great customers. They wanted the big heavy sole on them cause they were on their feet all day pounding the beat. A big heavy black boot they'd wear. And now the army men used a polish and they boned it. They 'boned' the polish on. That's how they got this [shiny] skin over it. It was a natural full film of polish *caked* on to the shoe. It was spit and polish. You'd put the polish on and then you'd actually have an old bone of a knife, the bone handle of the old knives, the smooth ones, and you'd actually bone it in. Spit on it and actually bone the polish in. And just continue to do this and it'd actually cake the polish on. Well, this took some time to do. I mean, you didn't do it overnight. I tried that at one stage on a pair of my shoes and you'd see your face in it like a *mirror*. But if you caught it on a nail or anything sharp there was a lump taken out and there was a channel put in that shoe. And it would take you months and months to build that channel back up again. So all your months of doing this was just out the window. But the army men used to do this for the officers. Oh, I did it as a youngster when you'd want to impress the girls with lovely shiny shoes. I used to spend *ages* doing this.

"We had aprons with the leather front on them, a heavy leather so that if the knife slipped or went through too fast it'd slice through this leather rather than their chest. Cuts were common. Oh, you'd want to see some of the older type men, their hands. Oh, their hands were nearly *deformed* with so many cuts and bruises. I've seen men cut nearly down to the bone, and healed over. And every man had his own set of tools. And he'd wrap them up in his apron when he'd be going home each evening. Some of them would take them home if they were doing 'nixers' at home. A nixer was a home job. They all did nixers. They'd do some of their neighbours' shoes. Your hammer and your awl and your pinchers would last you a lifetime but your knives would wear out. And on the hammer the handle would break and it was easy to put a new handle on it. And the handle would [eventually] get your own shape [of hand] and you'd find it very awkward using somebody else's hammer. Like, with knives, everybody had their own way of sharpening and if one lad went to his dinner and I came along and was doing a job and grabbed his knife and used it, well, he'd come back and *he'd* know that somebody was at his knife. Oh, yeah, he'd take it up and say, 'There was somebody at this.' He'd know *straight* away. He could tell by the feel of the blade going through the leather that somebody had interfered with his knife, that somebody had interfered with the edging on his knife.

"People used to queue up at the door looking for their shoes [to collect] at that stage. There were so many. Especially at lunch hour. You could have five, six, maybe eight people waiting for their shoes. At that time they didn't have so many shoes and they really *needed* their shoes. I have one pair of shoes there now and I think it's the fourth sole on them. If it's a good shoe it'll take the repairs. See, the oils dry out of the leather as time goes on and it'll become brittle. It used to be that some people'd bring in shoes and leave them and say, 'New sole and heel', and there'd be dung and everything on them. Now that's *no way* to hand a shoe to anybody. It happened to me on one occasion and there was dog dirt on them. And I called the woman back and says, 'Listen, take those home and clean them. I'm not going to have those around.' I wouldn't take them from her. So she cleaned them. Even if I was to lose a customer I wouldn't accept the likes of that from anybody.

"Now my father worked till he was 83. He was *here*. I reckon this building must be a 150 years old, at least. He's dead four years now. It was a way of life. He loved it. He knew *everything* about a shoe. He kept going till as long as he could. And he took *pride* in what he did. In his day you had to make your thread. You got your hemp and you got your wax and you got so many cords and you waxed your cords and then you'd get your awl and perforate the leather and stitch. That's a skill, a beautiful thing to be able to do. It was perfect work. But *now*, people in these Heel Bars working, they get a weekend course, or give them about four days' training and they're turned out and they call them fully fledged shoe repairers! Using staple guns and all that. They don't do the likes of this . . . they wouldn't have a clue about stitching. You still have older people coming in but the younger people, they don't want to have the one pair of shoes for ten or fifteen years now. The old customers, they love a yap. But some people have no time for talking now."

JOHN BRERETON—PAWNBROKER, AGE 78

When he came to work in his father's pawnshop on Capel Street nearly sixty years ago there were about thirty thriving pawnbrokers in Dublin serving the poor. Back then the little local pawn was truly the "people's bank" where the struggling tenement folk could always get a few shillings for the sake of survival. On Mondays and Saturdays, especially, hordes of women would queue up, bundles in hand, chatting amiably as they awaited their turn. In those times, Brereton's took in pyramids of old clothing, tattered shoes, holy pictures, irons, vases and what have you. By contrast, most of the business today is devoted to jewellery and appliances from the middle class. It is now one of only four remaining pawnshops in Dublin.

"I only came into the business by accident. I didn't like the business when I was a child. I preferred to be out playing. My father was anxious to get me interested in it but it didn't appeal to me. I was going to go on to dentistry or accountancy. I only came in here by accident at age 18. I was home from college for Christmas holidays and one of the staff got sick and I came in to give them a hand and help out—and I've been here ever since! Once I started working at it I got interested in it . . . got fascinated by it.

"I had a seven year apprenticeship. I started at the bottom and clothing was the main part of the business and it was *very busy*. I started by pinning on the numbers, sweeping the floors. The approach at that time was different altogether in the way that fathers would approach their children. The approach was that you were very lucky to have a business to go into and you had better do what you're told and learn it quick and be earnest about what you're doing. And, of course, I was put under the manager and treated just the same as anyone else coming in as a stranger, maybe a bit worse. The first year you wouldn't be let near the counter. Even after seven years' apprenticeship you wouldn't as a rule approach customers as regards taking in pledges and that. See, it was four years' apprenticeship, three years junior and then you became a senior assistant or a wareroom handler. Wareroom handlers never came down to the shop, they were packing stuff up into racks and keeping them in rotation of number.

"It was a different business altogether then. It was a weekly trade mostly. They pawned on a Monday and took out on a Saturday and we knew the customers. People were *very poor*, a lot of poverty around at that time. It was very hard to make a profit out of second-hand clothing. But people also brought in tools, the men who worked as carpenters, or in trades. They would pawn tools and irons and people used to pawn the old [wicker] basket cars. Oh, it was a type of bargaining. They'd want £3 and maybe you'd offer them £1 and then they'd say, 'Make it two.' They were mostly women back then and we had a separate office for the men because the men used to be shy about coming in. People used to queue out along the street, especially on a Monday morning. You'd open at 8.00 and the people would be waiting on the steps. It was like a *club*, they'd all know each other and they'd like meeting after a Sunday. People were very close at that time, you know. They all lived around the same area. It was *teeming* with people around here and we'd know most of them because they were regularly in and out. They'd *all* know each other and be talking—like a club—and the man at the counter would be writing in the book and sometimes my father would become infuriated and ask them to stop talking because the man recording in the book couldn't hear what the manager was calling out. In fact, we had to put up a notice, 'No Talking'. And people used to bring their children with them and they'd run around the place. We used to have to tell them to hold the children by the hands. Like, we would take in maybe a *hundred* pledges in half an hour if the man was a good writer. If he was a good writer he was very desirable. Although the people were poor they weren't downhearted, they were able to manage.

"Now the staff lived in at that time and downstairs was a kitchen and a housekeeper and a cat. And people's [staff] business was their relaxation, really, you know. It was their way of life. They didn't finish business and expect to go off and enjoy themselves. And when they were taking stock they'd send out and get in whiskey and they'd enjoy themselves. Once a staff member married he no longer lived in. For those who lived in there was a housekeeper who prepared their meals. At lunch there would be a big joint of beef there and as a child I would come home from school for the meal. It was very nice. There were seven men employed here at the time and it was very hard work. Everything had to be carried up. See, it's an old Georgian house and there's plenty of storage space and storage at the back in the old mews. See, everything had a number on it and had to be kept in rotation and as the stock came in it was put on the first floor and then was moved up to the top of the house—there were three floors—and when it got to the top it had to be got ready for auction. We had to keep everything for a minimum of six months and most of the stock was twelve months.

"There were over thirty pawnbrokers in the city at that time. There was pawnbroking houses that did much more business than we did. It was controlled by law and it dates back to the 1790s and 1800s, under George III, and that was the law we operated under. Everything you do is governed by law and you wouldn't really go into it if you weren't born into it. If you do anything wrong you can be taken to court and you have to apply for a licence every year and if you've done anything wrong on a person they can go into court and oppose you. I don't ever remember anyone being opposed for their licence, so the people must have been satisfied with the way they were treated. But the law says that if you're not satisfied you can go into court when the pawnbroker is looking for his yearly licence and you can oppose him and it's up to the judge to decide whether he gets his licence or not.

"People find it very hard to understand pawnbroking. They're simply fascinated by it just the same. They think we take in goods for little or nothing and sell them for huge profits and keep the money yourself. But, like, when the goods were sold by auction we'd very seldom make any money, profit, out of them. People always thought the pawnbroker made a lot of money out of the stuff that was left. But that was the *worst* thing for us, for things to be left, because it was very hard to make a profit out of second-hand clothing. There was no money in it . . . you know, a lot of hard work but no money. You'd bring the goods down and the market would be bad and no one would want to buy them. So we'd eventually sell it off for little or nothing. You *had* to clear it out because you needed the room. We made very little out of it. I don't know how my father reared our own family when I look back at the books and see what was made, how small the money was.

"It's just like a bank. We work it as a bank. We had the sense that we were serving the community. You had that feeling, all right. You helped them out as much as you could. And in the old days a lot of illegal money-lending went on and people were often subject to exploitation and extortion. Oh, there was no social welfare or anything like that back then and a lot of people would be very badly stuck for money. You know, pawnbroking, it was the forerunner of the social services, really. Back then it was to help people out. There was a *lot* of poverty.

"Now it's completely changed. It's no longer a weekly business, it's now a middle-class business. It's more interesting now because you're getting a greater variety of goods and from a cross-section of people. People always get stuck for money. Have you ever tried to get money from a bank? It's not the easiest thing. Or from a building society? Even if you have your own money in a building society you maybe have to wait a month before you get it back. If you want money *today* where are you going to turn? If you want to get money by the afternoon, where are you going to get it? It's ready money on your property. You can bring in a camera, get money on it, have it stored and it costs you very little. Or bring in a good watch. We've taken in motor cars. And pianos were pawned too. We've changed the pawnbroking business now. I suppose we changed with the times and we developed the retail sales end of it and pawnbroking became a sideline. Pawnbroking wouldn't survive on its own and it wouldn't pay. But it has a fascination for me so I keep it on. People put something up on the counter and you have to estimate its worth. You know, it's a challenge. And with travel now, people going off all over the world, you never know what you're going to be offered. You get a tremendous variety of things. We won't take clothing any more today. Our customers are almost all middle class today. It used to be mostly poorer classes. It's a pattern of life now for people to live beyond their means . . . spending money they haven't got. But we wouldn't enquire, it's very personal. They know it's private.

"My father would never put up with the business today. Too much legislation, book-keeping, and how hard it is to get good staff. And all the robbery and violence. Like, we used to leave all the stuff in the window at night and we only had wooden shutters. *Now* we have to have every kind of modern anti-burglary device and *even then* you're not safe. Society has deteriorated very much. Back then people were very poor but there was little crime and people were by and large very honest. So my father worked long hours but was not under the same pressure. And this shop's been here for over a hundred years, at least. I even thought of changing the outside of the shop. You know, there was a time when it was all the fashion to modernise the shop fronts and you weren't in business unless you had a modern front. I just decided to leave it as it was and I'm glad now that I did. It would be difficult to imagine past decades without the presence of the pawnbroker. A lot of poverty. And although they were poor they were nice people and you'd be surprised at the families they reared. It's very gratifying . . . people don't forget."

JAMES ROONEY—CHIMNEY SWEEP, AGE 85

The Rooneys, one of Dublin's oldest chimney sweep families, can trace their trade back to 1834. Oral family history recounts the old days when unscrupulous sweeps would "buy" stunted orphans and force them to climb into dangerous chimneys. He began by peddling his bike along northside streets laden with cane rods, brushes, scrapers and other assorted gear. The "toughest" job was extracting the thick tar from turf fires in old tenement houses. But it was always interesting since in a chimney one could find most anything from a child's note left for Santa decades ago to a precious parcel of the family's hidden jewels. At age 85 he is one of Dublin's last traditional chimney sweeps.

"It goes back in the family to somewhere around 1834. That's what my father said it goes back to. Me father was at it and me brother was at it and his son was at it. And there was another Rooney, Jack Rooney, a relation, and he was in it and his two sons. And then there was Mathew Rooney in Dun Laoghaire and another Rooney at North William Street. So we nearly had the whole northside. My father was 91 when he died and he worked as a sweep till he was 78. He *did*, indeed. They say soot is healthy.

"So we started in 1834. Now me father told me there was a painter on South Anne Street and he had two sons and the father died and then the mother had no way of keeping them then because there was no allowances for children in those days. And she had to put them into a home, an orphanage. And they used to sell them [children] out of the orphanages. The old fellas that used to be doing the chimneys, they'd buy them and they'd make them go up the chimney. They used to *beat* them up the chimneys. They were always small and they'd make them go up the chimney to clean them down. It must have been awful altogether. Oh, made to go up *into* the chimney. Well, those two children, the two brothers, *they* were the Rooneys! Me father told me. This was around 1825 as near as I can put it. Oh, that's how it come into our family. There's truth in it! Get the small children and they were *made* to climb up . . . with their feet. It was Lord Shaftsbury that fought to get it done away with. Oh, there was murder going on over it, over in England and all. That's how the law was brought out [against it].

"We lived on Annesley Place, on North Strand, and *all around* there was me father's area, Howth and all. And me father was out in all weathers. Like before he got the bicycle he was telling me about going out to Howth and there was open-deck trams at the time and the top was wide open. And it was raining out of the heavens! But they'd let him stand on the platform with his rods and things when it'd be like that. Get the tram to Howth and carry his rods around with him. Going out in the lashings of rain and he was soaked to the skin. He decided then he was going to get a bicycle. And then me father got used to the bicycle. Oh, I done it meself even. You tied the rods on to the crossbar. And you had a handbrush for cleaning down and taking it [ash] up with. So me father had to push all the way out to the Hill of Howth then, up to the top of the hill with his bicycle . . . carried cane rods with him. They were Malacca canes. We bought them here in Capel Street. At that time we used six foot rods. A sweep could go anywhere he wanted but we wouldn't go over to the southside. There was one fella, another sweep, and he used to go out by Howth and he used to be chasing me father and he used to threaten him and everything else. See, this fella used to do the area too. And this man had a pony and cart and me father'd be on a bicycle. He was opposition to him and he'd be giving out and abusing him.

"Now I was a bus driver at first but then I started to sweep. Oh, doing it the *very same* way, go out on a bicycle. On the bicycle I'd go out on any days, all days. The Malacca canes we bought, the six foot rods, we'd have enough for houses that were at least thirty feet. And we'd have spares as well in case any broke. You'd always carry maybe four or five spares. When you went to a house you'd never know what you were up against. So we'd have to have spares in case any broke. They could be riveted together—brass tops—screwed together, as many as you like. Ah, I done *ninety feet* one time, up on Dominick Street. It was a big old tenement house and I was down in the basement and the *smoke* . . . I was near choking. And I done ninety foot! And we had sixteen inch brushes. Some of them you could get very stiff. And you could get them eight inches if you wanted. You could buy them at Varian's in Talbot Street. And you had a big cloth to go in front of the fireplace. Calico we used. Covered the whole front down.

"So you covered the whole front down and I'd wear a boiler suit and tie it at the sleeves to keep ashes from going up your arm. It was for your own cleanliness. And you wore an old cap. But if there was a blow-down [draft] down the chimney and it was real light soot it'd come right into your face. But it didn't do me a bit of harm. And sweeps was big drinkers, they were indeed. Oh, they were devils for the drink! But you'd kneel to put the brush in and you couldn't see, you went all by feel. Start with one rod and then screw another one. We used our bare hands because you've more feeling with your bare hands. If you put gloves on you wouldn't feel the rod coming off, unscrewing—which it would do.

"At that time there was fireplaces in the bedrooms. And some chimneys had terrible bends in them. And people then were using turf. They were *tough* ones. Built up *tar* from it. Turf, it goes into tar. Oh, turf is worse than coal, *by far*. And then chimneys would go on fire and it'd crack them. It destroyed more chimneys. The heat would crack the lining in the chimney, if the chimney caught fire from all the tar. We used to use then what me father made up from an old gear wheel of a bicycle, to get the tar out. He got it rigged up so it'd fit on to the screws of the rods. It'd scrape it off. And I done another big house up on Stephen's Green, another ninety-footer. And I was down in the basement and, *oh*, it was terrible. A big old Georgian house. And there was grips on it for climbing *up* in the chimney. The old grips was still there. You could *see* the grips they used to have for climbing, when the old sweeps made the children climb up there. Oh, sweat would roll down me trying to get into it. I used to go up in the night time and do it for him. Ah, that was often two and three hours.

"And we'd find jackdaws' nests, birds' nests. Oh, some of the builders should take an example from them! Oh, they were devils. They'd build good houses. Oh, *solid*. Trying to get through, break through with a bare rod first, trying to break holes in it. They put sticks across and built it up and then there'd be paper and bits of metal they'd bring in and put into it. They were a devil for metal. Like flat metal. You'd be trying to break through that underneath with a rod, be banging and banging. And you'd have a sore arm after. It was just like concrete trying to break through. Oh, it'd block it up and people couldn't light it.

"Spring was our busy time. Spring cleaning, when carpets would be taken up and cleaned. We were real busy. And people'd give you tea regular in the morning time. And you got a few cakes maybe as well. Home-made cakes and all. And one woman, she'd sit there beside you and be chatting away all the time you'd be working. She was terrible jolly. And one time this lady had a white carpet. She had it cleaned just the night *before* I was coming. Now it was *madness*. It was a mad thing to do when I was going to do the chimney, because anything could happen. And I had papers all around on the thing and these two young kids she had was pulling them away and I was trying to shoo them away. And she ignored them. I wanted to give them a scalp. Oh, I can tell you I prayed that day! Oh, and Christmas time was real busy. And I used to tell children that Santa sent me to clean the chimney. And you'd find hidden notes up the chimneys [from children to Santa]. I reached up this one chimney in Clontarf and here was this note . . . 'Dear Santa, please bring me a bicycle.' And I brought it into the family and the father says, 'Here, I'll show you that little girl.' And she was about 25 years old. Oh, the father and mother laughed.

"You had a handbrush for taking up the ash with. Some people took it. People say soot is good for brushing your teeth. And people with gardens would ask you to keep it for them. We'd carry the soot away on the bicycle on the crossbars in a calico bag. It didn't come through the calico. Long ago O'Keefe's, the knackers, used to buy it. Me father had a big shed down the lane and he gathered up the soot in big sacks and would bring it home and O'Keefe's used to buy it off him. They'd get some chap to go with a pony and cart and collect the sacks. They could put eighty big sacks on a horse and lorry. Eighty big, huge sacks. I think O'Keefe's used to mix it with manure for fertiliser.

"I used to do about eight to ten chimneys a day. Regular customers. Oh, you got a name for yourself. See, we were renowned, we were *known* at the trade. And once you got the name, you got the customers. Sometimes with me father, long ago, people'd come to me father and they'd leave the key to their house for him to go in. He was very trusted. And he was dead honest. One time he was doing a house out in Clontarf and he was cleaning the chimney and a lump of cloth comes down the chimney, rolled up with a *load* of jewellery in it. He said it must have been put there hiding it during the troubled times. That's what he made of it. So he just showed it there to the man and he never as much as said thanks to him. Never even said thanks to him! And he gave it up to him. Always honest. If you ever got caught stealing anything or got a bad reputation you were ruined for life.

"Now if you were doing boilers that was a dirty job. Doing big boilers. I used to do Woolworth's in Henry Street. They had two huge big boilers. One of them would take up this room. You had to clean out the flues on them and, of course, the chimney going from it. It was nearly two days working, only meself. With the boilers, you'd be destroyed with them. You had to *scrape* it out with a scraper and a rod and it'd be coming into your face. They used oil in the boilers and it got caked on to the sides of it. Now me father and brother used to go to Downes's Bakery and they had to get *into* the boiler. They used coal. But one would stay outside in case the other got weak in the heat. See, it'd been used that day. They'd be out all night doing it. Oh, I had to go home and right into the bath after the boilers.

"You'd be tired at the end of the day. You know, with the weight of the old rods on you, pushing them up, and you can get ninety feet of rods and swinging your shoulder. Ah, it's a one-man job. No one can help you. But you're your own boss and that means a lot. Now the new crowd [of sweeps] uses vacuums. I bought one once but I never used it. It was a nuisance. No use to me. It was better the way we were doing it. And some of them were trying to clean the chimney with the vacuum and naturally you *can't*, because it's only a little pipe. You're not going to get it up the chimney. But people are fooled into thinking it works and they pay the money for it. Sure, one day I saw a fella and he had an ordinary little *house* vacuum cleaner, going to clean the chimney! Two young chaps going around asking, 'Do you want your chimney cleaned?' Ah, the world is full of chancers!"

11

Caravans and Visions

MARGARET DORAN MURPHY—LEGENDARY TRAVELLER,
CLAIRVOYANT AND ORACLE, AGE 70

She is seen by many as a modern-day Biddy Early, able to foretell the future, soothe or cure human sufferings and set people on the right course in life. Her reputation now transcends Ireland as people from around the world seek her out. To most Irish she is simply known as the "gypsy fortune teller". As a child of travelling (tinker or itinerant) parents, she roamed the roads of Ireland in a caravan and at age 7 realised that she possessed psychic powers that were clearly extraordinary. When she married a "settled" man it broke the tradition of tinkers marrying within their own clan. She had great difficulty adjusting to the tight confines of a home. For decades hordes of distressed, often desperate, souls have sought her powers and help. She uses the crystal ball, tarot cards and reads palms. In her eyes, the meek and the mighty are equal and many regard her as more important in their lives than doctor or priest. This responsibility or "burden" takes a heavy toll on her emotional welfare—but she has never turned a person away from her door. Countless beneficiaries credit her with literally saving their lives. Of her fourteen children, only two have inherited the "gift". One senses that she will be relieved when they can take over her role so that finally she can find more rest and peace for herself.

"We were the travelling people so I was from all over Ireland—*every* place was our home. But, funny enough, I was born in Dublin in the old Coombe Hospital when there was a big snowstorm. I remember me father telling me about the big fall of snow and he'd all his horses and caravan out and we took a tenement room in a place called High Street. That's the *real* old Liberties. And I was born in this big storm. My father was a man that took houses for winters, you know, and then he'd take off. He was never a settler.

'There was *always* distinction about our life. We were the *travelling people* and we wasn't wanted in many spots in the country with our caravans and horses and if you started to put a fire on the ground the police would come and might kick it up in your face. Ah, the police were very hard on us years ago, not because we'd be robbing or doing anything but just because we were the travelling people. We were on the move all the time and we were looked down on very much to a great extent. But then we met some nice people like farmers, and some great people. Our caravans were the colourful big square ones, not the round ones. We had the square ones with the cupboards and beds and mantelpiece for delft. My father used to go down in the west and buy all these little Shetland ponies, black and white ones, and horses and he used to ship them away from Galway. He'd be up in the mountains getting the herds. And then he did the tinsmithing and trading as well and—I shouldn't be telling you this—but he'd make stills for the farmers for making the poitin. Oh, and the police would be looking about and, you know, you might find a policeman that wanted it for himself! Now there was another thing I remember, about the old Queen Victoria when she was over here. My grandfather, he was a *great* bagpipe player. Oh, you wouldn't *believe* the sound, it'd bring the people out of the woods. But he played for her and she thought it was fantastic. And when she was going back she sent him a gold and silver set of gilded bagpipes. And when he died he couldn't give them to anybody, they had to come back to the museum in London. See, he had made a promise to her that they would go back.

'My father lived to be 100. Oh, he was the hardiest man in the world. He *never* went to a doctor in his life, even when his shoulder got broken. He was leading two horses on O'Connell Street, big mares, and the trams was then in Dublin and one of the horses bolted and went under the tram and one of the horses fell on me father's arm and he was knocked out. So in those times they had to do the setting of the arms without anaesthetic. And travelling people, they had healing and they wouldn't be running to doctors if a man got a bad cut or a bad going over. They were able to pick a dock leaf out of the land and they'd have it in a jar maybe and they'd have it in their caravan in case anyone would get hurt. It was a big green leaf with all the ribs going through it and that was the remedy. They'd put this dock leaf on them and the skin would go back the same way and the wound, the blood, would stop. It was the *belief* they had—they were able to help themselves because they were healing with their mind and that was very hard to explain. Like, you could see them very sick and the next day they'd be all right. Oh, I saw cancer being cured! I *know* persons that has been cured.

"In Kerry now they'd get the pitchfork after you, after healers and fortune tellers. There's parts of Ireland in the west where if they heard of a fortune teller some of them wouldn't like it. They'd say, 'That's bad.' The priests would. Of course, in the old times they had the greatest fear of Biddy Early. You might have heard of her. Now Biddy Early was just a very good woman that *really could* heal. And she didn't ask for money either. People used to give her shelter, a night's lodging. But some'd go down and burn down her little cottage because she was a healer and they called her a witch. Anyone who could outsmart a doctor then was called a witch. If a man was dying the doctors would say, 'Throw him in the poor house to die!' There was no hospitals in those times. Well, maybe this family would keep this man [at home] and they'd say, '*Get Biddy.*' So they'd have to get up on a horse's back or old coach and go miles to old Biddy and bring her back. And Biddy'd have her little [curing] bottles. And she'd say, 'He's going to *stand up.*' And he *would* stand up! And he might live for fifteen or twenty years after. Now that happened all the time. And the priests used to come on horseback and really hit her with a whip and say, 'Throw her out of Ireland!' Now that was in the west of Ireland. The west of Ireland is very holy country altogether and it really genuinely is. The real old customs is still there.

"Traveller's news was even quicker than telegraph. If one of them was sick in a part of Ireland they'd travel *all night* in their horse and caravan. They'd get there to tell the news that their cousin was sick. Through hail, rain or snow, thunder and lightning, they'd *get there* to tell the news that someone was very sick. Or if there was going to be a marriage. Arranged marriages is dying out but there's still a few. A girl might *never* [before] see the chap in her life. He might just pull up and come to stay near her parents for the very first time and in twenty-four hours there could be a marriage made up. And even if the marriage took three months to take place she wouldn't be let go from here to the gate with him. That was the tradition. You wouldn't be left to see him at all, until the day of the marriage. That's the funny part of it. Wouldn't be let go for a bottle of milk with him or go even for to get a cigarette or a sweet with him. Couldn't walk down the road with him. All through that time she would be watched by her family and he'd be watched. That was the old tradition. Oh, if you went with him to the end of the road they'd say you were no good. Something was wrong. That wasn't supposed to be. Oh, that was as old as time itself . . . as old as time itself. But on the day of the marriage, ah, all the families was there and great celebrations.

"When I got married my life changed completely. He wasn't a traveller, he was a builder, a very good man. I got married very young, two years after meeting him. I was 18 and he was 29. How I met him was I used to sell things out of the basket. You know, buy all the cheap stuff and sell it and he come along in his car and he says, 'Oh, I wouldn't buy any of those things.' And going home that evening then he stopped again and says, 'Does you want a lift?' 'Ah, not at all,' I says. And he says, 'Ah, sure, you wouldn't say that if we were going to the pictures. If I see you tomorrow evening I'll bring you to the pictures.' And he was a man from a house and I just wasn't going to lead him on . . . and I was very young. But he used to follow me around all over to different parts of Ireland to see me and maybe only talk to you for an hour. And we used to say to him, 'There must be loads of lovely girls in Dublin.' And I'd say to him, 'What's wrong with you? . . . we're *different*. I'd never fit in with your life. It wouldn't be fair to you.' See, my being used to the open air . . . and to go into a house like that.

"I married him, anyway, and then I had to stop me travelling life. It was very unusual at that time. Not many of them married out of the race. My particular family and their generation, with them, once you married—good, bad or middle—once you made your bed you had to lie in it. There was *no way* there was going to be a broken marriage over little titter tatters. And now I had *fourteen* children. And it wasn't easy, especially the first year, being so used to the *free life*. I didn't know what any responsibility was until I got married. And then I had a husband, a different life to control. And I couldn't see all Ireland then the way I used to see it . . . the freedom, the flowers, the valleys, the lakes, the moon, the stars that we always used to stay under. I'm in a house now and that is *for ever*! But that spirit is still there. Me husband understood that it wouldn't be easy. Even the priest that married us said, 'Well, Margaret, you're coming away from the sun and the stars now. We have to clip your wings now.' So, strange enough, I did stay. Which I'm not sorry about now. That was the way my life was [meant] to go. Some things are destiny. But a *boring* life coming from such a free life and seeing so much life. It wasn't easy. But, to me, marriage was *sacred*, no matter what happened. Marriage was marriage, that's the way it was in the eyes of God. And I wasn't going to run away from him and the children. I said [to myself], 'I *have to stay* with those children, I have to adopt a different sort of life, I've *got to be able* to make myself happy.' And it was a fairly happy marriage and it lasted thirty-six years and he died of heart trouble.

"Some of the travelling women told fortunes. Now my mother could *feel* things, but she wouldn't tell a fortune, not if you were to give her ten million pounds! Many people many times asked her to do it. But she wouldn't tell it. She *knew* she had a gift but she'd always say, 'I'll never use it that way.' How I knew I had the gift was in another way altogether. I was always able to see things before they happened, even when I was 7 or 8 . . . as far back as I can remember. My sister was married at 14 and the man she married was 30. In the old times it was matchmaking marriages, you see. Now she was only a child going away from the family after being married and she asked me father could I go along for a few weeks just to keep her company. So I went along for a few weeks just to keep her company. And the first night I went to bed—and I was only 7—I saw something that came to me. There was a lady with real red hair and a white gate and a gate latch. I was supposed to come to it. So, I just said to Katy the next morning, 'Katy, there's a gate latch there somewhere, up in the big woods.' And she says, 'Oh, no, there's no gate latch around here, only farmers' houses.' 'Oh, there *is*,' I says. 'There's a white-washed house and a lady with lovely red hair and she has something for you.' Now she didn't *believe* this, you see, and this particular man she married was from this district and everybody knew that he was going to get married to the young bride at 14. 'It's a present, the lady has a box for you', I said. So we're going for a walk, anyhow, that evening and down this back road there was primroses and we went through that field and on to another road and *there was the gate latch*. And we went in. And 'Oh, hello Mrs Ward,' the lady says, 'I have your wedding present. I couldn't get to your wedding,' the lady with the red hair said. It was things like that!

"And like I've seen, like, houses before we're even *in* them, what shape they would be inside them. And if there was anyone that was evil or dangerous I could *sense* that straight away no matter how well they are covered or what way they looked. No matter how well they are covered or what way they looked I'd sense that *straight* away. Or when we were travelling the road with some houses I could sense that there was danger [that the people might be unfriendly] *immediately*. And my father used to say, 'Oh, nonsense, child, don't be thinking too much about it.' And it all used to *come true*. And people were coming to me [to tell their fortune] by the time I was about 15, coming all around me. And the priest comes to me and says, 'I don't believe in that stuff at all but I'll tell you, there's a carnival coming here for the Black Babies [mission] and there'll be a little box for to get a few bob in and you can do it [fortune telling] for them and all you can charge is two shillings.' So I says, 'Well, Father, I'll do it.' 'Well,' he says, 'you've done a great job, but I still don't believe in it. But if it's a gift, go ahead and use it.'

"The gift was *always* there. I'd tell my daughters things, forecast things that'd come true. I wasn't able to tell everything now but I could tell a lot. In the old time it was only two and sixpence to get your fortune told. But I think that any power you have is a gift from Him. But there are frightening moments as well, things you can *sense* about things around you. You can get *feelings* about things. Nobody showed me *nothing*. Not one thing. When I get the feel of a person's hand I can tell what they're lost about. And it's not the greatest thing or the best thing to be able to do. You'd rather not be able to do it, you'd like to get rid of it, give it to somebody, give them that sort of power—but you can't get rid of it. It *doesn't go away* . . . it's *there*. You have to *use* it, put up with it, *help* people with it.

"I look at the tarot cards and I know the crystal ball. My crystal ball was made in Waterford. Now tarot cards, they belonged to the fifteenth century. Nobody knows how far back they are. But tea leaves in a cup can tell you just as much as a crystal ball. The crystal ball will tell you the *immediate* future, about now and next month. And the tea leaf will tell you what's happening tonight, tomorrow night and the next month. The crystal ball is a very old thing. Now the hands [palms], from the hands you'll get all of the past but you won't get the future because you weren't given the power to do *that much* with the hands. You can get around the sides, about children and different things like the road to the unknown, the road to the future, the past . . . the two particular roads in life . . . whether a person is career wise or which they want first, career or marriage. Or you can get a hand with two marriages or no marriage in it. You could also see a ring for somebody, a very glittery ring, but it wouldn't be marriage. They could be going into a religion [priesthood]. So you'll always get those different roads in the hand, but you still wouldn't be getting the *whole future*. No way! *Never let anyone tell you* that you're going to get the whole future from that, from the hands. You'll get a little bit of the immediate future. You'd only be getting part of it, glimmers of it. But you'd be getting a lot of the past all right. And no two people in this world is the same, not even twins. And their roads in life are never the same.

"With a reading I try and get all the major things first. I go back to their past and can tell if they've come through a few storms or whether they were born in Ireland or whether they were adopted or about their parents. And then I go direct to the present time and I go right into the future. And, like, they could be at the crossroads and I would tell them whether to go to America or to Australia or stay in Ireland. And some people [women] could have two men in their life and some person might have no person in their life and might be looking for the right person. Some people are genuine frightened because they've never had a fortune done before. You can feel the tingling through them and through the cards and you can tell them to relax. And some are very scared of it and won't come in, but then a week later they'll come in with a friend. Some people, you can't get through to them. There's blockages surrounding them . . . *barriers*. But you can get the blockages out of them and bring them right. And people'll come to test you sometimes. Oh, *yes*. But, of course, you can expect that. And if you told them what they had for their breakfast that person will say, 'Now how could you tell me that? *How* did you know that?' You have to be nice to them.

"Men and women, the young and the old come . . . barristers, lawyers, priests, police, solicitors. Every one of them. And the *businessmen*. The businessman could have three shops, a big house, tennis courts, swimming pools, but *still not happy*. So much pressure on the poor man. Or the business falls through. And there's some poor people that comes about health or about their marriage or about their husband that has left them and run away or a man's wife who has maybe gone astray, and dealing with drink and people with diseases and maybe there's no hope. But there *is* hope—but they *think* there's no hope. If a thing is not going to go right I'll tell them. And secrets that shall never be told have been told to me. Everything under the sun! The biggest thing in the world doesn't surprise me. I've come through it, you see, in my lifetime. *Nothing* would surprise me. It's not going to be new. I help them all through and they keep coming back. And I bring them right. I take away their pressure and carry it with me. Oh, I've brought many of them through and some that did not want to go on, they did *not* want to live, I can tell you that. I've changed their life and helped them and put things right. They depend on me and keep coming. And I'm always relaxed. I'm *never* in a bad mood. I never *can be*.

"Sometimes I tell them where they're wrong in life. To bring them right I have to be tough on that part of it. It's too big of a responsibility for one person like me. I've often wanted to come away from it . . . *several times* in life. But you *cannot* get away from it, because they want me back. And then you've people coming from the west of Ireland, people coming to me, and even from America, and some comes over twice and three times a year to me. Oh, from *everywhere*. All the nationalities. India. I couldn't get on a train or a bus in any part of Ireland . . . I'm *known*. People come to talk to me and get their fortunes. They know my name, they know me to see, but I just remember their voices. And if I go to England I'm known. It's because I help them. And I don't charge them much money. It's something I was given as a gift to use.

"Most people come to see me for very serious reasons. Some could be coming every week in. They depend very heavy on me. People *confess* to me everything in their whole life, and it's left there with me. It's never told to another. You'll meet someone very, very distressed and they could have money, they could have power but they wouldn't want to go on in life, the pressure would be that strong. A doctor, *no* one, could get through to them and you'd be meeting them after all the help has failed. A good fortune teller can help that person more easier than all the doctors and advices that have failed. You can bring that person through . . . a good fortune teller can. And the older people, some of them are very lonely and very afraid, very frightened in their little flats, living alone. And with some people there's such sadness that they don't feel they'll ever live again, ever rise again [from depression], that they'll never see anything good in this life. But the *road is there*. And it's easy to start again, a new environment, a new life. But sometimes a person is blocked off for years. And they're afraid to talk to *anyone* about it. But they'll tell it to *me*. They'll break down. It's better when they cry because we've broken the barrier then. Whatever contact there is between me and them they know they're saved, some of them. I *know* . . . they've told me. Absolutely. Given them a reason to live, a reason to go on. And they say, 'God bless you. I'll get a Mass said for you.' I don't need much money, but I help others. You can't abuse it if you have the power. It's a power in its own, but it wasn't meant to be used for money. It'll leave you straight away if you take a lot of money.

"There's a lot of light around people . . . you see a lot of light. And there's all kinds of unfairness in life . . . a lot of badness going on behind closed doors. And you see danger points, like a young man on his motor bike [facing an accident] . . . and drugs. And I see evil all the time. Police have come to me a couple of times [for help in solving cases]. Like, there was five chaps came here to this house one night. This was about eight years ago. All young men about 25 and I never seen them in me life. But they got the address from one of their sisters. And they all had this plan set, the time, the place. And I told them, 'Turn back at this crossroads and you'll come out in the right. If you turn back now there's twenty-four hours, plenty of time. If you don't,' I says, 'I *know* what's going to happen. It'll be on the southside of Dublin and there'll be police and shooting and one policeman will be shot, but he'll live. And one of the gentlemen here will be shot but he'll live.' But the chaps went and done whatever they *had* to do and *out* they went. They didn't listen. The next day, *exactly what I had told them*! It was in the newspapers. It was a bank robbery. One got away and the others were captured. One was shot, wounded. Things like that you don't like to have to tell them . . . but you *have* to.

"I've been very lucky through life, with health and that. I'm old now but I always had that belief that I'd come through everything, that I'd come through the health things . . . with the fourteen children and twelve normal deliveries and a couple of sections. There was a few shaky moments. I have two daughters that have a little bit about the mind and are able to feel things. They sense things and can tell you some things. Very good photographic memories from about the time they were 3 or 2, which shouldn't have been there, but it is. All of life is fate. As I look back now . . . nine daughters and five sons and loads of grandchildren, that's the way it was supposed to be. That's the way my life was to go. Some things are destiny.'

Terriss Mary Lee Murphy—Famed Fortune Teller, Age 70

She is the daughter of the legendary "Gypsy Lee" Dublin's most famed fortune teller of this century. Her father, a traveller (tinker), took his family in their colourful gypsy caravan to the notorious Monto in the 1930s. As her mother's reputation spread, people swarmed upon the little caravan seeking her visions. By age 7 she realised that she had inherited the "gift" since she could often see things in her mind before they occurred. Not only does she use tarot cards, gaze into the crystal ball and interpret palms, but she "reads the water" which is a gift even her mother did not possess. There is a constant stream of the "faithful" to her door on the northside of Dublin. Men in expensive business suits sheepishly slip in and out, as do fashionably attired women. But most visitors are common folk with heavy worries upon their mind. "Some people think I'm God", she says, "but I'm not." At day's end she might have seen twenty people and she is visibly emotionally fatigued. She wearily confesses to often wishing she had never been given the power because of the dire dependency so many people have on her . . . "You're like a prisoner."

"My name, Terriss, my father fought very hard for that name. Actually, when I was being christened he wanted me called that and the cleric wouldn't have it. He had to put a Catholic name behind it as well. So I was called Terriss Mary. In fact, he delayed my christening for a fortnight with his stubbornness. He said, 'I want Terriss and *that's it*—I don't want any other name!' But he had to eventually put the Mary at the back. So I am unique from birth!

"I was born in Birkenhead, near Liverpool. My father came to Dublin I think when I was 5 years old. I remember coming over with my mother on the boat and it was very, very stormy, landing in Dublin and my father meeting us there and taking us to Amiens Street. Then we went to Railway Street and then Foley Street . . . the Monto. We just moved into the Monto, just woke up one morning as children and we were on the move again. It was just packing up, we put the horse on the caravan and you went. As children we thought we were going on a long, long travel, but we didn't. From Railway Street to Foley Street. And I have vivid memories of the Monto. A very exciting place, a very *rough* place where 'dog ate dog' but very nice people. If they got to know you and like you, they *liked* you. If they didn't, they'd *cast you out*! They wouldn't bother with you. But my father and mother and all their family were very well liked and, you know, my mother got established there. In the Monto my mother's reputation became known very quickly. Oh, *very* quickly. On Railway Street and she followed from there. She was *known*. I knew that my mother was a fortune teller and, see, being the oldest of my mother's lot I had to watch the younger children. That was my job. Our caravan was in a yard on Railway Street and the yard would be *packed* with people queuing up. And you'd see people coming out of the caravan saying, 'Oh, thank you, Mrs Lee. Oh, you've made me ever so happy', or 'Your advice was good and I'll take it.' You know, as you were a younger one playing you'd hear all these women talking.

"Now my father was married twice. My mother was the second wife. There were three stepbrothers and four stepsisters. And I was the eldest of my father's second set. See, at one time you didn't marry outside of the Romanies, you married into them. But my father married outside. Now my grandmother, my father's mother, was a very brilliant woman. A *brilliant* woman! She was clairvoyant. But most of the travelling people couldn't read and my grandmother was a very God-fearing woman and my mother would have to read stories out of the Bible to her. She loved the Bible. And my grandmother had the *gift* and could relay the gift to others in the family. But nobody outside the family. See, my mother, in Romany [language] was a 'gorger'. That's Romany slang for outsider. She was a gorger. Now I wouldn't say that you had to 'earn your bones' but they wouldn't take you too quick. They would wait. Your kindness, your goodness goes a long way with the gypsies. They read your goodness, they read your kindness and if they see anything wrong they'd cast you out! You follow? They won't embrace you.

'But the Monto . . . a rough area. The Corporation Buildings—they were called 'the buildings'—God, it was like a *prison*! Balconies of one-room little dog boxes. Two big sections of that with balconies, like a prison. But a lot of good families were brought up and reared in that. Nice people, but rough. And they had the animal gangs at that time. Oh, they were known all over Dublin, the animal gangs. It was poor times, depressing times and people had to live. And they were a clan within their own, the people in the Monto. And there was prostitution. Now maybe one particular lady would have a 'name' and she was known as a loose woman, but no finger would be put on her. In other words, a very nice person but that was her game. And in the public houses I remember ladies coming out and at that time there was a lot of shawls worn and the ladies would have their hair in buns and these long kind of pinafores down to their ankles, like you'd see in the Molly Malones now. The older ladies all wore shawls at that time. There were very few coats. If you wore a coat in those days you were very respectable . . . you were 'up'.

"Now as a child there was always rows and you'd run at that time and they'd make a ring [around men fighting]. There was no such thing as rushing in and hitting people with hammers or a stick. They'd make this ring and they'd fight it out. Oh, many a fight I seen. And they had their own set of rules in the Monto. Like, for child molesting now, they'd beat and *kill you* for that. Or if you interfered with a lady and her family, you really got it for that. Oh, I remember one argument in those buildings and whatever this man done anyway they *threw him* over the balcony, about two or three other men did. He done something totally which they wouldn't put up with, you know? Now what this man done I don't really know but it seems that he was carrying on with one of these men's brother's wife and the husband didn't know—but the brother found out! They beat him to a standstill and threw him over that top balcony.

"At the Store Street [Police] Station there was a policeman and he had a number '123', that was his number. He was a tall, very, very skinny bloke. Oh, my God, he was like a reed! And if any robbery had been done he would go *alone* into this complex and shout so-and-so's name. He'd come down and say,

'Where's the goods?' 'Oh, number 123, I haven't got them. I didn't do it.' 'I *know* you done it! *Where are they?* You'll *fight me now* and if you beat me you've got away with that robbery. If you don't, I want those goods!' And this particular policeman, he never came with a back-up. He was very, very well respected. See, a lot of policemen walked the beat back then and you got to know them.

"My grandmother was a very brilliant woman . . . she was that clairvoyant that before her last child was born she fell asleep and she was expecting the child. And in the little wagons [caravans] in the corner there was a little place for dishes—they loved their nice dishes!—and there was a little glass thing [case] for good cups and plates. And she fell asleep and she woke up and in that glass she could *see* this room and a child choking with its throat, a child as she described it then of about 10 or 12 or 13 years of age. It was all blue, with a number 7. And she could see this big cross. Now she was expecting this child at the time. Now that child was born and years afterwards my grandmother and grandfather decided to come over here [Ireland] to travel. And coming down by Amiens Street in the caravan there was a little funeral place and in this window was a big cross. Now the baby, her son, was now 13 years of age. And he's sitting on the footboard of the wagon. 'Oh, Mammy,' he says, 'isn't that a beautiful cross? Would you buy me that cross?' 'Oh, go way,' my grandfather said, 'that's only to put on coffins. Don't be silly, boy, you can't have one of them.' 'Oh, I like that,' he said. And they were going on to travel down in the country towards Kildare and he took very, very ill and he was taken into Naas Hospital and he was brought into the hospital she had seen—the *very room* that she had seen [in her vision] before that child was born. And [door] *No. 7!* She comes out of that hospital *screaming*, 'My boy will *never* come out of there!' What did he die of? Diphtheria. She could see very, very far into the future.

"My mother had the same experience with her own son that died at 6½. She said that she could see this very big tall building and a lot of tall steps, and the number 3, and she could hear this child's voice screaming, 'Oh, Mammy, Mammy, Mammy, tell them to stop, tell them to stop.' Now she could see this before he was born. And now that child was a huge child. He was over 14 lb born! He was *huge*. But he took ill at 6 years old and died. He went like a baby six months old . . . oh, terrible. My brother was 6 and took bad with headaches and eventually had T.B. And he was put in the Cork Street Hospital. It was a fever hospital at the time. And my mother was going up to see him on the first night and she heard him screaming, 'Oh, Mammy, Mammy, Mammy . . .' and there was a number 3 over his bed! Now she didn't want to believe in her head that he's not going to come out. She tried to block it out of her head. Now my mother is a very God-fearing woman and we were doing these nine weeks novena, every Tuesday. Now this was the last night of the novena and we were just after coming from the hospital. Now to me, you know, it just didn't hit home that he was going to die, but the change in him shocked me. I seen such a change in his appearance, from a big robust boy to just a little thing like that. And my mother said to him as we were going, 'Goodbye, my angel . . . goodbye, my angel.' And he kissed her *ever so hard*. 'Yes', the Sister said, 'he is a little angel.'

"So we were just after coming out of the hospital and we were rushing to do the novena and my mother realised that we didn't bring scarves. And now at that time you could not go into a chapel without a scarf to cover your head. You'd be shamed. And it was raining and the ground was mucky and we're in the middle of O'Connell Street and my mother said, 'My God, St Anthony, please send us something to put on our heads.' And this is as *true as God*! I said, '*Look*, Mammy, on the ground.' There was a handkerchief! This is as *true as God* what I'm telling you. We walked another few feet and there was *another* one! Not a blemish on them. Now in my eyes and mind they should have been put away as something [religiously] symbolic, but wherever those two handkerchiefs went from then till now I couldn't tell you. Those two scarves, those two men's handkerchiefs, honest to God, I don't know where those went to. And I was saying, 'My God, Mammy, in the rain, in the road, in the muck—and not a *blemish* on them!'

"So we went, we done the novena, and me mother said, 'Lord, if he's for me, make him better tonight—if not, take him tonight.' We went home then and then me father would go up the last thing at night to see my little brother and he had to walk all the way up to Cork Street Hospital. And he went in and the bed was empty! The bed was empty which means that he was in the morgue. He was dead. 'Why didn't you let me know?' he said [to the Sister]. 'But your wife was up here and I'm sure she knew your little boy wouldn't last,' she said. Me mother . . . she *cried*, she *cried*, she *cried*, she *cried* for nearly twelve months non-stop. Done nothing! 'Oh, God', she said, '*please* send him back to me again.' Finally she said, 'Lord, if you show me where that child is . . . if he's in heaven, I'll never cry over him again.' And she went to bed and she fell asleep that night.

"She got up the next morning so excited. 'I've *seen him*', she said. 'I know where he is and I'll never, never cry again to want him back.' She said she was asleep and she was being led up these *beautiful marble steps* and he came running down to meet her halfway in the same clothes he had been wearing before he took bad. 'Mammy, Mammy, *quick*,' he said, 'I want to show you somebody.' And he rushed her up these steps and when he got to the top there was Our Lord sitting there, Jesus Christ, she said, sitting there and he had a hold of Our Lady's hand. She described everything Our Lady was wearing . . . and Jesus Christ sitting contentedly. 'Oh, Frankie,' she said, 'this is a beautiful place, but will you come home with me?' 'Oh, no, Mammy, I want to stay here, let me stay here,' he said. '*Don't cry* now,' he said, 'I'm *happy*.' With that, he led her back down the steps, he went back up the steps and he waved her goodbye. She was content. She went straight after that to a Father McNevin and related all that she had seen and he said, 'Don't you know, Mrs Lee, that your son is dead and with the Lord and he's trying to tell you not to cry any more.' And she never did.

"Now I'm not an educated woman but I only know that I could *see things happening* before they happened . . . at round about 7. But at that time they had no meaning to me. So I got the gift round about 7 but I didn't use it at 7. From an early age I didn't realise what was coming into me. It *is* a gift from God, dear.

All knowledge, everything we have is from God. Being from deep Romany origins they have the powers to pass it down. Maybe it was my grandmother through my mother passing it into me. I don't know. But it wasn't just like a wave of a magic wand . . . now you've got it! It *didn't*! It came on over the years. Like, a friend of ours lived across the road in Foley Street and she had a big, huge knee. There was something wrong with her knee. And I remember her being taken ill when she was playing with us all. And I remember it was a Sunday, and I'd be about 10 years old, and a lot of us girls went to see her in the hospital. And when I seen her I *knew* she'd never come out of that hospital. Yet they were all brimming and brewing how she looks well and she'd have this big operation. I remember going home and saying, 'Mammy, she looks very well but she won't come out of there.' It's things I can *see*, sometimes trouble for other people. And she never come out!

"And when I was around about 12 one of my friends in school said to me, 'Your mother is a great fortune teller, surely *you* can tell fortunes?' And at this time this girl hated her teacher and she was concocting a lot of hardness for the teacher who had hit her. And I said, 'I *can* tell fortunes. What do you want to know?' I said, 'You're planning a lot of badness for this teacher.' She was very unruly and because she was reprimanded she was very vindictive, she wanted to get back at this teacher. I said, 'Within the next three weeks you're going to be put out of school.' 'When I get out of the school I'll leave it *myself*,' she said. 'Well,' I said, 'we'll *wait and see*.' I said, 'Don't do what you're planning to do because you could be put in a [reform] school.' See, at that time children would be put away for *years* if you were unruly. Anyway, I wasn't in school that day when it happened but she comes behind the teacher and she hit the teacher at the back of the neck and she dragged her to the ground by her hair. She was brought to court and she was put out of school. And she was put away! And I could *see* what was going to happen to her.

"I started using cards, telling fortunes, when I was about 20. My mother said to me one day, 'I have to go out, you take over for me. You've got the intelligence. You can *do it*.' And my mother used to say to me, 'Whatever you do, whatever you see, you must always *tell* what you see *truthfully*.' In other words, say you come to me through that door and you want to hear what *you* want to hear—I *can't do that*! I can only show you the best possible way you must act, what you must do. If it hurts you going back out, I can't help it. But by hurting you maybe I'll be more help to you in the long run. Anyway, I done *twenty people* that first night, using the crystal and cards. My mother said, 'You'll be able to do it.' I was using tarot cards then. And I was *able* to just do it.

"With the cards you tell your own fortune, you pick your own cards out, I don't do it for you. What you throw out, I read. But in a crystal ball and the water there are visions . . . sometimes maybe not very clear. In other words, if your mind is terribly befuddled it won't come as clear as it should come, the visions. Past, present and future visions are in the crystal. That crystal ball, oh, I've had that for years. It's handed down from gypsy to gypsy. If an old gypsy lady died you get her crystal ball but you'd have to be favoured before you'd get it. An aunt left me this one, my father's sister, who was also clairvoyant. Now I'm the only one that reads water. I said to a lady once, 'Let me do the water for you. I won't do the cards.' And that was the beginning of the reading of the water. Water is life! It's life. The blue is healing. Both combines. And it goes into more depth for your future, I can tell you. It's more *specific*. Something just said to me 'Blue, blue, blue, blue' . . . it was like a *knowledge*. Blue is like a knowledge, like a healing power. For me to explain it to you, what I have, I'd have to have an educated brain and I haven't got an educated brain. But blue is *healing* to the gypsies, a soothing colour. I got the blue [glass bowl] and put the water in and I said to the lady, 'Let me do the water for you.'

"All kinds of people you'll get. Some are curious. Girls will come in in trouble, emotional. One lady would come and her reading would be fantastic, you'd ease her worries, her troubles, you'd show her the right road to go on. Some people are very upset with maybe a son or daughter going wrong, going astray, and you show them what way they must react. And I've got solicitors and they won't make a move without me. And gamblers. I have women here who cry bitter tears. Priests will come to me and ask me to do garden parties, for charity. Now this one priest came to me for a chit-chat and I told him that he wouldn't remain, he wouldn't wear the collar, he wouldn't remain in the Order and that he'd marry. And he did! He left the Order and he's married now with children in Wales.

"And I see bad as well as good. Accidents and danger. Yes. I told one gentleman to watch his drinking habits going into a car. And a friend of his was killed and he was left very badly injured [in a car accident when he was driving]. Now if I seen somebody very, very ill there's no point in me saying, 'You're going to die tomorrow.' Because tomorrow will come and take care of itself. Do you follow? Anybody that's very, very ill, I don't like upsetting them. I don't think it's right to upset people very emotionally. Yes, I can say, 'There's details to be looked into, things to be done, settle business, settle affairs.' But I'm not going to tell somebody that they're going to die. No, I won't do that. I will *not do that*! Oh, I've *seen it* before.

"There are three ways everybody must balance—home, heart and career. And there's two roads to everybody's mountain. Was there ever a time you wanted to go on another road? Some people, you see, would wait for maybe six or seven years to take an opportunity to maybe go on another road which could bring them total satisfaction and happiness. Some people block their own head. I can only try to bring out what's *there*, what's *hidden*. You can never create. A person's got to have it or they don't have it. You can show them the way. See, the head rules and predominates the body. And it's up to me to try and solve that person's head for what they should do for happiness. I mean, oh God, in this life there's no immortality for nobody, but there is long life for some people. It's how we *use* our days and our weeks constructively. It's how we put our life in order. And dates and times are very important for people if they have to make decisions in a space of time. And if they don't use their head and act, then I can't help it. It's like being born . . . we're all ruled and dominated by our signs, you know. All ruled and dominated. There's no point in saying, 'Oh, I should have done that', when your signs are totally against it. Life is planned . . . it's already *predestined*. Because, dear, if we were all the master of our own fate, my God, wouldn't you have everything you want? Wouldn't you? No, I believe that three-quarter parts of our life is ruled and dominated by fate, from the day and hour you're born. But it's the other quarter, how we rule our life with decisions. If we don't use our head to make the right decisions we can totally throw fate around for a while, juggle it around.

"It's like if a person wants to commit suicide. Oh, I had a girl yesterday sitting there now crying bitter tears to me over a broken relationship. 'The mere fact,' I said, 'that you have contemplated it [suicide] is a sin against God. So go and ask God for forgiveness for what you planned to do. This gentleman is not for you. The new road that will come your way will be a very happy road, very contented.' But she wanted to end it all. *Tears, tears, tears, tears!* Dreadful. See, some people can't handle rejection. They can't handle disappointment. They can't handle defeat. I'm like a counsellor. But some counsellors, they'll say, 'Oh, you'll be all right tomorrow.' But they're not looking *into* that person's head. First thing they'll ask is, 'What is going wrong and can you make your marriage compatible?' But how does he know what that woman is suffering in that marriage? How does he know that perhaps maybe she is married to a drunken gentleman that's coming home beating her and molesting her and having a life of misery and torturing their children to death? *How* does that man know the depth, the *depth*, of what that woman is suffering? Oh, the gentleman has it all, his house all attached and he's a great gentleman. But there are house devils, you know, and street angels. A devil in the home behind the door but charming outside. Behind that door you get the devil—but no one *sees* that devil. And she's expected to remain in that marriage and she's like a reed that's broken and her children's minds will never be healed for what they've seen and what they've gone through. I can't stand hypocritical people. I can't stand people who set out to do harm and danger and injustice to other people.

"Some people are curious. Now I got a big write-up in that magazine, *Image*. Now these two ladies [writers] came to me and now I didn't know them. They came through the door and I take one of them in. And *everything* I told that lady happened. Now she didn't tell me she was a journalist, that she was working for a magazine. But I said, 'You're very good with a pen and you sell yourself well.' But whatever I was saying to her about her own [personal] life at the time, it fell to happen! And she wrote this article about me. And her friend then came afterwards and got a reading and everything I told *her* happened! That's why they wrote me up in *Image*.

"Fortune telling is very much *misconstrued*. They think you're God sometimes! Nobody is God. It's a lot of pressure. Look, businessmen come and they say, 'Should I sell? Should I buy?' And if you tell them, 'No, don't sell', and they should have, you could *break them*. It's a lot of pressure. It impairs my health. It does. You don't eat properly. It's head-racking sometimes to see people. Sometimes you don't seem to get enough oxygen at the end of the day, to the brain. You get flagged. Your mind gets weary. Oh, God, I couldn't stop now! If I *wanted to* now, I couldn't stop. Because people that come to me regularly won't make moves, they live their lives by my words . . . because they *know* that what I tell them is the truth. It varies, but I could see maybe fourteen people during the day and ten at night. Sometimes you can get weary with your power. You really can. Very, very tired. See, you give so *much* to the outside that you think, 'Am I giving enough to my own [family]?' Then you've got to come back to your own family. I've seven children. Your head is divided, in other words, and the most important part of your head is the part to the *people*, not to yourself and not to your family. Oh, I go up to bed sometimes with a very heavy head and it impairs your health sometimes. Oh, you've no idea! It *does* impair your own health. Because you carry too much.

'You build your own reputation. You build it honestly. I've one girl now who has the ability. Maybe sometimes I sorely wish that I never had this gift, that I could rest my head like a good housewife and plan a holiday and plan to go here, plan to do that. I can't. You're like a prisoner. Really, you're entombed in your own body. Now there was a murder over here [recently] and the police came to my mother. And this girl was dead and my mother could see that girl in the bottom of the river. And she was *found* in the river weighted down with lawnmowers. My mother saw that. My power is not as great as my mother's. I would never, never want to take one inch of my mother's brain. My mother has a brilliant brain. Maybe in time to come I'll be as well known as my mother, but my mother is the *main person* in this town. While she lives she is the main person. She has been *the most* important fortune teller in this century.'

12

Inner-City Natives
and Survivors

AGNES DALY OMAN—A NORTH CITY CHILDHOOD, AGE 72

She is the youngest of eleven children whose father, a stone cutter, went blind and died young. Poverty around the northside was rife and times were hard as her mother struggled to put food on the table. But some had it worse. Behind her house on Clarence Street were three dark, dismal lanes where the "poorest of the poor" lived in small stone dwellings known as Quinn's Cottages. Local folk christened the three lanes "Hell, Heaven and Purgatory". On Saturday night two feisty sisters from the cottages would go on the drink and roll about wildly on the ground fighting viciously before a gathering crowd. But there was also the kindly chap with the ice cream cart and groups of men clustering on corners to sing in lovely harmony. At age 14 she went to work in a shirt factory and at day's end played with her dolls. It was an age of sexual innocence and ignorance when pubescent girls still believed babies were delivered in the black bag carried by the nurse or doctor. In 1941 she narrowly survived the North Strand bombing, just a few yards away, which damaged her house beyond habitability. Today she lives on Summerhill Parade, only a few blocks from her childhood origins, and cherishes her treasury of northside memories.

"I was born on Clarence Street. There were seven girls and four boys. I'm the youngest. My father was a stone cutter and he died when I was only a year and a half. All my father's people were stone cutters and two of my brothers were stone cutters. My father, he was working on the lions [statues] on the Custom House. The British had bombed the Custom House and they were restoring it. Then his health got bad and he got neuritis of the spinal cord and he'd be walking down the street there falling from side to side and people'd think he was drunk, but he just couldn't walk. He *tried* to work but he couldn't. But the people on the job were good, they knew he had a big family and when the foreman would come around the men tried to cover him up so he wouldn't see that my father couldn't do the work. Because you *had* to go out to work— or you *starved*. And sometimes he used to scream in pain. And then he went blind. He *never saw* me. No, he was gone blind by the time I was born. And my mother said that I'd be running in and out and he'd say, 'That's a grand little one. Who owns that?' He didn't *know*, cause he never saw me.

"I was only a baby when he died. And we were called orphans. See, if your mother or father died you were called an orphan. After me father died me mother had an accident on her head and she didn't bleed but she started to lose her memory. And when me father died the man down there in O'Rourke's Bakery knew the story of what went on and for pity's sake he gave me brother Paddy a job at driving a van. At that time me mother had a pension from the government and that man that gave it to her is in heaven. Me mother a *hundred times a day* said, 'May the blessings of God be upon that man', cause she was getting nothing and then suddenly she was getting a pension. See, she took it that it was that one man that gave it to her.

"Where we used to live you had to go up a dark lane and bring down buckets of water, cause at home you washed yourself in a tin basin. And at night time you'd hate going up in the dark for fear of your life. And we'd just candles. And the bucket of water'd be *so heavy* with them big iron buckets that going down the lane we'd go swinging the bucket around and that was easier to carry then cause it'd be swinging out and we'd be turning *with* the bucket. We found that doing it that way it wasn't as heavy. And we used to make sheets out of flour bags. Get flour bags and you'd sew them all together and make big strong sheets. And you only got a certain amount of time to cook your meal and then you had to put out your gas because this man called the glimmerman used to go around to all the houses and he'd make sure you hadn't got the gas on. And you couldn't fool him cause he'd feel it and he'd cut you off.

"At the back of our house was little one-room cottages, little stone cottages. They were Quinn's Cottages and the poorest of the poor lived in them. There were three lanes and at the top of one lane there was a toilet and one water pipe. People put the name on it 'Hell, Heaven and Purgatory', for the three lanes at Quinn's Cottages. That's what the people christened it. Some of the poor really had nothing. There was one woman used to come around there singing and she was a most beautiful singer. She looked like somebody who had been very well off and had crashed. But she was a beautiful singer and she'd sing around here and maybe they'd give her a ha'penny. She was like a trained singer. I heard that she went to America after and became famous. And I remember Mrs McDonagh and she had a black man and you never saw a black man over here in them days—you never saw an airplane, you didn't see *anything*! You just saw the crowd that was around you. But I remember that this black man came to live with Mrs McDonagh down the lane there and we'd stop everything when we'd see them coming [to watch].

"And a Mrs Byrne lived up the last lane, a very good looking woman. And Mr Byrne used to go around pushing this ice cream cart and when he'd be finished with his rounds we used to go over and get a bit of ice off him and you'd be sucking the ice. He had this round thing and all the ice was around the ice cream in the middle and he had this gadget for to put the wafer in and get the scoop and put the ice cream on it and then put the other wafer on top and then he'd press the thing and you'd get that for a penny. Now Mrs Byrne had a sister that lived down the lane here and her name was Mary Bourke and the two sisters were terrible fond of the drink. Alcoholics, yeah. And on a Saturday night the two of them would go up and fill themselves with beer and next thing there'd be *murder!* The two of them would be rolling down the lane boxing one another. And everyone'd run out and 'Ruggy up! Ruggy up!' *Everyone* would run out of their house on a Saturday night to see this. Just stand watching. *Every* Saturday night. Oh, they'd *kill* one another. They'd throw their shawls off and they wore white aprons then. Oh, and they were very good looking, very refined looking. Pulling out bunches of hair and everything. Oh, they'd be *really* fighting. See, they'd get the drink in the pub. But Mr Byrne, he was a very nice man and he didn't drink.

"All our gang used to play relieve-io. And we'd get huge big ropes from men who worked on the docks and we'd play skipping and the mothers'd come out then and turn the rope for you. See, the mothers didn't go out and work cause there was no work anyway and they had gangs of kids. And we had a great time swinging on the lampposts. And we used to call the lamplighter 'Billy with the light'. Then the policeman would come and cut your rope off the lamppost. And the police would even hit you back then. Number 50 [badge] gave my brother Kevin a box in the ear cause he was playing handball. 'Number 50' he was called, and he hit him and nearly knocked him down. And they were *only kids* and they'd nowhere else to play and they were just playing handball up against a big blank wall. Then there was a Protestant hall there and we'd go up and be saying, 'Proddy, waddy on the wall, half a loaf'll do you all, a farthing candle'll show you light, to read the paper on a Saturday night.' We'd only do it for a kick, just something to have fun with. We were all Catholic and had *no* education really and the Protestants kept apart from us because we were all just ragamuffins.

"We went to the convent school over there with the Sisters of Charity. Now they have little black bonnets but then they had, like, big wings. At the convent school anyone whose father wasn't working or whose father was dead—and our father was dead—they'd bring you down underneath to a big long table with stools and you got soup and bread. Oh, a *beautiful* cup of soup. One day you'd have barley soup and the next day pea soup. And on a Friday you'd get jam and bread. But the nuns were very strict. They taught us Irish but we didn't understand a word of it. It made us ignorant really. They should have taught things in English. The only thing we were taught in English was catechism. Everything was in Irish and you *didn't understand* it cause you grew up with English. Now Sister Philomena, she was a little nun but, oh, my God, she was a walking demon! Oh, your poor hands! You'd have to hold out your hands and she had a big cane. I remember me mother wanted to throw one of the nuns into the canal. Because me father was on his deathbed and a sister of mine, Tessie, she didn't know her catechism because there was no money and she hadn't got tuppence for the book. And the teacher makes a show of her and brings her around by the ear to all the classes. And when me mother heard about it she went off. She'd enough with my father dying and all them kids, and she went over to that nun and says, 'If you *ever* do anything like that again I'll throw you in the bloody canal!'

"We were terrible innocent in those days and we knew nothing about sex. We never knew the word 'sex'. And there was eleven of us. You know, the word 'sex' has only come out since well after the war. Eighteen years of age and you didn't know anything. Oh, you never spoke about anything. You didn't know where babies came from. You'd see the nurse coming in with a black bag and you thought the baby was in the black bag. Nobody knew. Now down there around Foley Street, that was all called 'Monto' when the English was there and all these ladies of the night down there. I mean, we didn't know about that then. Your mother never spoke about you having a baby. You were 'in a family way' and that's the way it was pronounced. You never said, 'She's having a baby', or 'She's pregnant.' 'Pregnant', I never heard that word. And a girl [unmarried] having a baby . . . *oh*, that was terrible! Oh, she'd be *thrown out*, get a hiding and be thrown out on the street. She had to go down to Gloucester Street [convent] and the nuns down there used to take all them poor girls in. They had a kind of prison, like, for them and they had a laundry and the girls worked there.

"There were shops all along on the North Strand. There was a kind of grocery and dairy and that was kind of a meeting place for the men and they'd have about two pence and they'd have a big pint glass full of milk and a cake. They had a big long counter and they had gur cake. There was nothing packaged then and the milk was out of the churn and butter came in a big slab. And there was Crowe's public house and me mother used to send me down there for tea and sugar and he had weighing scales up on the ceiling and he'd pull it down and weigh your tea and sugar. Ah, there wasn't much work then and there was a shop, a grocery, down here on Portland Row called McQuaid's and all the men would stand around there. They had *nothing to do*. They'd be all standing there just talking—and they were great for singing and wise-cracking— and the police'd come down and chase them, just for standing there. And women would be going around with their baby in a shawl. There was no prams then. Women used to go into the public house into the snug, the men sat at the bar. But the women went into the little snug and there was a little window in it and would have their order in there. And my mother would go into the pub and have a little tiddly, a little sup of whiskey, a baby Power's, in Moran's pub. She could go into the snug and have that, and you could go down for a can of porter.

"The day you were 14 you went to work. I went to work in a shirt factory and when we'd come back we'd go out to play, like, play mothers with our dolls. I went to work in Todd Byrne's at 14 and it was slave labour really cause you worked for buttons really. We were on piece-work and I remember I often came home with only two shillings. And I was 14 and only a kid . . . sure I'd go home and play with me dolls. Todd Byrne's was a big department store and they used to make their own shirts and that. Up on the top was the factory part. Maybe a hundred working there. My wages were very small. You were shown how to use the machine and I remember one type of shirt I used to be making, they were called horickses. They must have been for big farmers, big heavy *good* shirts. They were *huge* big shirts, one shirt would make two of me! We worked from 9.00 to 6.00 and no tea breaks. And there was a forewoman there and she was an old rip. *Oh*, an awful old rip. You were only 14 and the *way* she'd be looking at you. And if you broke a needle, cause the material was so thick that maybe the needle would snap, you'd have to go up to her for a needle and she'd leave you standing there for about three minutes and she'd just keep looking at you. I *hated* that woman. They all hated going up to her. She'd *never* open her mouth, she'd just *throw* you the needle. And the price of the needle would be stopped out of your wages. Oh, yes. I only stayed there for about nine months.

"Me sisters then worked at the Afton Knitting Company and they got me a job there and that was great, but the money was small. And very hard work. This was a knitting place where they'd make up jumpers and cardigans. It was in Linenhall Street. By machine. You learned how to do all the stitches on this machine. There was an English couple owned the factory, Mr and Mrs Hurst. But I liked the atmosphere. The girls were just a jolly crowd and we'd be *singing* all day long. We were on piece-work and I didn't make much money. It was kind of slavery but you were happy there. It was a very homey feeling, free and easy. Maybe six or eight of us after work now in the summer, we'd all meet then with our bikes and we'd *cycle* all the way out to Portmarnock and we'd dip into the water—but we didn't know how to swim. But we'd paddle around. It was *great*. And we'd cycle all the way back and you never had any worry about traffic because there was no cars. You had the road to yourself and you'd *fly* along. The only snag was the tram tracks and your bike could get caught in the track.

"Now at the time of the bombing, in 1941, I was working in Todd Byrne's. We never bothered about the war then cause we didn't read newspapers and we'd no wireless. You didn't ever think the war would come here. Cause the only thing happening here was we were short of tea and things. And we had a cat named 'Hitler'. And I heard that Hitler said that Ireland was a land of saints and scholars but when he got over here he'd make it a land of tombstones. Now it was just an ordinary night and we went to bed about 10.00 and me mother said, 'Did you say your prayers?' And we got into bed. And I just conked out. And I was sleeping facing the window. And the next thing I heard me mother shouting, 'C'mon, Agnes, get up *quick*, we're being bombed!' Now she heard the bomb that smacked down this house, but I didn't, I was asleep. And I opened me eyes and the window was facing me and I saw *all* these lights . . . they were like fairy lights. *All* these lights. Now we never saw a Christmas tree and we never had a birthday. There was nothing like that. But I saw all these searchlights going and the flares were going and I could see all these lovely lights. Oh, it was *lovely*, it was beautiful. Because we had no electricity and when we would go up to bed we had to bring a little altar lamp. But it was *all lit up*, lovely . . . and I wasn't a bit frightened.

"So we got up and got dressed and went out. Now we lived on Clarence Street and ours was the corner house and the North Strand was at the end of Clarence Street. So we were right in the very middle. And I come out of the house and I stood there and there was a few others around me own age, about five of us standing there, and the *next thing* we hear is the plane coming back. It was a *clear* night, a *beautiful* night, and we could see everything. Now we saw that plane as clear as if we were sitting in it. We were looking up at that man [German pilot] with our mouth open. We heard the drone of the plane first and we said, 'Oh, Jesus, Mary and Joseph, he's back!' And the next thing we heard *'Boooomb!'* And next thing a big piece of tram tracks came flying over. This big explosion and the tram tracks fell here. Sure, we know one person, Mrs Boyle, who lived up the lane and her son was married and lived on the Strand there and had a young baby and the mother got up to give the baby a bottle when the bomb dropped and she was blown to smithereens. But the baby was OK.

"Everyone stayed up and no one got any sleep that night. And the next day the men came around to see if the buildings was safe and our house was ready to fall in like a pack of cards. And me mother says, 'Where are we going to?' So me married sister had a flat and me mother went over there. And there were ambulances and they took Ginny [sister] and I off and they drove us over to the Theatre Royal and there was mattresses all over and on the stage. We were put up on the stage and that was the biggest theatre in Ireland. Now this was for people whose homes were gone. And all night long there was a child crying and this one woman was singing hymns to this child to keep him quiet.

"So then the next morning we came home and sure me mother was back in the house. We saw this big crater in the road and people were coming from all over Ireland to see the bombing. And the next morning after the bomb *everyone* was going to church, going to Confession, naturally enough. Now our house was condemned. The man said it was going to fall in like a pack of cards—but me mother didn't care! Me mother says, 'Sure, what else can we do? We've nowhere else to go.' So Kevin and meself and me mother slept there, and Ginny, for about four or five nights. And one day me mother was cooking on the fire and the man outside saw the smoke coming out of the chimney and he runs in the hall and he got the surprise there cause me mother had the table set for eating and all. So the next thing, we got a lovely house up in Cabra. It was a new house, a beautiful house, three bedrooms, a lovely big living room and a kitchen and *bathroom.* Cause we never had running water. And we got electric lights and you just had to switch on a light and the light came on. And we couldn't believe that! And we got compensation then from the German government. We got £10 and army mattresses and army blankets. And the blankets were beautiful. Cause we'd no clothes. And there was a tailor around there and there was no work for him and all the people got beautiful coats made out of the blankets. We all got a coat made out of this. He was a lovely tailor and he made coats for *everybody,* out of them blankets.

"During the war years Phoenix Park was loaded with turf, *walls* of turf. Because we got no coal. And me brother used to go down to the dumps and collect cinders. They used to empty the bags of cinders from the trains there and he'd pick out a bag of cinders and bring it home to me mother for fuel. And if you found a jam jar in them days you could get in the pictures with it [money from sale]. But the poor, anyone the like of me mother that was on the widow's pension, they got a voucher from the government for a sack of turf from Phoenix Park. And *everyone* made a boxcart with two wheels and two handles. Made it out of a wooden box, crates from a shop and get two wheels off an old pram and put that on it and put an axle through it and that was for turf. The lorries would go up and collect it in Phoenix Park and bring it down to different depots all over the city for turf. Ours was down in King's Avenue and you'd have to go down with your boxcart and collect it. I used to have to go down and I *hated* coming up the hill pushing it. And the men down there giving it out were terrible cranky. They almost threw it at you to get it away for the next person to come. Ah, some of it would be only like sawdust and wouldn't light and it'd be smouldering away. Sometimes you'd be lucky to get a good bag.

"And do you know another thing that happened during the war? When they were trying to get the wheat in they used to get the army lorries and we'd go off in the lorries down in the country to help take in the wheat. *We* would. I was in the army lorries. We'd all be allocated to some farmer to help him take in his wheat. Some of them [helpers] would do great and get lovely tea, but we got nothing off the fella we went to. They were covered-in lorries and we were all in that and you'd spend your day out there. We *loved* it, being driven along. It was great for us. We just went into the fields and they showed us what to do and we just put it all in stacks. We thought that was marvellous, being brought out in a car. And it was lovely and coming back we'd have a sing-song."

Nellie McCann—A City Quay Original, Age 86

Her father, a sea captain, died in a tragic accident leaving behind a wife and twelve children in a tenement house on City Quay. Though life was a struggle, she relished growing up in a community alive with dockers, seamen, horses, tradesmen and the sight of great sailing ships right outside her front door. But she was "terrified" of the brutal Black and Tans who menacingly prowled about, broke into pubs for whiskey and went on wild shooting sprees. History unfolded before her eyes the day the British ship Helga steamed up the Liffey and fired its mighty cannon at the Custom House and Liberty Hall. It was a shocking sound and sight. One day nearly a half-century ago the Blessed Virgin was said to have appeared to a person facing death in her house. Accepted on faith by most dockland natives, the event has become part of the folklore of City Quay. After seventy-eight years of living in the brittle brick house a "hurricane of a wind" raged up the river causing walls to collapse into rubble. Today she lives only a few blocks away in a small flat but her heart clearly remains on City Quay.

"I was born in 1910, No. 25 City Quay. And the house was a tenement, eight rooms in it. My mother'd never leave it. When housing was cheap I could have bought the house for £90. This was back in the fifties. My father was a sea captain and he went all over the world and he *loved* City Quay. There was twelve of us children. My father drowned in England. He was coming home and he fell between the ship and the quay wall. My father used to say to me mother, 'Susan, when I die I'll come back as a seagull.' And after he died, for years after, this seagull used to come and knock on the window and she used to say to me, 'That's your father knocking.'

"City Quay was beautiful, and beautiful people lived in it. Kind. We had nuns and priests and ship captains and they all came from City Quay and all very respectable. Highly respectable. The quays was a very busy place, all horses and carts. Oh, and lots of public houses. And the coal boats and cement boats were coming in. They all came as far as the bridge on City Quay and we'd be up to our eyes in coal dust. An awful lot of people living there in tenements, you know. I seen a family of fourteen all reared in the one room on City Quay. And, I'm telling you, they turned out the loveliest family. And what they used to do, they turned the table upside down for to put so many into the table to sleep in, cause there was no *other* place. Turn the table upside down to put so many children into it to sleep. Cause most people only had the one room. But you were never down cause if anyone hadn't anything they helped out. My mother was very kind to people and she never drank or smoked. A lovely person she was. Anyone that would die and wouldn't have the money to be buried, she'd take them up to Fanagan's the undertakers and he'd say, 'Mrs McCann, you bring me the rich people [to be buried] and I'll do for the poor people with you,' and he'd *bury* them. She done things like that. See, and he'd *charge* the rich. Do you understand? And at Christmas time all the people'd come out, everyone would come out with trays and they'd have whiskey and wine and tea and pudding and all those things and they'd be dancing in the streets out on the cobblestones. Ah, I can remember that *well*.

"Oh, and I remember the Black and Tans. I had a brother on the *Blackrock* [ship] at the time and he knew some of the Tans from England. He was bringing different papers and things across for Sinn Fein and me mother used to say, 'One day he's going to be caught.' But he never was. And they smuggled de Valera over on the *Blackrock* as a fireman. Now did you get that? As a fireman —he was supposed to be shovelling the coal. That was 1916. See, they smuggled him over to England and then brought him back from some business he was on. And they were never caught. And my brother knew some of the Black and Tans. They had the little hats to the side of their head. Oh, we were *terrified* of Tans. The Tans, they were definitely villains. When the Tans would go on the beer nobody could go outside their doors! They were going into public houses and they were supposed to be going in to search but they were taking the drink themselves, the beer and everything. We used to see that from the window. And there'd be all blinds and curtains pulled over. And then we'd be peeping out. And me mother'd say, '*Get away* from that window!' Cause there'd be sniping. Oh, they used to shoot people down and we had curfew and everyone had to be in at a certain hour. I remember one man, Gerry Farrell, and he went over to the quay wall and they *riddled* him with bullets. And my mother and a man named Corrigan went across to the wall and brought him over and put him in our hall. And my mother was a woman who never cursed, she was a very polite woman, but she said, 'Those *bastards*!' I remember that as a young one now. Then they buried him when the shooting stopped. Oh, it was *dreadful* . . . we had terrible times.

"I had sailing ships right opposite my window. And I remember when the ship called the *Helga* came up the river and we were looking at it and the *next thing* Liberty Hall was blew up—and *then* the Custom House. We didn't know what was happening, you see. It was just the boat came up the river and nobody knew what she was doing, came up slowly, and it stopped *dead* at the bridge cause it couldn't go any farther. And the gun was right on the front—I can *see it now*—right in the front of the ship. And next thing, Liberty Hall went! Oh, a *dreadful* noise, and the two buildings was blew up. Oh, my God, it was a '*crash*'! It all crumbled. And my mother was only after just coming back from the Custom House. She was only after being over there paying the father's tax and she said, 'The place is blew up.' And the boat backed right out then into the bay. Ah, sure, people then went out in *droves*. Oh, God Almighty! It was just only in the river facing us. And we were out in the street, we all run out. *Crowds* on City Quay, *everybody* out in the streets. And then there was looting going on. They were looting down in the city. We were very badly off for stuff, you know. You see, the people were all taking what they could be getting, clothing and bread and everything like that, that the people couldn't get. Oh, sure, they got clothing and everything. And the lads was bringing flour and everything. I remember me mother got a bag of flour. And there was a great big detective called Martin and everyone was terrified of him, a big tall man. And he was going around to see who got this robbed stuff, cause they were given it, and someone shouts up my mother's name, 'Susan, Johnny Martin's around!' And the flour was all thrown down the toilet.

"You could leave your door open on City Quay to every sailor that'd come in [to port]. They were the greatest crowd. There wasn't a dirty sailor among them all. They'd stand and talk with you and they'd dance with the kids and we'd be in the thick of it. City Quay was a great place, no really bad people on it. Oh, the sailors, they were *terrific*. And many of the women on City Quay, they married foreigners. Married foreigners, men that came in from different countries on boats, from Canada and all over. Met them on the quays, cause everybody came out and we were always chatting and that. And they were lovely men and they had lovely families. I met *my* husband standing at the door, talking. Yeah, he was a Cork man. He came up on a ship called the *City of Antwerp*. Well, I picked up with him at the door and it was a lovely courtship. We'd go to the cinema and we'd go dancing. He was a great dancer. I'd see him and then he'd go off to Antwerp or somewhere and he'd bring back lovely things, like a chain with a photograph in it. It's 54 years old and I love it. He was a very good looking fella. And sometimes when he'd come into Cork I'd go down and meet him for five shillings on a train excursion. And I'd meet the boat down there and I'd stay with his mother. On City Quay they were house weddings then, beautiful. And you'd have a ham and a turkey and a wedding cake up so high, and a barrel of porter. Oh, *tons* of beer. And the wedding would last for a week. And dancing in the house and it'd end up in the street. Oh, you had a melodeon and a violin. Children and all the neighbours would be out. I remember when I got married I danced the lace off me dress! Oh, they were great times.

"And a wake was like a wedding. As a kid I'd go to a wake with me mother. Oh, you'd go into a wake and you'd be telling frightening stories the whole night and you'd be afraid of your life to come out then and so you'd stay till dawn. And the banshee would be around, always come for someone that'd died. The dead was there for three solid nights. And maybe my mother'd go in and wash them and do them out and put the habit on them. At wakes you'd get everything, *jokes* and *singing* and everything! And they'd go around with the snuff. Then they'd all come and carry the remains to the church. And on the day of the funeral they'd stop at the Punch Bowl [pub] and make a day of it. You'd be in a horse cab. Some wouldn't come home till night and the jarveys would be drunk . . . they'd *all* be drunk. Oh, the wakes were great.

"Me brother Richard was a docker and two other brothers were stevedores. Some of the men, the coal tippers, used to [purposely] spill coal on the docks for the people. And I used to hate washing after the coal men. Black! My brother's clothes, you'd have to put them into Rinso and steep them and then you had a washing board and a big tub. You almost had to bleach them. And they used to work *very hard*. The stevedores'd pick out so many men and it used to make enemies cause they'd *all* want to be picked out and they'd only pick maybe twenty people and they'd go over with their shovels. My brothers who were stevedores made an awful lot of enemies and the women'd say, 'You didn't give *my* son a job', and all this. And in 1925 there was a strike and, my God, it was *dreadful* then. And we'd nothing to eat. They used to go around looting. Then they brought in scabs and there was *killing* going on. Oh, some of the dockers had great principles. Oh, the dockers and the scabs used to kill one another, I'm telling you. Yeah, we used to *see* it on the quay wall, when they'd be working the boats. We used to be looking over at them, several of them killing [fighting with] one another. There was one man that lived in Townsend Street, a Mr O'Toole, and he was a big man and he went in and scabbed it and he was *always* a scab till he died. He always went by the name of a scab *all* his life and nobody'd talk to him nor work with him.

"Now on City Quay the Blessed Virgin was seen in our house. I'm telling the truth. I had a sister, Maud—she was the eldest, and she picked up with a sailor. His name was Robert Evans, he was from a little town in Wales. Oh, he was a handsome man and he was on the ship with me father. Now they were going to be married and he turned his religion from Protestant to be a Catholic. And his people then wouldn't have *anything* to do with him when he turned his religion. And next he cut his arm on a winch and then Bob took to die. Now let me tell you the story—and this is the *truth* now I'm telling you. He had his apartment upstairs where we lived on City Quay and there was forty-four stairs up to the top. And before he went [died] Bob was going up to the toilet and this night he comes down and says to me mother, 'Susan, I've seen a lovely lady in the corner of the stairs and she was all in blue and she was in the corner of the stairs and her hands were joined.' So me mother sent up for the priest, Father O'Shea, and he says, 'Well, that was the Blessed Virgin you seen . . . that was the Blessed Virgin you seen, Bob.' And the priest says, 'Mrs McCann, he's going to die.' And he died. Died about a month after, because of the accident he had that affected his heart. And he was only a young man. A lovely fella he was. Now that *was* the Blessed Virgin. I'm telling you the truth. And now anyone would tell you that now, that came from City Quay. In *our* house.

"The side of the house fell four years ago. It was 9 February and I remember it was a terrible gale. I was born in that house and was in it for seventy-eight years. I never left it. See, our house collapsed cause they were after knocking down the house beside it [for support] and we knew that'd happen if there was a gale. And it was blowing a hurricane of a wind that night on 9 February four years ago. And I was *in* the house when it fell. I was doing the dinner. And all I could say was, 'Jesus and Mary!' And I put up me hands like that. The *whole side* of the house fell down and you could see in, see the bed and the wardrobe and the pictures on the wall. And all the fellas on the quay wall were shouting. They thought for sure I was done. They could see *right in* the side of the house. And *all* the furniture was left up there. Oh, I'll never forget it. And if I had been in bed . . . cause all the bricks come in on the bed. Oh, I'd have been killed. I got out and the police come up and wouldn't let us [back] in. Hundreds of people around and barricades. And I said, 'There's valuable things up there that I want.' There was money and jewellery and stuff. So he came up with me and I got it and I got me clothes.

"I *loved* that house, I did. And it was the *salt of the earth*, City Quay. I was the oldest one left on City Quay, of the originals. We were the last family on City Quay. So I moved down here to Macken Street—and took me memories with me. Ah, there's nothing on the docks now. Oh, you'd never see the days that we seen. Great memories of it and they were marvellous people. I have great memories so I can go back on every day of me life. I *remember* all that. And they say memories live longer than dreams."

MICHAEL LYNCH, AGE 95, AND DAUGHTER MAUREEN LYNCH, AGE 70
CANAL-SIDE COTTAGE DWELLERS

From halcyon to hellish—that is how they describe their life over the past sixty-five years. They live in a 200-year-old whitewashed stone cottage embroidered with roses and gardens beside the Royal Canal at the North Strand. Back in the 1920s Michael, who worked for the railway since age 10, acquired the derelict cottage from CIE and renovated it for his wife who was a country woman. Here they happily raised seven children, kept horses, pigs, poultry and tended lovely vegetable and flower gardens. It was an idyllic country cottage life in the heart of old Dublin. Passing bargemen became close friends and tenement neighbours were grand. Canal water was pure enough to drink and elegant swans and ducks abounded. During warm summer months "fancy" excursion boats hosting gala parties passed by as formally attired passengers smiled and waved. Even movie stars like Tyrone Power and Jean Tierney stopped to visit and chat.

But it was too good to last. First came the German bomb in 1941 which fell directly across the road and cleanly ripped the roof off the cottage. The structure itself was spared only because it was situated in the canal basin about ten feet below the general ground level. But the rickety tenements nearby were demolished by the blast. Upon the site in the 1960s a new flat complex was built, bringing in new elements of residents including some "bad apples". Today the Lynchs live a "tormented" life, daily harassed by adult hoodlums and mean teenagers who hurl verbal abuse and threats and pelt them with stones and bottles. Father, Michael, who is now totally blind but finds small pleasure sitting in the warmth of the sun, has been struck several times, once having his head severely gashed open by a crude missile. Fish, ducks and swans are gone as the canal has become a stenchy cesspool of waste and debris ridden with huge rats. It is all terribly dispiriting and frightening. Coping with bouts of depression, Maureen confides with profound sadness, "It was lovely here . . . the good days . . . I'm a survivor."

MICHAEL:

"Mister, there was great days here. We're living here now for the last sixty-five years. When I come in now to this house there was only meself living here then and me family. We'd no next door neighbours. None at all. You'd think you were living in a real country place, a country village. The missus, she was a country woman too and she died a young woman. And she used to have about fifty or sixty fowl here. I had fowl here and I had pigs at one time. We were never short of anything. I had a garden up here and chickens and six and seven fresh eggs every day from them. When I came to the canal here you wouldn't want to go to your water tap. You could take it out of the canal there and drink it. It was that clean. And I used to have six pairs of horses, bargemen's horses, and I used to get four shillings each night for each horse for feeding them and giving them their bedding. And they were no trouble. Oh, you were never short of a shilling here. And they'd [bargemen] throw you a bag of potatoes. You didn't have to buy anything, the boatmen would bring you in maybe a leg of something and maybe a pair of rabbits. Cause they'd be down in the country and maybe have a dozen rabbits.

"There was eleven barges on this canal when I come into this house first. Oh, they were carrying all cargo and corn and wheat, coal, timber, carried everything down in the west of Ireland. Used to carry barrels of Guinness. They was carrying furniture, people from the country ordering stuff. When they'd lay up here at 7.00 at night to go to Ballina, if it was bad weather they wouldn't go. And there'd be a cook on the boat and he'd bake all the bread. Ah, there was the best of cooks on them boats. They'd exchange the cakes they made for the white bread [made by his wife]. And one of the lads would make a can of tea and he'd go to the canal there and make the tea out of that water and it'd be the *best* cup of tea you ever drank. Got the water from under the boat. Got a big can that'd hold about three or four quarts of tea and they'd have that for four big men and they'd have good potatoes. And, oh, they were *big* men. They were seven and eight foot!

"Now the barges used to carry barrels of Guinness. And then there was complaints going in that the booze was getting taken, the boatmen drinking it, you know? And the owners used to hide up behind the hedges along the canal to see if they could catch them. Now the Leaches [bargemen family], the son,

Jack, was a hard chaw for the beer. There'd be about three or four bargemen on each boat and they'd have to get their beer. And they'd get a gimlet and bore holes in maybe two or three barrels of beer on the boat. And when they'd get full of beer they had pegs made to put in where they were boring to get the beer. Wooden pegs. And you'd never think they were interfered with. And they'd be half-drunk! They used to come into the house here, two or three of the bargemen, and they'd be drunk. And they'd have an old sing-song. This house was never empty in them days. The door was always open from morning to night. The bargemen, ah, they were hard chaws.

"And there used to be pleasure boats with the ladies here. Ladies from Greystones and Dalkey, and they used to have a small little barge and they had their family on it. And they'd have electric light on the pleasure ship and the best of cooking and everything. They'd open the locks to let them get through. Wealthy people. Oh, the best of everything. And they'd be up till 4.00 in the morning and they'd be out on the deck there getting the fresh air and you'd see them there in the best of clean clothes on them. And they'd have a melodeon playing and a small little piano. Ah, they were great times. You know, when I look back to the days when I come here . . . it kills me to see what's going on now."

MAUREEN:
"Well, it's a long story. From the time me father was 10 he worked on the railway selling papers. And he went straight through till he was pensioned off as a train examiner. And at that early beginning when we were all small—going back now into the 1920s—he saw this house being vandalised. CIE owned it. Somebody had been living in it but they had gone. Grass was growing inside it. Oh, it was *horrible*. The house would be over 200 years old. It was a CIE cottage and Daddy applied for it and he got it. And we came here when we were only tiny. It was my two brothers and meself and the rest were all born here. There were seven of us children here and not a one ever fell in the canal. We were taught not to go near it and that was that! My mother, Lord have mercy on her, she came from the Grand Canal. Now the lock-keeper's house, it was on the *far* side. So we've nothing whatsoever to do [officially] with the canal. We've just lived here as CIE. And, see, I'm not married. I gave up me life when me Mammy died and there was no one to look after me Daddy. He's 95 and there's only myself and my brother and Daddy.

"Ah, it was lovely here. I used to cross the lock cause I went to school over there. Walk across and Mammy'd make sure I was all right. And there was another stone cottage up at the top. We used to have cabbage and rhubarb and potatoes up on the banks and we used to sell it. We had a pony, Molly, and a nanny goat. And me mother loved animals and she'd have a hundred cats if she was able. We often had six and seven here. And we used to sell all the beautiful cabbage. And there was swans and geese in the canal. And it was really nice when you'd see the horses and all. We had two or three horses that belonged to the bargemen and we'd put them up for the night. We used to get manure and we had the garden and lovely flowers. And the itinerants would eat eels out of the canal. Oh, they're in the thousands there. About that length [three feet]. We didn't mind them fishing. The tinkers would eat them.

"Oh, I lived on the barges, really. Especially Leaches' barges. They were wonderful people, the Leaches, and the Caffreys. Hail, rain or snow they'd have to go. But if it was [extremely] bad weather they'd stop out there. They were elderly men but young in spirit. Poor Mr Leach must have been 60 or 70 and still doing it. The majority of them were countrymen, except for the Leaches. Hard-working men, and honest. And they always had money. Some had farms down in the country and their own house and cattle. The boat would pull in here and the men would sleep in it. Oh, it was their home. And they wouldn't come to *me* for water, they'd get it out of the canal—it was *that clean*. I'm talking about the twenties and the thirties. Make their tea out of it. Oh, many a cup of tea I had on the barges. The water was that lovely. They were the *real* good days.

"Many a time I got a lift [on barges] up all the way. It was *great*. And you could eat your dinner off it! They'd *scrub* it, the barge, and everything was spotless. You'd be surprised. And their shirts would be in a bucket of cold water. And yer man then would have the big, big pot and he'd be boiling hell out of the shirts. Then dry them on ropes and they'd be pressed. Sometimes three men on the barges. And they were the *real* bargers. They were *history*, beautiful people. They were the real old thing. You'd never get the likes of them again. They were a different race in that generation. You wouldn't hear a bad word out of them . . . *gentlemen*.

"The barges were carrying wheat and timber and Guinness and all stuff for the country. They were a good workman's boat. They'd come very frequent. There was the Metcalfs' boat and the Leaches. They run the whole lot. Like, you'd have maybe one barge this morning and you'd have maybe one this evening. And the boat would stop here with the horses. We used to know their names and walk up along with them. And then they might have a bit of wheat or something that they'd throw me for the hens. And they always gave me ten pence. And they'd sleep in the barges. It was great. And if there was anything valuable [cargo] then one would have to do the watch. They were like my second parents. They'd have their drink and you'd never see cigarettes, it was always pipes. And the smell of the pipes used to be lovely. And they used to have beautiful coffee on the boat and, mind you, you could *smell* it. And the tobacco . . . *every night* here at 12.00, coffee and cigars. It's not like coffee you'd smell anywhere else, it was the *real* coffee then. They were good people and you'd never see the like of them again. And they were fond of the loaves of bread my Mammy would make here and they'd exchange the cakes they made for the white bread. Many a good dinner I had on the barges. They'd have bacon, cabbage, potatoes and pig's cheek and pig's feet and ribs. And they'd have a whole chicken, maybe a live one, and maybe two or three that's going around in the boat. And they'd say, 'I'm going to kill me dinner now.' And they had fresh milk from the country in the cans. And they'd bring back nice bacon and butter that was churned down in the country and that was nicer than our own butter here. Ah, you'd hear them singing in the boat, like 'The Old Bog Road', 'Come

Back Mavourneen, Mavourneen' and 'I'll Take You Home Again, Kathleen'. And the 'Wings of the Swallow'. And card playing on a fine day.

"They'd wear their old clothes on the boat but on Sunday morning they'd be at that door and say, 'There's a few rashers for you', and sausages and maybe black pudding. Bring it to our door. And you'd look at them and they'd have a lovely serge suit and a round soft hat and a snow white shirt and black tie and they'd be after washing their feet in the canal. And shoes polished. Oh, you could eat off their shoes. On a Sunday. Sunday was the sabbath and that was that. And they'd have their rosary beads and their prayer book. And they had their gold watch and chain. And they'd be over to Mass then. Then they'd sit on that bridge and they'd read the paper and we'd have the tea ready for them and they'd come over for a cup of tea. And then they'd walk down to the pub and have a pint or two and maybe one man'd stay back and cook their dinner and you'd *smell* that dinner! Then they'd have their rashers and eggs and ham and brown bread and white bread and that was their meal. And the boat used to be pulled in here and I used to get up on the plank and go down into it and they'd say, 'Ah, there she is.' And it would be dished up rough and ready, but the *best* you ever ate. And porridge or custard for your sweet. And marmalade and home-made jam! And then your glass of milk out of the churn. They'd all go for a walk then and do you know what they'd do? They'd all go over there in the grass and take off their coats and they'd play cards till maybe half seven or eight. The next thing then, you'd see them over at the chapel again cause there used to be Mass in the evening. Then go back and have a pint and an old chat and back up, stand on that bridge till 1.00 in the morning. Oh, a good life.

"At Christmas time you always got little Christmas stockings. One of the bargemen would knit the stocking. And you got a slice of brown bread and a cooked chicken and well stuffed, and a lollipop. And maybe Mammy'd get a calendar and a holy statue and a lovely card from the barge people. And Daddy would get two cans with a lid on it with beer in one and whiskey in the other and a little ribbon and a miraculous medal on it. Always, always, always. And they might leave us £5 to go down to the shows, down to the pantomimes. They were wonderful people.

"Then you might get a fancy boat, a pleasure boat, coming up. Looked like a house! And lovely curtains. They were very well-to-do and going down to the Shannon mostly. Some were foreigners. And they'd stop and have a chat and we'd always have a cup of tea for them and a biscuit. Very friendly. And some of them would give you a dollar and we were ignorant and didn't know what it was till you went into a shop. And the shops wouldn't change it. So we had to go to the bank. There was Tyrone Power and Jean Tierney and John Huston was on one boat when they were making a film. They'd sleep aboard, like a caravan. And they had engine power. Ah, a long time ago . . . honest to God, they were beautiful.

"Now in 1941 a bomb fell and that's how the flats is there [across the canal] now. I was about 14 and I was in bed. We were all in bed, except me Daddy. He was just coming in after night work. A German plane come over and he's too heavy and he let go two of them [bombs] and over on the far side were lovely houses, they were Georgian type. And the bomb just came and it just *blew everybody* and the roof come in and we went flying. And all the stuff come down on top of me and knocked me out. And blew all them lovely houses down. It took five houses altogether. Just a land mine dropped here. There was twenty of them killed. Now when I say there was twenty killed I'm including the North Circular Road. I think there was about four or five killed here. And so many injured. I didn't understand it at the time. I didn't know what a bomb was. And when I woke up there was a St John's [Hospital] man and a Knights of Malta man leaning over me in the bed. They were after taking all the mortar off me and didn't know I was there and they got a shock. 'Where's me Mammy, where's me Daddy?' He took off his coat and threw it around me and carried me out of the bed. And they took us around to this house and on this slab there was a little child that was dead. Only 3 or something. And the father was blown to bits. And his wife killed as well. The whole house come down on her. Oh, I couldn't believe it. The Strand was *demolished*. It was like an earthquake in a foreign country.

"I couldn't find me mother—for nearly six or seven days! They took her away, she was unconscious. We didn't know if she was alive or not because everybody was scattered. Everybody was confused to know who was dead and who was not. My brothers and sisters was taken over to the convent and I couldn't find nobody. And I got back here, got through the barrier, and I run screaming and when I got back here I couldn't get into the house, it was that bad. And I sat there. And I was sitting there and poor Alfie Byrne was the Lord Mayor and he come down and he had the medal on him and he was a great gentleman. And he put two and sixpence into me hand and said, 'Go and get yourself a gur cake.' So my pal, Mary, lived over there and I wanted to find out how she was. She just scratched her leg and she was sitting in half of the parlour. The other half was gone. So I went over and said, 'C'mon, let's go and gallivant.' And when we were going down the stairs didn't we fall three flights down because the banister broke and we were nearly killed. We landed out in the back yard and couldn't get back up to come out the front. And we had to climb out. And there was a shop on the corner just *blazing*. See, they used to sell oil and there was an awful blaze. There was a huge crowd but everybody had to get back. Oh, fire brigades and everything. And ambulances. We [children] went up to Phibsborough to my aunt and stayed there for nearly seven weeks. They said this house wouldn't stand for another ten years, they said it was really gone with the bomb. But my father says, 'I want it done up again.' So they put a new roof on and done the best they could. And [later] I got a toilet in meself. The company [CIE] wouldn't do it.

"In that generation of ours an awful lot drowned here. We saved more children and brought them into that coal house and put blankets around them. And we never got as much as a thank you. Another fella fell in and I couldn't save him. A very well-kept fella and all I could do is scream for someone to bring me the lifebelt. It's always hanging there. And a little girl looking for crabs and she fell straight in and she drowned and she was only about 9 . . . and a lovely head of hair . . . gorgeous. There was a write-up [a few years ago] about along here—which was the truth—that anyone that fell into that canal ended up with polio. That's what they're saying now. And we've known two or three cases that has polio from falling in there. The canal is *rotten* at the moment. And if you fall in you're bound to drink some of the water. And the rats! Oh, you'd want to see the rats over there. Shocking! See, we can't control the [tall] grass and CIE won't do nothing.

"It was really nice when they used to do the cargo and you'd see the horses and all pulling the barges, before these lorries went on the road. And then when the lorries went on the roads the barges was left with *nothing*. About thirty years ago. That's what done the canal in. Oh, I lived on the barges, really. Especially Leaches' barges. We had the *best* of times here—until them flats ruined it. You never knew nothing bad here. Now for the past fifteen or twenty years we are *demented* [tormented]. See, we're a right open cockshot [sling-shot]. On my windows I'm fed up putting in panes of glass. There's bars now to block the windows. And the roof, I'm fed up getting slates into it [from being smashed]. It's *torture* here now, with the kids and the big fellas. People don't know the *torment* we have. Maybe four little blackguards there and throwing stones. And they use a sling. I'd like to do the place up and even run it as a bed-and-breakfast, but what's the use? I always enjoyed meself, but my bit of enjoyment is gone. Too many frights here, and getting the windows broken in. I'd even have it thatched but maybe a [fire] bomb they'd throw on it. Set it afire. And if you send for the police and they see the police coming, that's the *worst* thing you can do cause you'll get *twice* as much trouble then for doing that.

"I know there's good and bad [people] in the flats. Mind you, there's some *bad* ones around here. My father doesn't get four minutes peace sitting out here. See, when they knock the eel's head off they don't care where they throw them. They catch an eel, chop the head off it—just bash it off the wall . . . ill treat the poor thing—and this is why the rats is accumulating here, because of the dead eels. The smell! Me father was sitting here and got hit in the face with an eel's head and had to get stitches. And they throw batteries and they're heavy.

"We used to have cabbage and fruits here but then the kids was taking the vegetables. And then me Nellie goat was getting persecuted . . . Nellie was her name. And poor Molly was the horse and she was getting persecuted by the kids. So it went from drip to drip. Then the place was getting *bashed*. Then they were letting out the pigs and the pigs was running into the water. They weren't all young kids, they were big enough to know what they were doing. It started then from all that. And now I never go to bed till 5.00 in the morning. I'm sitting up reading books when the television's over. I sit in that kitchen. I get nervous and I hear prowlers at the back. It was 3.00 one morning and I decided to just go to bed. And they gave the door one *bash* and I heard two fellas saying, 'Give it a good bang.' And I went on the phone but I couldn't get a policeman. And they really tried their best to get down the door and I was an hour with this going on before a policeman come. Anyway, I don't go to bed now *at all*, until maybe three or half three, or five.

"It's been my life here and I know of nothing else. I was only a baby when I came here. We had the pony, Molly, and a hackney car. And Mammy would send me down for gur cake. That was our dish at 10.00 and a pint of fresh milk in the can. And if Daddy wanted a pint of stout I'd take the jug and pay fourpence for a pint of stout for him and bring it back. The good days . . . we had them . . . but there's none of that now. It's only abuse and threatening. And the dirt and the rats. I'll hold on. After all, we've put so much into it. They've got their slings and their bottles. I'm a survivor . . . I *am* a survivor. And CIE, they're just waiting for me to move. They want us out. I think to meself, 'If I got a flat over *there* and lived with them I'd have peace.' But you hear the water falling here and I'd miss that. I remember the best days . . . the *really* good days."

Notes

1. W. B. Yeats, *The Autobiography of William Butler Yeats* (New York: The Macmillan Company, 1953) p. 19.
2. Ben Savage and Terry Fagan, *All Around the Diamond* (Dublin: North Inner-City Folklore Project, 1991) Frontispiece.
3. E. Estyn Evans, *Irish Folk Ways* (London: Routledge & Kegan Paul, 1957) p. xiii.
4. Paul Thompson, 'History and the Community', in Willa K. Baum and David K. Dunaway (eds) *Oral History: An Interdisciplinary Anthology* (Nashville, Tennessee: American Association for State and Local History, 1984) p. 50.
5. Louis Starr, 'Oral History', in Willa K. Baum and David K. Dunaway (eds) op. cit., p. 4.
6. Alice Hoffman, 'Reliability and Validity in Oral History', in Willa K. Baum and David K. Dunaway (eds) op. cit., p. 68.
7. ibid., p. 72.
8. ibid.
9. Richard M. Dorson, 'The Oral Historian and the Folklorist', in Willa K. Baum and David K. Dunaway (eds) op. cit., p. 292.
10. Larry Danielson, 'The Folklorist, the Oral Historian and Local History', in Willa K. Baum and David K. Dunaway (eds) op. cit., p. 177.
11. Thompson, op. cit., note 4, p. 49.
12. Hoffman, op. cit., note 6, p. 72.
13. Evans, op. cit., note 3, p. xiv.
14. Alan Dundes, *The Study of Folklore* (New Jersey: Prentice-Hall, 1965) p. 2.
15. Betty Messenger, *Picking Up the Linen Threads* (Belfast: Blackstaff Press, 1988) pp 3–4.
16. Thompson, op. cit., note 4, p. 48.
17. Thompson, op. cit., note 4, p. 39.
18. Thompson, op. cit., note 4, p. 40.
19. Charles T. Morrissey, 'Introduction', in Willa K. Baum and David K. Dunaway (eds) op. cit., p. xxi.
20. Thompson, op. cit., note 4, p. 40.
21. Bernard Share, *The Emergency: Neutral Ireland 1939–45* (Dublin: Gill and Macmillan, 1978) p. 69.

22. ibid., p. 121.

23. Dermot Keogh, *The Rise of the Irish Working Class* (Belfast: Appletree Press, 1982) p. 88.

24. Joseph V. O'Brien, *'Dear, Dirty Dublin'* (Berkeley: University of California Press, 1982) pp 200 and 204.

25. Phil O'Keefe, *Down Cobbled Streets: A Liberties Childhood* (Dingle: Brandon Press, 1995) pp 32 and 104.

26. Elaine Crowley, *Cowslips and Chainies: A Memoir of Dublin in the 1930s* (Dublin: Lilliput Press, 1996) p. 33.

27. Pete St John, *Jaysus Wept!* (published by the *Midland Tribune*, 1984) p. 55.

28. Eilis Brady, *All In! All In!* (Dublin: Comhairle Bhealoideas Éireann, University College, Belfield, 1984) Frontispiece.

29. John D. Brewer, *The Royal Irish Constabulary: An Oral History* (Belfast: Institute of Irish Studies, Queen's University, 1990) p. 18.

30. Donald A. MacDonald, 'Fieldwork: Collecting Oral Literature', in Richard M. Dorson (ed.) *Folklore and Folklife* (Chicago: University of Chicago Press, 1972) p. 413.

31. Starr, op. cit., note 5, p. 4.

32. Sherna Gluck, 'What's So Special About Women? Women's Oral History', in Willa K. Baum and David K. Dunaway (eds) op. cit., p. 227.

33. ibid., p. 227.

34. Conrad M. Arensberg, *The Irish Countryman* (Gloucester, Massachusetts: Peter Smith, 1955) p. vii.

35. ibid., p. 227.

36. Kevin C. Kearns, *Stoneybatter: Dublin's Inner Urban Village* (Dublin: Glendale Press, 1989) p. 138.

37. Hoffman, op. cit., note 6, p. 72.

38. Thompson, op. cit., note 4, p. 48.

39. Gluck, op. cit., note 32, p. 227.

40. Adrian McLoughlin, *Evening Press*, 5 September 1986, p. 16.

41. Thompson, op. cit., note 4, p. 40.

Bibliography

Arensberg, Conrad M., *The Irish Countryman* (Gloucester, Massachusetts, Peter Smith, 1955).

Barrington, Sir Jonah, *Personal Sketches of His Own Times* (London: Routledge & Sons, 1869).

Baum, Willa K. and Dunaway, David K. (eds) *Oral History: An Interdisciplinary Anthology* (Nashville, Tennessee: American Association for State and Local History, 1984).

Bolger, Dermot (ed.) *Invisible Cities: The New Dubliners* (Dublin: Raven Arts Press, 1988).

Brewer, John D., *The Royal Irish Constabulary: An Oral History* (Belfast: Institute of Irish Studies, Queen's University, 1990).

Carmichael, Rev. Canon F. F., *Dublin—A Lecture* (Dublin: Hodges, Figgis and Co., 1907).

Chart, D. A., *The Story of Dublin* (London J. M. Dent & Son, 1932).

Clarke, Desmond, *Dublin* (London: B. T. Batsford Ltd, 1977).

Collins, James, *Life in Old Dublin* (Cork: Tower Books, 1978). A reprint of original 1913 edition.

Corkery, Tom, *Tom Corkery's Dublin* (Dublin: Anvil Press, 1980).

Cosgrave, Augustine D., 'North Dublin City', *Dublin Historical Record*, Vol. XXIII, 1969, pp 3–22.

Cosgrove, Art, *Dublin Through the Ages* (Dublin: The College Press, 1986).

Cronin, Anthony, *Dead as Doornails* (Dublin: Poolbeg Press, 1976).

Crosbie, Paddy, *Your Dinner's Poured Out!* (Dublin: O'Brien Press, 1981).

Crowley, Elaine, *Cowslips and Chainies: A Memoir of Dublin in the 1930s* (Dublin: Lilliput Press, 1996).

Daly, Mary E., *Dublin—The Deposed Capital* (Cork: Cork University Press, 1984).

Davies, Sidney, *Dublin Types* (Dublin: The Talbot Press Ltd, 1918).

Dickinson, David (ed.) *The Gorgeous Mask: Dublin 1700–1850* (Dublin: Trinity College Workshop, 1987).

Dickinson, Page L., *The Dublin of Yesterday* (London: Methuen & Co., 1929).

Dorson, Richard M. (ed.) *Folklore and Folklife* (Chicago: University of Chicago Press, 1972).

Dublin Explorations and Reflections, written by an anonymous Englishman (Dublin: Maunsel & Co., 1917).

Dunne, John J., *Street Broad and Narrow* (Dublin: Helicon Ltd, 1982).

Evans, E. Estyn, *Irish Folk Ways* (London: Routledge & Kegan Paul, 1957).

Fagan, Patrick, *The Second City* (Dublin: Branar Press, 1986).

Gahan, Robert, 'Some Old Street Characters of Dublin', *Dublin Historical Record*, Vol. II, 1939, pp 98–105.

Gilbert, John T., *A History of the City of Dublin* (Dublin: Gill and Macmillan, 1978). A reprint of original three volumes, 1854–59.

Gilbert, John T., *The Streets of Dublin* (Dublin: no publisher cited, 1852).

Gillespie, Elgy, *The Liberties of Dublin* (Dublin: O'Brien Press, 1973).

Glassie, Henry, *Irish Folk History* (Philadelphia: University of Pennsylvania Press, 1982).

Henchy, Deirdre, 'Dublin 80 Years Ago', *Dublin Historical Record*, Vol. XXVI, No. 1, 1972, pp 18–34.

Humphreys, Alexander J., *New Dubliners* (London: Routledge & Kegan Paul, 1966).

Johnston, Mairin, *Around the Banks of Pimlico* (Dublin: Attic Press, 1985).

Joyce, Weston St John, *The Neighbourhood of Dublin* (Dublin: M. H. Gill and Son, 1939).

Kearns, Kevin C., *Dublin Pub Life & Lore: An Oral History* (Dublin: Gill & Macmillan, 1996).

Kearns, Kevin C., *Dublin Street Life & Lore: An Oral History* (Dublin: The Glendale Press, 1991).

Kearns, Kevin C., *Dublin Tenement Life: An Oral History* (Dublin: Gill & Macmillan, 1994).

Kearns, Kevin C., *Dublin's Vanishing Craftsmen* (Belfast: Appletree Press, 1986).

Kearns, Kevin C., *Stoneybatter: Dublin's Inner-Urban Village* (Dublin: The Glendale Press, 1989).

Kelly, Bill, *Me Darlin' Dublin's Dead and Gone* (Dublin: Ward River Press, 1983).

Kennedy, Tom (ed.) *Victorian Dublin* (Dublin: Albertine Kennedy Publishers, 1980).

Keogh, Dermot, *The Rise of the Irish Working Class* (Belfast: Appletree Press, 1982).

Longford, Christine, *A Biography of Dublin* (London: Methuen & Co. Ltd, 1936).

Lysaght, Moira, 'My Dublin', *Dublin Historical Record*, Vol. XXX, No. 4, 1977, pp 122–35.

McCourt, Desmond, 'The Use of Oral Tradition in Irish Historical Geography', *Irish Geography*, Vol. VI, No. 4, 1972, pp 394–410.

McDonald, Frank, *The Destruction of Dublin* (Dublin: Gill and Macmillan, 1985).

McGregor, John James, *New Picture of Dublin* (Dublin: Sealy, Bryers and Walker, 1907).

McLoughlin, Adrian, *Guide to Historic Dublin* (Dublin: Gill and Macmillan Ltd, 1979).

MacThomais, Eamonn, *Gur Cake & Coal Blocks* (Dublin: O'Brien Press, 1976).

MacThomais, Eamonn, *Janey Mack Me Shirt is Black* (Dublin: O'Brien Press, 1974).

Maxwell, Constantia, *Dublin Under the Georges, 1714–1830* (Dublin: Gill and Macmillan, 1979).

Messenger, Betty, *Picking Up the Linen Threads* (Belfast: Blackstaff Press, 1988).

Munck, Ronnie and Rolston, Bill, *Belfast in the Thirties: An Oral History* (Belfast: Blackstaff Press, 1987).

Neary, Bernard, *North of the Liffey* (Dublin: Lenhar Publications, 1984).

O'Brien, Joseph V., *'Dear, Dirty Dublin'* (Berkeley: University of California Press, 1982).

O'Donovan, John, *Life by the Liffey* (Dublin: Gill and Macmillan, 1986).

O'Keefe, Phil, *Down Cobbled Streets: A Liberties Childhood* (Dingle: Brandon Press, 1995).

Orpen, Sir William, *Stories of Old Dublin and Myself* (London: Williams and Norgate, 1924).

Peter, A., *Dublin Fragments* (Dublin: Hodges, Figgis & Co., 1925).

Peter, A., *Sketches of Old Dublin* (Dublin: Sealy, Bryers & Walker, 1907).

Redmond, Lar, *Show Us the Moon* (Dingle: Brandon Books, 1988).

Rich, Barnaby, *A New Description of Ireland* (London: Thomas Adams, 1610).

Robertson, Olivia, *Dublin Phoenix* (London: The Alden Press, 1957).

Ryan, John, *Remembering How We Stood* (Dublin: Lilliput Press, 1987).

Savage, Ben and Fagan, Terry, *All Around the Diamond* (Dublin: North Inner-City Folklore Project, 1991).

Share, Bernard, *The Emergency: Neutral Ireland 1939–45* (Dublin: Gill and Macmillan, 1978).

Sheehan, Ronan and Walsh, Brendan, *The Heart of the City* (Dingle: Brandon Books, 1988).

Somerville-Large, Peter, *Dublin* (London: Hamish-Hamilton, 1979).

Warburton, J., Whitelaw, J. and Walsh, Robert, *History of the City of Dublin* (Dublin: T. Cadell and W. Davies, 1818, two volumes).

Whelpton, Eric, *The Book of Dublin* (London: Rockliffe Press, 1984).

Whitelaw, Rev. James, *An Essay on the Population of Dublin* (Dublin: Graisberry and Campbell, 1805).

Index